Once again, Rodanthi Tzanelli offers a high-quality and promising book, where she theorizes on the cultural borders of the Olympic City in the ceremonials of Rio 2016 and Tokyo 2020. With delightful prose, her development exhibits a fertile ground to understand media events as the juxtaposition of two economic forms: the artificial economy, which focuses on the doctrine of security; and the economy of imagination, more oriented to the production of architectural legacies as artificially fabricated and externally imposed.

Korstanje Maximiliano, *University of Palermo, Argentina*

This book makes a major contribution to understanding mega-events through a cultural sociological analysis. Grounded in a multi-disciplinary literature, it will appeal to readers coming from a wide range of perspectives. The central theme of *Mega-Events as Economies of the Imagination* provides an innovative and compelling lens through which to understand and explore mega-events.

Paul Lynch, *Professor of Critical Hospitality and Tourism, The Business School, Edinburgh Napier University, UK*

The planning of Olympic mega-events for Rio 2016 and Tokyo 2020 involved not just pragmatic aspects of logistics and engineering, but also what Rodanthi Tzanelli describes as imagineering. This fascinating study of global mega-events brings together recent theoretical approaches to atmospheres, aesthetics, technologies, economic development, infrastructural urbanism, hypermobility, and dark tourism to give us new insights into the staging of "mobile situations" and their symbolic "choreomobilities." It is an intriguing contribution to the literature on mobilities, global urbanism, and the performative arts.

Mimi Sheller, *Professor of Sociology, Department of Sociology, Drexel University, USA*

Mega-Events as Economies of the Imagination

Atmosphere, the elusive ambiance of a place, enables or hinders its mobility in global consumption contexts. Atmosphere connects to social imaginaries, utopian representational frames producing the culture of a city or country. But who resolves atmospheric contradictions in a place's social and cultural rhythms, when the eyes of the world are turned on it?

Mega-Events as Economies of the Imagination examines ephemeral and solidified atmospheres in the Rio 2016 Olympic Games and the Handover Ceremony to Tokyo for the 2020 Games. Indeed, highlighting the various social and cultural implications upon these Olympic Games hosts, Tzanelli argues that the 'Olympic City' is produced by aesthetic *imagineers*, mobile groups of architects, artists and entrepreneurs, who aesthetically 'engineer' native cultures as utopias. Thus, it is explored as to how Rio and Tokyo's imagineers problematise notions of creativity, cosmopolitan togetherness and belonging.

Mega-Events as Economies of the Imagination will appeal to postgraduate students, postdoctoral researchers and professionals interested in fields such as: Globalisation Studies, Mobility Theory, Cultural Sociology, International Political Economy, Conference and Event Management, Tourism Studies and Migration Studies.

Rodanthi Tzanelli is Associate Professor of Cultural Sociology at the University of Leeds, UK.

Routledge Advances in Sociology

For a full list of titles in this series, please visit www.routledge.com/series/SE0511.

Twentieth Century Population Thinking
A Critical Reader of Primary Sources
Edited by Population Knowledge Network

The Synchronization of National Policies
Ethnography of the Global Tribe of Moderns
Pertti Alasuutari

Retail and the Artifice of Social Change
Steven Miles

Theorizing Social Memories
Concepts and Contexts
Edited by Gerd Sebald and Jatin Wagle

Addiction, Modernity, and the City
A Users' Guide to Urban Space
Christopher B.R. Smith

Medicine, Risk, Discourse and Power
Edited by John Martyn Chamberlain

Pragmatic Humanism
On the Nature and Value of Sociological Knowledge
Marcus Morgan

Shared Experiences of Mass Shootings
A Comparative Perspective on the Aftermath
Johanna Nurmi

Mega-Events as Economies of the Imagination
Creating Atmospheres for Rio 2016 and Tokyo 2020
Rodanthi Tzanelli

Mega-Events as Economies of the Imagination

Creating Atmospheres for Rio 2016 and Tokyo 2020

Rodanthi Tzanelli

Routledge
Taylor & Francis Group

LONDON AND NEW YORK

First published 2018
by Routledge

2 Park Square, Milton Park, Abingdon, Oxfordshire OX14 4RN
52 Vanderbilt Avenue, New York, NY 10017

Routledge is an imprint of the Taylor & Francis Group, an informa business

First issued in paperback 2019

British Library Cataloguing in Publication Data
A catalogue record for this book is available from the British Library

Library of Congress Cataloging in Publication Data
A catalog record for this book has been requested

ISBN: 978-1-138-30028-6 (hbk)
ISBN: 978-0-367-89087-2 (pbk)

Typeset in Times New Roman
by Taylor & Francis Books

For Majid, as always

Contents

List of figures   x
Acknowledgements   xi

1   Staging the mega-event: Militourist imaginaries in an
    Olympic city   1

2   Globalising utopias: Imagineering the Olympic event, making
    the world   29

3   Tomorrow never comes: Rio's museum of our futures   53

4   Choreomobility and artistic worldmaking: Retrieving Rio's
    submerged centre   88

5   The Opening and Closing Ceremonies: Migration, nostalgia and
    the making of tourism mobilities   101

6   Tokyo 2020: Urban amnesia and the technoromantic spirit
    of capitalism   134

7   The Handover Ceremony: Digital gift economies in a global city   148

8   Conclusion: Dark journeys and hopeful futures   165

References   176
Index   221

List of figures

3.1 Museu do Amanhã, Gaia entrance   77
3.2 Museu do Amanhã, under construction on the waterfront   77
5.1 Amazonian Brazilian Genesis: The Tree of Life   103
5.2 The arrival of Japanese labour migrants in Brazil   104
5.3 Representations of urban Rio   106
5.4 The boxes in which athletes place seeds   120
5.5 The Olympic Cauldron overseeing the Stadium   124

Acknowledgements

The book's thesis benefitted from 'Populations Mobilities', a reading group hosted by the Bauman Institute and the Centre for Ethnicity and Racism Studies at Leeds in 2015–16. I am grateful for discussions with the group's regular members (Adrian Favell, Austin Harrington, Thomas Campbell, Ruth Holliday, Bobby Sayyid and Mark Davis). Discussions with Maximiliano Korstanje (University of Buenos Aires, Argentina) and Nelson Graburn (University of Berkeley) on things we (dis)agree on have also been valuable.

I remain in debt to two scholars who acted as my teachers in theory: John Urry, with whom I interacted in person over the years, and Zygmunt Bauman, with whom I never did, but whose work I consumed voraciously, if not fast enough.

The clash between thanatology and hope, as well as the ways of escape we devise from disaster, were inspired by my Greek and Pakistani families, who make ends meet in the current socio-economic climate. A word of gratitude goes to my companion, Majid Yar: his intellectual and moral support has been invaluable; his invisible labour as homemaker helped me create some of the following pages; and his presence in my scholarly discourse is significant.

1 Staging the mega-event
Militourist imaginaries in an Olympic city

Mega-events: enterprises of time, explosions of spaces, non-spaces

Officially known as the Games of the XXXI Olympiad, the 2016 Summer
Olympics (*Jogos Olímpicos de Verão de 2016*) of Rio de Janeiro, Brazil, fit
into a form of conduct dictated by the ethical regulators of the inter-
nationalised sporting market, the International Olympic Committee (IOC):
they should be a major international multi-sport event held in a formally
selected host city (Rio de Janeiro), within a designated time frame (5 August
to 21 August 2016). The 'host' should provide for international guests/athletes,
food, drink and a place to stay, train and prepare for the competition
(Lashley and Morrison, Eds, 2000). Over 11,000 athletes from 207 National
Olympic Committees, including first time entrants Kosovo, South Sudan and
the Refugee Olympic Team, took part in Rio 2016 (Rio 2016 Olympic Wiki,
undated). A series of other training and event-making venues should be ready
to host the actual athletic and ceremonial performances: thus, 33 sporting
venues in the host city, and five more in São Paulo, Belo Horizonte, Salvador,
Brasília, and Manaus, were made available.

Rio de Janeiro was announced bid winner at the 121st IOC Session in
Copenhagen, Denmark, in 2009. Under the leadership of IOC President
Jacques Rogge, the thirteenth Olympic Congress would bring together all the
constituent parties of the Olympic Movement (IOC members, representatives
of National Olympic Committee (NOCs), International Federations (IFs), the
Organising Committees of the Olympic Games (OCOGS), athletes, coaches,
media, sponsors and other stakeholders) to discuss the current functioning of
the Movement and define the main development axes for the future (XIII
Olympic Congress – Copenhagen 2009, undated). The 'future' of the Movement would figure prominently during the Rio 2016 mega-event, in both ceremonial and architectural formats, which brought to the fore the role of
technology in event-making milieus of a solidary, peaceful nature. The thirteenth Olympic Congress had already discussed the implications of the digital
revolution for humanity and the Movement itself, thus implicating Rio's successful Olympic bid in both from the outset. The theme of the digital revolution figured in Rio 2016, as it had in London 2012's Opening Ceremony and

the host city's statement of contribution to global civilisation (Tzanelli, 2013b, Chapter 2). It was present in the advertising of the brand-new Olympic Channel in Rio's ceremonies (Olympic.org, 27 July 2016), which inaugurated a new era of global connectivity superseding the achievement of satellite TV that paved the way for post-national, globalising initiatives (Curran, 2011) and the intensification of cultural mobilities (Castells, 2009).

Harsh criticism of Rio's involvement in such a risky enterprise amidst one of the greatest economic and socio-political crises Brazil suffered was almost inevitable. When Brazilian President Luiz Inácio Lula da Silva (in office 1 January 2003 to 1 January 2011) celebrated the successful bid in 2009, the world was not in deep recession, wars in the Middle East were yet to induce vast waves of refugee movement that would destabilise global societies, and Brazil was yet to suffer the worst ever economic dip in its contemporary history. The second decade of the twenty-first century would remove the bliss of celebration, sparking protests across Brazil, but especially in its urban centres, where people suffered most. The dream of 'hospitable Olympic staging' came at a steep price, and when the flow of tourists began to dissipate the host city faced the consequences of seven years of intense Olympic preparation (Cavalcanti, 21 August 2016): the state government had now run out of money to keep police vehicles on the roads; the health care system was in a precarious position; Rio's universities were on strike because, just like the state's 500,000 public servants, their staff was not paid regularly. Construction work had ceased and unemployment was increasing, prolonging Rio state's declaration of a state of emergency and regional accusations of incompetence of the federal government, which had handed it 'almost a billion dollars to prevent chaos during the Olympics' (Soares, 21 August 2016).

Such controversies exacerbated fears that the instability of the country's federal government and the subsequent impeachment of President Dilma Rousseff (in office 1 January 2011 to 31 August 2016) would not allow for sufficient administrative coordination and order within Brazil for the mega-event (Segal, 7 August 2015; Flynn and Soto, 14 March 2016); health and safety concerns surrounding the Zika virus and significant pollution in the Guanabara Bay, where sporting events were scheduled (BBC Sports, 29 January 2016; Khazan, 31 March 2016); the usual riots and violence in the city, which became more socially polarised and potentially less safe for visitors, as the day the Olympics would start drew closer; and a doping scandal involving Russia, which affected the participation of its athletes in the Games (Olympic.org, 24 July 2016). But the fear that Rio de Janeiro would not be ready in time, or the suggestion that its preparations were worse than those for Athens 2004 (Gibson, 29 April 2014), were mere symptoms of something more serious. The true anxiety was that the world and its localities were changing in unpleasant ways and someone had to step in and help to rewrite this 'script' (Fincher *et al.*, 2002). From a dispassionate perspective, Rio 2016's mega-event was merely symptomatic of cosmogonic, global events, affecting mobilities of cash, people and ideas, hence national and international connectivities. A mega-event is nothing in the grand scheme of world things, in which the possibility of several systemic failures connected to capitalist mismanagement, consumer excess, terrorist violence, epidemics and environmental destruction come together under the ambit of a true and final 'mega-event': the end of human happiness and life.

Chapter 2 examines the identities and roles of its 'artistic *imagineers*' (distinguished architects, ceremonial directors and choreographers) as producers of the host city's cultural futures and legacies. Thereafter, we proceed to examine specific artistic interventions: Chapter 3 debates the ways the Museum of Tomorrow, the product of an international artistic contingent and Rio 2016's neo-futurist educational-touristic landmark, debates humanity's survival in the context of climate change and unrestrained capitalist development. Chapters 4 and 5 examine Rio 2016's Opening and Closing Ceremonies as artistic statements on *Carioca* culture. The Olympic directors and choreographers do not work independently from each other in terms of a political, cultural and overall philosophical stance: their artwork crystallises into a uniform narrative of *Carioca* and global worlds, asserting varied degrees of solidarity and coexistence in the difficult context of recession. Similar analysis is applied in Chapters 6 and 7 with regards to the forthcoming Japanese mega-event context. Chapter 6 outlines Japan and Tokyo's cultural, political and economic development, to consider its contribution to Olympic culture, whereas Chapter 7 considers the Handover Ceremony to Tokyo 2020 as a dual national and transnational narrative of belonging that supersedes memories of war and imperial domination. The final Chapter considers *imagineering* as artistic practice of engagement with contemporary national and global concerns to argue that the mega-event's artistic economy is generative of dark and bright, negative and positive future frames. Such aesthetic frames negotiate the principle and value of hope for human betterment, respect for fellow humans and nature in an enlarged cosmopolitan sense – an *Event* subsuming all mega-events.

The geopolitical and cultural coordinates of this *Event* – its aesthetic contextualisation, every four years – are of immense significance. The slow but sure 'unlocking' of capitalism from old world centres in Europe and the West (Wallerstein, 1974, 1980) has not necessarily resolved global power hierarchies, it just complexified them further. Mega-event organisation is not dissociated from these new complexities, both because new multidirectional flows of capital influence are influenced by new decentred forms of corporate power (the mega-event's investors) and because the new imaginations of geopolitical belonging and legal connectivity prioritise the urban over the national-state unit (Sassen, 2006). Today entrepreneurial urban governance, including that of creative content, appears to have replaced the national or even broader regional government with more localised patterns of capitalist urbanisation of potent global connectivity and networking (Sheller, 2008). Thus, spatial reconfigurations of belonging, legislating and acting upon the social have come to favour a peculiar local aesthetic of internationalisation, in line with new communication and transportation technologies, the dismantling of constraints on cross-border financial transactions (Urry, 2014), or the intensification of international labour migration. Brenner (2004, pp. 17–20) discusses this in terms of a qualitative transformation of rescaling that involves crisis-management strategies. Such strategies affect perceptions of time and space – which for Lefebvre (1979, p. 290) bears testimony to a post-industrial 'explosion of spaces', and for Augé (2008, p. 65) gives rise to 'non-spaces', spaces defined by capitalist signification and not entrenched belonging, a globetrotting rationale rather than rooting (Urry, 2007).

In addition, we must consider how old cultural and aesthetic hierarchies diffuse in global markets, thus leaving the 'custodians' of various cultural and aesthetic formations (post-colonial nations) unable to protect their very own populations from indiscriminate commoditisation. The additional toll of safety for mega-event hosts adds to these old hierarchies a shadow of 'doubt', suggesting that the designated urban hosts are not quite 'ready' to deliver a good and safe spectacle. But as already hinted at, this is symptomatic of the ways more localised (or nationalised) political and economic transformations play out on an interactive 'glocal' (Robertson, 1992) template. This results in the intensified urbanisation, industrialisation and transnational connectivity of 'developing' nations and urban hosts of the Southern global hemisphere at an unmanageably fast pace (Black and Van der Westhuizen, 2004; Cornelissen, 2010). It therefore helps to situate Rio 2016 chronologically and spatially on a generic mega-event mobilities 'map' to understand its significance in terms of capital flows (Girginov, 2016, pp. 147–148): the Global South figured as host to sporting events several times in the twentieth century (Mexico 1968 Summer Olympics and several FIFA World Cup finals, including Uruguay 1930, Brazil 1950, Chile 1968 and 1986, and Argentina 1978). In the twenty-first century, one Summer Olympics was hosted by Beijing (2008) and one Commonwealth Games meeting by India (New Delhi 2010), and two World Cups took place in 'emerging nations' (South Africa 2010, Brazil 2014) (Giulianotti and Klauser, 2010, p. 51; Millington and Darnell, 2014, p. 191; Giulianotti *et al.*, 2015). This transnational policy of cultural openness and inclusivity becomes problematic with the implementation of Western technologies to counter terrorist risks, spectator and political violence, poverty, inequality and urban crime.

Although mega-events of a sporting (such as the Olympic Games and the FIFA World Cup) and non-sporting (such as international Expos) nature may be seen as exceptional, they now involve organisation 'unmatched outside of wartime and planning that requires significant alterations to the governance of the host city or country' (Fussey and Coaffee, 2012, p. 269). The ephemerality of the actual occasion aside, mega-events usually have a long-lasting legacy for the host (Roche, 2000, 2002): in terms of urban renewal (for example, the 1992 Barcelona or Sydney 2000 Olympics); in terms of infrastructural alterations (the 1964 Tokyo Olympics); in terms of cumulative debt (the 1976 Montreal Olympics and 2004 Athens Olympics); or in terms of aspiration for global recognition through distortion of, or accommodation into Olympic values (the 1936 Berlin and 1968 Mexico City Games, respectively, as well as Qatar 2022 – Carter, 2016) and its status as a global media event (Tomlinson and Young, Eds, 2006). These concerns, which mirror the focus of the existing (and rapidly expanding) literature on mega-event management, prioritise traditional 'critical realist' and 'hard policy' themes, often displacing, with some exceptions, the publication of research on ceremony and cultural activity in the Olympic city to other fields. Few studies attempted to consider the notion of 'event' and urban 'eventisation' as self-contained queries, with their own cultural idiosyncrasies and representational capabilities (Tzanelli, 2015c; Hannam *et al.*, 2016).

The present study considers the mega-event's 'globetrotting' rationale across two dimensions: the space in which different movements of business, people, ideas and performances are concentrated for the duration of a few weeks; but also the non-spaces of capitalist production of such movements that are not physically located in the host's territories, but across the world. The idea is that we bring together symptoms and causes of an impending 'catastrophe' so as to examine who tries to imagine better futures. This 'mapping' of spaces and non-spaces has to be matched with considerations of the experience of space and non-space by mega-event visitors, creative labour and hosts. 'Official' conceptions of space would merely superimpose the logic of territorial belonging, authority and security onto experience (Sassen, 2006). Mega-event cities and venues have their own histories and heritages that local game-makers and artists and architects (this study's focus), use to produce new forward-looking temporal templates (Salazar, 2016, p. 9). The mega-event's notion of time is peculiarly two-dimensional: its principles obey to the 'slow' movement of old Olympic traditions and values – Baron de Coubertin's heritage to the world (Toohey and Veal, 2000) – and the hyper-speed of globalisation, its systems of mobility, its markets and development demands (Tzanelli, 2013b, Chapter 1). The mega-event's 'arrow of time' is very much a product of Enlightenment notions of 'progress' mostly associated with Northern European traditions of modernity and understandings of Heideggerian mechanical clock-time (Heidegger, 1967). Contemporary human societies experience an existential crisis in post-industrial times, connected to a true proliferation (or, for some, intentional production of representations and simulations) of risks, which feed especially the imaginary of environmental catastrophism (Giddens, 2009; Urry, 2010, 2011).

Some may object to the relevance of such observations about mega-events as real festivities: the end of times is more befit for a movie, or should be consigned to the Olympic Ceremony, they may argue. This book suggests that social sciences should make space for an analysis of such imaginaries of the future. Teleological takes on temporality rooted in Western philosophical traditions attribute causes of historical events to abstract transhistorical processes, leading to some future historical state (Sewell, 1990, p. 3). Transhistories of this sort often render themselves as explanatory frameworks in

Olympic ceremonial contexts, where memories and events pivotal for the host communities are compressed, so as to weave an overall central scenario of cultural development for the Olympic host (McKee, 1999, pp. 45–46). In ceremonies we discern connections between 'cosmology' as the experiential dimensions of social ordering and framing (Herzfeld, 2008; Tzanelli, 2013a, 2013b) and as a branch of astronomy that studies the universe as a whole from its observable parts (Sewell, 1990, pp. 3–6), with a note that the treatment of human action as a component of the universe's mechanical functioning is valid only as a mythical analogy. Olympic ceremonial texts also render themselves vulnerable to fusions between internal and external (to the event's narrative) explanations of development – a practice akin to that of 'freezing time' to extract and shuffle some of its components (Burawoy, 1989). The artificiality of 'freezing' and 'fracturing' temporalities does not allow space for an explanation of the ways happenings between significant events affect their outcome or emergence (Sewell, 1990, p. 14).

Yet, it is precisely such potential fusions that reveal alternative paths to the future – 'pathways' that may not be 'scientifically verifiable' (Popper, 1959), but do provide problem-solvers with a new perspective. Lakatos would have cast this as a 'positive heuristic' (Lakatos, 1976): the creation of a new narrative made up by fusions of models that might enable the defence of the hard core of theory (problems faced by host societies) by means of problem-shifting (Burawoy, 1989, p. 761). The practice is not just applicable to the Olympic Games' artistic ceremony but their *performative* (in Butler's (1993) terms) nature: the embodiment of the Olympic principles of solidarity and fairness, which is performed in ceremonies by artists, athletes and public functionaries, provides a different context, every four years, in which, often globally applicable challenges can be addressed within the material constraints and limitations of the era. Still, the thesis is too post-structuralist, like Butler's, who notes that, although subjects repeatedly perform the teachings of discourse, the experience of repetition ceases to be mechanical: 'as the appearance of power shifts from the condition of the subject to its effects, the conditions of power (prior and external) assume a present and futural form' (Butler, 1997, p. 16). For me, no repetition is structurally binding, because humans possess interpretative skills. It is this power to interpret that supports a positive heuristic, allowing ceremonial text and context to transcend constrictive social and economic realities.

Here we can detect how heuristic 'engineerings' of the Olympic ceremonial type can produce imaginaries of the future. The whole Olympic enterprise of knowledge has European epistemological roots, which new systems of mobility (technology, professionalisation of athleticism and migration, tourism and hospitality) constantly challenge – a phenomenon transferred onto the mega-event's double conception of time. The 'slow' time of cosmology, to which the Olympic 'event' belongs, produces an ontology of labour: this is what Arendt (1958) saw in the *Homo Faber*, the slow and plodding man, an ideal type of worker, who, in Olympic contexts produces versions of human nature. The idealisation of slow mobility in calibrations of the host's 'unique' ethno-cultures or the display of athletic ability and integrity in Olympic competition, are part of the Olympic heritage. Yet, the suggestion that 'slow is beautiful' also informs contemporary leisure rituals originating in Europe, such as the Italian *cittaslow*, a movement involving the consumption of local food cultures in cities (Fullagar *et al.*, 2012, p. 4). A growing number of authors (Bertman, 1998; Odih, 1999; Honoré, 2005; Urry, 2007; Howard, 2012), implicate modern constructions of time in creating stress and dissatisfaction. We are inundated with suggestions as to how to spend our time and what kind of activities we may perform as fast as possible (Bauman, 1988; Paolucci, 1998). As Bauman (1996, pp. 10–11) explains, contemporary fragmentations of time into 'episodes' structure our experience as that of a player, who cannot distinguish accident from necessity.

The onus of constant clockwise labour is relieved by the provision of hospitality to and for us in a different social and cultural context, in which we are cast in the roles of the leisure-seeking human. Thus, against the first impression that notions of hospitality as the provision of food, drink, accommodation and entertainment (Lashley, 2007; Caffyn, 2012; Lynch *et al.*, 2011) are shallow, their genealogies reveal that they are implicated in the production of multi-scalar socialities, beyond the scope of small communal interactions (Lashley and Morrison, Eds, 2000). I do not disregard the importance of hospitality and tourism generation for countries of the Global South as a developmental path or a regional leadership strategy (Beek and Schmidt, 2012), but focus more on how ideas of societal 'giving' (the basis of hospitality) can also translate into unconditional generosity to strangers (Tzanelli, 2011, p. 133; Derrida, 1994; Derrida and Dufourmantelle, 2000; Still, 2010). Such traditions are as European as that of the Olympic Games: O'Gorman has argued after Derrida that the proto-Indo-European root *ghos-ti* refers to 'stranger, guest, host: someone with whom one has reciprocal duties of hospitality' (2007, pp. 17–18). He suggests that both terms 'host' and 'guest' connect to words denoting sacrifice and to the term *philoxenia* as the love of alienness/strangerhood. Olympic hospitality in particular obeys norms and values of peaceful place-making for guests – whether these are tourists, refugees, business travellers or labour migrants. And that is how hopeful future-making enters our lives.

Much like the Olympic movement, *cittaslow* bridges the gap between the mythical time of *kairós*, in which (food) cultures as ethnic properties and heritage emerge, with that of *chrónos*, the uniform and quantifiable time of everyday life (and consumption) (Heidegger, 1967; Howard, 2012). Much like the Olympic Movement, *cittaslow* resolves capitalism's contradictions in a touristified 'bubble' (the Olympic city), by turning tourist-visitors from the 'fast world' into pilgrims of the host culture (ibid., p. 12). At the same time, the Olympic 'event' functions on a speedy temporal plane, where tourism and hospitality services are organised and the mega-event is literally staged in the city. This productive contradiction supports the logic of 'life politics' (Miller and Rose, 2010), the principal human negotiation between sustainable and responsible behaviours on the one hand, and unbound consumerism and exploitation on the other (Rojek, 2010). Notably, slow tourism is also connected to the organisation of tourism for social justice and environmental sustainability (Hall, 2009). Thus, for social movements with a broader eco-systemic (human-nature) vision, it articulates demands for fundamental changes in the organisation of tourism while also advocating particular ethical decisions and collective identities (Dickinson and Lumsdon, 2010; Dickinson and Peters, 2014; Fullagar *et al.*, 2012; Guiver and McGrath, 2016). For social movements with a specific political-ecological vision, a 'life politics' articulates demands for fundamental changes in the organisation of tourism while also advocating particular ethical decisions and collective identities.

Capitalist organisations of time introduce instrumentalism in the ways we use various enabling technologies. For academics who provide empirical calibrations of relevant theory, 'the rejection of this goal-orientated, linear time is symbolised by the spiral motif for the slow travel movement' (Guiver and McGrath, 2016, p. 13). For them, slow travel represents a circular and more abundant vision of time, one that allows us to exercise our freedom (Germann Molz, 2009). Instituted as a movement and as an ideal of mobility, slow tourism responds to modern time scarcity – which is why it was connected to the institutionalisation of employment time and the subsequent reorientation of our leisure activities. Circular organisations of time – a reaction to employment constrictions – stand at the heart of capitalism as an economic system with its own ideological variations (Sewell, 2008). For post-Marxist scholars, capitalism is not just a mode of production but a production of worlds through the disciplined coordination between minds (Lazzarato, 2004), which is now regulated with the help of technology. The genealogy of this capitalist process is not flattering even for 'progressive' political systems: in socialist contexts, factories were competing for medals to motivate workers in a society alternative to capitalism (Negruşa *et al.*, 2015, p. 1175). Thus, the principles and qualities of 'softness', 'dedication' and engagement with the local communities or the environment that slow tourists display do not actually counter or eradicate, but modify capitalist contexts.

Engineering time in Olympic mega-event contexts takes into account these parameters of international mobility. The *modus vivendi* is that of generative human empowerment: the transformation of 'labour' without a particular cause other than capitalist accumulation into *movement* for betterment (of human nature and nature at large). In this respect, as space-bound enterprises, all mega-event contexts implicate host cultures to the politics of place-making, which in turn sustain mobility constellations (Cresswell, 2006, 2010). Olympic engineering (dubbed in the book '*imagineering*') necessitates the involvement of international experts, hence a strict division of labour in the production of mobilities. Discussion in Chapter 2 of what I term the *homo mobilis* is informed by the consideration of the mega-event as a functional and structural reality: though based on an ideal (Olympism), today mega-events are primarily organised as transnational enterprises, in which the mobility of ideas, humans and materialities acts as the governing principle (Bærenholdt, 2013). I do not start my analysis from the institution (the nation-state or the business firm) but from the interlacing of the mega-event's production of distinctive life-worlds (after Habermas (1987, 1989b)) as both consumable practices and conserving ideals, with their workers/artists and their consumers. Thus, I view the mega-event as an enterprise engaged in knowledge production about human environments and the aesthetic landscapes humans inhabit – 'worlds' within which subjects exist as labour, in short.

For reasons I explain later, although legally the cities of Rio and Tokyo as mega-event hosts operate within a national polity, in reality, their enterprise points to a form of international relations policy informed by centrifugal political manoeuvring. This 'style' of political engagement is also a style of cultural association and an interpretation of the Olympic norm of hospitality, in line with post-neoliberal global transformations that favour a sort of collective individualism (Brenner, 2004, pp. 16–17; Lazzarato, 2015, p. 73). Every mega-event depends on a double notion of 'debts' embracing both economic (private contracts with various Olympic partners) and political domains (public contracts pertaining to variations of citizenship and solidarity extending those entrenched in the nation-state (Lazzarato, 2015, p. 77). Often, the idea that mega-event mobilities are conditioned by 'political debts' is Protean in nature but Manichean in strategy. This is so because such 'debts' might be *seen* to stem from colonial scripts of power in order to symbolically overwrite economic ones in the eyes of different native and foreign audiences (Tzanelli, 2015c). And yet, colonial pasts themselves may also be overwritten ('forgotten') by their guardians (post-colonial polities) when they are called into account for the enduring social inequalities in their dominions. The city of Rio was pressurised into operating like an egoistic individual in hypermobile environments of consumption in preparation for the mega-event – like a monad, exemplary of wider, global social processes. And this is where its distinguished creative labour – its nationally and internationally contracted *homines mobilis* – intervenes in revolutionary ways to reshape native *and* international systemic worlds.

The contribution of the book to urban atmospherics

Viewing artistic and architectural labour as contracted labour with independent priorities, personal cultural alliances and even revolutionary commitments flies in the face of established literature on the mega-event's Manichean organisational strategism. The book seeks to challenge precisely this scholarly mindset, which views the cultures of Olympism as 'only politics and money'. My deviation from the norm is based on the realisation that, currently, most of this literature (to which I contributed) reproduces developmental failures: its unilateral focus on variable polemics – the 'evilness' of Olympic industries, the justice shortcomings of the host city and state, the avarice of Olympic art and festivals – presents vulnerable segments of the host as populations in need of salvation. The same pens will valorise us, authors (often white, middle-class and mostly, though not exclusively, male academics), as committed activists, thus reproducing/relocating the gaze of power of which we accuse the host in academic communities of experts. Current analyses of Olympic art and tourism as mere 'profitable enterprise of knowledge' do more than racialise work: they produce perversions of 'gender orders', casting distinguished service providers as corrupt hermaphrodite businessmen and women. Paralleling constructions of 'Camp' as fake depoliticised sensibility (Sontag, 2013, p. 260), such interpellations – for this is what they are for critical theorists – validate old problematic discourses pertaining to 'cultures of narcissism' (Lasch, 1991, pp. 39–40), coincidentally, also rooted in patriarchal constructions of gendered social role-playing. Whether corrupt or just, Olympic infrastructural policy-makers always enter academic discourse, but artists and tourist-makers are often displaced to 'cultural' or 'tourist studies' as inessential case studies.

The book contributes to cultural sociological theory in an alternative fashion: it looks at the semantics and contexts of culture-making via the products and practices of its distinguished artistic/architectural labour in globalised contexts. As such, it seeks to analyse ways in which urban ecologies are reworked symbolically in cultural economic frames. Artistic symbolisations of urban ecologies capture overlaps between silent racialisations and salient glamorisations in urban development, often granting both with political and economic depth (in Rio's case they stretch back to colonialism). Of course, local cultures receive and rework the forces of globalisation in creative and disruptive ways, thus also propelling disconnections from past patterns and life forms. So, *live culture* matters – which is why such 'urban ecological journeys' communicate with the book's other half, focusing on the cultural economy of the mega-event. I argue that at the 'morphogenetic' level (Archer, 1995), the level of phenomenal and material shaping of culture, materiality and culture are interwoven in complex, dialogical ways that disrupt the Marxist dialectics one retrieves from conventional theories of art and aesthetics (on revisions see Sheller and Urry, 2016; Freudendal-Pedersen *et al.*, 2016). Host cities are microcosmic parables of globalisation constantly re-imagined at the figurative level. This level of urban form-shaping is phenomenal and based on design – all the things we cannot take for granted when we talk about the ways the 'city image' is formed through interactions among the city and its internal and external observers (Lynch, 1960; Hasson, 2002). In political and economic terms, global exchange can do more than one thing at the same time, here opening up cultures to affluent and positive futures, there increasing inequalities, ecosystemic risks, urban stretch and unsustainable lifestyles (Urry, 2011).

In this combined thesis mega-event management, as well as the idea(l) of the Olympic Movement, speak the language of 'mobility' in cultural politics. As a pre-eminently international cultural movement in global society, the

Olympic Movement was always conditioned by political and economic choices (who hosts the Games), the imperatives of urban renewal, the catering for global guests and tourists, the principles of transnationalism and the imperatives of corporatisation (Roche, 2002, pp. 165–166). Yet, politics and economics sit at the surface of a cultural core: what imbues human associations with meanings. As Appiah ([1991] 2009) notes, in our post-modern culture which, for him, is a global cultural phenomenon, different post-modernisms might operate in synergy and/or competition to forge different ideas and ideals. With this in mind, I place the cultural and political dimensions of my study under what Alexander (2006; Alexander and Smith, 2001) has defined as cultural sociology: a sociology informed by the centrality of culture in everyday life and, more appropriately, a project of retrieving, studying and evaluating different textures of meaning that allow space for considerations of hermeneutics and structure. I need interdisciplinarity to realise the book as an ambitious project that views the urban host's social development and aesthetic sensibilities in coexistence and collaboration, but also in conflict (Born, 2010). The fact that Rio's variable inflection and rejection of Olympic heritage during its hosting of the mega-event reminds us that utopian renditions of mobility as the promise of frictionless movement, speed and freedom can and have to be challenged.

As a former colony and national capital, a regional city rife with problems of inequality and racism, emanating from colonial pasts and current socio-economic developments, Rio was asked to both meet the standards of the mega-event's phantasmagoric policies set by international players in the field, such as the IOC, and to conform its societal order to the demands of other international policy coordinators, such as the UN and UNESCO, in issues of climate change, violence, refugee crisis and urban renewal (Millington and Darnell, 2014, p. 198). In an age of uncontrollable 'speeding up' (of technologies, systems, work and leisure/tourism patterns – Hannam, 2006; Beaverstock *et al.*, 2009) and 'stretching out' (that flattens out national, regional and cross-border capabilities – Kesselring, 2016), we cannot disregard the consequences of applying seamless strategies of growth across the globe. But we also need to learn to stay detached from discourses of development, 'bracketing its familiarity, in order to analyse the theoretical and practical context with which it has been associated' (Escobar, 1995, p. 21; Nederveen Pieterse, 2010). The utopian ideal of hosting a mega-event in a 'zero-friction society', where seamless mobilities can be neatly coordinated, is a problematic ideological relic of Western European notions of cosmopolitanism (Horne and Manzenreiter, 2006; Cresswell 2001, 2006, 2010; Delanty, 2009; Jensen and Freudendal-Pedersen, 2012). But in the same cultural locus the mega-event as situational expression of an Olympic Movement can seek solutions – for, in European spaces, notions of humanity were problematised with consequences haunting global presents.

However, I will not be dealing with cultural policies at large, but with particular instances of socially astute cultural creativity in Rio's and Tokyo's ceremonies and show-stopping architecture. The book does not place the cultural workings and distinguished workers of the mega-event under indiscriminate ethical attack (à la 'political ecology'), but considers how they partake in the 'schematisation' (Stiegler, 2011) or reimagining of urban ecologies. Political economists analyse the reciprocal influences among economic, social and political factors, as well as how these impact on the regulation of activities in different institutional contexts, thus capturing patterns of inequality and restructuring in a post-Fordist now economic landscape (Piore and Sabel, 1984; Esping-Andersen, 1994). In mega-event contexts, this approach condenses the analysis of different phenomena, often confusing the cultural with the social and the political (Close *et al.*, 2006; Tzanelli, 2010). A cultural economic approach would emphasise how changes in the everyday life of a city and the ways its futures are imagined partake in the production of its contemporary cultural codes, mores and lifestyles.

This aspect of the study looks to the ways distinct social spaces or 'moorings' orchestrate new forms of social and cultural life – how new utopian architecture and performance propel *Cariocas* (Rio de Janeiro's citizens) to think about themselves in present and future worlds (Merriman, 2005; Hannam *et al.*, 2006; Kesselring, 2009; Obrador-Pons *et al.*, 2009). Thus, a cultural economic approach would note the concerted contribution of all human mobilities (including business, tourism and activism) in the articulation of global reciprocities as glocalised interactions. And although economy and inequality are not off the table, the focus is the type of cultural communications, ideas and ideals such interactions bring to life. Without a dip into the localisation of reciprocity in the mega-event, we cannot really study its most prominent feature: the articulation and engineering of hospitality for global visitors (Lashley and Morrison, Eds, 2000). The point is not minor, given that especially Rio's *favelas* (shantytowns), now more touristified than ever (LeBaron, 2014; Freire-Medeiros, 2014; Korstanje, 2016a), present us with a unique variation of urbanisation through an increased involvement of former slave (rather than rural – Tilly, 1964, p. 11) communities in sets of the city's activities, norms and relationships that reach beyond the limits of their own life-world. Not only was Rio's *favela* formation a 'mega-event' in its urban chronicles, it would eventually evolve into a twin marketable and destructive trope in its 2016 Olympic mega-event, because of social tensions (Tilly, 1984). Regarded by their former masters as non-human populations and living in the present in a recognitive purgatory, communities of *favelados* (*favela* residents) attain some form of cultural citizenship through their insertion into the new tourist markets (Tzanelli, 2016c). But how are these tensions received in the mega-event's artistic spaces?

Favela engineerings in the mega-event's creative spaces also present us with a phenomenon exceeding the usual overlap of global and local capitalist structuration (Giddens, 1985; Robertson, 1995). Art is cultural *praxis* that does not obey structural rules at all times; much like organised travel (Henning, 2002), it produces counter-worlds and alternative future possibilities.

The mega-event's art and architecture may be subsidised by capitalist networks, but their propensity to revise their structural conditions – to be utopian – renders mega-event artists and architects as articulators of the host city's atmospheres. By 'atmosphere' I refer to an elusive and intangible feeling, 'taking form between people, objects and physical settings', which is often modified by business in brand-making (Löfgren, 2014, p. 255). The notion of atmosphere connects with terms such as affect, emotion, ambience and attunement or 'collective affects' (Anderson, 2009, p. 78), holding in tension a series of opposites, such as 'presence and absence, materiality and ideality, definite and indefinite, singularity and generality' (ibid., p. 80). A bundle of all these things is imagined and 'engineered' by creative labour – what I term in Chapter 2 '*imagineering*'. To consider Rio's atmosphere, I focus on its *Carioca* ethno-style: as denomination of the natives of Rio de Janeiro, '*carioca*' emerged as a pejorative for the residents of poor neighbourhoods but would eventually evolve into a mark of pride for the entire city. As the city's 'accented' Brazilian Portuguese and as embodied style (a modification of samba, an interaction style), *Carioca* is now disseminated via the second largest TV network in the world, Rede Globo, 'so it is a sign of global cultural mobility' (Tzanelli, 2016c, p. 74).

Atmospheres are a 'force field' giving life to lived spaces, with the ability both to affect and be affected by broader changes (Stewart, 2011). As the material consolidation of atmospheres and a potential aspect of local heritage milieus, such 'brands' are by-products of imaginary formations, blending native self-understanding and tourism fantasies that constantly recreate place and its people (Salazar, 2009, p. 50, 2012, p. 869). Mega-event imperatives can exercise immense pressure on the host or even its global sponsors to 'use' such local affects as consumables. Often, although the host city's brand ought to contribute to its sustainable future, a breach between its mobilisation in the mega-event as symbolic capital and urban structures (Scott, 2010) induces a crisis in its cultural life-worlds. In the following section I analyse how *Carioca* and samba are not mere 'products' but deep-seated atmospheric formations sustaining Rio's social and cultural rhythms, and in the next section I explain how their historic associations with 'slum dangerousness' feeds into a global but locally implemented military tourist imaginary of securitisation. Artistic formations of the *Carioca*-samba ethno-style use the principal sensory tool of such 'war frames' (Butler, 2009), the gaze, to contest their brutal logic by polyaesthetic means. Examples are provided by Santiago Calatrava's Museum of Tomorrow, Rio's new atmospheric landmark of 'good' future living, the Olympic Ceremonies by Fernando Meirelles, Daniella Thomas and Andrucha Waddington, as well as the Handover Ceremony to Tokyo, as equivalent cultural prognostications.

Drawing on the work of philosopher Gernot Böhme (1993, 1995), Urry *et al.* (2016) consider how atmospheres are today constructed or staged from such disparate locations as architecturally enhanced urban environments, the home, sports stadiums and museums. Much like its embodied and digitised ceremonies, the mega-event's foremost architectural creation, the Museum of Tomorrow, encloses a form of 'pictorial intentionality' (the perception of an aspect-specific entity as part of its physical presence) that shapes and conditions the world around it on a deeper level (Heidegger, 1993, p. 192). In Chapter 7, I highlight a similar trend in Tokyo 2020's programmatic ceremonial narrative, through representations of the future host city's architectural landmarks. Poetic formation is accomplished in the city by the mega-event's architectural 'hearth', which acts as a homestead unique to Rio and Tokyo, thus projecting both cities' legacies as their new authenticity. Especially for Rio 2016, much like its con-temporary samba rhythms, the mega-event's architecture attunes Rio's urbanite atmosphere to landscape, thus joining spaces of social activity (Heidegger, 1993, p. 105). And while buildings direct our perception back to elemental properties (mass, solidity), formal features (symmetry, harmony, balance) and designs (sculptural, curvilinear, dynamic), as architectural structures such 'landmarks' awaken our imagination 'to the organic, irregular and fluctuating forms of nature as a living, evolving life-world' (Anderson, 2011, p. 78). Only for this, we should consider Rio's material urban development for the Olympics as a suc-cessful marriage between architectural craft as technology and decorative design as art (but see also Jensen A., 2011; Jensen O., 2014).

These examples are products of globalisation, not of some mystical, intro-vert ethno-culture. They were generated thanks to the free flow of ideas, individuals, investments and industries in a globally interlinked economy that speeds up the erosion of national sovereignty 'as the power of information directly touches local communities' (Ohmae, 1990, p. 269). The picturisation and audio-visualisation of *Carioca*-samba has certainly led to its hybridisa-tion as an embodied (dance, singing) and technological genre (in its cinematic renditions). Local atmospherics are fictionalised self-narrations of place in games of make-believe for hosts and guests, although, of course, they are anchored on mythical histories of the land. Because *Carioca*-samba atmospherics also affect mega-event guests, they are subjected by its artificial machine of sur-veillance to further scrutinisation, so that they 'fit' into the projection of an impeccable urban ecological picture. And as local and foreign 'cosmopolitans' gain more in capacity for knowing others categorically (in the abstract), rather than personally (through tacit neighbourly interactions) (Hofland, 1973, p. 177), the city turns into the nature of the modern human, 'holding for him [sic.] the same fascination, opportunity, and terror that the forest held for our ancestors', with the demand that we adopt a logic 'in which the cate-gories are not filled by parts of plants and animals but by different types of our fellowmen' (Cohen, 1975, p. 1026). Rio's atmospherics are, therefore, concomitant with the emergence of the city's own strangerhoods (Wolff/ Simmel, [1959] 1971; Bauman, 1991): the *mulatta Carioca*, the *favelado sam-bista* and *capoeira*, as well as their cultural development through new, emer-gent music and dance subgenres. Rio's atmosphere is complete only when the cityscape is populated with socially marginal ghosts, stripped of their anger and tamed for the visitor's gaze.

Rio's eurhythmic and arrhythmic flows

The amelioration of Rio's 'edgy' atmospherics for mega-event visitors is not dissociated from the predicament of its Brazilian stylistic modernism, its pathway to modernisation or its intellectual encapsulation of modernity. Although all three expressed resentment towards the lures of European colonialism, they budded into a coherent cultural programme after the dawn of the nineteenth century and the European rise of national cultures. It is significant that Rio's urban design ignored or concealed inherent contradictions in favour of a modernism based on formalist excess and exorcising darkness and hierarchical social arrangement (Conduru, 2004; Lara, 2011). Achieving metropolitan status in 1808 and following the declaration of Brazilian independence in 1822 and the advent of the Republic from 1889, the city would embrace the positivist European tradition of *Ordem e Progresso*.

Until almost the mid-twentieth century, the national flag's motto would not achieve structural implementation. Whereas the military and trade elites enjoyed some technological or industrial improvements and an emerging intelligentsia embraced European mannerisms with a tropical twist, the masses would have to wait for these promised changes. Such carefully concealed contradictions, usually known as symptoms of the country's 'incomplete modernisation' (García Canclini, 1995), have always been disclosed in potent ways in artistic performances. It is no coincidence that, to date, although the country's artistic cosmopolitan ethos is characterised by an interweaving of adventurous narratives of 'physical movement and imaginative migration' (Sheller, 2004, p. 14), its ceremonial projections in mega-events cannot shake off the aesthetics of 'sedentary' *indigenismo* altogether (Tzanelli, 2015c). This domesticated version of cosmopolitanism – what Aravamudan (1999, pp. 6–7) terms 'tropicopolitanism' – maintained a dialogue with the former colonial and late capitalist powers on the nature of Brazilian character. Hence, the aesthetics of Brazilian tropicopolitanism are not altogether disconnected from the Western European 'beautiful' world image (Heidegger, 1975) and the picturesque renditions of cultural nature as a way of 'world making' (Duncan, 1999, p. 153; Dann, 2002, p. 6).

Ironically, the country would achieve order and progress after 1930, with a revolution that allowed General Getúlio Vargas to seize power. What the Republic did not achieve in welfare provision, such as education, export diversification and organised urbanisation, was accomplished under the authoritarian vigilance of the Commander (Lara, 2011, p. 132). The notion of the *Estado Novo*, the new state that brought about the birth of a hybrid nation, was engineered with the help of modernist intellectuals, who would produce a selective template for Brazilian heritage. More of a 'safe' (for the authoritarian regime) *bricolage*, this template mobilised the intellectual richness of the country's colonial past, streamlined its dissemination into the educational system and consolidated its *faux* primordiality in architectural constructions akin to those we associate with European artwork (Segawa,

1994, p. 64). This blending of European avant-gardism with versions of tradition foregrounded a haphazard compromise between nationalism and internationalism and guided the creativity of architects such as Oscar Niemeyer. From the outset, authoritarian Brazil had to achieve a symbiotic relationship with extreme communist visions of the future.

Alternative paths to modernisation and nation-birth, including those of Afro-Brazilian origins, were discarded – or, better, displaced in the netherworlds of emerging slum formations in cities such as Rio de Janeiro, rapidly re-engineered into touristic commodities. It is important then to note that the alleged prevalence of Brazilian avant-garde modernism from the 1940s did not eradicate earlier traditions, it just attempted to relocate them to an outside (non-national, tourist) territory, thus acting as a precursor of postmodern 'non-places' (Augé, 2008). This spatial reconfiguration of cultural politics fits into a concerted political programme armed with intellectual tools – for, Vargas' desired 'national unity' was strongly influenced by fascist corporatism and European nationalist trends, thus favouring revisions of the old Brazilian cultural 'profiling'. From roughly the late 1940s, 'appearances' would matter more and more in global presentations of the country's 'racial democracy'. Pivotal in this peculiar game of native-style *branqueamento* (symbolic 'bleaching' or 'whitening') was the work of the first Brazilian race relations analyst, Gilberto Freyre (1963), who managed to present the ensueing colonial 'racial miscegenation' as the core of Brazilian national prowess, allowing for Brazilian 'character' to participate in multiple Euro-African experiential mobilities.

Augé astutely notes that any empire, 'like the world of Orwell or Kafka, is ... "para-modern"; a botched modernity ... [the] exact negative [of supermodernity] ... blind to the acceleration of history' (2008, p. 92). Vargas' urgency to meet the race of progress by ordering Brazilian populations produced its Nemesis in the amplification of his project's internal contradictions. Ruling Brazil with Rio as its capital with an iron fist between 1930 and 1945, and then again between 1950 and 1954, he both initiated welfare provision for the poor and the emerging working classes and repressed their ethno-cultural core, brewing trouble for his successors. Having a culture of international nationalism is paradoxical, if not systemically catastrophic, so his peculiar partnership with a champion of the Moscow-endorsed Communist Party, Niemeyer, exemplified Brazilian political life's mid-century impasse. The promises of Lula's *abertura* as a much softer programme of left-wing liberalisation in the footsteps of a frail constitutional reform (1988), would not necessarily remove the thorns of Vargas' anti-democratic ideology, nor would it eradicate the legacies of slavery in the country. Note also that for urban research, this 'opening' can only lead to rigid reproductions of a structural opposition between a putatively 'non-urban' realm as a 'constitutive outside' for any empirical and epistemological analysis (in Rio's case, its slave and labour populations and their cultural habitats, zones and cultural formations) and the wider global context 'as "obviously" playing some constitutive role in the local process' (McCann, 2011, p. 114). Without disregarding the empirical significance of urban locales and milieus, this book attempts to supersede bounded territorial understandings and assumptions that locality somehow gestures up to globality or the global manifests in localised milieus. Its substantive focus is the mutual constitution of the urban and the global in the 'ongoing art of being global' (Ong, 2011), not as a constitutive spatial imaginary informed by hard policy standards (Baker and Ruming, 2014), but through imaginative reflections of its cultural worlds. The book substitutes the idea of 'worlding' (Roy and Ong, 2011) with what is discussed as 'world-making' both in political theory and philosophy (Arendt, 1958; Goodman, 1978).

Today Rio de Janeiro accounts for a population of 6.5 million, and is known for two diametrically opposed reasons: its high homicide rates (18,243 between 2005 and 2014), mostly of black male populations and mostly in the poorest neighbourhoods in the North Zone (*Zona Norte*), and its popularity as an internal and international tourist destination (Soares, 2016, pp. 10–12). *Zona Norte* extends away from Rio's Centre, the city's administrative, cultural and consumption node, to include suburbs of various income levels but mostly working class. The wealthy South Zone (*Zona Sul*) neighbourhoods of Botafogo, Copacabana and Ipanema, which figured amongst the Olympic Games' most-visited areas and venues, seem visually and socially worlds apart from Rio's shantytowns: they concentrate world famous beaches, are full of shops, high-rise apartment blocks and restaurants and are surrounded by upscale residential neighbourhoods such as that of *Jardim Botânico* (Botanical Garden) (Moehn, 2008, pp. 176–177). The meeting of Afro-Brazilian traditions with Western-looking, Europeanising modernity is strong enough to drive the city's brand, now carefully updated by its Olympic visionaries. The move of the capital to Brasília in 1960 continues to partake in a neoliberal game of urban competition, casting the new capital as 'reason' and the old one as 'nature'.

A prominent singularity enmeshed into such capitalist cultures is what we associate with Rio's particular inflection of *Brasilidade* or Brazilian-ness (DaMatta, 1991). Interpellated identifications of *Brasilidade* with the Brazilian 'land' as a touristified 'landscape' (Urry, 2004) include a sort of 'cultural cannibalism' (*antropofagia*), the appropriation of cultural artefacts and practices from foreign civilisations (Sneed, 2008, p. 66). This conveys what Nederveen Pieterse has termed 'cultural hybridisation', a mixing of cultures previously considered independent 'categories', with a degree of subsequent recognition of shared characteristics as well as 'difference' (Nederveen Pieterse, 2006a, p. 672). Displays of affects, friendliness and musicality are also coupled in *Brasilidade* with political corruption signs, sensual androgyny and *malandragem* (macho deviant or criminal street smartness) – all three gesturing to 'Camp'. But it is problematic to consider this list of 'characteristics' in line with legalistic readings of property – especially intellectual property. In the professional context of the mega-event, Brazilian *anthropofagia* ought to be examined in lieu of organised hospitality as a mode of engagement with reputed international political and cultural players, whose cultural codes often remain as perplexing as the Brazilian ones. Because especially artistic appropriations of foreign properties are displayed in public with some degree of acknowledgement, they communicate sharing, hence belonging to a community, rather than 'stealing'. As we will see in the Opening Ceremony, such sharing signifies mergers between the slow time of national cultures and the fast time of foreign, especially European, cultural mobilities. In this context, 'cultural hybridisation' has to be matched with a 'structural' one, allowing Rio to harmonise temporally and spatially (infrastructurally) with global centres of governance. Enabling further translatability of native cultural practices, Meirelles and his associates performing *anthropofagias* in Olympic Ceremonies are symptoms of globalisation: not only do they produce Rio's atmosphere, they connect Brazilian art-scenes to powerful global centres of cultural production.

The artistic inflection of an essentialised *Carioca* habitus is deeply rooted in the city's Brazilian-style modern contradictions. Soares (2016, p. 228), who includes in such stereotyped *Carioca* aptitudes a natural talent for dance, a flair for music and the gift of the gab, suggests that such myth-making masks the native urbanites' darker side. The carnival atmospheres of Rio, its Dionysian touristic style and legendary beautiful women complement an entrenched 'machismo, prejudice … and image-peddling to bring the tourists in', as well as the city's 'constant violence and abiding inequality' (ibid.). The 2016 mega-event's host is essentialised by the *Cariocas* themselves as a crafty low-class or feminine con artist at the same time as its international Olympic image-makers strive to present the city as a spectacular media-controlling magician. This gap between intimate self-recognition and public self-presentation (Herzfeld, 2005), a simultaneous slippage in meaning and convergence in voices or *diforia* (Tzanelli, 2008c, p. 491), is not mere quirk displayed by Rio's natives but also part of the local, federal and the national administrative machine and its press mythologisation. Far from communicating fictional scenarios, such second- and third-order performances and representations *make* Rio's cultural worlds in as diverse spheres as those of politics, jurisprudence and economics. The making is also present in global contexts, given the city's indeterminate position in global urban hierarchies. The post-colonial condition has been absorbed in urban policy in such a way that reproductions of binary oppositions between the 'real global cities' of the post-industrial Global North, and the putative 'provincial cities' of the Global South or 'Third World' have turned old imaginaries of development into 'geographies of authoritative knowledge' (Robinson, 2002, p. 531; Roy, 2011; Robinson, 2011), obscuring the many ways the global is 'in play' in context (Ong, 2011, p. 12). And this 'obscuring' generates its Nemesis within the international political system(s).

The inability or refusal to admit cruelty (embedded in Soares' cultural mugshot of Rio), is also a rejection of the new confessional practice sketching the economic human's relation to capitalist development. Such 'development' contains traces of a promise based on a bond of indebtedness that the Brazilian human *polis'* governors seek to modify. Clean brand-making is a policy of cultural and social environmental cleansing not so dissimilar to the racial whitewashing we find in so-called 'developed' parts of the world. Much like the 'reality' of personal misdemeanours tarnishing former President Dilma Rousseff's public image maintained by right-wing propaganda in the country and abroad, which calls for an *exagoreusis*, a repentance addressed to a human master of development as representative of God (Foucault, 1988, p. 44), the 'reality' of image surveillance calls for public accountability within and without the nation-state. The idea of urban regeneration is thus guided at a formal level by the penitential logic that has been shaping the European disciplinary system since the eighteenth century, and which might prevent Rio's disciplined body from the 'possibility of being – of arriving – otherwise' (Beard, 2007, p. 31). In this system of symbolic 'incarceration', an artistically crafted response based on the preservation of habitual uniqueness (Rio's high spirit, hospitable atmosphere and untamed enthusiasm – DaMatta, 1991) is hardly unexpected: not only does it reject the 'imported' alien logic of a unitary self-managed self as a form of sovereignty (Balibar, 1991), it appropriates its aliens tools (the mega-event as spectacle) to achieve 'character development' on one's own terms.

The end game is ambiguous in terms of actual achievement, as in capitalist life-worlds no development can happen without the rule of the market. Here, as a self-declared Marxist and a career socialist, Rousseff threatens both Truman's post-Cold War capitalist utopianism and the uniform rhetoric of 'Third World underdevelopment' that Truman's Doctrine brought to life (Beard, 2007, pp. 157–178) – the very ideas Rousseff's right-wing enemies used against her in their cries for impeachment. Rousseff's welfare reforms *and* neoliberal 'opening' have been at such odds that they enabled further suspicion of foul play. Transfer such observations onto the mega-event's host now to observe homologies: an attempt to bring the values of nation and development together under the discourse of international market management (Scott, 1998, pp. 92–93) brings Rio's 'unruly' status on a par with the status of the country's 'unsuitable' governors, who must comply with the expectations of an interdependent global system – or else. It is forgotten that North American development in particular had to *be engineered*, as it was never presumed by international policy coordinators to exist in and of itself (Cardoso and Faletto, 1979). Intervention projects are designed specifically 'to "bring" development to those amongst whom it is lacking' (Kaplan, 1999, p. 24). The omnipresence of corruption, 'crony capitalism' and 'relationship-based banking' (Martin, 1999) – all the economic facets a celebrity Brazilian individualism of Rousseff's stance allegedly possesses (DaMatta, 1991; Barbosa, 1995) – have to be addressed by greater foreign ownership control. By the same token, we should not consider the ubiquity of 'transparency' references (see Rio 2016 official website) in the public management of Rio 2016 as an isolated regional Brazilian occurrence: their 'grammatological significance' (Derrida, 1976) as ways of 'discovering the truth' and establishing knowledge ensures eurhythmic patterns of interaction between the host and 'her' various international policy and market partners.

It is this international response to an *oeconomie artificialem*, an economy that turns the artifice of technology into instrumentally rational means to an end (equivalent to Giddens' (1990, 1991) 'cognitive reflexivity' (Lash and Urry, 1994, pp. 32–44) that art aspires to transcend. But in the context of the Olympic Games, Rio's 'sinful' political ecology has to be 'fixed' both for internal and external audiences and powerful stakeholders. The *locus* of corruption can only be placed outside the nation's respectable image: Rio de Janeiro's *favelas*, whose life stretches as far back as the late nineteenth century, have always been associated with criminal marginality. The verdict that *favelas* are characterised by a collapsing civil society and by weak 'civilising processes' (ibid., p. 324) is a construct imposed on their inner realities from outside and above. The idea of an expansive 'outlaw territory' embracing or overlooking the urban core and occupied illegally by freed slave labour, poor immigrant populations from Northeastern areas and decommissioned soldiers (Perlman, 2010), contributes to the denial of the city's own memory in the wake of cosmetic mega-imaginaries of mobility. Where upper class and mainstream popular discourse sees risk and damage by arms of gangs and drug traffickers, the *favelados* experience housing they can afford with their poor salaries, protection by shadowy criminal organisations and easy-to-reach illegal connections that secure their electricity, water, television services and sewage. Limiting the *favelados'* contact with the state to encounters with armed police (ibid., p. 201) further enables local gangs to operate as an alternative 'rule of law' (Leeds, 1996, p. 62).

Rio's 'de-criminalising' enterprise necessitates the involvement of partners that belong to different scalar hierarchies (business residing abroad, local recruits and urban as well as IOC administrators). These hierarchies do not involve fixed scaffolds of social interaction but are themselves produced and modified through various specific virtual and terrestrial interactions and policy-making meetings. Thus, Rio's urban ecologies are being redefined and redesigned on the basis of a new political economy of scale (Jessop, 2002) and as part of new globalising spaces of financial (Castells, 1996, 2004; Urry, 2007, 2014) and criminogenic flows (Franko Aas, 2007). The polarised but integrative development between dynamic urban cores (the phantasmagoric city) and peripheral areas (the city of ruin) may allow Rio to reap the benefits of other external scale economies but can certainly contribute to the destabilisation of its cultural rhythms (Brenner, 2004, p. 13). Notably, the Brazilian state's militarised approach to public security has historical depth, when it comes to its applications in impoverished areas and marginalised populations. In terms of urban securitisation policy, it is significant that, from the mid-1990s, a series of police programmes targeted *favelas* located in the southern part of Rio, where all the wealthiest and touristified areas are located. In this sense, 'white' (in symbolic terms and matching the *Carioca* language of race as comportment of class and wealth) mobilities produce the *favelas* as spaces of racial and class inequalities. Rio's symbolic whiteness is enacted in this instance through privileged ways of moving in the city with security, even where its inhabitants may feel insecure (Braathen *et al.*, 2015).

The prevalence of negative feelings in the *favela* is constitutive of the various mobilities and immobilities that redefine it in spatio-temporal and phenomenological terms, and which communicate with the mega-event's management of identities, images and reputations (Salazar, 2016, p. 2; Andranovich, 2016, p. 53, p. 55). In the grand capitalist scheme of things, slums figure as 'world's waste spaces', 'Third World' miniatures that either carry too much history to include in the city-host's mega-event narration or no history worthy of mention, hence fit for instant integration into Western chronologies of humankind (Nisbet, 1969, p. 241; Agamben, 1998, p. 122). To align this with the more general social and cultural rhythmanalysis of Rio in this study, like all human beings, the *favelados* must be able to both actively extend themselves through imagination and action in a happy future and be granted the right to have a future in existential terms. 'Futurising' is an act of establishing firm links between action, knowledge and ethics for the maintenance of meaningful temporal bonds (Brun, 2016, p. 401; Adam and Groves, 2011). Yet, for any such futurisation in the *favelas*, the presence of an emergency discourse within Brazil and abroad must become more diverse than that proffered by the current business-orientated project of 'police pacification'. The state of poverty and the experience of racialisation and criminalisation remove the act of futurising from these communities, whereas their displacement in an informal (tourism or otherwise) economy, suggests a sort of phenomenological disappearance from future urban possibilities (on experiential modes on 'seeing the city' see Donald, 1999). To attain a future as spaces of grotesque beauty, the *favelas* look outwards, to embrace the world of travel, business and tourism; their international 'network capital' (Larsen and Urry, 2008) comes from their potential for modification by the 'gardening state', that weeds out those populations it deems unpresentable to foreign onlookers (Bauman, 1989, 1991). And this is how they enter the imagination of the mega-event's distinguished artistic labour.

Enrique Dussel (1995, pp. 76–77) called for the actualisation of 'transmodernity' as a process in which both modernity and its negated alterity (silenced populations in post-colonial statist formations) 'co-realize themselves in a process of creative fertilization'. Rio's *favelas* are raw material for the implementation of transmodern ethics, but their hastened (by the state) neoliberal networking halters such reflexivity in favour of mobility. Note that *favela* network capital is constitutive of Rio's urban rhythms from a musical point of view. As a composite musical form and dance, samba emanated from the black and *mulatto* working classes in the city, making the lyrics of relevant songs historical documents (Shaw, 1999). Samba is the quintessential silent rhythm of the subaltern and thus constitutive of transmodern utopian possibilities (on utopia, music and silence see Levitas, 2013a, p. 239). Authoritative scholarly voices locate the origins of this art-form in the Western African cultures of Salvador, Bahia, during the late nineteenth century abolition of slavery. Abolition led to migrations to the mines of Minas Gerais, the coffee plantations of Rio and the city of Rio, in which migrants could take up jobs at the dockyard, as street vendors or domestic labour, but live marginalised to the *morros* or hills surrounding the city (McGowan and Pessanha, 1991). Under conditions of marginalisation, samba songs became escapist utopian narratives focusing on the twin themes of love and nocturnal life, and giving life to the figure of the *malandro* or hustler that challenged the work ethic of the government (Barke *et al.*, 2001). The genre itself mutated to reflect internal urban divides: in the affluent parts of Rio, *samba-cançao* became a melodic variation of samba with sentimental themes figuring on the radio and selling records, whereas *samba de morro* remained a classical version of the same genre, associated with black working-class issues and the organisation of social protest. Given the genre's roots and increasingly widespread routes in global musical art-scenes, samba would eventually transmute into a question of Afro-Brazilian heritage in a society openly hostile to black practices and resistant to what was regarded as its 'lowly' popular culture (Ortiz, 2000).

The low is 'kitsch', if not also 'queer': it turns the human body into the locus of cultural and social assignation, pushing its bearers to perform roles. For a country constantly symbolising its ethno-cultures in gendered terms, this is pivotal. Note again how Rio is stereotyped by *Cariocas* themselves as a beautiful feminine crook – a *Citade Maravilhosa*. The gendering of 'beauty' allegorises space and culture as much as it embodies it in whitewashed now spaces of consumption, whereas the marvellousness of 'deceit' draws on the disreputable heritage of the (migrant) pedlar and the *malandro do morro* (Acerbi, 2014, p. 99, p. 110). The hermaphrodite effect of such self-stereotyping is totally disregarded in popular parlance, which flies in the face of real everyday homophobia (Silva 2014). Almost simultaneously, the disreputable heritage of hustling that we also find in other South American contexts, rife with sexualised tourist encounters (Sánchez Taylor, 2000; Sheller, 2003; Simoni, 2008, 2013, 2015), proceeds to supplant the notion of *Carioca feminine mystique. Cariocas* as makeshift 'ideal types' excel at bodily revelation, strongly associated with liminal *carnivalesque* beach cultures only the affluent enjoy. Encoding the city's and the whole nation's love-hate regard of 'First World' encounters, conceptions of this feminised marvellous being enmesh those of the so-called *suingue* (literally 'swinging'). This refers to *Carioca* body's musical way of moving as both 'a sort of embodied sense of rhythmic deportment' (Moehn, 2008, p. 179), and indecision pertaining to cross-cultural fertilisation.

Embodiment is not just a gendered business; it brings questions of race in play, in an allegory of skin whitening we find across cultures consigned to the 'developing world' but also amongst migrant black populations living in the 'developed world' (Tate, 2007, 2009). Cresswell (2016) suggests that blackness and mobility are mutually constituted through as diverse registers and activities as sports, dancing or policing. Amongst these movements he highlights transnational events in black histories, such as slave trade and migration – pivotal in the formation of some of Rio's out-of-the-city *favelas*. As much as such pasts inform the social make-up of these sites as sources of national and transnational creativity and expressivity in the arts of dancing and the crafts of sports, contemporary black mobilities in *favelas* are also defined by social protest. Despite the fact that the mega-event's atmospheres and brands are 'refined' by distinguished international artists and other such labour, art and social protest continue to form the two poles of samba history and inform Rio's rhythmographic atmospherics.

These glocal atmospheric formations provide a blueprint for the city's mega-event design, allowing us to understand how and why the mega-event itself becomes a lightning rod for protest, how to resolve security concerns and what the ethical implications of socio-technical innovations that connect communities with professional spokespeople (or not) are (Büscher *et al.*, 2014). Only for these reasons, we cannot bypass the exploration of the ways samba, *capoeira* (a touristified now Afro-Brazilian dance-martial art) and Rio's overall art-scene developed as a 'habit' inscribed in the minds, bodies and hearts of its populations, or consign their evolution to irrelevant 'histories'. To properly understand how such 'habits' are now being mobilised in the mega-event, how Rio's memories become cosmopolitanised in the city and how they assume planetary proportions (as a *mega*-event – Salazar, 2016), we must also account for their passage from mere local memories to artistic (re)invention (Lazzarato, 2004, p. 201).

Phantoms of militarism and utopian dreaming: on Rio's ethnic move(ment)s

It is precisely this, circumstantially cast as 'subaltern' popular 'radical habitus' (see Crossley's (2003) attribution of reflexive radicalism exclusively to middle-class activists), that provides justification for the redevelopment of urban enclaves, such as those of the *favelas*. *Favelas* develop cultural potential thanks to their schematisation by mega-event artists, in other words: their cinematic projection on big stadium screens and the *favelados*' embodied performances in ceremonies. This blended upper/lower class radicalism, which involves 'shedding light' on the city's dark corners, is closely tied to the 'festivalisation' of the host city and opens the door to foreign investors and consumers of working-class ethno-cultures as attractive locations for future festivals and public events (Klauser, 2011b; Giulianotti and Klauser, 2012, pp. 317–318). The festivalisation of the city has historical depth in post-colonial Rio de Janeiro's policies. The dominant thesis has it that to festivalise place, one has to turn 'land' into 'landscape' (Urry, 2004, p. 208), to transform illegible (to outsiders/guests) homeland territories and their organically arranged cultures into globally transparent maps, usually with the help of novel technologies of the eye (Scott, 1998, p. 53, p. 57; Herzfeld, 2006, 2016; Tzanelli, 2013a, Chapter 1). In late 1960s and early 1970s Rio de Janeiro, such practices connected to the relocation of populations into 'model villages' that could be scrutinised by the state (Perlman, 1976). Brazil 2014 and Rio 2016 marked another turning point in such policies: new techniques of control the state implemented in the *favelas* involved street naming and assigning addresses, mapping, painting and street widening (Freeman, 2014, p. 12).

It has been said that the city can be regarded as 'a work of art' (Olsen, 1986), both in the case of the outstanding natural beauty of the site (as is the case with Rio de Janeiro), which can be regarded as an alternative source of prestige, and in the case of its establishment as a cultural centre 'to the extent to which [it] house[s] leisure and entertainment industries' (Featherstone, 1991, p. 96). The willingness of city administration and private capital to encourage and seek investment in culture and their sensitivity to the importance of the city's image 'under conditions of intensified competition' (ibid.) are crucial factors in the context of mega-event mobilities (Urry, 2008; Lederman, 2015; Tzanelli, 2016c; Salazar, 2016). The stylisation/aestheticisation of the everyday privileges now the local and the vernacular as a manifestation of cultural uniqueness in the face of global competition. To this we could also add cities that have a digital, post-industrial organisation, in cyber-networks and with centres of global cultural governance, such as Los Angeles or London. As Lazzarato (2004, p. 193) notes, any competition between 'companies without factories', cities operating on a 'brain tank' rather than an industrial basis, as is the case with most cities these days, is not aimed at conquering a market but at 'capturing a clientele ... building a *customer capital* which is managed monopolistically' (ibid., emphasis in text).

And here we enter the usual mega-event research niche focusing on securitisation. Rio's *oeconomie artificialem* fits into a broader pattern of control literature, which happily enmeshes the (artistic) production and consumption of local style without further qualification. The project of turning style creativity into a clientele involves anticipating demands so that the city's experts/designers realise through various deliberations and arrangements of consumable 'signs', images and promised experiences (Urry, 2002b; Urry and Larsen, 2011). And here the dandy directors of Ceremonies and the contracted distinguished architects are seen as mere 'pawns' in a game of magical make-believe: as the story goes, touring the world is increasingly performed by connoisseurs and collectors of places, allowing for the amplification of mobility and the development of an urban 'experience economy' (Pine and Gilmore, 1999). The cultural de-classification the West experiences (DiMaggio, 1987), its slow removal from the aesthetic centre of the world, affects urban world peripheries such as Rio in ways that, ironically, give a head-start in event hosting, at least at an aesthetic/cultural level. The weakening Western ability to impose value hierarchies means that cities such as Rio can respond to the old colonial predicament of underdevelopment more effectively – albeit still not always as empowered players. In mega-event contexts of development, we may even be dealing with the projection of public culture as synonymous with the development of tourism (Horne, 1992, p. 113). The stories of peoples and places promoted by this multi-industry serve as philosophies of a '"heritage" or a "societal inheritance" genes bank', turning a Western tourist industry into a purely native business (Hollinshead, 1999, p. 271). This 'legendermain' of Rio's creative industry (or its industries, given the networked nature of the mega-event's business), is never wholly produced on site, but emerges as a fusion of opinions and knowledges of global experts in the field (Horne, 1992, pp. 10–37; Urry, 2002b, Chapter 1). It is such experts, as representatives of the mega-event's invisible 'company without offices' – Lazzarato (2004, p. 188) – that produce the city and refashion its various life-worlds as 'bits' of a picture-postcard.

This academic script also provides 'evidence' and 'uncovers' epistemic truths: following a Foucaultian framework, it can propagate that terrestrial and digital surveillance, ceremonial art, architectural production and tourism altogether simply answer institutional needs to repress dissent at home, inspect and control the mega-event host's multiple ethno-cultures, and 'reach out' to other global financial and cultural centres (Sassen, 2001, 2006). We are all familiar with studies of evictions *en masse* for the production of the host's impeccable Olympic image. And truly, the underlining logic of *favela* human capital as mere 'garbage dump', belonging to waste gene banks, contradicts the very biopolitical project of the nation-state (see also Bauman, 2003, pp. 123–124 on privacy and the *homo sacer*), as it turns social spaces into landscapes with thinning populations (Jacobs, [1961] 1992, pp. 271–273). *Favelas* are spatially separated from mega-event visitor 'fan zones', where supporters of different competing nations drink, party and watch fixtures on giant television screens. This allegedly allows for an efficient spatialisation of non-violent consumption activities (Klauser, 2008; Giulianotti and Klauser, 2010). But 'staging' fan zones in support of safe urban branding allows for a 'translation' of ephemeral policy tactics into a legally prescribed and globally transferable exemplar, with various good and bad consequences (Latour, 1999, p. 91; Klauser, 2011a, p. 3209).

The logic of 'segmentation' is only superficially spatial: the spirit of the practice aims to streamline flows of capital into consumption circuits at the expense of native practices of being and performing space and identity. To complement the Foucaultian explorations of the ways social space is defined by security stakeholders, a Bourdieusian conception of the 'security field' (Wacquant, 1989; Bourdieu, 1990, 1993; Crossley, 2002) is introduced, which nevertheless does not unpack discrepancies and contingencies in on-site performances of communal belonging. Such a Bourdieusian framework is tailored specifically to the needs of business, as it creates 'fan zones' conducive to 'intepretative flexibility' for security (Klauser, 2011a) and policy transfer purposes from mega-event to mega-event (McCann and Ward, 2010; McCann, 2011; Klauser, 2011b).

Of course, although this study sides with aesthetic reflexivity (what I analyse in detail in Chapter 2) as apposite alternative practice to cognitive instrumentalism in event-making (Zimmerman and Favell, 2011, p. 501), it cannot ignore pragmatic political concerns that mega-event management resolves effectively within the context of an *oeconomie artificialem*. There are, of course, suggestions that the artistic spectacles we attribute to human imagination and creativity (what I place in Chapter 2 under the ambit of an *oeconomie imaginationis*) have become constitutive of contemporary 'security iconographies' in mega-events – a thesis propagated by scholars such as Lenskyj (2008) and Rutheiser (1996), famously introducing a negative-capitalist conception of imagineering that I revise in this book. The realist school of International Relations considers this economy as a way of imagining security in terms of the sovereign and territorial integrity of the nation-state, thus treating the latter as a human actor (Wood and Shearing, 2007, pp. 64–66). This humanocentric vision of security, which the book's hypothesis treats with caution, given its emphasis on environmental imagineering, appeals to discourses of a cosmopolitan ethic, imagining humans living in a world of human beings only *by accident* and as monads (Held, 2003, 2004). However, it is acknowledged that we cannot disentangle the mega-events' cultural industrial products (their globally networked broadcasting, ceremonial aspects, cultural festivals and consumption regimes) from security concerns any longer. As mega-events are destined to globally mediate and even refashion urban identities, forge future possibilities and overwrite past linkages (Harvey, 1989), and cities are urged to participate in global competition (Degen, 2004; Hiller, 2006; Urry, 2008; Lederman, 2015), the organisation of security climbs up the host's agenda. But it may be wrong to confuse the two forms of reflexivity involved in imagineering in a typical Frankfurt School argument.

Frankfurt School approaches place industrial rationalisation and modern capitalism on a continuum because of the corruptive growth of a 'Culture Industry' (Adorno and Horkheimer, 1991; Marcuse, 1986). So, I will not follow Salazar's (2016, p. 4) elaboration of mega-event imagineering in this study as 'the conscious manipulation and promotion of the city, region or even country and their global image'. An overarching conception of 'spectacular economy' should not be underpinned by a reductivist understanding of creativity and intentionality: the goals of creation and their future orientations (security and artistic flourishing) cannot be merged, nor do they always obey the same laws of cause and effect (Williams, 1977, pp. 83–84; Hesmondhalgh, 2007, pp. 45–47). By extension, I do not wish to follow Foucault's suggestion of unilateral societal progression from spectacle to surveillance. Although I heed Debord's (1995) and Barber's (2003) notions of spectacular (especially visual) consumption as a contemporary capitalist mutation, I cannot accept the abstraction of the mega-event as a uniform spectacle, an exercise in appearances without meaningful and situated content. The fallacy on which such essentialisations play sketches a Western reduction of works of art (mega-event ceremonies) to statements of intent (e.g. figurative securitisation based on a monological narrative of the host culture) (Sontag, 2013).

Yet, the organisation of security in Rio 2016 often obeyed the logic of naturalisation of 'risks' (the evilness of human nature and environmental pollution – Beck, 2006) to produce a seamless urban ecology of environmental racism. If the mega-event's ceremonies hint at such ecologies, they do so in aesthetically reflexive ways that transcend the cognitive imperatives of the *oeconomie artificialem* (contra Boyle and Haggerty's (2009, p. 261) claim). The artistic expression of an *oeconomie imaginationis*, the economy of imagination, on which the book focuses heretofore, should not be confused with the display of military prowess. Such 'confusion' figured previously in analyses of the placement of ground-to-air missile launchers near the Bird's Nest Stadium for Beijing 2008, or Afghanistan-like drones patrolling the skies of London during the 'Olympic Handover Party' in 2008, and later on above the London 2012 Olympic Games, framing the mega-event like a Hollywood war movie (Boyle and Haggerty, 2009, p. 26; Roberts, 2004). Analyses of such 'display' comply in literature with 'military urbanism': the transformation of urban spheres into sites of martial experimentation and technological control (Coaffee, 2009; Graham, 2010).

Such transformations are implemented by groups of international security specialists, endeavouring to align the governance of urban realms with the contemporary neoliberal project of privatisation and commercially conducive visions of 'order' (Davis, 1990; Clarke, 2010). This form of governance looks to old models of 'militourism' or 'military tourism', based on a symbiosis of the gaze of the first-world tourists to occupied countries with the gaze of military surveillance (O'Dwyer, 2004). Militourism employed a twin technology of looking-as-devouring: 'the reproduction and dissemination of impeccable idyllic images of native culture for the tourist gaze and the fulfilment of touristic fantasies by violent means' (Tzanelli, 2016c, p. 70). The mega-event's 'militourist' rationale involves the coordination of security in accordance with the tasks involved in war preparation. However, the present study suggests that the old militourist technique is employed by artists and architects only figuratively, so as to both incite anxiety about the future and to generate utopian possibilities – therefore, to (re)make hope and life.

To conclude then: in the context of Rio 2016, artistic and scientific innovation (inter)weave Rio's cultural fabric in ways acceptable to, and/or contested by various foreign interest groups, local administration and informal living cultures. Incidentally, in the fields of tourist and hospitality studies, it is often assumed that the power dynamics are exclusively exogenous in host–guest interactions involving developing countries, with researchers all too commonly privileging the unidirectional impacts localities are believed to suffer (Lanfant, 1995, p. 6; Hollinshead, 1999, pp. 18–19). I consider this argument as an offshoot of the management of mobility in the Olympic city with regard to crime, alleged terrorist threats and epidemic or environmental risks. The staging of contemporary mega-events is always framed by discourses of risk reduction/elimination as part of the host's ritual and pragmatic legitimation in global public spheres. Technology in particular has opened up such processes to discussions of innovation, including also artistic-like crea-tivity, highlighting the significance of 'softer' power tools for the management of mega-event mobilities such as information and communication. Unfortu-nately, the host's real(ist) vulnerability to all manner of external and/or domestic threats tends to reduce artistic creativity to 'technical innovations' associated with *oeconomie artificialem*. Note for example how Büscher *et al.* (2016) recognise two distinctive functions of such technologies in disaster responses: the first celebrates their potential to increase the efficiency of response to them (Büscher *et al.*, 2016, p. 243; Whatmore, 1997; Sheller, 2013), whereas the second stresses the detrimental social effects of risk-reducing sur-veillance (Bigo, 2006; Graham, 2010). This book opens up with notes on Rio's militarisation as its main thesis's counterpoint, which brings to the fore critical artistic interventions in the form of futural imaginings, utopian scripts produced by various technological means.

No technology as such is evil, but all technologies activate interplays between space and time, affecting local temporal imaginings by various dif-ferent interests groups and communities. Thrift (2004b) speaks of a 'chron-ometrical sea': a space created from the endless calculations produced between network components, including time switches and data packet frag-ments. For Thrift, spatial reconfigurations will change in terms of vocabularies; a sense of direction will become 'given' and space 'will increasingly be per-ceived as relative' (ibid., p. 589). Space will become perpetually mobile – an environment generated out of what he terms 'qualculation', the new for-mulation of our sense of location and access to information (ibid., p. 593). Such amplified networking of time and space in the Olympic *événement* (Braudel, 1996, vol. II) suggests that we consider the multiple dynamics and consequences of digital and terrestrial urbanisms both with regard to the production of a new ethics of care for distant others and the ethics for non-unitary subjects (Braidotti, 2013, p. 190) – what Haraway (in Büscher *et al.*, 2016, pp. 242–243) recognises, after Latour (1993), as a sign that 'we have never been human'. The educative/communicational script of this projective ethics of care – for guests, fellow citizens and refugees, but also our global home, Earth – is not created by surveillance technologies. It is the visionary job of the economy of imagination, which may even feed into futural policy-making.

2 Globalising utopias
Imagineering the Olympic event, making the world

Homo mobilis: beyond traditional biopolitics

This Chapter considers in more detail how self-designated 'artistic' creators come to form in mega-events affective communities of interest, thus both transcending and affirming their public perception as disinterested international or local/national human capital. Subsequent Chapters extend observations on such affective/aesthetic engagement to the social contexts in which such labour is invited to work, suggesting that we also consider the broader implications (e.g. *favela* policies) of their involvement in the mega-event. There is no appropriate term to capture the work and activities of these 'artistic' creators (directors, architects, actors/performers and so forth). Bauman's (1996, p. 14; 1998) definition of such distinguished labour would classify them on the basis of status and income. The identification of such groups as (affluent) 'tourists', or (ethically committed or consuming) 'pilgrims' might produce fixed positionalities in hypermobile contexts, so we need further assistance from theory. Other scholars (Favell *et al.*, 2007; Favell, 2015b) call for a new vocabulary to describe these new global mobilities. But the designation of such middle-class labour as 'migrants' does not necessarily illuminate their contribution to cultural hybridisation, because the concept does not connect to 'their cultural and social practices arising in the context of migration and diaspora and the new modernities of the "emerging markets"' (Nederveen Pieterse, 2004, p. 88). If contemporary human mobilities point to blends of established social activities such as travel, tourism, business relocation, migration and the likes (Hannam *et al.*, 2006; Adey, 2010; Sheller, 2014b), then we need a term that can encompass all of them. There are two different aspects of mobility to address in new terminology: an internal and phenomenological (a term providing insight into self-assignations) and an external and realist (a term analysing the mobile human as a subject associated with various institutions and discharging various social obligations).

Bauman's (1996, 1998) conception of pilgrimage as post-modernity's condemnation of humans to eternal, rootless movement, is considered with some modifications attuned to Derrida's work: most of the artists of the study are far from rootless; on the contrary, they represent a national culture, reimagining it artistically. A different attempt to marry the institutional and existential/ phenomenal aspects of human mobility was provided by Urry (1990, 2002b) in his 'tourist gaze'. The term helped scholars deliberate on the ways tourists become interpellated by organised leisure industries to 'perform' their assignation as 'tourists/consumers' (Urry and Larsen 2011, pp. 16–17). Although Urry revised his thesis in a 'mobilities paradigm' context (ibid.), its original Foucaultian inception (Foucault 1976, 1979, 1997a, 1998) persisted in examinations of tourism through an all-encompassing surveillance apparatus associated with the noblest of all senses: sight. This European discursive organisation of our world persists to date in tourism studies and studies of social sense-making at large (Jay, 1993). An analogous comment could be made on the interpellation of migrants as vulnerable beings, subjected to the machinations of national or transnational governance (Anderson, 2013). In this case, the 'gaze' never belongs to them, but forms an abstracted and dehumanising 'technique' controlled by others (state apparatuses or 'privileged' social groups). Far from denying the presence of power and social inequality, I support more inclusive epistemologies and hence more flexible ontologies. It seems that social sciences and humanities still cannot address Foucault's self-acknowledged weakness in exploring human agency.

But I will not discard previous theoretical stances. Their core thesis that contemporary (Westernised) societies are based on the 'spectacle' (Debord, 1995) and surveillance (Foucault, 1979) still apply in festive occasions, such as those of the mega-event. To reiterate Lefebvre's ([1992] 2015, p. 52) observation, which also chimes with Luxembourg's (1998/9, p. 50, p. 65) notes on labour freedom, 'creative activity, as distinct from productive activity, proceeds from the liberty and individuality that unfurl only in conditions that are external (to them)'. But when this observation turns into an all-encompassing paradigm, explaining human action at all times, we are left with a negative Polaroid image of Marcuse's (1986) one-dimensional human, programmed to respond to market needs by replicating their 'artificial' desires and fears. To provide a modified analysis of artwork produced by the mega-event's distinguished labour, I examine them as examples of the new *homo mobilis*. There is a separate set of social considerations to account for, including the precarity of labour and the challenges various mega-event professionals on the move from mega-event to mega-event face, which stands outside this book's substantive focus. Sebro (2016), who furthers the new mobilities paradigm, argues that a focus on *homo mobilis* encloses potentialities to consider in the place of biological terminologies so as to study practices of everyday life (Cresswell and Merriman, 2001; Edensor, 2010, 2011, 2014). The term *homo mobilis* – a Latin neologism better reflecting the legal, rather than territory, kinship-bound, or 'heritage' obligations these subjects enter at work – involves a multi-sensory, aesthetic appreciation of the worlds they modify and 'engineer' in their (art)work. An attempt to classify mega-event actors as 'agents' and 'passive recipients' will not yield results without a situational examination of their actions and creative self-perception.

Situated action connects to the wider context in which it takes place: not only do we need to account for the complexities of the mega-event city's temporary visitor economy, we have to consider how resident natives and mega-event professionals experience urban spaces and atmospheres – for, this is what *hominem mobiles* schematise in their work. Narrowing down this pool of subjects to two contrasting 'ideal types' – say, some of the mobile professionals, especially those of celebrity status (artists and policy-makers) and the slum-dwellers (*favelados*) – provides crude and reductive results. At first, these two categories appear to fit into Urry's (1990, 2002b) Foucaultian binary of 'gazers' (the privileged, affluent mobile/tourist subjects) and 'gazees' (the poor, the disenfranchised, the objects of tourist fascination), but closer inspection, such as those proffered in *favela* ethnographies, problematise the dichotomisation. As I explained in my study of the Brazil 2014 ceremonies (Tzanelli, 2015c), not only are some mega-event artists social products of *favela* life, their personal projects seek to invigorate and empower these communities (also as policy-makers – one such artist figures in Rio 2016). Something proceeds the experience of upward mobility and re-stratification, the fortune of becoming affluent and/or recognised – and this might be the experience of being regarded as a non-citizen, or even a form of 'domestic labour' of sorts (Lister, 1997).

At the other end of the spectrum, the alleged objects of the 'gaze' are 'more than': performers of consumer desire and reproducers of native traditions; passive recipients of '*favela* pacification' policies; and immobile non-consuming humans (Maoz, 2006). I consider the *favelados* as the embodied core of Rio's popular culture, which becomes in the mega-event's cultural economy a mobile multitude transcending subject–object dichotomies (Buscema, 2011). As Rio's internal strangerhood, both very familiar to the nation and dangerously different to its middle-class aspirations, the *favelados* become the focus of official surveillance (Bauman and Lyon, 2013; Amoore, 2013). If we concede this, we must acknowledge that, likewise, because Rio's 'popular culture' functions as the abstract property of mega-event management, labour celebrities and artists (its 'engineers') also become objects of the official gaze. Correspondingly, such practices of surveillance result in counter-scrutinisations by all types of Olympic critics, activist groups, or even independent actors from within capitalist structures (Timms, 2016), ultimately 'enabl[ing] the creation of new circuits of cooperation and collaboration that stretch across nations and continents' (Hardt and Negri, 2004, p. xiii). *Homo mobilis*' capacity for empathy, his or her desire or impulse to act as a fellow human, transcends the imperatives of the gaze, enabling the making of art about and often for those in need of support (Marcuse, 1955).

The suggestion that the economy has shifted from the political to the biopolitical, so that it essentially articulates communities on the basis of cerebral productivity has become a given in political theory: such productivity does not involve 'capitalist investment' as we knew it, but an investment in social brains, '[with] the breaking of disciplinary relations becom[ing] the absolute foundation of creating wealth' (Negri, 1998, pp. 139–140; Dascal, 1987, pp. 16–19; Lefebvre, 1991, p. 33). The city or state of Rio and its global partners may seek to appropriate 'brains' in the mega-project (Horne and Manzenreiter, 2016, p. 35), but brains and souls do not necessarily 'follow the brief' of such biopolitical techniques. The *oeconomie artificialem*, an artificial economy based on 'technique' devised by the state, the city or global markets, cannot always encroach upon the *oeconomie imaginationis*, the internal organisation of imagination by communities of interest. This second economy forms the basis of what I will call *imagineering*, engineering by imaginative means. The affinity of imagination with unconscious processes of dreaming before (conscious) arrangements of ideas (engineering), highlights the civilising capacity of language (the power to 'articulate' social and cultural visions) (see Dascal (1987, pp. 23–25) on Leibniz and signs and markets) and its centrality in what is commonly known as global 'knowledge economies' (see Lash and Urry 1994, pp. 14–15, p. 132 on culture industries, and Eade and Mele, 2002, pp. 5–7 on the semiotics of urban imaginaries).

The 'brain control' thesis also encounters problems on the other side of the spectrum: biopolitical regulation is based on an investment in life, but the city of Rio's surveillance apparatus seems to be partly responsible for the deaths of young *favelados*, who constitute the main carriers and live investment in its popular culture. Such policies contravene the idea of preserving *favelas* as 'suprasensible things' (Virtanen, 2004, p. 222), one of the most marketable commodities of the city, replacing them with inauthentic (safer) enclaves that do not appeal to all global guests. For an assessment of imagineering from above (the main focus of this study) and below (from within the *favelas*), we must be cautious when using conceptions of a 'biopolitics of population' – a problematic conceptual tool in the mega-event's governmobile, fluid economic and cultural spaces. Deleuze and Guattari's (1988) original axiom of capitalism in the de-territorialised workers, who are free to sell their labour power in the form of abstract creativity, makes a valuable point on the changing nature of wealth, but does not assess its *ad hoc* uses by various groups.

Hence, imagineering reflects human resourcefulness and creativity in different cultural topographies of belonging to a class, a subculture, a cosmopolitan enclave and a nation, in ever-shifting combinations. Akin to political elaborations of cosmopolitan ethics as an individual agential project (Kaldor, 2003), the concept allows us to frame collective cultural, political and economic agency in ways that may transcend micro-political interests (Appiah, 2006). The primary ambition of imagineers is to select, rearrange and/or discard pasts with no future, so as to build a future in the present that liberates society and its cultures from former mistakes. 'Liberatory politics is ... not simply opposition but an expression of the impulse to create the new, an expanding sense of what is *humanly possible*' (Rich, 2001, p. 154). A way of rewriting practice, materiality and ideals on various *humanscapes*, such as those of the city, imagineering is bolstered by the artist and the policy-maker's ability to revive older but still viable forms of practice: to be a highly selective 'ghosthunter' of sorts (Alexander, 2010). My figurative reference to 'ghosthunting' is situationally critical: Hollinshead (1998) draws our attention to 'fantasmatics' in tourist consumption to discuss the ways experts exercise an emic reselection and reproduction of narratives from specific cultural cosmologies to 'make' tourism. Such imaginary significations of culture and its populations (Mosedale, 2012) may also be applied by governing and interventionist agencies in non-tourist contexts, with issues pertaining to environmental politics, cultural urban aesthetics and ethno-political sorting as cases in point (Wetzstein, 2013). The 'fantasmatics' of Rio's imagineering might inform policies on hospitality, with various consequences for the mobilities of the mega-event's hosts and guests (Kirschenblatt-Gimblett, 1997; Germann Molz and Gibson, Eds, 2007; Salazar, 2016).

Imagineering the 'humanly possible' invites the mega-event's artistic *homo mobilis* to fuse art with technology. At least in the domain of fine art display during the mega-event, the technological separation of 'high' from 'low' artistic production should not be placed within a discourse on inequality and unfairness but viewed first as an *innovation* that propels imagineering to new levels of artistry (DiMaggio, 1992; Goldfarb, 2012). Analogies between processes by which certain frameworks of analysis and categories came to be incorporated into the scientific canon (Latour, 1987) and processes by which artistic canons were established (Bourdieu, 1984; Bourdieu and Darbel, 1990; Zolberg, 2015) provide insight into the institutionalisation of imagineering. Still, a great deal of interpretative work of an affective nature is necessary by individuals and collective communities, the not-for-profit and for-profit creative sector and the city and nation-state's spokespersons to arrive at such institutionalisations. This affective work is the shadow agent of aesthetic processes in the Olympic city as part of democratic performance. I examine such deliberative democratic processes with caution, given Brazil's current political and economic turmoil. Similar caution is exercised in Chapters 6 and 7, which examine analogous phenomena in the case of Tokyo: the Olympic Handover contained just a series of concentrated gestures towards the forthcoming Japanese mega-event, but its cultural references still contained artistic micro-statements on Tokyo's and Japan's cultural state and social fabric.

Imagineering utopias

We must be clear about one performative constant in the imagineering of utopian futures, even if/when these draw upon resources of the past (Guffey, 2006, 2014): they tend to negotiate the makers' and their subjects' relationship with European modernity. At least when we speak about culture (separate observations apply to militarised technology), Brazilian and Japanese modernities entered a turbulent dialogue with an imagined European tradition of 'high art' from their birth, and with the formation of national imaginaries of belonging their intellectual elites often resorted to amenable hybridisations of ethno-cultural style. My aim in the study of these two, glocalised now imaginaries, is to operationalise *phenomenology with history* (Mannheim, [1936] 1968), so as to illuminate *cultural context*. Brazil's heavy intellectual-as-political heritage and present public culture (especially its imported and adapted *culturae digitalis*) calls for reflections on the relationship between culture and society (Giddens, 1979; Archer, 1995). Japan's, and especially Tokyo's post-imperial relationship with cultural industrial technologies also gestures towards complex formations of a public culture in which popular artefacts (movies, comics) reflect the country's social and political transformations at large.

The imagineering of utopia by intellectual elites (re-)constitutes at least two dominant 'belief systems', the ideological and the utopian, with each of them propelling stasis (with an emphasis on the past) or mobility (with an emphasis on the future) in society and culture. Imagineering, or imagining and engineering dreamed futures, especially in national contexts (Gourgouris, 1996), stands in between these two systems, because, both in its preliminary envisioning stage and during its policy applications, the past is often set as a (good or bad) standard against the impeding innovation (Castoriadis, [1975] 1987, p. 44; Levitas, 2013b). Significantly, especially in art and architecture, utopianism, which seeks social transformation, encloses anti-rational elements, either because imagination resides in the subconscious (Castoriadis [1975] 1987, p. 45) or because there is an orientation towards goals not realistically attainable as yet (Mannheim [1929] 1968, p. 173). Artistic utopias of a technological/cinematic range in particular, audio-visualise futural possibilities, thus allowing hard policy-making possibilities to enter the phenomenal world. The principal objective of art-making is to articulate what it means to be human (Campbell, 2008), with all his/her flaws and virtues (Bloch, 1986). The 'not yet attainable' but always 'in the making' (Žižek, 2013, p. xix) human nature proffers two forms of hope in the objective possibility and the 'aspiration of becoming' (Thompson, 2013, p. 4) – useful starting-points in my examination of two mega-event hosts with colonial and imperial pasts. Not only does the 'not yet' describe such hosts' post-colonial condition in today's neoliberal world as one of prescriptive and victim-inducing (or not) but creative adaptation, it prompts us to speculate on possibilities to de-colonise their cultural imagination (Nederveen Pieterse and Parekh, 1995).

Such de-colonisation resides in the subconscious properties of nationally appropriated artistic imaginations, which better connect to the alleged immaturity of working-class and youth styles – what is aptly summarised as 'kitschification' in Brazilian and Japanese contexts, respectively. Early associations of 'kitsch' with the 'faux' modernity of the masses connected kitsch to totalitarian visions of modernity in Europe (Holliday and Potts, 2012, pp. 62–65). The twentieth-century certainty that elites dealt with 'atrophied critical sense', spiritual laziness and physical sloth (Călinescu, 1987, pp. 258–263) matches current neoliberal displacements of working-class/underclass slum cultures and the virtualised cultures of the *manga* and *anime* range to the non-spaces of capitalist markets: tourism, post-national leisure regimes – both stereotypically considered as domains of 'non-work'. Yet, it helps remembering that it was an extension of belonging, the prospect of taking up a place in the new national cultures beckoning the extraordinariness of a holiday break that generated tourism as a projection of difference (Franklin 2004). Both such Brazilian and Japanese popular cultures produce the 'kitsch man': the inward looking, intimate face of ethno-culture, effeminised in terms of class habitus on global hierarchies of value, craft and know-how skilled but 'not quite there yet' in terms of aesthetic credentials (Polanyi, 1966; Giddens, 1984; MacKenzie, 1996; Ingold, 2008). Art-making of the conscious ('Camp') type relocates these displaced cultures within a 'social dreaming matrix', as fragments of individual psychic experiences that connect individuals to others and help the community make sense of social life (Lawrence, 2003, p. 619). Dreaming can be unbound from inhibitions and norms, but the social dreaming matrix can act as both the source of creative power and the expression of new authority (Gosling and Case, 2013, p. 714). Because we always experience the 'darkness of the lived moment', in which we are surrounded both by possibilities of failure and success, utopian and dystopian conclusions, and freedom and oppression (Thompson, 2013, p. 13), the dreaming matrix is part of a culture's interpretative toolkit, a contingent fusion of agency with structure. Binding aesthetics with ethics in a potent interpretative cycle, artistic imagineering makes and remakes our social world in infinite ways.

If utopia is other than the instituted society, and utopic transgression is 'the obverse of current institutions', then 'its critical negativity remains fictional' (Marin, 2016, p. 196). Almost all artists have the capacity to represent utopia and even the 'insurgent architect', in recognising that only common sense persuasion realises beauty, can participate in radical social change (Bloch, 1986, vol. II, p. 737; Harvey, 2000). Imagineering tends to retain traces of artistic creativity in that it does not allow the actual work (whether this is for ceremonies, architecture or speech acts) invested in a project to shift from imagination to memory, as may be the case with its frozen end products. This shift merely highlights how imagination as a human faculty combines the familiar and the alien, the knowable (*noeín*) and the unknowable (*légein*) in harmonious ways (Lazarin, 2008, p. 57). This combination produces a utopian moment that can also be recognisable 'in the absence of a direct reference to a better future: a mediation of absence and void can, after all, imply the desire or hope for everything' (Heynen, 1999, p. 120). Especially when imaginaries achieve institutional recognition, they insert themselves into discourses by virtue of representation or implicit understandings, and they become 'the means by which individuals understand their identities and their place in the world' (Gaonkar, 2002, p. 4 in Salazar, 2012, p. 864). The key here is to answer 'when' questions – 'when can actors be transformative (which involves specification of degrees of freedom) and when are they trapped into replication (which involves specification of the stringency of constraints)' (Archer, 2010, p. 231). The reproduction of past projects in contemporary imagineering can be transformative or calamitous, depending on the circumstances: if the past becomes the future, engineering imperatives subsume imagination and become ideology (Mannheim, [1936] 1968).

In mega-event contexts, artistic imagineers tend to form cultural enclaves (DiMaggio, 1987) or privileged 'multitudes' (Hardt and Negri 2000, 2004), anarchist-like social formations holding distinctively globalist intellectual outlooks, despite their situational belonging to national polities (Mannheim, [1929] 1993, p. 139). And although on an institutional-structural level their presence matches global patterns of unfettered highly skilled migration liberalisation by governments and nation-states looking to enhance their international profile during prestigious mega-events, micro- and meso-sociologies of interaction (Tzanelli, 2013b, Chapter 2; Tzanelli, 2015c, Chapters 3 and 4) suggest that even such mobile subjects operate in blends of filiative (ethnonational) and affiliative (professional, guild) networks, rather than as rootless 'neo-barbarians' (Favell *et al.*, 2007, p. 22; Clifford, 2013). Professional mobilities of artists, technicians and engineers working in the mega-event's multinational environment and on the move are often under the same pressures of surveillance and 'data-veillance' implemented on localities during mega-events (Hannam *et al.*, 2016; Nadler, 2016). Doing things via such international networking contradicts the 'capitalist and nation-centred order of things, emphasizing transnational actors' resistance and freedom in [transnationalism's] conceptualization of "agency"' (Favell *et al.*, 2007, p. 15).

The spaces in which imagineering is activated are physical (terrestrial sites), but also virtual (with remote communications, via new media technologies and tele-conferencing). To match the theoretical elaborations I presented above with practical considerations, I stress how the Rio Organising Committee for the Olympic Games (ROCOG) and the city of Rio's emphasis on smart mobilities enabled, amongst other things, the institution of such virtual 'key relational sites' (McCann, 2011), 'globalising microspaces', or 'interspaces' (Urry, 2007, pp. 274–277). This institution allowed the liaison of various pre-existing networks of expertise, 'connecting, for example, pre-existent police collaborations with pre-established partnerships between the event organiser and private security companies' (Klauser, 2011a, p. 3211; Horne and Manzenreiter, 2016, pp. 35–37). For Urry (2007) 'interspaces' can be imaginary and virtually projected zones that different subjects can traverse and in which different worldviews may meet under the auspices of new permutations of a global service class (Tzanelli, 2015a, p. 48). Normally, such service classes claim specific technological professions as status symbol, but as we will see in the case of Rio 2016 and the forthcoming Tokyo 2020, professional artists and architects can (in)form a different type of cultural action, participating in aesthetic adaptation and hence mediating between policy and ideational planning.

There is ample friction among the artistic imagineers' functionality, status, self-perception and situational community belonging, as is the case with all contemporary mobility situations of this kind (Cresswell, 2006, 2010; Adey,

2006, 2010). But the technologisation of artistic and architectural imagineering informs debates on the physicality and virtuality of identity boundaries – or, more correctly, how such boundaries become instituted by key policy players in mega-events. In both Rio's and Tokyo's cases, technology figures as both an imported tool (from Europe and Western (post)industrial spheres), a means of local self-aggrandisement or 'upgrading' on a global civilisational sphere, and an unspoken 'violation' of *Carioca* and *honne* habitus, which are allegedly embodied and emotionally rich. This clash is central to Rio 2016's branding, which elevates ideas of play (*jogo*) and joy as happiness (*felicidade*) to local and national values (Tzanelli, 2015c, pp. 45–46). A similar branding game informs the Handover to Tokyo 2020, which celebrates a slightly different shift from private notions of the Japanese Self and identity to the public cultures of individualised mobility. However, contemporary uses of technology in staging the mega-event, make Rio and Tokyo's entry into virtual 'webs of obligation', in which returns can have both abstract origins (Tzanelli, 2016a, p. 118) and very material gains, especially from a visitor economy (mega-event tourism and beyond). Such a case of virtual and material gains is explicitly connected to Santiago Calatrava's Museum of Tomorrow (see Chapter 3), which is (em)powered by technology and the display of digital exhibits. The Museum's use as an international tourist attraction brings to the fore the question of Rio's role as a reliable international political player and competent mega-event organiser. The overriding objective in a 'gift economy' of this sort is to give away resources to secure status (Currah 2007, 475; Bourdieu, 1997). But where would Calatrava and his consociates fit into this situation?

We are back to 'Camp': despite their international recognition as imaginative engineers, such distinguished mega-event labour suffers from old accusations of serving as functional pawns in the hands of the regulators of *oeconomie artificialem*. Their alternative situating as 'sensitive artists' bears the potential to damage their agential 'reliability' through considerations of their role as effeminate, equally inessential labour (Molotch, 2004) – for, dreams aside, we live in social formations still plagued by sexism, racism and the likes. This diminution of 'masculine capital' will be explored in the context of the mega-event's ceremonies (see Chapters 4, 5 and 7), with Brazilian director Fernando Meirelles also as a case in point. In line with Bourdieu's (1977, 1984) work on symbolic capital, this gendered-bound credit can be traded to compensate for what is stereotypically cast as 'non-masculine behaviour' in other spheres of human activity (de Visser and McDonnell, 2013; Robinson and Robertson, 2014). The urban and international Olympic organisers' ethics of care for the athletic team of refugees (a cosmopolitan initiative tellingly introduced in the Opening Ceremony – Chapter 4), provides an equally significant opportunity to explore critically such adjustments in men's 'ethical capital', because it mediates between the two extremes. Female artistic imagineers do not necessarily fare better: their professional identity can also be questioned when they display interest in aspects of event management not stereotypically considered as 'feminine' enough: political activism of environmental or risk-deduction type, or technological organisation (as opposed to 'caring' expressions of humanitarian type or decorative ceremonial creativity) (Bryans *et al.*, 2010; Bligh *et al.*, 2011). As I explain in the concluding Chapter, counter-posing these imagineers' *gendered* capital to pure *ethno-racial* capital helps us supersede their analyses as feminist, gender or racial issues, creating an allegory of anti- or counter-globalisation. Not only does this negative attitude towards functionality obey old European scripts that separate art from technology, it does not acknowledge that artistic imagineering involves 'edgework' (Lyng, 2005), forms of emotional and cognitive risk-taking not necessarily addressed in Beck's (2009) rationalised and homogenised definition of 'risk'. A variety of 'feeling rules' (Hochschild, 1979) associated with discourses of personal and social responsibility (Rose, 1999; Donnelly, 2004) creep into the picture, prompting repetitions and contestations of stylised gendered and ethnic performances of responsibility to the world by artistic experts (Butler, 1993, 2007; Grosz, 2005). Such stereotypes are negotiated in Calatrava's self-understanding as an artistic engineer and the city of Rio's use of the Museum as an educational tool; all ceremonial directors' use of technology to create embodied performances; the Olympic policymakers' invitation to refugees to use their bodies in technological mediations of heroism; and Meirelles and his associate directors, Daniella Thomas and Andrucha Waddington, as well as their Japanese colleagues Hiroshi Sasaki, Ringo Sheena, Mikiko Mizuno and Kaoru Sugano's digital/televised calibrations of a global compassionate gaze.

I will conclude, by rejecting Foucault's definition of 'biopolitics' (1988, 1997b, 2010), that the introduction of all these forms of virtuality and technology in the mega-event have one aim: to beat the past as (dark) death and create new hope horizons as the (good) life. This propensity to utopian meaning-making merges the old script of art as godless creation with artistic (and architectural) functionality into a post-biopolitical project of mobility and global cultural connectivity. This post-biopolitical endeavour enhances Hannah Arendt's empathic gaze (Benhabib, 1996), which disregards the significance of aesthetics as alternative politics in post-modern configurations of the self and of community. It also warns that our Foucaultian epistemophilia disregards experiential and phenomenological questions, better addressed in Merleau-Ponty's (1964) phenomenology of experience and Derrida's conceptions of hospitality (see Derrida and Dufourmantelle, 2000). The power of such aesthetically reflexive networks of actors resides in a sense of political non-affiliation, in the sense that their members act as 'citizens of the world'. As other scholars argue (Appiah, 1997; Inglis, 2014), such non-affiliations embrace several areas of action and deliberation on ethics, justice, social responsibility and cultural attachment – a branching and universalising process of aesthetics as beauty and fairness, in short. This form of aesthetic engagement matches the way Kant reworked Stoic notions of universal hospitality as resolution to world conflict into his 'world citizenship' as participation in the globe, hence globalisation. Given the insertion of artistic communities into global networks, such cosmopolitanisms become implicated in late twentieth and early twenty-first century configurations of international relations, in which mega-events partake. They clarify the limits of politics as a social activity and question the actors' (artists or activists) aesthetic propensity, while pointing to the nature and sources of power in Rio's and Tokyo's social matrix. Not only do they highlight the necessity and indivisibility of authority in a market society, they bring forth 'the anarchic nature of international society and the rational conduct of states as the unitary actors within [Rio's] society' (Strange, 1996, pp. 4–5).

Artistic and social critique

We must examine how the cultural domain of imagineering *ipso facto*, interacts with territorially defined social norms. The oxymoron defining the culture of the Brazilian mega-event in Rio de Janeiro, is that its manifestations do not reflect local peculiarity; they inflect global capitalist contradictions (Bell, 1976). The fact that Rio is (self)defined by the principles of joy but organises hospitality alongside Western militourist guidelines, or acknowledges the damage imported capitalist ideology does to the environment and the social fabric but pursues unrestrained profit-making as a policy of international development and prestige does not escape the attention of privileged artistic labour. I do not wish to erect a new ethical dichotomy between policy and art, as the former tries to address such contradictions, with varying degrees of success in Rio's case, whereas the latter cannot work without capital. Rather, I seek to examine the *modus operandi* of imagineering alongside its *modus vivendi*, which is the making of utopian futures. Also, considering capitalism as a system that does not include any ethical rules and norms may be problematic (Gudeman, 2015, p. 79; Gudeman, 1986, 2001, 2008; Sahlins, 2013). Forceful critiques of the capitalist system prompt its mechanisms to readjust, thus allowing for '*a positive improvement in terms of justice*' and even an incorporation '*of the values in whose name* [capitalism] *was criticised*' (Boltanski and Chiapello, 2004, p. 28, emphasis in text). In Rio's case, such readjustments allow distinguished artistic and architectural labour to propose both reformist and radical-revolutionary imaginaries of belonging policy-makers cannot afford to ignore altogether.

Boltanski and Chiapello distinguish between two principal forms of action to injustice in what they call the 'artistic' and the 'social critique'. The former is rooted in the invention of bohemian lifestyles, and the pronouncement of loss of authenticity and beauty. This critique is based on a contrast between stability and mobility in the tradition of Rimbaud or Baudelaire's urban *flânerie* (Lash and Urry, 1994, pp. 5–6, p. 47). The social critique is rooted in socialist and Marxist indignation for capitalist accumulation and incorporates morality of often Christian overtones to attack mobile individualism and artistic egotism (Boltanski and Chiapello, 2004, pp. 37–40). Though very useful, the distinction does not apply to Rio 2016's artistic production and meaning-making, which can promote blends between the two ends in symbolic (ceremony, urban renewal) and pragmatic (humanitarian) ways. As explained in Chapter 1 and will be expanded upon in Chapter 5, Brazil's political and cultural heritage is based on creative oscillations between socialist and Marxist planning and bohemian intellectual lifestyles, which often make their way to the highest offices of Brasília to date. Because Rio's and Brazil's cultural traditions are based on such a blend of social and artistic critiques, its mega-event's principal artistic labour can (and does) extend its artwork to both ends. Former Presidents Lula and Rouseff's *abertura* share much with a twentieth-century political turn to the centre, neoliberalism-with-justice mechanisms and intellectual expertise that we identify in Western left-wing parties, such as that of the United Kingdom's 'New Labour'. The similarities also extend to a respect for and investment in culture and creative industrial development. Yet, although Rio's enterprise of mega-event knowledge should aim at distributing our beliefs across different populations evenly and equitably – what Ranciére (2004, p. 8; Ranciére, 2011) identifies as a process concerning 'the distribution of the sensible' – it actually hones our emotional intelligence anew and towards a post-human, eco-centric re-education.

Fluctuating between narratives and performances about the end of the world and the possibilities to promote new beginnings, Rio 2016's artistic critique *is social and utopian*. Throughout the book I stress that the economic surface of the mega-event's enterprise has aesthetic depth (Alexander, 2008) – indeed, it is about a particular aesthetics seeking to modify the machine of expression endorsing contemporary capitalism (Lazzarato, 2004, p. 189). Such aesthetic production is, by turns, productive of new life-worlds that counter or circumnavigate cold rationality through artistic expression, public protest and activism (contra Lazzarato, 2004). Transcending the Cartesian dualism of mind and body allows us to understand how Rio 2016, and to some extent also Tokyo 2020, do not always subscribe to Western-imported production and consumption subjectivities – how, in other words, especially but not exclusively, native communities and their subjects think of the good life otherwise. On this point, it helps noting that neat distinctions between local and foreign participation in the mega-event's enterprise on the basis of some essentialised notion of cultural difference do little justice to the interpenetration of globality and locality.

This is especially significant for activist collaborations stemming from artistic communities, local and foreign, that meet and form during the mega-event. Deslandes and King (2006) draw on Ruggiero (2000, p. 178) to stress how activists often engage in 'a form of sociological self-investigation' – what Lash and Urry (1994, pp. 49–50) otherwise dubbed 'aesthetic reflexivity' – to critique both entrenched official registers of action and external critiques that gaze upon what they purport to examine. A blend of self-with-other-reflection but with art allows artistic communities to develop an intersubjective sense of solidarity that both acknowledges power imbalances between local and foreign activist groups (Deslandes and King, 2006, p. 318) and seeks to restore cosmopolitan solidarity. Such solidarities enable forms of self-determination and activate a sense of relative autonomy that can be achieved by aesthetically reflexive means and not through 'cognitive reflexivity' (Giddens, 2002) of instrumental nature (Foucault, 2007). Cognitive reflexivity does not account for those emotional and embodied aspects of the reflexive process that amplify one's creative capacity (Hochschild, 1983; Kurosawa, 2004).

By the same token, it is essential not to discriminate between high artistic and low, folk/popular registers in the mega-event to establish what is aesthetically acceptable, right and fair. As I explained in other mega-event contexts (Tzanelli, 2013b on the London 2012 Handover to Rio; Tzanelli, 2015c on the 2014 FIFA World Cup), it is wrong to assume that soul and body instantly produce for the Olympic enterprise 'luxurious' and 'rubbish' subjectivities, because Brazilian cosmologies (a) are based on fusions of mind, body and soul that (b) as holistic ontologies cannot be regulated by disciplinary institutions (of the market or the state/regional authority). The same principles apply to the Tokyo 2020 Handover's artwork, which looks to embodied performances as revelations of an inner Self in public. The capitalist innovation in Rio's enterprise does not reside with its direct surveillance policies of street life, the *favelas* and consumption enclaves, but their liberation and embracement as production sites (of meaning). Tourism and leisure, but also ceremonial performances, agree better with Rio's established social and cultural rhythms and are better starting points even for capitalist invention (Tarde, [1890] 2001), allowing for more capital accumulation and potential redistribution (Barry and Thrift, 2007).

Where it discards distinctions between body, soul and mind, Rio's mega-event translates Western discipline into the organised indiscipline of Brazil. This provides a special social rhythmology incorporating both the Brazilian formalism of samba, *pisco* (wink and alcohol), *Caudillismo* (militarism), Carnival and mirth (DaMatta, 1991, p. 270) on the one hand, and a belief in geographical (urban centres versus peripheries), monadic (networked persons versus socially alienated individuals) and global hierarchies, with some degree of resignation (Tzanelli, 2015c, p. 20; DaMatta, 1995). Against the suggestion that, because all contemporary polities embrace technology and financialise life they march towards conservatism in the same straight line and towards the same conclusion (Strange, 1996), I consider technologies as tools used in various ways and with varied, not always negative results. To contextualise, I see 'technology' as a worldmaking process implanted with intentionalities we find in bodies, intellects, machines and emotions, not the impersonal market forces of political theory. I therefore argue that Rio's creative potentialities emerge, in Leibnizian terms, in the interpretation of individual 'talents' as a collective activity, and their projection as properties (e.g. Rio's and Tokyo's heritage matrix) by poly-aesthetic and multi-sensory means (Dascal, 1987). There is no 'evil' market *in abstracto* to identify for failures in the delivery of mega-event imagineerings, only particular implementations of mobility

policies by various actors – including activist networks. The point is methodological, because it invites situated analysis – a sort of 'methodological
glocalism' that enables the researcher to avoid 'the trap of global determinism,
while recognizing the robustness of national scales' (Holton, 2008, pp. 199–200;
Brenner, 2004, Chapter 2).

Methodological glocalism and context-bound research can comfortably
match with the ontological and epistemological position of grounded theory.
But I do not want to move to methodological questions yet. Sterilised observations on Brazilian social reality are useful at this stage for the pursuit of our
encounter with Brazilian social realities and, most importantly, their cultural
surplus: the situational cultural resources with which imagineers are invited to
work and incorporate into the mega-event as Rio's (Tokyo's) Olympic 'legacy'
to future generations. As legacies, culture and art 'work' to exceed the rationale of sustenance or biological growth of a society: they are a sort of 'excess
energy' humans generate and expend in ritualist ways through animate or
inanimate sacrifice, festivals and occasions such as those provided by mega-
events (what Bataille, ([1949] 1988) terms the 'accursed share'). The very
expenditure of excess requires a 'sovereign' use: not an *árchon* as a person or
a government (though both are involved in it these days), but a more general
'philosophical intent of political prospect' (Romano, 2015, p. 87; Romano,
2014). Intent and ritual give meaning and hope to individual and collective
life, so all communities (localities, nations and transnational formations)
devise their own rituals of expenditure or *depénse*, which is governed by specific
sovereign processes (Berking, 1999).

When such processes are disrupted, or excess energy accumulates with no
relief mechanisms in place, human societies experience a deep existential and
material crisis: by not using their excess energy, they do not exercise their own
freedom. The crisis is averted in mega-events by the massive expenditure of
public funds, hospitality and ceremonial narratives of what the host city and
its (multi-)culture(s) offers to the world. Olympic ceremonialisms are, in
effect, narratives of gift-giving (Bataille, [1949] 1988, vol. I, p. 115) – which is
why the Athens 2004 ceremonies focused on Greece's 'gift' of philosophy,
sports and education to Europe and the world (Tzanelli 2004, 2008c); Beijing
2008 ceremonies highlighted the 'true' Chinese origins of various technological discoveries, such as calligraphy and exploratory travel (Tzanelli 2010); and
London 2012 stressed Berners Lee's invention and generous dissemination of
the World Wide Web as a technological 'gift' to world civilisation (Tzanelli,
2013b, 2016a, 2016c). Ritualised *depénse* allows different cities and their
nations to enter a global reciprocal cycle that can only be completed through
processes of financial remuneration and international political recognition of
the host.

This cultural 'bread and butter' of international relations is concomitant
with the experience of modernisation across the world, the demographic
explosion in industrial and post-industrial urban formations and various
other social by-products of this shift, including the privatisation of family life

and individualisation (Giddens, 1990, 1991, 1992; Beck and Beck-Gernsheim, 1995; Beck, 1999). Today's individualised societies experience a crisis in processes of consumption of excess energy and because of their inability to put a stop to their own growth, which leads to the generation of more energy and unmanageable crises. Such crises are not merely existentialist, as Brazil's environmental and cultural problems attest: they are key policy and everyday cultural issues for the nation's and the city of Rio's citizens, who acknowledge them as 'critical'. Urry's (2010) observation that we 'consume the planet to excess' explains why both Calatrava's architectural and Meirelles, Thomas and Waddington's ceremonial imagineerings focus so heavily on resolving dystopian scenarios for Rio, Brazil and the world. Korstanje (2016b) discusses this ceremonialism as symptomatic of a rise of a society of spectacles, in which crises are 'invented' so that societies follow a thanatic capitalist ('thana-capitalist') 'script', whereby deaths are images to be consumed. We must make allowances and adjustments in our case: for Korstanje, in such 'scripts', often televised and broadcast globally, death and darkness (natural and human-made catastrophes) satisfy our human death drive in Freudian terms, feeding back into capitalist processes of consumption. But in line with my utopian thesis, I would stress that every death bears the promise of life and new beginnings – a cyclical process that can also alter the cognitive framework in which the catastrophic imaginary emerged in the first place. Our distinguished imagineers work towards this aim: though their allegorical tone seems to feed into thana-capitalist mechanisms of gazing at death as consumption, their stories conclude by questioning how audiences of all classes, cultures, races and genders can think about life *otherwise*. Their oscillation between employing the means of capitalist 'excess' (to do their artwork) and an imaginary of 'degrowth' (turning their back on capitalist ideology currently experiencing a world-wide systemic failure) is symptomatic of a negotiation of the constraints imposed by what Romano (2015, p. 88) recognises as the dominant culture. This is the culture of gift-giving that, despite its local variations, retains a universalising cosmopolitan ethos, so essential for international peace-making. In the following section I explain how this cyclical process is not, as others maintain (Sewell, 2008), fixed but generative of new cultural politics and alternative life-worlds.

Worldmaking and the methodology of post-growth imaginaries

The book's blended positive heuristics (Lakatos, 1976) addresses problems enclosed in particular theoretical legacies. The structuralism of Marxist discourse forms a well-established line of critique in the social sciences, but my use of agency-structure variations from other compatible traditions is less obviously problematic in the context of a young federal democracy, such as Brazil, which has been constantly injected with global mobilities since its institution. Drawing on Heidegger and Wittgenstein, Nicolini (2009, p. 1392) prioritises the analysis of practice as 'the unspoken and scarcely notable background of everyday life' that we must bring to the fore to turn into an epistemic, discursive object. 'Practice' in research often necessitates plural methodological frames and the ability to blend epistemic registers in order to rectify problems, close up gaps and harmonise ideas. The resulting 'transitive methodological framework', which is closer to the rationale of mathematical science, locates notions of agency not in individuals but the networks to which they belong, asserting the heterogeneity of social action (Law, 2004; Latour, 2005; Shove *et al.*, 2012). Yet, any study of practice as *praxis* or imagineering must consider various secondary data and their relationship across different populations (Morley, 2014). I return to data analysis later in the section.

Especially in my elaboration of the mega-event's ceremonies, I do not wish to replicate lapses from popular culture (Rio's self-declared site of joy sitting at the intersection of global banal leisure/pleasures) to populism with the help of discursive frame analysis, because populism is continuously being treated as a 'thin-centred', omni-applicable ideology (Aslanidis, 2016). Instead, I consider critically the context in which populism emerges in Rio's political ecologies of the slum as a site of ethno-national or regional birth and pollution. Any definition of 'populism' includes in its repertoire the themes of a 'noble people', the presence of 'corrupt elites' and the value of popular sovereignty as sufficient preconditions (Mudde and Kaltwasser, 2013), so it matters to consider the correct site of its application (Müller, 2014). At the same time, the ways media sites 'frame' even mega-event ceremonies to debate the current state of affairs in crisis contexts with the use of diagnostic elements (Moffitt, 2014) from a 'cultural toolkit' familiar to audiences (Swindler, 1986), suggests that I consider them in the context of a mediated meta-performance, in which populism becomes a central theme. I set the well-meaning actions of imagineers against their personal social aspirations, as well as the consequences of those actions' implementations, while also considering whether artistic imagineers were actual agents in the process. The small-scale analysis of an ephemeral artistic network's individuals is meant to produce 'valid knowledge' with some potential for transferability, rather than generalisability (Denzin and Lincoln, 1998; Lincoln and Guba, 1985). Finally, given my focus on cities, I need to tease out points of connection and departure of Rio de Janeiro, and now also Tokyo, from the national whole and other comparable regional urban centres. The insertion of digitality in the mega-event's staging also cautions me to assess the presence of transnational actors and emerging life-worlds and systems, so a national theoretical or empirical view will not suffice.

I will be tracing alliances and conflicts in triadic arrangements of 'space-time-energy', 'melody', harmony and rhythm, to arrive at laws on the ways the world is imagineered in the Olympic mega-event (Lefebvre, [1992] 2015, pp. 22–23). These laws are produced by a group of actors designating itself as a collective innovator/producer of meaning and with its acts 'inscribing [itself] on reality' (ibid., p. 24). Rhythmic repetition and frequency allow for methodological observation on the nature of political action in the case of Rio 2016 policy-making but also of localised (re)action to it, and they mask ethical (more local manifestations) and moral (generalised, global) principles. We can only understand how Rio 2016's plural (institutional and unofficial) worldmaking changes the city's social, cultural and political fabric through a combined study of socio-political actions, their interpretations and consequences. Considering Arendt's (1968, p. 152) claim that principles informing political action become fully manifested 'only in the performing of act itself' and that they are immanent in inspiring, guiding and organising political action, suggests that no source can be judged without some idea about its situated interpretation by communities (of artists, activists or politicians). But as principles (of Olympism, equality or well-being) are only the guiding criteria by which actions in the public realm 'are judged beyond the negative yardstick of lawfulness' (Arendt, 2007, p. 65), and their situated spontaneity opposes the imposition of 'transcendental sources of authority, power and control' (Muldoon, 2016, pp. 124–125), we have to consider how they translate into events of long-scale or planetary proportions (*événements*) (Arendt, 2007, p. 66; Girginov, 2016, pp. 145–147; Braudel, 1996). I am therefore mindful of regarding art-making as shallow a-political action. This reintroduces evaluations of artistic performances and cultural styles as populist kitschification or 'Camp' reflexivity.

Arendt considered the judgement of taste as a problem analogous to that of the political: 'an inter-subjective realm that requires criteria through which discrimination and judgment can be communicated without relying on objective laws that would command obedience' (Muldoon, 2016, p. 129). In Olympic contexts, producing judgement for future events is an essential aspect of mega-event imagineering. However, Arendt resorts to differentiations between political and aesthetic judgement, thus validating regressive constructions of activism as the edge in artistic-activist edgework: the world is meant to change for the better by taking risks traditionally perceived as masculinist or feminist activities and rhythms (Newmahr, 2011, p. 685) – an unfortunate reiteration of both Butler's performativity and Connell's hegemonic gender performance. I argue instead that imagineering mega-events artistically combines aesthetic and political action in terms of principles and forms of judgement. Blends of artistic and social critique enable us to better understand how, though mega-events are mostly based on formulaic fusions of Olympic and host values, the friction between them always bears the potential to suggest new principles that create a rupture in the present, 'a hiatus in the continual flow of temporal consequences' (Muldoon, 2016, p. 131). When it comes to structural constrictions on aesthetic-as-political action I disagree with traditional Marxists. Lefebvre ([1992] 2015, p. 63) sees capital as a force that erects itself on a contempt for life, concealed beneath an ethic – a process activated in the history of human civilisation with the help of 'ornamental' compensations, such as the proliferation of sports and sporting ideology as exaltations of life. Because, according to Lefebvre, especially in

Western modernities, capital tends to kill social richness and support privati-sation, it halts investment in open monumentality, such as gardens, squares and avenues (Davis and Monk, 2007). In late capitalist conditions, archi-tecture and the architect, 'threatened with disappearance, capitulate before the *property developer*, who spends the money' (Lefebvre [1992], 2015, pp. 63–64, emphasis in text). And yet Lefebvre, as is the case with recent distinguished economists (Piketty, 2014), refuses to acknowledge that it is not capital that drives inequalities but the collection and privatisation of riches, especially those based on inheritance (Gudeman, 2015, p. 77). As an instance of heritage/legacy, Olympic imagineering counters Lefebvre's thesis to a great extent, because Rio's ornamentalism and Olympic monumentality are in principle open to the public. Moreover, in Lefebvre's account there is a missing agent of economic and social change: the much-maligned entrepreneur, who can be a positive economic and creative force.

We live in difficult times and the idea of a world economy caught in recur-ring recession appeals to the imaginary of globalisation pessimists (Steger, 2008, pp. 178–179), who see a dangerous proliferation in 'allegories'. Benja-min's use of the term, which refers to the ways stable and hierarchically ordered meaning is dissolved, leaving behind kaleidoscopic fragments, which resist any coherent notion of what they once stood for, may fuel such pessi-mism (Featherstone, 1991, p. 23). For many social theorists, the replacement of stable meaning with signs (Lash and Urry, 1994), allows for the deep aes-theticisation of everyday life in the big cities. The collapse of some boundaries between art and everyday life, coupled with a 1960s *avant-gardist* movement's use of art as a vehicle for public engagement (Zukin, 1982), is speaking a very old political language now transferred into digital common spaces. Today's digital commons, and the uses of new and old technologies in art-worlds and by artistic communities, enable the insertion of art and aesthetically pleasing architectural creativity into world markets (Becker, 1982). Globalisation pes-simists ask: if distinguished artists are now capitalism's cogwheels and art is an old language, what can the artistic critique offer to the world that we cannot get from organised social movements?

I will not try to conflate the two here, because 'politics' in art primarily refers to the 'distribution of the sensible' (Ranciére, 2004). But the making (imagineering) of the sensible in art-worlds is always orientated towards the production – and subsequent audience and user-proliferation – of various worlds. This refers to Nelson Goodman's (1978) notion of 'worldmaking', which is based on the predicament that neither are we able to encapsulate the 'world' as such, nor can we ever know that it exists as a uniform or frag-mented totality, or as plural totalities. The only thing the human mind can capture is 'world versions', ways the world *is*. These versions are symbolic systems that attain several forms via language, dancing, pictures or other symbols and symbolisation processes. To reintroduce Zolberg's (2015) dis-course on art and science, we have symbolic systems in science, which are literal and numeric, and systems in arts, which are free-formed (Ingold, 2008;

Geertz, 2000; Marcus, 2011). We cannot claim that either of these worlds is more real than others, only select one as our own reference system. Evidently, Goodman's thesis is closely related to ways of knowing, to epistemology. But as it can, and often does produce 'epistemic communities', groups or networks of experts, whose shared beliefs or ideas are, voluntarily or not, mobilised in national or regional policies (Haas, 1992; Tzanelli, 2015a, pp. 39–40), adhering to a particular symbolic system is also ontologically productive.

Shared symbolic systems often rely on what Goodman calls 'sameness of meaning': two or more conceptions and expressions of the same 'world' having the same meaning because they share the same extension (Cohnitz and Rossberg, 2016). In this respect, Goodman's thesis allows us to replace the pessimism of allegorical proliferations in contemporary societies with a more hopeful process of community-bonding via agreed *synecdochical arrangements* of meaning. In other words, humans create communities by sharing the same arrangements (extensions) of symbols. Far from being an objectivised process, worldmaking involves the realisation of knowledge about society, both 'in the sense of apprehending the objectivated social reality and in the sense of ongoing producing of this reality' (Berger and Luckmann, 1966, p. 66). The synecdoche is thus not mere economy, but *an economisation of signs* not present in indiscriminately marketised allegories but in selective arrangement that makes worlds (Fullerton and Ettema, 2014, p. 198). Such economisation supports the hermeneutic production of signification of belonging, consuming and producing life-worlds, and thus is reminiscent of cultural sociology's 'strong programme' of structuralism with hermeneutics (Alexander, 2006, 2011). A study of worldmaking in the context of Rio 2016 – and the context of any mega-event – must consider seriously the independent power of justifications of action framed in terms of a common good across political, legal, technological and cultural spheres (Boltanski and Thévenot, 2006).

So, an examination of the ways different artistic creators meet through sharing in the same world orientation also has immense methodological value. Goodman himself always refused to reduce his 'critique of worldmaking' to a methodology, thinking of it as a 'guiding practice' instead. However, worldmaking bridges a methodological gap created in this book by considerations of 'hard politics' and critical realism. Better, it helps us bridge unfounded phenomenological claims with an investigation into the production of culture as a reality. The critique of worldmaking can be conceived as 'practical orientation' comparable to Kant's critique of reason and Wittgenstein's critique of language games, so it should not be conceived of as an epistemology only – though it communicates with it, its scope is broader. For the social scientist in particular, Goodman's symbol theory is not so much a theory but a practical conception, 'a certain technique of thinking' (Leteen, 2012, p. 30). Much like Sloterdijk's 'spherological' aesthetics as a method of 'mapping' (Sloterdijk, 2009, 2014; Weibel, 2011), worldmaking suggests that the unity of the world as a totality can only be considered as an idea, so we can only critique, rather than theorise about knowledge – we can differentiate domains of judgements, thus finding a critical-as-thinking orientation (in Kant's tradition of the *Critique of Judgement of Reason*). This stance has its own consequences arising from suspicions of relativising 'reality'. Clearly, the book does not adopt a Mannheimian pro-historicist stance (which we would find in the works of Foucault or Greenblatt), as it accepts that, superseding the nexus of text-context, reaching the actual moment with its actual first-hand testimonies, might be unachievable (Lazarin, 2008, pp. 49–50). This study should be treated as an exercise in worldmaking, but with an aesthetic overdetermined by questions of gender, racial and class inequalities. More correctly, the study aligns with the distinguished artists' critical imaginaries of and on post-growth societies, stressing that these imaginaries challenge perceptions of standardised cultural creativity.

The latter point is pivotal. If we consider 'worldmaking' as our opportunity to systematise knowledge – as an explanatory enterprise (Goodman, 1951, p. 48) – then we are allowed to 'map' the statements and (un)ethical positions that are available to us in the explored social and cultural fields (Natanson, 1986). Goodman's refusal to get into questions of ethical rightness, however, underlines the lack of normative discussion – rightness is taken as an epistemological criterion that allows us to distinguish between acceptable and inacceptable descriptions. But when 'rightness' replaces 'truth', and is understood as 'multidimensional', we are left with no moral compass in a social universe plagued by divisions, inequalities and conflict. Moreover, economic regimes shape 'truths' in compliance with what appears to be the 'right' market strategies. The world is not 'disclosed' in these regimes, it is promoted via a 'primacy of practice' to allegedly reject epistemological foundationalisms. A look at another successful field-shaping use of Goodman's work will convince us that this is the case. Hollinshead's (2004, 2009; Hollinshead *et al.*, 2009) adoption of 'worldmaking' for the production of tourism stands between the two options I outline above: on the one hand, as a 'categorical tool', worldmaking can be appropriated by tourism management to promote ethical relativism in decision-making; on the other, it can allow for the production of an ethical 'meta-theory' of mobilities that includes tourism, migration and technologies (Sheller, 2014a). For Hollinshead, the choice is displaced on the agent, who can be the scholar or the practitioner – does Charles Taylor not stress, in an otherwise more absolute fashion, that knowledge cannot be neatly separated from practical standpoints, that its 'fundament' is to be found in the agent ([1987] 1995, p. 14)? For Goodman 'we are all much in the same position of absolute but sane monarchs; our pronouncements are law, but we use our heads in making them' (Cohnitz and Rossberg, 2016). Theoretically, outside tourism studies, Hollinshead's worldmaking is not close to Goodman's but to Hilary Putnam's (1996) and Nikolas Rose's (1999) takes on Goodman: simply put, in cultural production contexts, what is ultimately 'real' as an idea, landscape, artefact or narrative, is what some 'finished science' will eventually say is real and thus ready for us to experience or consume.

As an 'absolute monarch', I can only direct readers to 'sites' of worldmaking. These also act as data pools for this study. My primary resources are mostly digital and digitised; they include international (especially, but not exclusively Anglophone) press articles, reports taken from Rio 2016 and Tokyo 2020's official websites, materials from Rio's official Museum of Tomorrow website and other web-posted materials about and of the ceremonies. This 'zooming in' and 'out' of contexts of imagineering allows me to consider how the mega-event as a trans-local phenomenon 'come[s] into being and persist[s] in time as effects of the mutual relationships between the local real-time accomplishments of practices' (Nicolini, 2009, p. 1392). The blend of official and unofficial or activist materials is purposeful in presenting readers with successive makings of different worlds. Published interviews with some of my key artistic worldmakers are also included in these materials as a 'counterpoint' to my own and other academic or political actors' interpretations. One always must have the notion of interest in mind: as is the case with blogs, Internet sites can serve different interest groups. However, online activism in particular is befitted by website profiling as a strategy for self-presentation. So, articles taking a critical approach to artwork are treated as juxtapositions of alternative worlds, not absolute realities. As Pink *et al.* (2015, p. 8) note, there is more than one way to engage with the digital, as digital ethnography is guided by specific theoretical frameworks connected to academic disciplines. Perhaps the most important feature of my search techniques is the de-centring of media as focus of the media research, in order to acknowledge their indivisibility from other embodied activities, technologies, materialities and feelings through which the media function (Alexander, 2010; Couldry, 2012; Pink *et al.*, 2015). Indeed, just as place is 'open' as a sort of 'event' pulling together activities, people and ideas (Massey, 2005), so is 'designing', imagineering the future in the cyber-sphere (Ingold, 2012, pp. 29–30).

Perhaps the most questioned digital source of information is not journalist articles but Wikipedia entries, which are often composed by journalists. Fullerton and Ettema (2014) note that what matters most is a useful convergence of world versions in the entry's collaboratively produced text – not some 'foundational *really* real version of events' but an acceptable overall organisation (Goodman, 1978, pp. 5–6). There are, of course, other epistemological issues to address, including the presence or absence of a traditional journalist or academic ethic in entries, which involves cross-referencing facts, presenting several different viewpoints, using quotation marks and providing a comprehensive sequence of events (Fullerton and Ettema, 2014, p. 186). In addition, there are several different ways of producing a narrative, which may cross the boundary of dispassionate observation to focus on versions of events and choose an angle from which to present them (Bal, 2006). The selection and organisation of images and photographs in the entry also partakes in this production of 'seriated' arguments, arguments placed on a single hierarchy

(Bal, 2003, pp. 21–22). It has been argued that Wikipedia entries obey the rules of 'organizational literacy', a way of writing and reading that takes into account 'how a particular document has been or will be circulated, interpreted, and evaluated within an organization' (Ford and Geiger, 2012, p. 27). The well-documented gender gap in entry creation and development matches the way techno-science and its institutions often marginalise female labour and make leadership positions unattainable (Ford and Wajcman, 2016). Such Foucaultian approaches do not fully address the interpretative power of readers. For a literate reader, well-crafted Wikipedia entries provide a wealth of hyperlinks and other unused meta-hyperlinks (press reports, blogposts and video links never figuring in the entry), from which the researcher can produce her own world, with its own hierarchies of relevance and irrelevance in events (Goodman, 1978, p. 11, p. 14; Tzanelli, 2011, Chapter 2).

The holistic take of the study carries within it an ambivalence towards methodology when it comes to the analysis of Olympic ceremony. Sontag (2013, p. 16) is adamant that art's marriage with interpretation is based on a high modernist assumption that works of art are composed of 'items of content' to be arranged into a 'mental scheme of categories' – a suggestion pretty close to Goodman's 'worldmaking' proposition. This allegedly violates the moral pleasure of gratification inherent in art, a unique fusion of ethics and aesthetics in our conscious life, which we do not find in stylised, rationalised and intention-orientated human creations. Herein lies the ambivalence, however: not only do all ceremonial directors answer to an authority, a collection of agencies ranging from national, federal or urban/local government and the mega-event's various market partners, they have to align their own creativity with a style that is allegedly representative of the event's host culture. Evidently, then, we deal with a worldmaking process, in which power over who makes and who is included in representations, metaphors and allegories – what for Ranciére (2004) produces 'silent speech' affecting the 'distribution of the sensible', damaging art – is not exclusively in the hands of artists but also 'in check' by policy-makers (Horne and Manzenreiter, 2016, pp. 38–41).

Notably, Rio 2016's and Tokyo 2020's ceremonial directors are nationals: it is assumed that they know the culture they schematise 'from within', with all its appropriate rhythms. The artist's relaxation or energy, his or her style (Sontag, 2013, p. 33), is thus invited to conform to political stylisation (i.e. representations of local character or habitus (Elias, 1982; Bourdieu, 1984)), so as to be made legible to the host city's guests/tourists. Standing between art as the naming of emotions or fluid aesthetic sensibility, and policy as the technical extension of human will to novel forms of social order, mega-event ceremonies *invite* interpretation by the researcher through their makers' statements. At the same time, respect for art's 'flow of energy' suggests that no conventional 'discourse analysis' or 'double hermeneutics' will do the business. Only a hybrid epistemology can support this study's meta-analysis, with room for error. Any interpretation by myself activates worldmaking processes from scratch, despite its anchoring to some real determinants, such as interviews and cultural developments in context. The point also suggests further clarification on the relationship between worldmaking and imagineering: if the former establishes bilateral connectivities between emotional and cognitive faculties, the latter transcends emotion through engineering processes (Ranciére, 2013, pp. xv–xvi). Perhaps works of imagination are imbued with emotion, but the interference of rational processes ('to make' ceremony, architecture, stadiums, laws and the likes) suggests non-artistic pursuits, with emotions displaced to the margins. Worldmaking and imagineering negotiate both individualised and collective-cultural notions of the 'edge', the boundary of risk itself, as critique, (social) movement or production of reality – as *discourse* of wild nature, in which individual actors and communities can achieve 'an undomesticated, fully feeling self' (Olstead, 2011, p. 88).

Much like Rio 2016's principal architectural product, the Museum of Tomorrow (Chapter 3), I consider the Olympic Ceremonies as products of a sense of crisis, which, both in Rio and Tokyo's cases, is heightened by a more general lack of political and ideological direction (see Chapter 1). This frames the ceremonies in public debate and allows me to identify their supra-artistic principles of aesthetic organisation in terms of frame analysis (Hiller, 2016, pp. 129–130; Goffman, 1974). Contemporary events are framed by global media systems that produce relationships between performances, their makers and audiences, hence 'more-than representational mobilities' (Adey, 2010, p. 146; Hannam *et al.*, 2016, pp. 3–4). The ceremonies inspect the host cityscape and country through arrangements of aesthetic signs, thus producing their own meta-frames of reality. Brazil currently experiences a twin war. In Rio, this war is actualised on the one hand within and between its political elites, and its non-citizen masses, and on the other through a race against other Brazilian and foreign cities so as to make it to the top of urban hierarchies. Tokyo also battles to supersede Japan's militarised past while retaining a top place in global urban hierarchies, especially with regard to its cultural production. Unsurprisingly, both Rio and Tokyo's ceremonial renditions of social reality critique war frames (Butler, 2009), communicating with the cities' militourist policies. The plea for life is set against selective death of certain populations that ceremonial directors revive before their ultimate social obliteration from the urban map. Their 'first aid' toolkit sets worldmaking against unproductive policies of imagineering, confronting us with two alternative forms of action, which fuse only conditionally for the benefit of the resuscitated.

Kleist and Jansen (2016, p. 375) suggest that the destabilising effects of such 'events' are often grounded in unreflective Western perspectives, and better perpetrated by native commentators, 'ignoring that a sense of protractive uncertainty and precarious life conditions have long been widespread in big parts of the world' (Scott, 2004; Sassen, 2014). The 2016 mega-event was unexpectedly framed by the localised trend of the global financial crisis, prescriptive global securitisation, disease and environmental risks, and even the global refugee crisis. The localisation of these '*mega*-events' in Rio's Olympic mega-event would lead to pronouncements of 'the end of hope'

(Zournazi, 2002, pp. 123–124) under the neoliberal 'end of history', the establishment of neoliberalism as the ultimate human government (Fukuyama, 1992). Almost as much as new social movements such as those of environmentalism, feminism, post-colonialism and the like facilitate direct critique in the style of 'discourses of degrowth', art and architecture continue to enunciate atmospheres of degrowth as a *predicament*. Here countering, there modifying developmental ideologies of progress, Olympic art and architecture manifest that modernist metanarratives are far from irrelevant today – 'if anything else, they have afterlives, whether as lingering hopes or as disillusion after disappointment … shaping people's temporal reasoning in [the] present' (Kleist and Jansen, 2016, p. 377). In the following Chapters I suggest that, much like the notion of a 'crisis', 'degrowth' is very much a *predicament* in art, a *problematique* rather than a 'given'. Predicaments allow for hope to flourish in dark cracks, allowing humans to believe that another world is always possible.

3 Tomorrow never comes

Rio's museum of our futures

Calatrava's creative dreams and Brazil's environmental nightmares

The world evolves within a schema of chaotic ordering, superimposing structures of feeling upon forms of nature (Thrift, 1999; Maasen and Weingart, 2000). This 'neo-vitalist' making of our world (Fraser *et al.*, 2005) suggests that everything, from living beings to animated matter, constantly adapts to new circumstances, revising orders 'that remain in the edge of chaos' (Urry, 2005b, pp. 1–2; Urry, 2003). Such urgent change captures the human imagination, also producing new art and architectural art-forms to fit new needs. Yet, unlike the governance of social adaptation, art and architecture can imagine life otherwise, escape the constraints of situated biopolitics and manufacture alternative paths to the future. Such is the case with Santiago Calatrava's 'Museum of Tomorrow' (*Museu do Amanhã*), an otherworldly edifice that sits at the edge of the old port of Rio de Janeiro (*Porto Maravilha*). Funded by the City of Rio de Janeiro, the *Roberto Marinho* Foundation (part of the *Globo* media group and involved in *favela* redevelopment that forced poor people from their homes), Banco Santander, BG Project and the government of Brazil (*Dezeen Magazine*, 17 December 2016), the Museum is a corporate-state collaborative project, speaking the new language of multi-scalar globalisation (Castells, 1996, 2004; Brenner, 2004; Urry, 2007, 2014; Baldacchino, 2010). The implementation of multi-scalar 'development' through public–private partnerships is at least as old as the 1992 Olympic Games, which were infrastructurally organised on the basis of what came to be known as the 'Barcelona model' of management (Kennett and de Moragas, 2006, p. 188). It is not coincidental that Calatrava's architectural genius was pivotal in the artistic realisation of this model.

The building's peculiar form and content are not products of individual conceit, but serious prognosticating means facilitating dreaming about a better world. This dreaming begins for Calatrava and his associates (including Meirelles as filmmaking contributor) with the painful acknowledgement that several emergent contradictions stemming from shifts within capitalism, first in the rich North, and more recently also within the rich urban enclaves of the Global South, produce life-threatening conditions. Shifts from low-carbon to high-carbon societies, societies of discipline to societies of control and, most importantly, differentiated zones of consumption to mobile, de-differentiated consumption of excess, lead to accumulation of waste and global climate change (O'Brien, 2008: p. 156; Urry, 2010, pp. 191–192). Of more relevance to this Chapter's focus on artistic-architectural worldmaking is that the symbolic spaces, in which sociological modernity and artistic modernisms forged utopias and escapist romantic travel, are now used by post-modern social sciences and arts as non-spatial configurations of homecoming (Augé, 2008, pp. 62–64, p. 70). Travel to other places has been replaced by the desire to build an *Umheimlich* Paradise on earth for humans and now also animals, an Ark of plenitude and purity, constantly threatened by unfortunate glitches in contemporary capitalism.

As a hybrid of scientism and art, the Museum of Tomorrow is located within the non-existing places of a global social imaginary of self-preservation and betterment. But as an artificial construction, the Museum is situated within these contradictions of capitalism that, according to degrowthers, will bring about the demise of humanity. As a beautiful material structure, Calatrava's creation mediates the dilemmas of climate change brought about by thoughtless human action. This ultimate Fall without God, a failure to regulate excess as 'sin', is narrated through scientific notions of the 'Anthropocene'. A proposed epoch beginning when human activities started having significant, and for some, irreversible impacts on earth's geology and ecosystems (Ehlers *et al.*, 2006), the Anthropocene is scientifically involved in the recording of feedback loops and curves in time and process (Crutzen and Stoermer, 2000; Will *et al.*, 2011). It therefore stands for the complexity and unpredictability of events and creativity in a neo-vitalist fashion, seeing the future as organised in and through various non-linear dynamic systems possessing emergent or vitalist properties (Urry, 2005a, p. 236). Artistically, this proffers in Calatrava's *magnum opus* an organisation of episodic events or 'scenes' in a near-theatrical narrative of the self-destructive human struggle for progress. Incidentally, the fact that this consolidates a dystopian discourse does not preclude the ultimate search for a *eu*-topia, or even a *kalli*-topia, a better (*eu* as good) or beautiful (*kállos* as beauty) place. The roots of the term Anthropocene in *ánthropos* (human) and *cené* (novel) already include an arrow of time that looks upwards and towards a better and more virtuous life (*ánthropos* as the aspiring human in soul and spirit, rather than in body) (Tzanelli, 2008b, Chapter 6). Ironically, then, the term's adherence to Enlightenment notions of progressive time clashes with the scientific reality of pure chance and non-linearity in relationships between climatic (and sociocultural) causes and effects (Nicolis, 1995; Capra, 1996; Prigogine, 1997; Urry, 2011).

I argue that the building relays societal discourses on the demise of dense networks of interwoven socio-spatial processes 'that are simultaneously local and global, human and physical, cultural and organic' (Paulson, 2015, p. 45). As human–environmental interactions in Brazil and elsewhere, in urban regions, are now enmeshed into these dystopian socio-ecological discourses, the Museum's multiple meanings (as a form of art) and social contribution (as a form of ecologically friendly architecture) cannot be evaluated outside the twin problematic of degrowth and political ecology. In the domains of social sciences, a combination of the two rejects the cult of development and prompts a critical interrogation of political economic factors in environmental degradation, thus forming the epistemological basis of the (re)production of bio-physical landscapes and human nature itself. Woven into contexts and categories of knowledge production, the two *problématiques* together deepen the dialogue among ecofeminism, environmental justice and other related movements (ibid., p. 47). It is also worth bearing in mind that the movement of degrowth began from the Franco-European philosophical disputes of *l'écologie politique* – the very continental context from which tourism as an activity and an experience emerged.

Designed as a troublesome journey to human epochs, a visit to the Museum of Tomorrow is both an edu-tourist experience (Holdnak and Holland, 1996) and an alternative activist statement. Norum and Mostafanezhad (2016) use the term of 'chronopolitics' to highlight the role various times play in three areas of discourse central to tourist practice: authenticity, capitalism and ecology. The Museum fits into these three chronopolitical mobilities, casting their politics into the mould of art. Despite its *global* stylistic and epistemological contribution, the Museum's 'movement' angle fits nicely in broader *Latin American* debates on notions of *buen vivir* (well-being) and the Rights to Nature – both animated by glocalised social movements (Escobar, 2015, p. 31). If so, we can examine its contribution to global knowledge economies and urban imaginary formations also in deterritorialised ways, as a 'worldling' statement (Baker and Ruming, 2014).

Brazilian understandings of *buen vivir* highlight how the socio-political reality of upper-class convenience and consumption clashes with the desire for collective betterment and ecological balance. Culture and geopolitics are now orchestrated not by the region or centralised state players, but by disorganised and shifting networks of capital, demanding both efficiency and progress at all costs. Rio's response to such demands partly leads to the organisation of the rhythms of its bio-spheres in ways not always ecosystemically viable (Lefebvre [1992] 2015, p. 78). Tyfield and Urry (2014) stress that the BRICS countries (Brazil, Russia, India, China and South Africa) often contribute to the burning of fossil fuels because such fuels are part of the maintenance of modernisation structures and processes in which these countries wish to be included. From an imagineering policy perspective, there are also global responses to climate change contravening these practices, contributing to the production of alternative social imaginaries. The UN-funded Intergovernmental Panel on Climate Change (IPCC, est. 1988) brought scientists, NGOs and policy-makers across the world together, to counteract powerful commercial interests and to transform public opinion via media debates (Urry, 2011, 2013). The IPCC's organised campaigns called attention to the fact that climate change poses a threat to global security 'that eclipses global terrorism' (Dayrell and Urry, 2015, p. 258). IPCC reports adhere to a so-called 'gradualist' perspective, supporting the thesis that climates around the world are changing at a relatively slow pace, thus allowing economies to adjust to reduce the rise in temperature. The argument presupposes the development of new technologies to slow down or fix problems. As opposed to 'gradualists', the 'sceptics' stress the unpredictability of temperature changes, disseminating via think-tanks and the Internet the suggestion that we go about 'business as usual'. Finally, 'catastrophists' draw on historical and archaeological evidence to suggest that positive feedback loops 'will take the climate system away from equilibrium through positive feedback effects' (ibid.). The overall 'unpredictability' argument warns of abrupt changes that may lead to the disappearance of whole societies and human ecosystems (Giddens, 2009; Wynne, 2010).

We therefore have a repertoire of global imaginaries in place, from which the makers of the Museum of Tomorrow could craft political and cultural statements – some less dystopian than others. All three key perspectives on climate change, as well as their emerging variations, were consolidated as global paradigms in what Steger (2008) calls the 'roaring nineties', the decade of the death of Marxism-Leninism and the elevation of political and economic liberalism to a universal doctrine focused on technological problem-solving and the satisfaction of consumer demands (Steger, 2008, p. 178). Brazil did not escape this evolutionary utopian or *evotopian* doctrine we habitually associate with liberal thinkers such as Hayek and Friedman (Hodgson, 1995). Notably, the anti-utopian theses of the likes of Hayek, Friedman and Marx – the first two proffering a market system bolstered by the state and its experts in peculiarly 'spontaneous', hence anti-systemic ways, the third one basing the future on planning and/or a communist economy – have often ended up presuming or suggesting a utopia of their own (Hodgson, 1995, p. 205; Mittelman, 2004, pp. 18–19). And in spite of Malthus' (1798) motivation to write his work on populations to counter radical utopian ideas concerning the perfectibility of society (a work very much in line today with correlations between pollution, climate change and population growth in the developing cities of the South, such as Rio), the end product *was* about humanity's *evotopian* possibilities.

Drawing on Leahy's (2008, p. 481) dark premonition that 'capitalism as a growth economy is impossible to reconcile with a finite environment', Urry (2010, p. 194) suggests that diverse but interconnected changes within the earth's environmental systems create a vicious circle of accumulative disruption, with speed and violence far greater than those of terrorist incidents. Brazilian emissions result from agriculture, land use and deforestation, with the last accounting for as much as 60% of total greenhouse gases in 2005. A year later, the country proposed the creation of a global fund from corporations and countries to control deforestation (Viola, 2013) and in 2013 it made a commitment to reduce its carbon emissions regardless of international actions and to use renewable energy (Held *et al.*, 2013). Recent surveys indicated a significant pro-intervention shift in public opinion, with Brazilians endorsing climate change mitigation politics, whereas protest movements before and during the 2014 World Cup also addressed relevant issues of national governance (Tzanelli, 2015c). Pressures led to the inclusion of environmental issues and sustainable development on the political agendas of all major parties (Labour Party, with Dilma Rouseff as leader; the Socialists, with Maria Silva; and the Democrats, with Aecio Neves) during the 2014 election campaign. From the start of the twenty-first century dedicated environmentalists in key government positions and various NGOs also supported actions against deforestation on consumption practices. The Brazilian media have been very active in the promotion of debates against global warming and the detrimental effects of certain human activities, with a significant shift towards gradualist discourses in light of lower carbon innovations and hydropower projects and some less conspicuous catastrophist tendencies connected to the slow implementation of the Climate Law in Brazil and the reduction in taxes on oil consumption to stimulate car manufacturing as a response to the global economic crisis in 2012 (Dayrell and Urry, 2015, pp. 265–269).

Eco-technocracy and environmental racism

Law and heritage take a long time to integrate; the time and space required for transitions at this level. The idea(l) of 'green democracy', or its variants, such as 'environmental democracy', 'ecological democracy' and 'bio-cracy', which emerged to capture the purported positive relationship between democracy and the environment (Dryzek, 2000; Eckersley, 2000, 2004), obscure context-specific dissonances between democratic decision-making and sustainability (Wong, 2016). Ever since discussions on the limits to growth by the Club of Rome in 1972, the viability of a marriage between the two has been questioned. Instead, an authoritarian system of experts and professionals that determines governmental control on harmful human activities was deemed as the only effective form of action (Mannheim [1936] 1968, pp. 157–164; Heilbroner, 1974). Generally, Green politics centres today on the promotion of ecological responsibility and grassroots democracy, as well as the ideal of social justice and peace, with an eye to restructuring relations between humans and nature (Carter, 2007). The democratic dilemma remains at the core of such politics, which has to recognise the conflict between the preservation of rigorous pluralism, basic majoritarianism and collective rational decision-making. An eco-centric environmental ethics, which views the environment as intrinsically valuable and non-human entities as moral beings, raises more questions in Rio's political ecological context than those it attempts to answer. Apart from the fact that it can always degenerate into eco-fascism (Argyrou, 2005), it 'does away' with processes of deliberation over green values that consider specific human needs (Arias-MalDonaldo, 2007).

Currently, Rio's developmental project draws on an eco-technocratic model of governance that grants the decision power to elites, experts and professionals and involves more technology (Dryzek, 2005). Its policy imagineering is 'radical', because it does not support Marxist-Leninist planning; on the contrary, it looks towards neoliberal solutions. Proof of this neo-radicalism is provided by the involvement of the Brazilian centre in the construction of a series of hydroelectric dams across Latin America that have uprooted Amazonian tribes and threatened local ecosystems (Tzanelli, 2013a, pp. 172–185). In the context of mega-event development, Rio's eco-technocratic approach also interacts with an eco-libertarian model adapted to *abertura* needs, thus relying more and more on free market mechanisms to achieve environmental ends (Anderson and Leal, 2001; Roberts, 2011). Brazil's Labour Party found out, by trial and error, that business is managed better by a Malthusian-like mixed economy 'where variety and impurity are essential to test all structures and systems on a pragmatic, experimental and evolutionary basis' (Hodgson, 1995, p. 109, p. 210). This policy vision of the future avoids the Marxian and Hayekian extremes and allegedly relies on a will to retain the viability of the social bio-spheres *and* the eco-system, assigning active roles both to markets and to localised planning. But to what extent do Brazilian state agents or markets truly care for the needs of all citizens? And does Calatrava's project reflect on this problem, or are we left with an international architectural wonder to please the tourist gaze?

I will attempt to answer this question in the following sections, treating the Museum both as a utopian project and as a non-utilitarian piece of art. Eradicating or side-lining the growth of ecological consciousness or relevant artistic and architectural projects in favour of human welfare is not an answer to the endogenous presence of environmental racism, nor should the two be fused ideologically. Nor should we place the responsibility of making urban ecologies 'more inclusive' on the shoulders of specific imagineers (architects or artists), who are often commissioned to develop projects they envisaged otherwise. Unfortunately, in a globalised economic landscape, constituted by capitalist nodes (Harvey, 1985, 1989; Sassen, 2006) and mobility assemblages (Sheller, 2014b), the voice or the creative capital of individual actors cannot be felt or heard outside dominant ideological structures or global systemic arrangements. Agency in mega-event projects is more present in collective social and cultural action, which may build on visions propagated by individual imagineers – as it usually does.

Substantive environmental rights, including the right to live in clean, healthy environments, issues of stewardship and heritage as well as local empowerment in decision-making, are often seen as a set of human rights. Their absence in the management of social and cultural ecologies could be detrimental to human populations. It is no coincidence that the UN Commission of Human Rights and the Environment of 1994 states that 'all persons have the right to a secure, healthy and ecologically sound environment' (Elliott, 2004, p. 148), including 'the right to freedom from pollution and environmental degradation' (ibid., 29–30). As these principles are incorporated into constitutional environmental provisions in Brazil, the question of such rights is not merely projective but a legally binding reality (Ekeli, 2007; Birnie *et al.*, 2009; Wong, 2016).

But legacies can also turn into legitimations of questionable action, producing new variations of unwanted atmosphere, where they are supposed to supplant contentment, pleasure and joy of the affluent *buen vivir* type (Andranovich, 2016 on Los Angeles 1984). The question of 'rights' brought together problems of environmental governance and class exclusion as a form of environmental racism. Rio's particular brand of environmental racism was activated when the Olympic city decided to combine its 'clean-up' environmental policies with the 'pacification' of its *favelas*' life-worlds. Freeman (2014) recognises in this new civilising project a form of 'internal colonisation' (Scott, 1998, p. 82), which has as its motor the Police Pacification Program (UPP), involving the military occupation of *favelas* and the imposition of bureaucratic control. The federal Programme for Accelerated Growth (PAC) that funds accompanying infrastructural projects in larger *favela* complexes is financially assisted by external partners. The UPP programme and its bureaucratised machinations have focused on the *favelas* of the affluent South Zone, 'the central business district including the multi-billion dollar Porto Maravilha port revitalization project, strategic corridors leading to the international airport, and the middle class neighborhoods of the Tijuca basin bordering the strategic Maracanã stadium' (Freeman, 2014, p. 8). Making these areas safer communicates with an updated militourist ideology, whereby occupation of 'foreign' lands follows and is followed by their transformation into global consumer/tourist paradises (Hollinshead, 1999; O'Dwyer, 2004).

We must be cautious here: *Porto Maravilha* was a largely abandoned and crime-infested area of the city in desperate need of revamping for the then forthcoming Olympics. Much like the Chatham Historic Dockyard on the River Medway (part of London 2012's urban regeneration), the Museum of Tomorrow was built in one of the city's poorest and most crime-ridden areas to successfully transform it into a touristic and gentrified business area (Watts, 17 December 2015). So, the initiative itself was beneficial for the development of an area largely consisting of crime and nothingness as unproductive space. Conceptions of emptiness as capital in tourism are not new – nor are their connection to visual industrial framing (Robinson and Picard, Eds, 2009). Often prompting reinventions of the authenticity of place (Florida, 2002, p. 232), nothingness produces tourism where heritage spots become increasingly congested (Ousby, 2002). However, ROCOG's and the city's inability to respond to urgent environmental needs, ensuring the safety of its athletic guests and *all* its citizens, placed the port's costly regeneration under scrutiny. Promises to 'regenerate Rio's magnificent waterways' dating back to the days of the Olympic bid, through investment in sanitation, would not yield any results (the state of Rio de Janeiro had committed to install sewers and water treatment facilities in 80% of communities ahead of the Games). The piles of rubbish and unprocessed waste flow that washed into Guanabara Bay, where the Museum of Tomorrow was built, were not removed for the aquatic sports season. Even with international sustainability experts recruited at the last minute, innovative proposals on the table and Rio Mayor Eduardo Paes' promise to launch a brand new sewage treatment plant under United Nations and the World Health Organization's (WHO) director of Public Health advice, Olympic athletes had to take precautions while training in the sea and have a team of medical doctors on stand-by in case of infection (Vidal, 3 August 2016).

According to city authorities, about 70% of residents living in the Guanabara Bay watershed lack basic sewage treatment, and the crowded *favelas* make it difficult to bring in sewer lines (ibid.). Lack of coordinated action between the 12 cities around Guanabara Bay and the state further complicated Rio's initiative in the matter (Watson *et al.*, 2 June 2016). However, Environment Secretary of Rio state Andre Correa's statement that Brazil's 'difficult financial conditions' are to be blamed, with its federal system making waste management impossible (the federal Navy is responsible for surface pollution, the Municipalities deal with waste and the Environment Ministry with industrial waste) (Bernal, 29 June 2016), is only part of the story. Suffice it to mention that, in search of last-minute solutions, the World Bank and the Dutch Development Bank paired up with WWF and the non-profit Plastic Soup Foundation to tackle Guanabara's environmental pollution through projects recruiting litter-pickers from *favelas* such as the Carioca River, close to the city's iconic Christ the Redeemer (Balch, 1 February 2016). If we consider this initiative alongside the spread of Zika virus in South America and its flourishing in stagnant and polluted waters, the recruitment of *favelados* as litter-pickers for the Plastic Soup Foundation is problematic. In contradistinction to litter-picking, the municipal authorities provided evidence of coordination with the WHO in the case of the Zika virus, launching preventative measures in infestation areas (Rio 2016 News, 2 February 2016).

Approached from this angle, Calatrava and his associates' (art)work is not mere pastime, because it encloses the possibility to articulate radical *praxis*, an activity that acquires situated meaning in a world-wide professional network of artists, architects, policy-makers and political patrons (Albertsen and Diken, 2003, p. 12; Tzanelli, 2013a, p. 9). Traditional museums retain direct connections to warfare and violence, fictionalising and purifying war causes and aligning practices of image management with narratives of ethnogenesis or imperiogenesis (Korstanje, 2015). Inversely, the Museum of Tomorrow relocates the logic of war within the collective human psyche: 'we are at war with ourselves', its exhibits pronounce, 'capitalism feeds our death drive, leading the planet into sure obliteration'. Nevertheless, a rationalist assessment of the Museum of Tomorrow as art-*work* will not do justice to the emotional and aesthetic processes involved in its production as a piece of *art* (as Calatrava insists), nor will it acknowledge its makers' own ecological beliefs and consciousness as non-prescriptive (by 'patrons' and funders) realities (Bourdieu and Wacquant, 1992, p. 87; Bourdieu, 1993, pp. 106–111, p. 252).

The state and the city of Rio's advertising of the Museum as an educational or tourist destination does not necessarily coincide with its makers, creative aims and objectives.

There is also evidence that the Museum's creative makers recognise that we are past the era of boundless 'Epicurean materialism', which allowed us to pursue refined lifestyles and sensuous experiences as forms of happiness at no cost (Bauman, 1997, pp. 2–3; Smith, 2009, pp. 263–264). Such notions of well-being acted as the 'mid-wife of political economy' to stimulate Enlightenment imaginaries of progress (Robertson, 2005), further assisting in the rise of urban tourism for the bourgeoisie that could now consume the poor masses in slums with a great deal of *schadenfreude* (Tzanelli, 2015a, Chapter 8). In the following section I consider the Museum of Tomorrow as part of collective and successive 'worldmaking' (by architects and scholars): the product of a pliable system of knowledge that does not merely represent the world (make knowledge available), but arranges what we know (makes knowledge workable), thus disclosing facts 'we could hardly learn immediately from our explorations' (Leteen, 2012, p. 32).

The suffering artist and his art-forms

The proposition that ideology and dreaming stand worlds apart often supports a peculiar concoction of aesthetic naïveté, social self-denial and strategic political planning. Suffice it to consider how the Museum of Tomorrow is already enmeshed into Rio's 'infrastructural urbanism', an assemblage of infrastructures exceeded 'by other logics than those considered by conventional transport design' (Allen, 2010, p. 39 in Jensen *et al.*, 2016, p. 34). In contemporary urbanism we need to consider infrastructural design as a project of engineering not just matter but also life possibilities capable of triggering 'complex and unpredictable urban effects' in excess of a building's 'designed capacity' (ibid.; Birtchnell and Urry, 2012). The shape (*morphé*) is constitutive of a building's harmonisation into a landscape; it speaks of its utilitarian or otherwise content. However, *morphé* and landscape together are also produced by the multiple life-worlds, within which the architectural structure resides. In other words, architectural *morphogenesis* or birth of shape is part of intentional designing as much as it is a consequence of this design across multiple arenas: material/urban, social/intimate and public/private. The aesthetics of design correspond to regimes of beauty as physical appeal, justice as a competence displayed by the building's makers and patrons (Boltanski, 2012) and pragmatic rightness as a certain technique of thinking (Leteen, 2012). Architecture maps the world socially and aesthetically, consolidating spheres of knowledge, being and experience. As a 'world orientation', such material mapmaking resembles Wittgenstein's *übersichtliche darstellung* or observable representation as a *process* of forming the world, only when it enables human subjects to comprehend their own understanding of the world (Goodman, 1978, p. 21).

To deny that human societies 'secrete ideology as the very element and atmosphere indispensable to their historical respiration and life' (Althusser, 1969, p. 232 in Steger, 2008, p. 4) is to also reject approaches of ideology as a critical investigative tool for interpreting social thought-patterns (ibid., p. 5). The support of critique does not entail the acceptance of any form of accusation as indiscriminate resistance to ideology. This often conceals lack of distinguishing or revealing differences in what, taken at face value, 'appears confused, obscure or difficult to grasp' (Boltanski and Chiapello, 2004, p. 535). The Museum of Tomorrow's principal designer is one such ideological conundrum to unpack in a more dispassionate fashion than that supported by left-wing radicalism. Because, as Albertsen and Diken (2003) state, 'works [of art] cannot exist ... without artists, their biographies and struggles of interest' (p. 8), and because artists are products of the worlds in which they grow, through which they move and in which they choose to cast material and emotional roots, it would be unwise to omit a few words on who Calatrava is, and why and how he engages in architectural worldmaking.

Born on 28 July 1951 in Benimâmet, an old municipality now part of urban Valencia, Spain, Santiago Calatrava Valls received a degree in architecture at the city's Polytechnic University and a second one in engineering at the Swiss Federal Institute of Technology in Zürich. Members of his father's family suffered during the 1930s Spanish Civil War and the dictatorship, instilling escapist tendencies in the young dreamer (Tzionis, 1999; Santiago Calatrava Biography, undated). His family's agricultural occupation exerted an indirect but lasting influence on his style, which bridges structural engineering and architecture. His personal signature is a tendency to bridge the 'hard' positivism of science with the 'soft' qualities of art in an experimental fashion. As sculptor and painter, he claims that the practice of architecture combines all the 'arts' into one, hence it is essentially poly-technic (*pole*: many, *téchne*: art). His artistic work entertained international exposure, including an exhibition in the Metropolitan Museum of Art in New York in 2003 (*Santiago Calatrava: Sculpture into Architecture*), and another two in 2012 in the Hermitage Museum in St Petersburg (Furuto, 2 July 2012) and the Vatican Museum in Rome (*Archdaily*, 5 December 2013). The latter included a series of architectural studies, watercolour paintings and sculptural works adhering to different artistic codes to direct the observer's gaze to 'different levels of interpretation of the architectural volumes, and of the vision of space and shapes, typical characteristics of Calatrava's artistic path' (ibid.). New York's Marlborough Gallery was also set to exhibit his work in May 2014, while eight of his sculptures were put on display along Park Avenue between 52nd and 55th streets in the spring of 2015 (Chaban, 21 March 2014).

Today known for his career-making construction of the Montjuic Communications Tower in Barcelona, Spain (1991) in the heart of the 1992 Olympics site, as a neo-futuristic architect, structural engineer, sculptor and painter, Calatrava maintains offices in New York City, Doha and Zürich. His claim to update the tradition of Spanish modernist engineering of Félix

Candela, Antonio Gaudi and Rafael Gustavino through his personal study of the human body and the natural world seem to rectify the fascistic-nationalist misuses of naturalism we find in Franco's authoritarian ideology (Montalbán, 1992). His long-term involvement with Barcelona's revivalist project, infused with Catalan nationalism's federalist, populist, regional conservative and literary renaissance ideologies (Bollens, 2007, p. 40, pp. 60–62), suggests an early link to Rio's peculiar cultural place in Brazil. Many see in his work a continuation of Finnish architect Eero Saarinen's neo-futurist expressionism, on which the Milwaukee Art Museum was based. The Quadracci Pavilion of this Museum, the first major work he was commissioned to do (completed in 2001), was designed as a futuristic, two-pronged shade that could open and close according to the atrium's lighting needs. The two fins, called Burke *Brise Soleil* ('movable shade' in French – see Santiago Calatrava Biography, undated) are not dissimilar to his artistic-engineering conception of a 'moving', helio-kinetic Museum of Tomorrow. Very similar to Klimt's modernist conception of two-dimensional time, which prompts the *Angelus Novus* to collect past fragments so as to build a future, Calatrava's 'movable shade' points forwards, as modernist architecture does, and upwards, as scientific-fictional imagineering does, with some dispassionate regard for forms and ideas that have outlived their use (Guffey, 2006).

At the same time, the architect-artist's work manages to preserve some retro-futurist principles we find in apocalyptic literature. What Kermode (2000, p. 58) sees in apocalyptic genres as the complementary 'tick of birth and the tock of death' recalls Heisenberg's note that both science and artform provide a human language by which we can speak of the more remote parts of reality (Halstead, 1989, p. 77). By interrogating pure nature, Calatrava places the most natural of all cycles, that of human life and death, in cosmic frameworks. There is a nature-friendly streak in his conception of movement, simultaneously showcasing the complexity of mobility as a new societal system spreading around the globe, in which the social fabric comes apart and is stitched back in novel forms, as several social scientists have debated (Giddens, 1994; Bauman, 1998; Beck, 1999; Urry, 2007). Significantly, the Museum of Tomorrow's incorporation of cinematographic techniques matches the role Calatrava's City of Arts and Sciences (July 1996–April 1998) occupies in *Tomorrowland* (dir. Brad Bird, 2015), an American science fiction/post-apocalyptic film with evil machines and ambiguous human motivations also connected to the futuristic-themed land at Disney theme parks (Tully, 28 January 2013). Film director Bird noted that the complex is 'very unconventional, based on natural forms but at the same time abstract' and actor George Clooney concluded that it is the creation of 'a dreamer' (*Dezeen Magazine*, 21 May 2015).

The film tells the story of a disillusioned genius inventor and a teenage science enthusiast, who enter an alternate dimension to find out that their actions directly affect the world and themselves – what the Museum of Tomorrow's 'alternate paths to the future' logic propagates. Located in the former riverbed of the Turia in Valencia, Spain, the City of Arts and Sciences comprises a cinema (L'Hemisfèric), a landscaped walk and sculpture garden (L'Umbracle), the Príncipe Felipe Science Museum, the largest aquarium in Europe (L'Oceanográfico), and the renowned Palau de les Arts Reina Sofia. The complex was constructed in stages commencing in July 1996, and opened to the public in October 2005. Unique and strikingly futuristic, the iconic group of buildings caught the eye of *Tomorrowland* producer Jeffrey Chernov, who mentioned at a press conference for the film that Calatrava's work reminds of a skeletal construction, 'like you're looking at the vertebrae of a dinosaur or prehistoric fish' (Arcilla, 23 May 2015). The Allen Lambert Galleria at Brookfield Place in Toronto, Canada (1992), with an interior close to the spine of a prehistoric animal, and the Puente del Alamillo building for the Expo '92 in Seville, which has both a worm-like and spinal shape, like the Museum of Tomorrow's, obey a similar design logic. The City of Arts and Sciences' spectacular feel explains why Calatrava's home town and 'host' of the complex, the city of Valencia, holds it as its most important modern tourist destination and one of the twelve Treasures of Spain.

Arches and vaults associated with a Byzantine style but adapted to modern purposes, particularly in spanning very large spaces, such as the Olympic Stadium are also part of his design signature. Calatrava's 'Byzantium' for Athens 2004 was already hybridised – as he noted at the time, 'the sequence of the [civic] space in plan is very classical, with the central axes, Agora, Plaza of the Nations, and stoa-like entrance plazas' (*Architecture Week*, 20 October 2004). His 'Agora', a curving promenade running along the northern edge of the Olympic site with ninety-nine tubular, vaulted steel arches, connected to a beautifully landscaped band of water and trees resembling the Museum of Tomorrow's spirit of a futuristic 'garden city'. 'So I would say', he concluded, 'that the plan is classical, the elevations are Byzantine, and the spirit is Mediterranean' (ibid.). If arches and spinal design dominate his work, so do cupolas and curvilinear forms. The two together speak of premodern architectural transitions from Hellenic to Byzantine artwork, and from pure mathematical to spiritual and then intellectual-artistic configurations of space and light that would dominate most of European artistic heritage (Johnson, 1991, pp. 583–586).

The illumination of the spherological form we find in many of the City of Arts and Sciences' buildings connects to Calatrava's design of another iconic building, reflecting one of the Western World's post-modern traumas, the 9/11 terrorist attacks. The St Nicholas Greek Orthodox Church across from the World Trade Centre figured in a seductive sketch to win over the congregation of the small parish that was destroyed on the day of the attack. Calatrava based the design on the *Hagía Sophía* in Turkey, and more particularly an icon of the Madonna and Child in the building. The two figures inspired a series of seven drawings, in which they were transformed into abstract circles and lines, so their ethereal Christian meaning attained the secularised properties of organic matter: a mother fused with a child. At the same time, the promise to build the church with steel and concrete (Sirigos, 8 March 2014) with the exterior clad in stone, betrays that a lot of the background work is done in the mind of an engineer, rather than an artist.

The creation of the new shrine replicates a hegemonic spatial logic (Jameson, 1995): the original Church dated back to the use of a nineteenth-century building as space for congregation in 1916 by Greek American immigrants. It housed the remains of St Nicholas, St Catherine and St Savas, which the last tsar of Russia (Nicholas II) had donated to the Church and which were never recovered after the attack (*Religion & Ethics*, 9 September 2005). So, for Orthodox communities in New York and elsewhere, the new building is erected on holy ground, thus observing Christian traditions of entombment, mourning and pilgrimage. Calatrava received news of this commission while sailing with his daughter around the Greek Dodecanese, renowned for its white vernacular architectural forms that we find in St Nicolas' illuminated design. He admitted in interviews that he was influenced by the way *Hagía Sophía's* interior 'sublimates matter into pure space through the sheer force of the natural light' and by the Pantheon's 'synthesis of form, proportion, and beauty, realized as a perfect sculpture' (Scarros, 8 March 2014). The design has a utopian quality, because it acts as 'anticipatory illumination' (*vor-schein*), a configuration-image tied to concrete utopias 'lit up on the frontal margins of reality … [to] rearrange social and political relations so that they engender *Heimat* ['homeliness']' (Zipes, 1988, p. xxxiii; Coleman, 2013, pp. 139–140). Placing the building amongst the monsters of global capitalism in the heart of Manhattan and very close to the site of the terrorist trauma 'choreographs' not an ancient Greek or Byzantine, but a contemporary narrative of place and belonging within post-modern non-spaces. With the end of certainty and the transcendence of the two alienating images – one of a deterministic world, where everything can be planned, and an arbitrary one, which is governed by pure chance (Prigogine, 1997, p. 189) – we find that events such as that of 9/11 produce systemic rearrangements in the way we live, feel and think, always on the verge of change (Beck, 2002b). As Urry (2002a) notes, such 'systems' possess a history that irreversibly evolves and in which past events 'are never "forgotten"' (p. 59).

Calatrava's new Church serves as a 'signpost' (MacCannell, 1989) of such an irreversible but uncertain movement to the future, where mourners, pilgrims and tourists habitually meet to 'see' the site of disaster. But as Sather-Wagstaff (2011, p. 47) notes, the historic significance of commemorative places does not connect only to their material link to events of bloodshed or landscape destruction, but also 'through ongoing human practices in time and … across multiple spaces and places'. The 'chronopolitics' (Norum and Mostafanezdhad, 2016) of tourism and pilgrimage in and around the temple operate beyond traditional ecological or capitalist principles, as cultural spatial configurations of events. Calatrava's intervention in Ground Zero's built landscape contributes to such interpretative (*art*)work in two ways: in line with Orthodox Christianity, it illuminates a place of death and suffering, thus involving the artist-architect in this collective mourning. When asked how he receives critiques of his financial excesses in construction, Calatrava responded that 'there is so much vulgarity in the everyday, that when somebody has the pretention to do something extraordinary for the community, then you have to suffer' (Jacobs, 18 December 2014).

Sontag (2013, pp. 46–47) would identify in this response one of modernity's transformations of the Pauline and Augustinian traditions of introspection into psychoanalytic 'confession', in which self-discovery mirrors the discovery of the suffering self. Suffering is constitutive of the economy of art, as all those who can suffer completely can own the feeling as their very own creation and choice. The artist-architect's suffering of criticism is thus like the saint's suffering for virtue, but with benefits: it turns anger, frustration or grief into art owned by the maker, who can at least claim that he makes the ultimate offer to the community: his soul and creativity. Where Eiserman, known for the Holocaust Memorial in Berlin, saw arrogance in Calatrava's silent drawing session during a visit to Yale, the artist-architect insists that aesthetics cannot be compromised for practical or monetary reasons – ultimately, it is the system of commissioning and contracting work that leads to structural or blown budget disasters, with which some of Calatrava's works are associated. The very 'massaging' of the form of Madonna and Child into a post-modern 'tidy, symmetrical domed structure' (Jacobs, 18 December 2014), produces the ideal of a comfortable hearth, a motherly feel in one of our century's most devastating events.

Calatrava's creative engagement with Ground Zero situates his artwork within a global dark tourist economy, in which loss casts roots on soil to become first national and then humanity's heritage. The mechanics and politics of a 'digital gift economy' seem to inform this project as much as they become implicated in Rio's Museum of Tomorrow as the gift of life: a story about the rise, fall and (potential) regeneration of all living things on earth, if only we try harder. I referred in Chapters 1 and 2 to global transformations in conceptions of reciprocity by technological means, as well as the role of imagineers in it as secular creators. St Nicholas' Church is an excessively illuminated 'dark spot' in American multicultural history and a gift erected from the tragic death of hundreds of 9/11 victims. The inevitable marketisation of such a spot as 'dark tourism' (all Ground Zero tourists will be able to visit the Church) still enters a web of invisible obligations, because the memorial is connected to a territorially situated dark history and, much like the Museum of Tomorrow's tale of ecological destruction, will still be handed down to younger generations. The obligation to respect this heritage existed independently from the altar/memorial's 'invention'. Yet, an exactly balanced exchange of technological-*cum*-economic (architecture) and cultural (the memories of the dark site) capital is never feasible, as the two forms of capital are not identical, only analogous (Sahlins, 1972, p. 193; Ardener, 1989). The projection of St Nicholas as a heritage spot with dark tourist histories will become implicated in the global governance of giving, which is progressively more diffused across private (travel companies with websites) and public sectors (national tourism organisations).

Rio's Museum faces similar obstacles. Born in the throes of a difficult Brazilian economic and social curve, it has to negotiate a pact among the necessity to generate cash (as an international tourist/visitor attraction), the desire for international recognition (as Rio's tale on the gift of life) and the potentiality of exiting such global obligations altogether – what I discuss below as *dépense* or deliberately wasteful spending that 'undoes' the capitalist logic (D'Alisa *et al.*, 2015). As I explain below, despite the diverse objectives of the sectors and actors involved in the venture, tourist attraction as the most immediate cash-generating option compels the building's custodians to focus on the aesthetic principles of darkness (Tzanelli, 2016a, pp. 118–119). Unsurprisingly, especially in the case of Meirelles' cinematic projections of this potential catastrophism, the darkness of dark tourist design is morally hued in sepia, red and dark colours – all things appealing to an aesthetically reflexive visitor, who knows how to consume the 'exotic' (Beck *et al.*, 1994; Giddens, 1994). Alternatively, Calatrava's illumination of possibilities and architectural brightness speaks about life and *genesis*, through a return to humanity's 'motherly hearth'. But let us proceed to consider both ends as indispensable components of the Museum's utopian meaning-making.

Architectural utopia in an ornamental museum

Described in the official Rio 2016 website as a giant 'spaceship-like building' and the 'centre-piece of a generation', the Museum of Tomorrow is seen by Calatrava, 'like sport, [as] a tribute to humanity. Both are creations which give us dignity, that exalt human beings and their origins' (Rio 2016 News, 18 December 2015). Situated in the previously abandoned *Praça Mauá*, it is part of a huge project to revitalise *Porto Maravilha*, with the demolition of an elevated highway and the construction of underground traffic tunnels, a light-rail tram service, a new art museum and kilometres of walking, cycling and leisure areas opening up along the city centre's waterfront. Previously, the area was plagued by chronic flooding and sewage seeping into the drainage system of the city. Its *Belle Epoque* buildings along nearby *Avenida Rio Branco* would never be visited. The overall *Porto Maravilha* project was set to include hotels, office complexes, residences, leisure space and more. But the Museum itself was placed under the auspices of Rio World Heritage Institute in collaboration with Daniel Van Raemdonck de Lima, supervisor at the Port Regional Urban Development Co. The involvement of Rio World Heritage Institute has been inevitable, because 70 heritage buildings in the original port area were set to be renovated and 530 new housing units to be built. But the shock has been the unearthing of the wharf where slaves disembarked, the cornerstone of the Old Customs House and several artefacts of heritage value. The fear that high-rise projects adhering to the rule of vertical privilege will displace port-area residents was also expressed vociferously, when the adjoining community of *Mora da Providência* saw hundreds of homes slated for removal. The priorities are evident in the ways space networking is orchestrated: tourism is a byword for mega-event regeneration. The construction of a subway link running through the posh seaside area of Ipanema to *Barra de Tijuca*, three major highway and bus rapid transit routes and new services for the *favelas* turn the renovated area into a much-needed urban node (Whitefield, 3 June 2014).

Here I wish to concentrate mainly on the Museum of Tomorrow's creative routes and possibilities. These provide unique insight into the ways imagineers such as Calatrava or Meirelles mediate, subvert or revise certain 'mobile situations' staged 'from above' (Jensen, 2013) in terms of planning, design and regulation, and then acted out or staged 'from below' by consociates in interactions (Jensen *et al.*, 2016, pp. 27–28). Though relevant to considerations about the built environment, *Porto Maravilha's* regeneration is first placed in a wider non-representational framework (Thrift, 2007; Vannini, 2015), to examine performances of Self and communal belonging. This also necessitates considering emergent, immanent or extant relationships between nature, human and technology, with the latter featuring as an 'actant' (as in Latour, 2005), a bodily or 'live' extension. In the Museum technology as 'live extension' of the human mediates stories about the beginning, end or future of earth life – the central scenario of the Museum's 'journey', which provides my analysis's second (phenomenological) stage. When considering the impact of such performances on social institutions and the (re)formulation of public attitudes and discourses, it is important to examine design as a way of thinking (Jensen *et al.*, 2016, p. 29): as practical imagineering. This prompts an examination of the agents/actors' world orientation, which I have already outlined in previous Chapters and in the preceding section. As my analysis of 'worldmaking' includes but exceeds the potentialities and practicalities of tourism planning, it is essential to build a record of creative and experimental action, with all its consequences.

Following modernity's foremost proponents of utopian thinking, such as William Morris and John Ruskin, Ernest Bloch lamented how the culture of capitalism restricts the possibilities of architecture. For Bloch 'true architecture' shares with 'ornament' in that it manages to communicate ideals of a better world, thus exceeding the engineering principles adhered to material construction (Coleman, 2013, p. 137). The argument is echoed in Calatrava's much-criticised take on architectural creativity and his implicit message in the Museum of Tomorrow's 'style', that good architectural work provides a habitat for humanity and all living beings, in the stead of a bankrupt bureaucracy, surveillance, control and death-making (Bell and Wakeford, Eds, 2008). Architecture's 'utopian vocation' is to critique and disrupt a repressive society's established codes, to act as a mediator between politics and aesthetics (Jameson, 1985; Hays, 1998) and to enable active participation of the public in the city's commons. As a 'counterform' of our 'homecoming', a 'tacit coefficient' of Utopia (Coleman, 2005, pp. 255–256), the

Museum of Tomorrow is a 'stranger' inhabiting the non-spaces of Rio's glocal capitalism.

Is the Museum of Tomorrow art, is it architecture, or mere educational 'tool' for Brazilians and the mega-event's globetrotters? The Museum's current Chief Curator, Luiz Alberto Oliveira says: 'Other Museums offer a collection of artefacts. We offer a collection of possibilities' (Steel, 23 August 2016). Its multiple private partnerships, including those with British Gas and Santander Bank, allow it to attract and support international researchers, thus contributing to the formation and/or maintenance of international scientific networks, and mobility (Fontes *et al.*, 2013; Leung, 2013). Note that the Museum of Tomorrow was built on 'empty grounds' for the twin purposes of scientific education and tourism, so we can safely associate it with other scientific initiatives and resources in physics and bio-technology, including observatories, laboratories, advanced technology installations and more conventional science museums (Weaver, 2011). The Museum of Tomorrow's Audience Development Director Alexandre Fernandes and Chief Curator Oliveira attended the 2016 Museums Association Conference and Exhibition in Glasgow (7–9 November 2016) to join discussions on best practice about museums and heritage sites engaging local communities and volunteering (Steel, 23 August 2016).

Much like the Rio 2016 Olympic Games, the Museum was based on the ethical pillars of sustainability and conviviality. Artworks are set up in museums for public display and are conserved so that they are available as models for future artists and the education of the public – 'in short, artworks are set up in museums to save the past' (Lazarin, 2008, p. 53). But the Museum of Tomorrow is about the future and about interactive public education, so it stands between something 'other than artwork' that 'sets the earth' (produces cosmopolitan notions of home) and a self-contained world (of activities, decisions and involvements) setting the horizon of space. Hence, it is intended as a transformation of mere matter, earth, water and fauna, into a story that enacts a philosophical plot about potential future living. Significantly, Calatrava and Meirelles' collaboration (examined below) also manages to blend austere Brazilian philosophies of *buen vivir* with the popular-cultural medium of film that assisted in the production of Rio's urban modernity. For anyone with elementary knowledge of Brazilian and Rio de Janeiro's history, blending technology with nature stands at the heart of the country's tropicopolitanism. In Rio's case this involves a unique adaptation of European notions of modernity and belonging to a world locally overdetermined by *Carioca* cultural behaviours and their specific environmental extensions (Aravamudan, 1999; Tzanelli, 2015c). A 'spectacular' fusion of technology with nature stands at the heart of the Museum's inception in the bromeliads (a family of monocot flowering plants native mainly to the tropical Americas) in Rio's Botanical Garden (*Jardim Botânico*) (Rio 2016 News, 18 December 2015). South American civilisations used bromeliads for food, protection, fibre and ceremony, just as they are still used today, but European interest in them began with the inclusion of pineapple in European art and sculpture after the Spanish conquest. Today, several bromeliads are popular ornamental plants, grown as both garden and houseplants.

Located in a district in the *Zona Sul* (South Zone) of Rio de Janeiro, the Botanical Garden shows the diversity of Brazilian and foreign flora. It also houses monuments of historical, artistic and archaeological significance and an important research centre with the most complete library in the country specialising in botany, with over 32,000 volumes. The Garden was a product of colonial contacts with native cultures, flora and fauna, highlighting the bio-technological dimensions of European natural adaptation in a completely alien climate: founded in 1808 by King John VI of Portugal, it was intended for the acclimatisation of spices like nutmeg, pepper and cinnamon imported from the West Indies, but in 1822 the Garden was opened to the public. Its unique global function as a twin artistic and technological conception of 'preserved otherness', resembles the early twentieth-century Western concep-tions of the 'garden city': the engineered relocation of luscious green suburbia into the urban centre. The relocation of this specific British vision of urban regeneration in Rio de Janeiro led to the production of a 'dormitory garden suburb' of the seaside for the middle and working classes (examples are Fla-mengo and Botafogo), 'thus defining space in environmental and social terms' (Tzanelli, 2016c, pp. 69–70; Almandoz, 22 May 2003). But historical experi-ence 'evaporates before [what is essentially] an imperial gaze' (Carter, 2010, p. xxii) to allow for legitimation, first by colonial and subsequently by various generations of local authoritarian power. This colonial discourse of moder-nisation is thoroughly revised by the Museum of Tomorrow's makers and sponsors in that they translate the idea(l) of the 'garden city' into a technologically (and digitally) empowered utopian vision of and for Rio.

Technologically, the environmental ethics on which the Museum was based become manifest in its use of 40% less energy than conventional buildings (with about 9% of its power derived from the sun) and a cooling system tap-ping deep water from Guanabara Bay. The Museum's solar spines and fan-like skylight were designed so that the building adapts to environmental condi-tions (Watts, 17 December 2015). In this respect, the construction's technolo-gical playfulness supports sustainable behaviours and renewable forms of energy (Negruşa *et al.*, 2015). But its triumph is that it turns mere 'equip-ment' and matter into essential components ('actants' in actor-network theory terms – Ingold, 2008) of a *technopoetic* (technologically geared, or informed making) process (Tzanelli, 2013a, Chapter 1). This process of technological *poesis* bridges (as in Japanese *en*: edge and connection) the rift (*Riss*: clea-vage) between nature and its manipulated artefacts (Lazarin, 2008, p. 56; Anderson, 2011, pp. 68–69). Here we shift focus from technology to art: the fact that the Museum is discussed for its sculptural form suggests a slippage of building toward sculpture, hence of mere 'equipment' to artistic ornament with thrusting curvilinear shapes. As a non-representational form of art (Thrift, 2007), the Museum of Tomorrow's 'earthbound', material presence can communicate true beauty that is not trapped in Enlightenment scientism but is in harmony with its (artificially) produced 'natural elements' (Anderson, 2011, p. 71). As a futural scenario, it is a means of imagining the future and hence formulating anticipatory action; as a performative structure, it invites visitors to enter and experience this alternative future world – a true 'worldmaking' assemblage bound up with practices of invention, imagination and performance.

The two-storey building features a cantilevered roof and façade with moving elements extending almost to the pier's full length, thus 'emphasising the extension into the bay, while minimizing the building's width' (Lomholt, 15 July 2016). Its northern location also maximises a continuous landscaping strip along the southern part of the pier and complements the view towards the historical Monastery *da Sao Bento do Rio de Janeiro* on and off the site. This 'situationist' inspection reveals that the building is set to be of ornamental nature, as it blends into the natural and built environment of the area, illuminating, rather than hiding heritage spots. As a building-symbol, the Museum manages to glue together past and alternative futures, thus creating a synechdochical arrangement of materialities and new mobilities. Calatrava is set to not simply suggest that the future is an incomplete project, but also emphasise that 'the very concept of a developed world is no more than its own fantasy of wholeness not yet completed; a synecdoche' (McFarland, 1981, p. 27). Such synecdoches extend to the overall mega-event's project. There is a synecdochical connection between how Rio de Janeiro comes to *be* as a mega-event host for global tourists, and how the collection and arrangement of global and local 'signs' of consumption by communities of mega-event imagineers produces our knowledge about the city (on the conditionality of language for intellectual ability see Dascal, 1987, p. 9, p. 13). We deal with intrinsic and unstable connections between epistemologies (how we 'read', understand the world) and ontologies (how the world is), in what we can term the *ontogenesis* (birth of being) of the (*mega*) event and the (*mega*) city through such artefacts as Calatrava's.

Urban presence is thus tied to how people learn about and experience place and heritage. Carter (2013, 2015) speaks of the ways places are made after their stories as a sort of choreotopographic art. Places (or *tópoi*) are inscribed or mapped (*grafō*) as terrains through specific collective human movements (*chorós* as the ancient Greek tragedy's group of actors reciting the chorus) in them, so that their landscapes are orchestrated in human narratives of their forms, their buildings and their 'soul'. The Museum continues this 'orchestration' of natural form, material thinking and artistic practice in its interior spaces, where the visitor is invited to become a hyperreal traveller to humanity's epochs.

Choreographing mobility: between *Ubuntu* and social thanatology

To fully comprehend the Museum's philosophy as part of a philosophy of movement to the future, one may have to accept an unlikely partnership between popular notions of (technology-assisted, including cinematic and virtual) travel and social notions of thanatology (the ways we experience, comprehend and feel death as the end of our social existence). Whereas the former adheres to capitalist philosophies of 'investment' for future returns, the latter stresses the omnipresence of *dépense* or wasteful spending, so that capital is burnt out, taken out of circulation altogether (D'Alisa *et al.*, 2015, pp. 217–218). To understand social – individual and collective – death in the context of irreversible environmental decline, to be a 'catastrophist' (Urry, 2007, 2011) also entails an acknowledgement of capitalism's suicidal greed, ruthless human and natural source exploitation and, ultimately, eradication of the 'good life'. Calatrava's usual tendency to blow budgets out of proportions in his work so that he delivers true art for the community, reflects a *dépense* logic befit as a response to catastrophist degrowthers.

The same non-utilitarian imaginary is present in the African philosophy of *Ubuntu* defining Brazilian notions of well-being (Tzanelli, 2015c, 2016b). Notions of 'human' in *Ubuntu* are based on the idea(l) of giving, receiving and passing on the goods of life to others (Griaule, 1965, p. 137 in Ramose, 2015, p. 212); care for oneself and others; protecting the environment and avoiding killing (Bujo, 1998, p. 77 in Ramose, 2015, p. 212). As a philosophy of wholeness, *Ubuntu* is rooted in customs of pre-capitalist societies (see Sahlins, 1972, 1976 on 'primitive exchange'; Bohm, 1980 on 'wholeness'), but the persistence of its principles in new social movements connected to environmentalism (eco-feminism and deep ecology) and more general welfare philosophies (care for humans) is indisputable. The suggestion that communal well-being and individual *praxis* are part of the same moral universe and that their unity is actualised in the triadic presence of the living, the living-dead (ancestors) and the unborn or yet to be (future generations), produces a social imaginary of rootedness in the past for the sake of the future (Ramose, 1999). To maintain harmony and avoid illness and bad luck, the community remembers the living-dead through rituals, while also avoiding the pursuit of profit-making as an end in itself (Ramose, 2015, p. 213). Contemporary Brazilian popular cultures rooted in folk aetiologies of evil include 'spiritual characters' such as those of *Umbanda* and *Catimbó* (or *Catimba*) *Zé Pilintra*. Originally figured as a sort of benevolent patron spirit of bars, gambling dens and gutters, but subsequently seen as an evil mercenary spirit, relieving people of their riches (Tzanelli, 2015c, p. 62), *Zé Pilintra* allegorises the new spirit of capitalism and its propensity to theatricality, mobility and greed. *Zé Pilintra's* association with the gutter ethics of *favela* crime blends causalities (greed, avarice and thoughtless pursuit of profit at the expense of fellow humans) with consequences (poverty, environmental racism) in folk explanations of social unhappiness.

Ubuntu's communal rootedness does not exclude the practice of mobility, but internalises it, turning it into a form of existential travel to the netherlands of ancestral spirits. There, the subject can achieve artistic and spiritual 'uplifting' by creating a good unified image for the community through her art, which is seen as part of the community's ancestral properties. The thesis resembles the connection of European heritage to the custodianship of 'national lands' and the regulation of citizenship rights (Lowenthal, 1985, pp. 37–38). It also points to the iconological principles of movie-making (Stiegler, 2011, p. 71), allowing us to associate 'moving images' with Christianity's utopian desire of perfection (Fuller, 2008, 2012). Thus, contemporary adaptations of *Ubuntu* in multi-partner projects, such as the Museum of Tomorrow, promotes cultural hybridisation (Nederveen Pieterse, 2006a) or cosmopolitanism as a fusion of cultural horizons (Delanty, 2009). Especially the inclusion of European ways of 'seeing' (hence arranging – Foucault, 1980) space within and around the Museum (Cosgrove and Jackson, 1987), complements its blended international and Brazilian artwork, rejecting cosmological insularity.

Ubuntu's environmentalist translation of ethical involvement in the world of yesterday, today and tomorrow clashes with commercialised travel in what we know as 'dark tourism': physical, emotional and now virtual/digital visits to physical sites and landscapes marked by death and suffering by ancestry. Korstanje (2014, p. 2) notes that dark tourism sites are considered to be important because they enhance the social cohesion of communities, in order to domesticate future death scenarios. Like Seaton (1996), he invokes the principle of *thanatopsis*, the inspection of death by the living. He discusses the feelings of relief (for temporarily evading death) and anxiety (for it cannot be avoided forever) this now commoditised exercise of visiting sites such as those of old slave castles, Ground Zero and the Auschwitz camp induce in a collective context of gazing as speculation upon communal mortality. *Thanatopsis* is part of *Ubuntu's* thanatological prognostication in capitalism, according to which our earth is murdered slowly but surely, with our daily contribution. Incidentally, darkness, existential travel and death produce a cosmopolitan portmanteau applicable in other cultural contexts, in which traumatic collective memories reproduce social solidarity, including those of human-made and natural disasters (Alexander *et al.*, 2004).

There is also a cross-cultural resonance to darkness and grime, which are in Chinese and Japanese cultures traditional virtues. At least in architecture, they are translated into colours and textures associated with the past and with metaphysical depth (Tanizaki, [1977] 2001, pp. 18–20). An essentially pessimistic aesthetic, 'not of a celebrant but of a mourner' (Harper, [1977] 2001, p. 71) communicates in traditional Japanese contexts authenticity. As I explain in Chapter 7, traditional qualities of existential mobility persist in contemporary Japanese popular cultures of tourism. In the context of post-1980s Japanese degrowth, they often blend ancient Japanese notions of a 'journey' into one's publicly concealed, inner self or *honne* (Graburn, 2012) with post-modern ones of individualised mobility (digital and physical travel, constant professional movement), prevalent amongst younger populations. The apparent individualisation of *honne* threatens the aesthetics of propriety. The latter is based on concealing uncivilised aspects of the Self in favour of community development, which is promoted by the *tatemae* or public Self. *Tatemae* allows individuals to be part of civilisation – to realise the so-called *satoyama*. Much like the accommodation of *Ubuntu* values into the technological innovations of the post-modern city, *satoyama* 'equates the in-between landscape' of cultivated land and urbanised civilisation with 'the soul of Japan', promoting the unity of the Japanese with the landscape and enabling post-industrial *machizukuri* (community building) (Favell, 2015a, pp. 150–151).

Thanatopsis is part of Calatrava's artistic-architectural practice and aesthetics of suffering, which are actualised in the Museum of Tomorrow's virtual installations with the contribution of Meirelles' filmwork. Both artists cannot avoid connecting individual tourist experience to the real(-ist) conditions that actualise cosmopolitan travel via global automobility networks and tourist transport systems (Edensor, 2005; Beeton, 2005; Gwerner, 2009). Contra *Ubuntu's* philosophy of rootedness and communal sustainability, partaking in such mobilities facilitates breaks from the past and a critique of affective codes of communal nostalgia, which connects to national memory (Guffey, 2006, 2014) – hence a renegotiation of the non-representational politics of mobility and stasis (Thrift, 2007). So, the Museum projects a reappraisal of human errors, hence a new cultural politics of memory, replete with seriation and ruptures. In fact, the role of sequence is firmly embedded into discussions on climate change, with many scholars considering the Anthropocene and the preceding epoch of the Holocene of coeval or identical geologic time span, and others insisting that the Anthropocene is more recent. The recognition of the Industrial Revolution as the start of the Anthropocene complies with discourses of Western modernity (see Urry, 2005a, pp. 242–243 on 'proletarian adaptation' and Giddens' (1984) 'duality of structure'), broadening understandings of the human impact on the planet (see Crutzen, 2002 and Douglas *et al.*, 2002 on chronologies). At first, we see in the Museum's rough organisation of temporal sequences a sort of 'stratigraphic' method, the building of layers of geomorphological and environmental change that correspond to epochal change (from prehistoric and premodern to post-modern). The three 'recorded' phases are organised so as to foretell the possibility of the 'end of civilisation' (Scranton, 2015) after the 'end of history' in neoliberal excess (Steger, 2008: p. 192; Fukuyama, 1992). This 'doom and gloom' cleverly mobilises what Bauman (2000, pp. 10–14) recognises as the post-panoptic conceptions of power. The feel of 'power' in the Museum's audio-visual displays is not based on the imposition of force or persuasion but on elision of direct engagement with the help of technological artefacts and computerised means of sharing information (Bauman and Lyon, 2013).

Virtuality, materiality, abstraction and possibilities serve as ontological categories in the Museum's spaces of flows and as narratives of 'becoming' (Shields, 2003). This 'becoming' binds humans and things, such as computers, with virtualities, to produce a temporal sequence of the earthly and human story. The Museum's displayed narrative of ecological development with a human touch is a way to map the temporal development of a 'problem' but also a way of 'tracing associations' between various causal connectors (human, material or more) (Latour, 2005, p. 5). The modes of flow from one component to another create our common past as a montage (*dérushage*) that stands for the retentional finitude of human consciousness: the fact that memory is originally all about selection and forgetting (Ricoeur, 1984–1988, vol. III, p. 55), or a rushing assortment of frozen images (Stiegler, 2011, pp. 27–28). Mackenzie (2003) terms this processual thinking 'transduction', thus casting technologies as 'events', rather than objects, 'as contingent the whole way down, rather than covering over or reducing contingency' (pp. 4–6). The Museum's technological assemblages (the building, its artistic material exhibits and virtual displays) and spaces 'perform' potential futures for visitors. What assembles them in its space is its makers' technicity, the general properties of technology as human (electronic and material) prosthesis (Gallope, 2011, pp. 48–49). Mackenzie's (2002, 2003) take on technicity as a transductive way of understanding technology allows one to consider the Museum's technological whole (of structures, installations and moving visitors-interpreters of its exhibits) as an evolving way of *inscribing*, of constantly 'translating' knowledge claims about the past, the present and future of earth (Latour and Woolgar, 1986). And since the Anthropocene overshadows the Museum's take on transduction, its narrative's temporal heterogeneity (of slow moving, punctual and erratic temporalities) seeks to both highlight and reject what maintains capitalism's destructive *modus operandi*: the repetitive mode of the business cycle (Sewell, 2008, p. 521).

Meirelles and Calatrava debate what is *revealed* in the worst possible future scenario of irreversible environmental decline via a dramaturgical projection of thanatology as the end of life and the social at large. This is achieved through colour and shades in the Museum's white interior (bright like St Nicholas' Church that commemorates the dead) and its cinematic canvas (dark, red and yellow like the *City of God's favela* representations of harsh social realities). Such plays on 'black', 'white' and 'grey' are not dissociated from European moral codes of 'evil' and 'good' and their artistic mobilisations in great pictorial arts such as painting, sculpting and filmmaking (Tzanelli, 2015a, p. 55). In fact, they even hint at the Hellenistic art and architecture from Pergamon and other ancient cities displayed during the Berlin 1936 Olympics – at the time, in a German attempt to move away from racist-nationalist propaganda while silently promoting a Nazi discourse on European origins (Guttman, 2006, pp. 71–72). The Museum's artists calibrate artistically an 'inverted sublime' (Bell and Lyall, 2002, p. 72, pp. 92–93): they use both natural planes (the horizontal sublime) and man-made industrial structures (the vertical) in their articulation of depth codes, ideas of (emotional) abyss and (moral) descent. Thus, the Museum's installations connect the Western and European 'high arts' to Brazilian notions of *buen vivir* and the city of Rio's realist policy planning in allegorical ways (Kracauer, [1960] 1997).

Calatrava's oppositional use of brightness matches his recurring use of sculptural curvilinearity in his architectural design. Reminiscent of the 1960s concrete modernism of Oscar Niemeyer, the renowned communist-allied supporter of nationalist state-centred development and creator of several Getúlio Vargas monumental structures (Soares, 2016, pp. 225–227), Calatrava's 'bright' stylistics is recuperative and subversive of past discourses of development. In urban Brazil brightness came to signify an uncomfortable marriage of hospitality with sterilisation and to stand for architectural symbolisations of the late 1970s and 1980s 'shift to the right'. The evolutionary ideology of the machine banished the industrial soot from 'good' spatial aesthetics, in favour of clean and clear lines and colours (Bloch, 1988, p. 187). But the Museum's architectural style is also subversive of the ideology of *Brasilidade* or Brazilianness espoused by the French-educated director of *Academia Imperial de Belas Artes* (later *Escola Nacional de Belas Artes* – ENBA) Lúcio Costa, who used Le Corbusier's ideas and radically reformed the *Academia*'s art and architecture curriculum on Bauhaus pedagogy (Lara, 2011, p. 133). Rio's Brazilianist vision during Costa's directorship also followed Vargas' delicate balance of 'progressive' and 'conservative' forces, thus coming closer to Niemeyer's unresolved fusion of Baroque legacy with modernist European *avant-gardism*.

This unresolved tendency between the archaic/national roots of art and the modernist/colonial pressures of European architectural modernisation is often seen as pivotal to the instability of the 1960s, which was accelerated by labour migration from rural to urban building industries and which led to the military coup (ibid., 134). Although such histories seem remote, they relate to the rise of *favela* enclaves and the verticalisation of Rio's urban form in apartments. In line with the newly erected capital of Brasília and the European pattern of building in São Paulo, Rio's verticalisation reproduced class and racial hierarchies, with the working and poor classes occupying the *favela* outskirts or working as servants in the urban centre and the upper and middle classes opting for high residential towers in a textbook fashion of Foucaultian Panopticism, or moving towards gated communities (Macedo, 2009, p. 82). Instead, the Museum's planar, horizontal construction speaks of a pan-human 'hearth', not a barricaded tower for the affluent, and is blended in an innovative way with its fluid marine surroundings. It includes temporary and permanent exhibition areas, a 400-seat auditorium, an education centre, a cafe and a gift shop. Its all-white interior has curving walls, staircases and ceilings, and is populated with displays created by US-based exhibition designer Ralph Appelbaum (*Dezeen Magazine*, 17 December 2015). The introduction of curves and movement is not as evident from outside, where we see an elongated arrow-like roof. But within, just above the Museum's opening 'mouth', we encounter an illuminated globe, a Gaia-like curve framing continuous harp-like windows surrounding the building and flooding it with natural light. The inside and the outside are harmonised with the help of artificial and natural light that reflects curves on the promenade's marble stone and the sea.

Figure 3.1 Museu do Amanhã, Gaia entrance
Source: Image by Leandro Neumann Ciuffo, Flickr/Creative Commons Licensing.

Figure 3.2 Museu do Amanhã, under construction on the waterfront
Source: Image by Brian Godfrey, Flickr/Creative Commons Licensing.

Thus, artist-architectural imagineers add to the built environment a mechanical overtone, without brushing aside the organic aspect of nature's rhythmed movements (*contra* Lefebvre, [1992] 2015, pp. 15–16). On the one hand, the illuminated 'Gaia's' presence reproduces a secularised version of the 'Madonna-with-Child' narrative of ecological wholeness, in which humans are mere atoms in a universe of beings. On the other, the architectural design trades natural movements and life cycles for a manufactured, sculpted kinesis akin to that of Tatil's Rio 2016 'dancing' logo. The logo's reference to the female *Carioca* body as native *phýsis* and the Museum's external (fallopian-like) and internal (curvilinear) shape, point to reproductive human areas, as is the case with traditional philosophies of bodily image and Brazilian music (Moehn, 2008, p. 179) and future-loving *Ubuntu*. So, nature, environment and technology are not separated but fused into a discourse of civilising movement. This fusion is majestic, given that the Museum was created to debate climate change and population growth, changes in bio-diversity, genetic engineering and bio-ethics, and new advances in technology (*Dezeen Magazine*, 17 December 2015). Following Nairn (1997), one can conclude that this biopolitical focus on the built environment projects a tendency towards the international as an alternative to the national gaze, but pairs the former with the heterogeneity of national history to blur the vision of would-be nation-builders. In the Museum we deal with an unacquainted desire to embrace the de-colonial moment, as is the case with previous Olympic hosting optics: the fusion of gazes in the Museum of Tomorrow's style, purpose and narrative comes close to the architectural modernism of Mexico City that, during the 1968 Olympic Games, would clear the streets of indigenous populations and promote the 'alabaster finish' of contemporaneous Mexican culture and society through pre-Columbian, Aztec design and ancient Greek-inspired material exhibits (Brewster and Brewster, 2006, pp. 101–103, pp. 108–109, p. 110).

The theme of population rise in growing mega-cities (incidentally, also Meirelles' allegorical projection on Maracanã's digital canvas in the Opening Ceremony) is far from mythical. Echoing Malthusian premonitions, the narrative is aligned with the moment the world's urban population exceeded the rural for the first time (23 May 2007), with an impact on the size and numbers of global slums, where the poor are concentrated (Davis, 2006; Homer-Dixon, 2006; Urry, 2010). Here, the feel of power is mediated in two very different ways: through the distant gaze of the projector, the naïve visitor-gazer is lulled into a peculiar masochist engagement with the story, as (s)he is, literally, entwined 'with the processes that [s]he himself [herself] is exercising' (Mulvey, 2006, p. 351) but also implicated in the social processes of the story itself. But in the grander scheme of things, the Museum's scopic practices replicate the eye of power, introducing uncomfortable 'mobility intrusions' into local life (Hiller, 2016, pp. 132–134). Currently, such scopic practices serve to expose once hidden communities to the eye of the state and the public – note, for example, the construction of cable cars over Alemão, a large *favela* complex with 60,000 population, bordering the Federal

University and two major road arteries, hence nestling within global mobilities (Freeman, 2014, p. 27). Closer to the Museum, the construction of the cable car for *Providência*, a *favela* overlooking *Porto Maravilha*, was implicated in the destruction of *Americo Brum* plaza, the heart of the *favela's* communal space and the location of the only soccer court in it, as part of the municipal *Morar Carioca* project's creation of a station with one line heading north to the City of Samba and another descending south to the Central train station. The project looks to the areas' upgrading, but the community has now fallen under the multiple gazes of the UPP patrols, local bureaucracy and swarms of journalists (ibid., p. 28). The absence of an economy of care in such settings (Young, I.M., 2006; Adam and Groves, 2011) displaces the idea of a brighter future from the communal core of the *favelas* to policy headquarters, which are geared towards tourismification, hence a guest-orientated future. In the Museum of Tomorrow two different gazes, from outside (dispassionate-political) and from within (existential-personal), structure the future of ecosystems antithetically.

If this connection between social reality and digital mythopoesis seems spurious at first, we must look to the histories of automobility to rectify our impressions, as they link such urban projects to the worries about climate change. It all begins with the car: commencing in Europe as a system of private transportation, it would soon be embraced by urban planners both in East and West and become synonymous with modern life in high-modernist planning (Scott, 1998, p. 103). Especially in the anthropocenic context (Urry, 2011), criticisms of the car focus on general health risks due to noise and pollution, whereas its decline as status symbol in world and peripheral cities and its steady replacement with bikes, suggests 'greener' alternatives (Gehl, 2010; Freudendal-Pedersen, 2015). The Museum of Tomorrow stands as an objection to such harmful social habits of mobility. Another greener path to the future is provided by digital technologies that minimise some of the societal costs host cities incur before and during the mega-event. In the context of Rio 2016, wider societal access to digital communications has a double green face: first, it allows the organisation of transport for global mega-event visitors via the Internet and new portable hardware in more environmentally friendly ways (Germann Molz and Paris, 2015); and second, it contributes to the production of a utopian façade for the city, allowing the mobility of local cultures in the cybersphere. So, although technologies of gazing are a communal anathema, they can also function as a 'greener' alternative to education to consider seriously.

Intended as a pedagogical tool, the development features photovoltaic panels on its steel roof, which tilt to follow the sun's course across the sky, so the building changes 'like a flower or a plant' (Murdock, 4 October 2010). The project's developer, the *Fundação Roberto Marinho*, reputed for making abstract concepts concrete practice, has been involved in other educational projects of an interactive (audio-visual) nature, better connected to native Brazilian philosophies of embodied well-being. The project has inspired other architects to design interactive sustainable projects, including the Swiss RAFAA Solar City Tower, aiming to represent 'an inner attitude, a symbol of society facing the future' (ibid.). Thus, the Museum of Tomorrow is built on the urgency to manage environmental risks by technological means – its infrastructure uses natural elements, such as sea and rain water, to generate electricity. Its inner structure, leading visitors from a ground-floor plaza upwards and then volte-face through a nave-like gallery to exhibits, represents an absent womb as human rebirth within, but at the centre of a hybrid natural-machinic ecosystem. In this respect, it does not necessarily avoid the deficit in democracy characterising post-industrial risk societies, because it liberates humans from the doubt of a future catastrophe only hypothetically (Argyrou, 2005, pp. 84–85). The hypothetical move resembles that which we associate with the construction of Munich 1972's Olympic Stadium as a political modernist portrayal of Germany's democratic transparency (Young, 2003). At the same time, the design's classificatory nature in the Museum of Tomorrow, which is enclosed in identification binaries (a navel/womb is the symbol of feminine reproduction, after all), resembles the aspiration enclosed in the design of Beijing 2008's iconic Olympic Stadium (Bird's Nest) to master human nature (Tzanelli, 2010, p. 224).

'When people think of the "Future"', says Hugo Barreto, Head Director of Content, 'it usually seems very far away. [But] it depends on what we do today' (Watts, 17 December 2015). The Museum's main exhibition attempts to bring the future a tad closer by virtual means. The exhibition has five areas or epochal segments: Cosmos, Earth, Anthropocene, Tomorrow and Now. It asks questions about where we come from, where we stand and where we are heading towards as a species and a civilisation, leading visitors along a hall through various (digital) visual and aural displays. Lash's (1988) elaboration on the figural nature of post-modern culture is of relevance to the function of digitality in the Museum's presentation of the future. For Lash this culture promotes the immersion of the spectator, their immediate engagement and investment of desire in objects – what he analyses as 'de-differentiation' by analogy to the removal of aura from art in cultural industrial spaces of advertising, cinema and consumption at large (Featherstone, 1991, pp. 70–72). This is the Benjaminian culture of the *flâneur/flâneuse* and aesthetic reflexivity (Lash and Urry, 1994, pp. 49–50), which is generally centrifugal (it characterises the symbolic or actual 'tourist', the more affluent spectator) and urban in orientation. But such disengaged *flânerie* says little about the orchestration of epochal movement in the Museum – its 'staging' (Jensen, 2013) of an organisational catastrophe in human and earth affairs. Anticipations of apocalyptic situations are incorporated in the Museum's narrative structure, which takes into account three broad phases of events: an incubation period, a critical period and a potential aftermath (Stein, 2004, p. 1244).

The centrifugal 'tourist' attitude would also not explain aesthetic engagement: situating and investigating the nature of visual/virtual art and beauty in terms of judgement. One may even argue that the resemblance of the Museum's long 'corridor' to that of an airport fosters such (dis)engagement. Or that the exhibition's resemblance of the design and organisation of airports as transient places of sociality, where one can access everything in one multi-site (Kesselring, 2009), without attaining knowledge of social problems 'from within' (Hollinshead, 1999, p. 272; Dann, 1996; Selwyn, 1996) is problematic. This is because the global traveller rarely engages deeply with the city's inner cultures and agendas to become involved in its 'commons' before or even during the visit (Rifkin, 2014). The exhibition's audio-visual premises may reinstate detachment or disengagement from the themes it explores. As Wolff (1984) suggests, an aesthetic attitude is formed through engagement with various objects and experiences in everyday life, and the digital sphere can only gesture towards them. As part of global capitalist systems, the digital world is both hugely enabling in terms of mobility of culture and disabling in terms of immediate knowledge (Berman, 1982). Yet, the airport space also presents us with the perfect form of globalisation optimism with regards to experimental knowledge and regulative accessibility: its utopic atmosphere 'is then copied, simulated and rolled out in towns, cities, resorts, islands, festivals, and events around the world' (Urry *et al.*, 2016, p. 13). And if the Museum is a utopic transfiguration of the cityscape, then the inclusion of equally modified, harmonised urban sounds or cacophonies produce the perfect stage for social engagement (Tzanelli, 2015c, Chapter 2; Donald and Gammack, 2007). In line with Afro-Brazilian philosophies of wholeness and cinematic audio-visual techniques of audience engagement, important segments of the exhibition involve the use of music. The holistic design allows visitors to develop 'deep listening' of the problems confronting humanity (Erlmann, 1999, 2004; Oliveros, 2005).

The entrance to the Museum, where the Gaia-Globe is elevated to the sky-ceiling, is meant to be a 'cosmic portal' and contains a film co-directed by Meirelles. The film compresses 13.7 billion years of geological change and natural evolution 'into eight minutes of sensory overload projected by nine projectors inside an egg-shaped cinema' (Watts, 17 December 2015; *Dezeen Magazine*, 17 December 2015). This fast travel emulates the digital framing of tourist destinations, the organisation of industrial design of touring. Hollinshead (1999, p. 8) reminds us that tourism participates often unsuspectingly in the production of dominant narratives and attractions of place, while suppressing other traditions and storylines. Though the Museum reveals, rather than conceals, the outcome of human mobilities on a diachronic scale, its discourse is still based on the ways the 'gaze' of professionals and institutions embraces 'the complex interlacing of language and vision' (Jay, 1986, p. 183; Hollinshead, 1998; Rose, 1999), hence the philosophical tenets of mobility. Of course, the 'language of tourism' (Dann, 1996) is always malleable in the hands of individual tourists, because every *flâneur/flâneuse* crafts his/her own autobiographical path in the city (Parkhurst Ferguson, 1994, p. 28; Germann Molz, 2012). Matching visual ethnographies (Pink, 2008), such touring practices are producing new worlds (Hollinshead, 2009).

We do, of course, deal with an experience exceeding that of the fun-loving tourist, as the Museum's next three displays suggest in three different languages (Portuguese, Spanish and English). The first display is an ethereal installation commissioned from American artist Daniel Wurzel representing the flux of matter; the second discusses biology, the DNA structure and the connectedness of life within and without our bodies; the last looks into our nervous system, human relationships and culture through 12,000 images 'arranged as pillars of prayer, sensations, relationships, home life and other themes' (Watts, 17 December 2015). The installations are nothing short of a translation of *Ubuntu* wholeness of being into ecosystemic complexity in today's globalised life-worlds: close to an actor-network organisation of life on earth, it signifies that humans are monads in a small living universe enclosed in an even larger one (Dascal, 1987). The Museum's essential contradiction between tourism and degrowth is reflected in the provision of several viewpoints in its exhibits. For actor-network (ANT) theorists, the multiplicity of alternative paths to the future is seen as 'the only way to repair the danger of giving a functionalist account of programmes and anti-programmes' (Latour *et al.*, 1992, p. 42). To avoid controversies about what counts as 'function', it is essential that visitors can compare contradictory accounts.

Accordingly, the Museum's central story is experienced in a cluster of 10-metre tall digital totems projecting data and images that overwhelm the visitor. This is our 'Now', the Anthropocene, in which the human exerts immense power over geological change resulting in social, cultural and political transformations across the globe (Urry, 2011). The experience is audio-visual, so every message is spoken out loud from huge speakers. It is not meant to comfort, but to unsettle: we are shown clips of burning forests, melting glaciers, dense traffic and 'Brazil's recent toxic mudslide … along with a real-time counter of global births and deaths … ocean acidification, ozone depletion and greenhouse gas emissions' as well as the latest figures on consumption of energy, water and beef (Watts, 17 December 2015). The images are framed with a dark soundtrack and in giant flashing letters we read in three languages how much we have modified the planet since 1950: 'We are more … We consume more … More … More' (ibid.). The creation of an atmosphere of imminent catastrophic failure manifests that the Museum is more than a didactic multi-medium, because it allows for the relocation of art to the digitised/cinematic plane (Witzgall and Vogl, 2016, p. 310; Gibson, 2006).

This also prompts considerations of the (non-)diegetic nature of music or the use of soundtracks as more than scores that accompany a film's or clip's narrative arc (Chion, 1994; Kassabian, 2000; Sider, 2003; Buhler *et al.*, 2009). Images of destruction mediate the human impact on bio-diversity, signalling humankind's entry to what has been called Earth's 'sixth major extinction' (Leakey and Lewin, 1995). The messages seem to be geographically rootless, but at closer inspection they are very local, Brazilian in nature. The Museum's use of digital media is uniquely 'locative': it turns the country and its ecological woes (deforestation, mudslides) into an unwanted celebrity, allowing for disaster to be located or 'found' in public cultures (Elmer, 2010, p. 20). By mobilising the geographic locale beyond its instrumentalised status as 'latitude/longitude coordinated point on earth', the Museum's use of Rio and Brazil captures their value as existential, inhabited and lived place (Bleecker and Knowlton, 2006, p. 22). The Museum's urban globetrotter is thus called upon to participate aesthetically and emotionally in a drama that is, after all, global and real, even if proffered in a representational scenario (Beck, 2009; Urry, 2011; Tzanelli, 2016b).

Scientific futurology also follows on from this: the next three exhibits feature interactive games that allow visitors to shape alternative futures. Projecting current trends fifty years into the future, the games involve measurements of the visitor's ecological footprint, the calculation of how many planets are needed to support mankind if everyone on earth had the same living standard, decision-making on energy sources, finance and land usage to support or diminish humanity's survival prospects, and more (Watts, 17 December 2015). Staging such interactive scenarios has become an essential feature of new smart cities in which – as is the case with airports (Fuller, 2009) – almost everything is informational. Like a website, the Museum embraces the new media's phantasmagoric principles, though it inverts their sublimation in its potentially dark scenarios. These days, phantasmagorias depend on the development and diffusion of Information Communication Technologies (ICT) so as to boost tourism. It is argued that digital connectivity enables the integration of information on tourism businesses, consumption and use of resources while interconnecting all the stakeholders to share relevant knowledge and manage data analytics tools for decision-making and tourism experience co-creation design (Zhu *et al.*, 2014; Lamsfus *et al.,* 2015; Del Chiappa and Baggio, 2015). But the mantra of 'sustainability', care for native human capital and provision of the right leadership for such projects (Lamsfus and Alzua-Sorzabal, 2013; Boes *et al.*, 2015), may in fact widen the gap between digital worlds (prone to neoliberal 'evotopias') and terrestrial life-worlds (especially those ridden with social problems). It is of course essential to stress that such projects can yield beneficial results, especially where physical proximity between projected guests (mega-event tourists) and hosts (slums) is limited or prohibited, or where mere visual/ digital connectivity puts the host on the global map (Gretzel *et al.*, 2015).

By capitalising on the advance of virtual reality technology, the Museum brings images, 3D simulations and cinematic narratives to life for 'armchair' and virtual tourists (Arnold, 2005; Hall, 2005; Germann Molz, 2012). The United Nations Environment Programme (UNEP) and the World Tourism Organization (UNWTO) define sustainable tourism in terms of developmental processes that 'meet the needs of the present without compromising the ability of future generations to meet their own needs' and by taking full account 'of its current and future economic, social and environmental impacts, addressing the needs of visitors, the industry, the environment and host communities' (UNEP/UNWTO, 2005). But 'gamification' does so much more than this for the Museum's visitors. Conventional gamification connects to tourism-making as place-making, because it allows prospective visitors to have 'taste bites' of places they might eventually visit – though these places are modified digitally. Gamification was used as a marketing strategy from the Brazilian Tourist Board (EMBRATUR), which released the 'Brazil Quest', an entertainment game intended to 'educate' prospective (digital-to-terrestrial) tourists during the 2014 FIFA World Cup (Corrêa and Kitano, 2015). The Rio 2016 official website for the mega-event used similar strategies of 'mapping' desirable places to visit in the city of Rio during the mega-event, to bolster urban tourism (Tzanelli, 2016c). Though practically connected to business models of sustainable development and tourist motivation (Kim, 2015), in terms of worldmaking, gamification often elicits memories of places, thus 'dragging', reshuffling and 'indexing' terrestrial sites from across the city (Rojek, 1997). But as is the case with Meirelles' imposing introductory clip, the Museum's digital games take visitors to non-places – not Rio's life-worlds, Brazil's terrains or a place nearby, but abstracted spheres of human activity endorsed by capitalism, asking them to affect pathways to humanity's collective future.

Contrary to tracing, firmly locating activity in terrestrial domains, 'which always returns to the "same"' (i.e. reproduction of specific places, their representations or branding), such individual map-making of the future is unique and 'can be torn, reversed [and] adapted to montages of every kind' (Galloway, 2010, p. 28). In this serious gamification, the scenarios' non-places are the opposite of utopia: they exist in our nightmares and in news reporting about the real effects of climate change and they do not contain any organic society (Augé, 2008, p. 90). They may simulate 'daily movements' or prey on audio-visual articulations of nostalgia with the help of soundtracks (Samuels *et al.*, 2010, p. 336; Gray, 2007; Sakakeeny, 2010), but they speak about the possibility of complete rootlessness, of turning tourist journeys into endless nomadic ploughings of arid earth in a future era of complete ecological catastrophe. The Museum's gamification techniques elicit emotional responses by the offered scenarios, thus encouraging and motivating for further positive activities and individual responses (Negruşa *et al.*, 2015, pp. 11162–11163).

The final exhibit maintains the Museum's ambivalent core attitude towards tourismification and degrowth, tourism and dystopian ecosystemic imaginaries, by suggesting collective existential rebirth as the ultimate form of travel. This 'rebirth' is achieved through a return to premodern values, symbolised in the wooden structure of an indigenous 'house of knowledge', where communities share stories. In the centre of the structure lies the Australian aboriginal *tjurunga*, 'a symbol of learning, fertility ritual power and the ability to cope with change' (Watts, 17 December 2015). The movements of visitors in the hall signal adjustments of lights and sounds as a reminder of how humans and their mobilities change the world around them. The exhibit is intentionally open to interpretation, but its hermeneutics seem to gravitate towards the non-rational and subliminal – hence open to reworking – future imaginings and responsive action countering 'the conventional techno-scientific hegemony of approaches to organization' (Gosling and Case, 2013, p. 706). The exhibit is intentionally used as a form of de-colonial allegory, because it turns its back on Western scientific narrative, even though it employs it in its staging. This ambivalence rests in the realisation that we may want to improve things and 'do good', but our hopeful attitude is not equipped with the appropriate concepts and tools with which action can be taken (Lear, 2006).

Despite the fact that the Museum has been set up by groups of male experts, its message is that positive change lies with technologically endowed reproduction, involving both female and male humans and drawing on ancient knowledge resources to maintain the inalienable process of the gift of life. This revised half-deep ecological and half-ecofeminist manifesto does not exclude technology from its agenda, nor does it suggest that biological labour alone can sustain change. The suggestion is twofold: on the one hand, the exhibit highlights that science's epistemic capacity to manage 'modality' (ways of doing things) determines the conditions under which possibilities can be realised (Fuller, 2012, p. 113). On the other, it brings to the fore the significance of socio-psychological conceptions of 'affordances', the range of choices available to humans within their particular world and the subjective experience of their socio-cultural environment (Michael, 1996, p. 149; Urry, 2007, p. 51; Tzanelli, 2016b, p. 8). *Tjurunga's* implicit association with a rupture in ecological fecundity – including human fertility – in the Museum's allegory, enables the narration of a '"cosmological episode" writ large ... a catastrophic point at which our own meaning systems are stressed to the point of breakdown' (Gosling and Case 2013, p. 712).

The Museum's concluding thematic appeals to the desire to escape the 'crowdedness' of concepts and scenarios populating its other segments, so as to allow visitors to engage in educative mind-walking (Ingold, 2010). The possibility of visiting places of the mind by technology produces the scientific sublime as 'a blend of aesthetic, religious and scientific elements' (Neeley, 2001, p. 39), but also an exploration of one's personal horizons (Sachs, 2006; Sennett, 2008). Such travels of the mind connect visual amazement with emotions, 'seeing' to feeling and spiritual uplifting that is often associated with the sublime. The *tjurunga's* rediscovered ethical singularity functions as a new dynamic site to elevate the mind, which is invited to contemplate forgotten greatness (Johnson, 1991, p. 158). The totemic nature of the 'thing' binds inanimate and animate entities in a holistic field of action, thus appealing to an 'ecocentric' ethics that displaces the human from this action's core, 'allow[ing] human interests, on occasion, to lose' (Gosling and Case, 2013, p. 709). Where we used to see versions of Nature manufactured for us by a tourist industry (Nicolson, 1997), or where we were trained to relate aesthetic sublimation to the botanical gaze of European poetry and literature (Raiskin, 1996, p. 41), the Museum's audio-visual media inject an element of novel kinetic energy in the projected landscapes of our future from a glocal indigenous perspective (Bell and Lyall, 2002, pp. 53–54). Here, it helps to consider the relationship between landscape and memory to unpack the Museum's take on interplays between nature and culture as an alternative cultural politics of our times (Schama, 1996). Much like Munich 1972's reflexive emphasis on architecture, which focused on 'fixing' the nature of 'nature-alienated cities' (Young C., 2006, p. 126), the Museum of Tomorrow aims to fix a human rupture from natural origins.

In the place of eco-tourist travel, a technologically mediated possibility to return to ancient human understandings of Nature focuses on horizontal (planar, flat) sublimation, and ideas of linear and curvilinear but retrogressive movement to a better future. This expands our temporal possibilities by giving us a glimpse into infinite time (Chown, 2007, p. 149), a life beyond a human life's span – and thus a way out of conventional dark tourism as visitation to sites of heritage (Lennon and Foley, 2000; Dann and Seaton, 2001; Walter, 2009; Cohen, 2011). The *tjurunga* replaces connections between heritage and loss, suffering or destruction, with the promise of (re)birth by the most natural means: the human life cycle. Where the inverted sublime of the abyss enabled artistic and religious creativity in celebration of the dark side of modernity, Calatrava and his associates' imagineering appealed to the life drive or *eros*, our appetite for enjoyment and satisfaction. At the same time, it appeals to our *epistemophilia* – our knowledge drive and the need for answers to deep existential questions (Fayos-Solá *et al.*, 2014, p. 664).

From there, visitors exit the Museum at the rear of the building, where the glass walls look out over to a 'reflecting pool' onto Guanabara Bay's views (Watts, 17 December 2015). Then, the Museum's potential dystopian/utopian scenarios are replaced with a certain challenge: what the visitor faces is a sea of junk, with spectacular views of mountains and the city's *morros*, where 'human garbage' lives without sanitation, further perpetrating the region's environmental problems. There is no better introduction to the immediate impact of techno-fossils, litter and debris carried by rivers and sewage into the sea and accumulating in the marine environment of the area than this shock (Waters, 2016). Such a 'panoramic perspective' (Czeglédy, 2003, p. 17) of the real issue at hand, here and now, suggests that the *favela* nature of its *Cariocas* floats amidst the sea's pollutants. And here, Guanabara's 'stratigraphic' landscape, the accumulation of waste sediments on the surface of its waters, meets Meirelles' and Calatrava's cine-stratigraphic (layer-recording) account of human self-destruction (Tzanelli, 2015a, p. 93). In many respects, the Museum's uneasy travel to epochs serves only as a preamble to the shock of the real: if its neatly organised 'iconic' events of the new world disorder showcase globalisation and global capitalism as the new 'structure', with nations and localities or individuals as 'agents' (Urry, 2005a, p. 244), what lies right outside it relocates these 'new structures' in the city. And as Rio's socio-political realities bring together the macro- and micro-structures in the visitor's affective and cognitive contact with 'local effects' (Latour, 1999), we are left with the feeling that problems are always much closer to 'home' than originally thought.

It helps recalling that *Gestell*, Heidegger's word for the much-maligned technology, is usually translated in English as 'enframing', thus ceasing to designate complex networks of machines and activities as such and beginning to refer instead to our 'attitude towards reality' (Žižek, 2014, p. 31). If so, the Museum of Tomorrow's 'enframing' is successful, in that it binds dramatic presentations of things as they are and things yet to come, by 'establishing powerful, pervasive and long-lasting moods and motivations' in its visitors, 'by formulating conceptions' and clothing them with such an aura of factuality that they seem 'uniquely realistic' (Geertz, 1973, p. 90). Thus, Calatrava and his associates' 'art' can be regarded as truthful as science (Alexander, 2011, p. 59): its performative power adheres to a symbolic order, a social imaginary under pressure by the hypermobilities of technological progress in contemporary capitalism. But is it not that this 'risk' encompasses the potential for salvation – for, 'the moment we become aware and fully assume the fact that technology itself is, in its essence, a mode of enframing, we [can] overcome it' (Žižek 2014, p. 31; Jameson, 1995, p. 260)?

4 Choreomobility and artistic worldmaking

Retrieving Rio's submerged centre

Shrinking budgets, shrinking worlds?

In 2015 data revealed that the Brazilian economy would shrink by 2.1 per cent, with an inflation rate of over 9 per cent and a deficit set to develop in the following crucial year of the Olympic Games (Butler, 23 September 2015). Under other circumstances, this would have been included in international press coverage with no commentary, save the usual notes on global economic fluctuations. But as a host to the Olympic Games, Brazil, and especially Rio, would receive additional undesired attention. The much-awaited Opening and Closing Ceremonies of the mega-event, now globally televised and attended, would certainly suffer the consequences. Because of this unfortunate economic turn, the Games' local and international organisers would find it difficult to keep people supportive of the enterprise. The common verdict that money was needed elsewhere, guided the game-makers' prudent strategy to make cuts without undermining a popular spectacle: subsequently, the plan to include high-tech gadgets, such as aerial drones, and moving stages, never figured in the event's Opening and Closing Ceremonies. Struggling to keep the Games' budget to 7 billion Reais ($1.7 billion) for the 16 days of the competition and the Ceremonies was challenging, as Sidney Levy, Chief Executive of Rio 2016, admitted. Brazil had budgeted a total of approximately 40 billion Reais for the Olympic preparations, including the *Porto Maravilha* and subway extension projects, on top of the 25 billion Reais spent on Brazil's FIFA World Cup in 2014 (Bloomberg, 22 September 2015).

As the global imaginary of growth and development – neoliberal globalisation's best partner (Steger, 2008) – received a reality blow in Rio, the Games' artistic labour prepared for a reworking of their understandings of 'commonality' and 'commons' – two key principles of *Ubuntu* philosophies of 'being in the world'. Art would be delivered, but within an ethical framework involving care for the host and their woes, not just the ephemeral guest of the spectacle. Goodman (1978) suggested that artists have a particular way of producing worldviews that does not always obey hegemonic templates of reality, but creates alternative routes to the future. I proposed elsewhere (Tzanelli, 2013a, 2013b, 2015a, 2015b, 2015c) under the term 'techno-poesis' (see also Chapter 2) that artists can adhere to the principles of 'sameness of meaning': their worldmaking practices converge, so that subsequently their conceptions and expressions of the same 'world' acquire the same meaning, because they share the same extension (Cohnitz and Rossberg, 2016). I suggest that the makers of Rio 2016's Opening and Closing Ceremonies (directors Fernando Meirelles, Daniela Thomas and Andrucha Waddington, as well as Rosa Magalhães, musical legends and organic imagineers Gilberto Gil and Caetano Veloso as advisors to the producers and ceremonial choreographer Deborah Colker), reflect *Ubuntu* notions of commonality and *buen vivir* as 'extensions' of hope, a visionary response to degrowth pressures. Omnipresent in expressions of musical, virtual/technological and embodied sociality in the ceremony, this 'sameness of meaning' articulated Rio's atmosphere, not as a fleeting feeling but as a battle between the entrenched 'Africanised' and labour migrant heritage of slum crime and the enthusiasm of tourismified mobilities of art (samba, *capoeira* and other derived contemporary music/dance genres).

There is an 'inside' (local, ethno-national) and an 'outside' (global) imaginary enclosed in artistic worldmakings of this sort – which is why a cultural sociological analysis of their underlying ideological formations and creative texts offers valuable insight into glocalisation (Robertson, 1992, 1995) as well as the routes of cultural mobilities outside the city and the national borderlands (Schein, 2002; Sheller, 2003, 2004; Sebro, 2016). The 'inside' or national logic of the Opening – and to a great extent, Closing – Ceremony is to be found in antithetical conceptions of fluidity vs. solidity that produce 'zero' or 'empty grounds' for Brazilian national identity, fostering a performative utopics not dissimilar from that of Calatrava's globalised Museum space. Nagib's (2007, p. 33) argument that Brazilian film of the *Cinema Novo* era (1980s) focuses on national identity's split between imaginaries of the fluid sea (hence, of mobility, migration, tourism and 'openness') and the solid *sertão* (the country's arid Northeastern back-lands associated with sedentarism) nicely matches Bauman's (1998, 2000) observations on the Manichean nature of contemporary subjectivities. But ceremonial texts of the Olympic variation are tied to global political contexts, thus stretching the idea of national land and identity to its uppermost limits. Where *Cinema Novo*'s allegories of Brazilian identity limited worldmaking in traversing the national land to make cinematic landscape (Urry, 2004; Tzanelli, 2013a), Rio 2016's directors (filmmakers, musicians and choreographers) would have recourse to a different game of hybridisation and touring (Thompson, 2005). Such hybridisation would allow the global logic of the 'outside' into the logic of national *poesis* in the world. Rio 2016's ceremonial worldmaking is extremely (in)fusing in this respect: not only does it acknowledge the interpenetration of global and local, as well as urban cultural forms (Nederveen Pieterse, 2004), it allows national allegories to be supplanted by the realities of degrowth in a 'cine-realist' style.

Old and new technologies have a role to play in this new post-national reality. Nick Couldry (2003, p. 2) speaks of the myth of the 'mediated centre':

the belief, or assumption, that there is a centre to the social world, for which the media speaks in various textual and audio-visual formats. To deconstruct the myth that different societies tailor to their needs – to perform a sort of 'recuperative surgery' to their social and cultural assumptions – we have to examine the 'banal practices of ordering' to which their representations of Self and other are subjected by media complexes in compliant or subversive ways (Couldry, 2000, p. 48). Erik Cohen (1979) complements Couldry and Bauman when he suggests, from a different disciplinary perspective, that each society acting as host in tourist encounters has a hidden 'core', with which its members form a special relationship of connectivity (as dwellers) or urgent departure (as travellers). If the centripetal urgency adheres to the principles of ethno-national or regional belonging, the centrifugal activates mobility constellations, including business travel, tourism or technological mediatisation and communication. In the mega-event's ceremonies we deal with combinations of media rituals enabling pilgrimage to the land (Rio's Brazil) visited by sports fans and tourists. Hence, every Olympic Ceremony activates a twin form of 'recreation': as a rebirth of the national community in global cosmic spaces, and as the community's 'experimental travelling', which internalises encounters with visitors-'others' (Tzanelli, 2015c, p. 63), but 'away from the spiritual, cultural, or even religious centre of [its] world, into its periphery [and] towards the centres of other cultures and societies' (Cohen, 1979, pp. 182–183).

Neither Cohen nor Couldry have much to say about the ways such spiritual or representational 'centres' are concealed from public spectatorship, or whether such a 'centre' is ontologically real. The assumption is that, once the mediated society develops centrifugal, globalising tendencies, its cultural core would always be exposed, even by and to itself. Yet, societies invent ways to conceal realities and self-representations from themselves in a make-believe political process of cosmetic nature, which contradicts Bloch's (1988) suggestion that forms of art and architecture ought to be public aesthetic goods. In what follows, I investigate the intricacies of what I term Rio's 'submerged centre', a core self-narration that adheres to the embarrassment of secret self-knowledge – what Herzfeld (2005) examines in another context as 'cultural intimacy'. A construct in the first place, which cannot realistically summarise the culture from which it emanates, but which always exposes some of its particularly potent features, the submerged centre borrows from marginalised identities within the represented community that are structured as the enemy of its *nomos* or law (Schmitt, 2001). As a 'zero institution' or empty signifier with no predetermined meaning, the *favela* is a fantasy of the pre-social, 'of what precedes difference' (Diken and Laustsen, 2008, p. 28), a peculiarly Brazilian archaic state of nature standing outside our responsibility as invitation to entertain our secret pleasures. Žižek identified in this move 'the future's primacy' (1999, p. 18), the preservation of pure national qualities by means of ritualistic, repetitive expulsion of what is selected to function as their 'outside'.

But the 'outside' is often part of one's repressed past that has to submerge, so that a movement to the future happens. Artistic worldmaking can reactivate such forgotten discourses of belonging in covert ways. This submerged centre is for Calatrava and Meirelles the politically 'expunged' (to the polluted sea) *favelas*. I suggest that the Museum of Tomorrow's creative 'expulsion' is replaced in the Olympic Ceremonies with a novel techno-political inclusion the *favelados* never experience in Rio's body politic. This inclusion is not, however, identical to the biopolitical strategies adopted by the nation-state (as per Wood and Shearing, 2007). Unlike the Museum's laconic architectonic configuration of the *favelas'* absent presence in the polluted cityscape, the Ceremonies' non-representational strategies of old and new *favelartes* showcase the *favelas* as hypermobile 'sites' of touristic consumption, networked spaces enclosing 'immutable mobiles', subjects and objects mediating traffic of all sorts of illegal and legal commodities and experiences (Latour, 1990, p. 32). Both illicit and licit forms of creativity are welcome in utopian choreographies of space and culture as mobile affects. The rule of law subsides in ceremonial contexts, even though it literally funds them. This is what makes utopia possible for a few hours, thanks to the multisensory education of the Ceremonies' cine-phile artists.

I argue that Rio 2016's ceremonial artwork is very much a legible text, against any pleas to respect its artistic autonomy (e.g. Sontag, 2013). Legibility commences with a focus on the border: Brazil's urban *favelas* are the start-up toolkits of its modernity, which all its urban centres had to exclude from their cosmetic programme and cast as their 'other'. But intensified urban globalisations diluted the divisions between 'inside' and 'outside' to further allow the penetration of global capital in the mega-event's host city (Hardt and Negri 2000, p. 188). The *favela* as the city's immutable post-industrial *sertão* and as an arrival and departure centre of various populations, preserves Rio's unstable memory magma, its fluid and internationally now networked cultural centre. The place of the *favela* in the Brazilian popular imagination as a liminal space that does not house ordinary citizens but marginal people excluded from the city (Caldeira, 2000, p. 78) appears at first to guide the directors' refusal to represent *favelados* as such in the ceremony. Yet, at a more careful glance, the directors give novel shape to Rio's memory magma by granting *favela* culture and art with a present *and a future.* In this projected future, technologies of a military nature are replaced with technologies of cine-tourism, in which gazers and gazees form a peaceful dialogics of care, in line with the Olympic Movement's principles. This lateral imagineering borrows from the portrayal of shantytown cultures in realist cinematic aesthetics (Jaguaribe and Hetherington, 2004, p. 156). So the ceremonial directors expect literacy from their audiences; at the same time, although with some exotic touches for the tourist gaze, there are some aspects of the ceremonial text only knowing insiders can fully comprehend.

The convergence that ceremonial directors and other principal ceremonial artists display in ways of worldmaking communicates with, but is not solely determined by the context of economic recession and state welfare retrenchment. The spending speed is curtailed in artwork in an accurate comparative display of virtue: China spent over $100 million on innovative technology for the Opening Ceremony of Beijing 2008, whereas London 2012's Olympic and Paralympic Ceremonies cost approximately £80 million ($112 million). Meirelles stated that, because Brazil is 'in a financial crisis … it wouldn't be fair to spend money that London spent in their ceremony' and that under these circumstances he was 'not sure [he] would approve an Olympics in Brazil' (Bloomberg, 22 September 2015). 'We will have a low budget but I'm happy to work with this budget', he continued. 'I would be ashamed to waste what London spent in a country where we need sanitation; where education needs money' (Butler, 23 September 2015). 'We don't have high culture', he added. 'Of course we have some pianists, some maestros and some orchestras, but that's not us … The beauty of Brazil comes from the roots' (The Associated Press, 22 September 2015). Virtue comes out of necessity, but in Brazil's case, necessity matches the country's historical relationship with a former colonial West, in which capitalist excess originates, after all. Leonardo Caetano, member of ROCOG, added in a distinctive Brazilian tone that the Ceremony 'will go into the heart … we will not have luxury, but we will have originality … we will spend less, but we compensate with creativity, rhythm and emotion' (ibid.). This more official statement matched plans for the involvement of Brazil's indigenous communities and about 12,000 volunteers from all walks of life in the show (ibid.).

A note is necessary here to avoid confusion of artistic intentionality and social imperatives. The treatment of Olympic Ceremonies as peripheral to eventisation processes connects to the fact that, as works of art, they are not meant as representations of reality but a reality in its own right. It is the Ceremonies' 'exisience' (how they allow us to live in the world poetically), rather than 'essence' (what is conveyed by directors and artists to audiences) that matters in an Olympic mega-event (Lazarin, 2008, p. 48). The rhythms that Ceremonies adopt, 'superimpose themselves on the multiple natural rhythms of the body … though not without changing them' (Lefebvre, [1992] 2015, p. 19). As we will see in Chapters 5 and 6, the harmonisation of indigenous music with the semi-sacred tempo of the Olympic mega-event frames ethnically specific styles in global terms, while allowing the particular Ceremonies of 2016 to set 'tropical truth' to work (Veloso, 2003). As a utopian parable, the Ceremony enacts a search to 'recover', but in the process it interprets, rather than matches, an idea with a 'thing' (produces televised or streamed audio-visual products) (Heidegger, 1935, p. 36, p. 39 in Lazarin, 2008, p. 52). At the same time, there is a positivist quality in what Olympic Ceremonies do in a world imbued with audio-visual media: to craft new 'worlds', ceremonial artists assume the role of rhythmanalysts, who measure and convey, interpret localised life-worlds, by using their own body and soul as a sort of 'metronome' (Lefebvre, [1992] 2015, p. 29).

Recovering social intimacy: towards a rhythmic sociology of belonging

Ceremonial makers act as aestheticians drawing on body rhythms, 'without privileging any … sensations', just learning to think with their body, not in the abstract, but in lived temporality (ibid., p. 31). Though certainly true for chief ceremonial choreographer Colker, the same principle applies to all reputed ceremonial makers, who connect individual to collective cultural and social rhythms in organic ways. In a compatible fashion, Sebro (2016, p. 96) suggests the launching of a '*choreomobility*' of the political as 'the choreographed – patterned, calculated and directed – movements of bodies (both dead and living) through spaces and through times'. *Choreomobility* allows for a historically situated analysis of movement transcending that of biological technologies and allowing for an exploration of interconnections between time, place and energy expenditure (Cresswell and Merriman, 2001; Foster, 2008, 2009, 2010; Edensor, 2010). It is precisely this 'methodology' that ceremonial makers apply to the explored Olympic host, which often leads them in investigations into their own homeland's cultural fabric and social structures. These *choreomobile* orchestrations enmesh musical art-forms, especially those that come to stand *for* representations of national style at large (Born and Hesmondhalgh, 2000, pp. 20–21), thus encouraging people to visit geographical places in person, or to travel to other places in an imaginary sense through music sounds, scenes and performance events (Cohen, 2005, p. 76; Connell and Gibson, 2002, pp. 231–233). Because they also stand *as* hybridised 'World Music', the same art-forms stir national consciousness or contribute to transnational political movements (Connell and Gibson, 2004, p. 343; Tzanelli, 2013b, p. 4, p. 6; Tzanelli, 2015c, p. 90). Hence, Rio 2016's artistic ceremonial contingent makes the world by measuring and redistributing energy to Brazilian society in symbolic ways, so that it addresses Brazil's accursed Western heritage following modernisation and urbanisation: the nightmare of a real catastrophe in human and natural ecosystems (Romano, 2015, p. 88). This is achieved by offering utopian exit strategies to its submerged *favelados* from what are, after all, Brazil's most intimate polluting qualities (Chauí, 2001, p. 8 in Nagib, 2007, p. 40): the viciousness of organised (black and white-collar) crime and an alleged 'corruption' of ethnic character that spills its bile into the natural ecosystem. This comes as close to environmental racism of (post)colonial origins as it gets.

After this introduction, the selection of Fernando Meirelles (born 1955) and his colleagues by ROCOG to narrate Rio's cultural biography in such difficult times makes even more sense. Born into a middle-class family and raised in Alto dos Pinheiros, a district of São Paulo's West Zone, a young Meirelles won several awards in film festivals as experimental video-maker, participated in a small independent company, *Olhar Electrônico*, and became director of a popular children's TV show in the 1980s. In the 1990s he started gravitating towards the production of social dramas such as *Domésticas* (2001), which featured São Paulo's invisible domestic labour. His early artwork would lead to his internationally acclaimed *City of God* (*Citade de Deus,* 2003), which he materialised with the recruitment of real *favelados* as actors (IMDB, undated). Associated with the Brazilian Film Revival of the mid-1990s, Meirelles made his name, along filmmakers such as Walter Sales (b. 1956) and Beto Brant (b. 1964) by addressing national issues through forms of revelatory realism (Nagib, 2011, p. 157). This Brazilian trend is exemplified by the co-directed (with Kátia Lund) *City of God*. After this film, Meirelles went on to direct high-budget films abroad, while also retaining a great reputation for his sharp critique of Rio's criminal socialities at home.

Where the *Cinema Novo* of the previous exilic era had produced critiques of domestic militarisms across Latin America, the mid-1990s Brazilian Film Revival signalled a 'homecoming' in the form of realism, complicated by transatlantic or trans-hemispheric migrations of talent and diasporic film production (Burton-Carvajal, 2000). Meirelles' ceremonial artwork is the product of his subsequent stylistic hybridisation abroad, not the reproduction of his 2002 domestic collaborations. A cleverly concealed ceremonial borrowing of (now hybridised) tropes from his artistic cinematic-realist critique of *favela* policy in *City of God*, which is both an aesthetic accomplishment and a skilful indexical diagnosis of Brazilian social problems, is part of my analysis of the Opening Ceremony. Although the *favela* appears nowhere in the ceremony's cinematic imagery, traces of its buzzing cultural rhythms punctuate its absence, tuning life into a movie-like spectacle. The insertion of realist *favela* epistemologies that we associate with Meirelles' cinematic artwork is replaced with an embodied utopian discourse of *favela* dance and music cultures in the Olympic Ceremonies. Although the theme of globalisation is also associated with European art cinema (Thompson, 2005, p. 218; Martin-Jones, 2013), the Olympic Ceremonies' *choreomobile* musicality casts new light on the value of cultural interactions under globalised conditions. And there is more: in line with tourismified cultures of slum consumption reminiscent of European industrial capitalism, a 'thana-political', or what Badiou (2013, p. 59) calls 'perishable spectacle', exists within a critically projected 'thana-capitalist' (Korstanje, 2016b) subtext in some of the 2016 ceremonial performances.

Continuations between film and ceremony are traced in Meirelles' early success. The *City of God*'s encapsulation of epochal change juxtaposes utopia as the unreal(ised) human condition with the religious motif of the Golden Age or Paradise Lost. This happens in cinematic segments through lyrical samba (until the end of the 1950s), waves of chaotic migration producing overcrowded and criminalised *favelas* and the production of localised pride through communal identification (Nagib, 2007, pp. 111–112). But in a state of law, such distinctions also wane – an observation nicely reflected in Diken and Laustsen's (2008, p. 57) take on the film's central scenario, as an Augustinian allusion, where *City of God* becomes an abandoned city without God: 'a state of being exempted from the domain of the law and ethical responsibility ... in other words, a "city without citizens" as well'.

If the 'City of God' – the real *favela*, its realist cinematic depiction – consists of fallen simulacra in the eyes of the digital God of Brazilian modernity, Meirelles and his associates' ceremonial urban spaces enact a rescue mission, a pacifying project for their forgiveness and inclusion in Rio's cultural polity (see Foster, 2010 on choreographies of empathy). This confessional process allowed human populations to fall prey to the old habit of secular *exagoreusis*, a repentance addressed to a human master of development as representative of God (Foucault, 1988, p. 44), so there are traps even for artmaking of this radical sort to be aware of. The Olympic utopia is, above all, a project of forgiveness and inclusion into an earthly Augustinian empire of athletes, commoners and elite policy-makers. Endorsed with its very own cultural industry's bright spectacular displays, in more recent decades, it has also been transformed into a 'narrative node' for capitalism and nationalism (Tzanelli, 2013a, Chapter 3). But this 'forgiveness' is also coupled with another hidden anger, a vital energy stemming from *favela* utopias, often excluded from Rio's officially sanctioned 'popular culture'. The inclusion of new street dance and music from the *favelas* and the spatial separation of *favelados* in the ceremonial cityscape, reminds global audiences that conditional implementations of empathy are risky, when social inequalities have already eroded community relations and become inscribed onto global developmental planes.

The inclusion of street music in the 2016 Opening Ceremony is reminiscent of Kátia Lund's co-directorship of *City of God*. Lund became known before her professional association with Meirelles because of a music video she created for the song '*A Minha Alma*' ('My Soul') by rap group *O Rappa*. The video portrays a young male *favelado* who is murdered by the police raiding a *favela* on his way to the beach. Lund, who was at the time member of the Salles brothers' production company, co-directed the video with Paulo Lins, author of the novel *City of God* (*Citade de Deus*, 1997) that inspired Meirelles and Lund's film (Nagib, 2007, p. 30). As I explain later, the theme of *favelados do morros*, who cannot access the privileged world of the beach to enjoy Rio's maritime Paradise, is also present in the Opening Ceremony's separation of street dancers from the beauty of Ipanema. Here, it is more important to note that Lund's absence from the artistic ceremonial team is compensated by the involvement of London 2012 Handover to Rio artistic co-director Daniella Thomas. Daughter of the famous cartoonist Ziraldo Alves Pinto and sister of Golden Globe Award-nominated film score composer, Antonio Pinto, Thomas (Daniella Gotijo Pintes), rose to fame from her early co-directing with Walters Salles of *Terra Estrangeira* (*Foreign Land*, 1995).

Matching Lund's allegory of the prohibitive (to *favelados*) maritime Paradise with an allegory of Brazilian middle-class fear of 'underdevelopment', and with inspiration from *Cinema Novo* and the New German Cinema, *Foreign Land* was produced during Brazil's short-lived economic Renaissance. The economic boost allowed the native middle classes to become global tourists, rather than immigrants, while also amplifying national insecurity concerning the country's incomplete modernisation. Thomas' involvement in the ceremonial text also reflected her involvement in *Midnight* (1999), another film she co-directed with Salles. As I endeavour to highlight in an analysis of particular ceremonial segments, the film's juxtaposition of 'the macho utopia that resulted in … [a] hollow land' (Nagib, 2007, p. 56), with the fecundity of female pragmatism, *forms a discursive cinematic trope in times of real economic and societal crisis in Brazil.* The clash between imperatives of degrowth and the desire of tourismification are most evident here: Thomas stated that the Opening Ceremony will be 'the biggest party there has ever been in the country' that will showcase 'the best of Brazilian music; not the songs from the radio, but truly the best' (Cantor-Navas, 15 July 2016). The 'best' hints at the presence of originality and authenticity, connected to ideas of place and culture, but given Thomas' professional biography, it may also allude to a utopia constructed on musical renditions of sociality. As I explain in the conclusion, notions of native affluence adhering to cine-tourist mobilities, also present in the production of Magalhães' Closing Ceremony, are constitutive of a global ambivalence towards conceptions of scarcity – and are of distinctive feminine undertones.

Also unsurprisingly, Veloso figures in the principal artistic team. Both Veloso and Gil, who served as Minister of Culture in Lula's administration from 2003 to 2008, are significant contributors to contemporary Brazilian politics and the music art-scene. Gilberto Passos Gil Moreira (born 1942), better known as Gilberto Gil, is a Brazilian singer, guitarist and songwriter, known for both his musical innovation and political commitment. His musical style includes an eclectic range of influences, such as rock, punk, samba, African music and reggae. Gil's interest in the blues-based music of rock pioneer Jimi Hendrix has also been described by Veloso as having 'extremely important consequences for Brazilian music' (Veloso, 2003, p. 191). Caetano Emanuel Viana Telles Veloso (born 1942, Salvador) is a Brazilian composer, singer, guitarist, writer and political activist known for his participation in the Brazilian musical movement *Tropicalismo*, which encompassed theatre, poetry and music at the beginning of the Brazilian military dictatorship (McGowan and Pessanha, 1998). Based on creative fusions of the popular with the *avant-garde*, as well as of traditional Brazilian culture with foreign influences, the movement merged Brazilian and African rhythms with rock 'n' roll. The *Tropicalistas*' anarchistic, anti-authoritarian musical and lyrical expressions made them a target of censorship and repression by the military junta that ruled Brazil. Veloso and Gil's participation in anti-government demonstrations made them targets.

The association of *Tropicalistas* with the new wave of American and British (e.g. The Beatles) psychedelic music of the period separated them from the traditional aesthetics and nationalistic tendencies of the Brazilian left, which regarded the *Tropicália* movement as the maiden of Western capitalism (Dunn, 2001). Vargas' oppression of dissent coerced Veloso and Gil (arrested and imprisoned by the military government over the political content of their work in 1969) to seek exile in London, where they continued their musical careers, until their return to Brazil in 1972. Gil's post-1972 political affiliation with the Green Party and his foundation of ONG Onda Azul, a non-governmental organisation fighting for the preservation of water resources, and his belief that music is the Brazilian nation's 'soul' (CNN, 1 September 2003), are in tune with Rio 2016's presentation of an ethically aware urban *Brasilidade*. Equally important is his adaptation of national allegories of mixing to the post-9/11 context. In his inaugural address (2 January 2003) as Minister of Culture, Gil expressed the hope that Brazilian hybridity featured a positive message to the world 'as an example of positives living side-by-side and of tolerance of differences, at a time when fierce discourses and banners of war are being raised across the globe' (Moehn, 2007, p. 180; Moehn, 2008, p. 198, fn.39). Evidently, in Rio's ceremony we deal with the projection of political ecologies on a cultural economic template through music.

The movement comprised the theme of the 2012 documentary film, *Tropicália*, directed by Brazilian filmmaker Marcelo Machado, to which Meirelles served as executive producer (*Tropicália* (2012), IMDB, 5 July 2013). The organisation of the Ceremonies' artistic contingent on the basis of a network-knit group is revealed in the involvement of Andrucha Waddington (born 1970, Rio de Janeiro) in their staging. As director and producer for films featuring female heroines and the theatrical stage (*House of Sand* (2005), *Me You Them* (2000) and *The Outlaw* (2010)) and director of video clips for Veloso (IMDB, undated), his role extends the artistic network's cultural dynamics and political-emotional commitment to Brazilian-Western techno-tropic fusions. It is not coincidental that in interviews almost a year before the Olympics he stated that the ceremony would reflect all of Brazil's roots 'from its indigenous slaves to the 5 million African slaves who arrived in chains' (The Associated Press, 22 September 2015): creative fusions of *Tropicália* with a feminine post-colonial aesthetic also permeated Brazil 2014's Ceremonies, suggesting a convergence of social (gendered and racial) and artistic hierarchies (non-European and non-Western vs. European and Western) (Tzanelli, 2015c). The comment echoes Meirelles' suggestion that Brazil's lack of 'high culture' is complemented by 'roots' or 'authenticity' – pivotal themes in the production of Rio's global tourist imaginaries.

Veloso's musical involvement in the development of *Tropicalismo* is better observed in his contribution to Carlos Degues' *Orfeu* (1999) as a take on Vinicius Morales' attempt to turn *favela* characters into Greek mythological figures in the play *Orfeu da Conceição* (1959). With a tourist view on *favela* life and the rise of black masculine pride, the film includes rap music that interrupts a *samba enredo* composed by Veloso for the fictitious school *Unidos da Carioca*. More is provided below on the subversive organisation of *favela's Carioca Brasilidade*, as well as its fall under the allure of a feminised post-modernity. At this point I want to stress that Veloso and Gil's appearance in the Ceremony also functions as an intertextual reference to a realist injection of *Orfeu's* plot with popular and old musical traditions (Nagib, 2007, pp. 94–95). The film's play on white European vs. Black Afro-Brazilian myths already suggests a problematisation of social-as-racial inequalities, which is silently transferred onto the Olympic ceremonial template.

The lyrical references of *Orfeu's* song to the Yoruba African traditions of Bahia, and Veloso's presentation of rap as an evolution of Brazilian samba (ibid.), also provide a link to the appearance of Anitta in the Ceremony. Born as Larissa de Macedo Machado (1993), Anitta is a Brazilian recording artist, songwriter and dancer. As an artist who promotes audio-visual fusions between Western and Brazilian genres and forms, Anitta appears as Rio's 'natural' evolution to a post-modern city. Anitta's Olympic-appropriate 2013 single '*Show das Poderosas*' (Show of the Powerful), with over 120 million views on YouTube, and her Warner Music Brasil latest 'Bang', have consolidated her as one of the new artistic generation's celebrities (Cantor-Navas, 25 July 2016). Because of their conspicuous political biography, the musical Olympic trio's propensity to cultural hybridisation also extends to a structural one, in which Brazil's urban morphogenesis negotiates home-grown tensions between social utopia and real inequality, post-modernity and tradition, national singularity and cultural polyphony (Archer, 1995, p. 179; Nederveen Pieterse, 2004, 2006a, 2006b).

The *choreomobile* network is incomplete without Deborah Colker (born 1960, Rio de Janeiro), a Brazilian writer, theatre director, dancer and choreographer. Managing more than 6,000 volunteers and more than 100 professional dancers for the Opening Ceremony, she insists that one has to demonstrate what one wants with body movement. Her experimental staging of shows questions the relationship between movement and space, with particular reference to the impact of gravity. The didactic content of the Opening event, which was supposed to also debate Brazil's colonisation, is at pace with her interest in embodied volunteer artwork. 'Sometimes volunteers respond better. They don't have bad habits, stereotypes, clichés. They bring naturalness, spontaneity and the desire to be involved in an artistic experience' (Rio 2016 News, 16 June 2016), she says. In charge of a FlashMob in 2015 to mark the 500 days from the Paralympic Games, Colker concludes that 'discipline is freedom. The more … you have, the more you will be able to achieve what you want' (ibid.). Deleuze and Guattari (1988) consider how physical entities as 'beings' moving at different speeds eventually come into contact. The contact, they argue, generates new compositions or assemblages of bodies that exceed the function of biology. Existing in such points of contact – what Lyotard (1984) calls 'nodal points' – produces specific circuits of communication. Colker's inception of bodies as being, gravitating towards one another to produce naturalistic assemblages, so as to tell a story of postcolonial ethno-genesis, showcases them as mediators between subject and the world (Merleau-Ponty, 1962).

Ethno-cultural traces of dance-movements, such as those we find in samba and its more recent transformations, produce an ethereal moving picture of Rio's life-worlds (Adey, 2010, p. 139). Not only does Colker's take on amateur naturalness connect to her conception of disciplining mobs/groups in creative ways to produce Rio's world, it also elevates the body to a site of artistic technology. As the right to free assembly, FlashMobs of the kind Colker 'orchestrated' with disciplined movement (dance), are momentary communities claiming space. But the fact that the assembly and the occasion, which framed the forthcoming Olympics as an 'event', figured in Rio 2016's official website, suggests that we deal with a 'SmartMob': a technologically and virtually organised (by administration) occasion of connectivity, with the help of Rio 2016's locative media (Salmond, 2010). The 'flat hierarchical' rationality of the ephemeral event, which is framed in a style appealing to Rio's left-wing traditions, is in fact co-opted by the official host as a world-making initiative. Colker's artwork is in agreement with her colleagues' anar-chist cosmopolitan style but also amenable to the city of Rio's advertising objectives as a mega-event host.

Cowan (1990) elaborated on dance in terms of a 'public event' in the tra-dition of Bourdieu's (1984) sociology of *hexis* and *praxis*: in 'warm' societies such as that of the Greeks (and Rio's Brazilians), people are culturally trained to dance in public for the creation of a positive self-image. But how can audiences, unfamiliar with native norms, attribute meaning to dance – and how do native performers maintain a feeling of achievement and global con-nectivity? For signification to happen in contemporary globalised contexts, we may consider the intervention of the Internet's mechano-sphere: people are not moving online, but mobilities do happen online and on satellite TV, enabling whole communities to insert themselves into global markets. The mechano-sphere is primarily iconic, but it is also enabling global translat-ability of local idiosyncrasies exceeding iconic dissemination. A globally dif-fused cerebral work (the making of the Rio 2016 website by international experts) incorporates embodied and territorialised intelligences and cap-abilities (Rio's samba and *capoeira* performers and performances) as tastes and know-hows, with which one can eradicate other convictions and passions (Lazzarato, 2004, p. 204). Both virtual and ceremonial worldmakings have this aim, so as to replace the angry and catastrophic passions of the masses with the gentle and civilising properties proffered by imagineers (Wenning, 2009, p. 93; Tzanelli, 2011, pp. 92–94). The raw material of imagineering is the 'rough' customs, habits and emotions of the masses that are transformed into 'cultural capital' by artists (Bourdieu, 1984, 1998) and into 'network capital' (Larsen and Urry, 2008) by the city's policy-makers.

The passage of such potentialities from cultural to network capital often suggests a shift from imagination to engineering, utopian art-making to poli-tical crystallisation (see also Zimmermann and Favel, 2011 on Bourdieu). This is how Rio's ethno-cultural mobilities are woven into a global template, not only in extensive (de-localising, marketing), but also in intensive ways: 'the cognitive, cultural, effective and communicative resources (the life of individuals), as much as territories, genetic heritage (plants, animals and humans), the resources necessary to the survival of the species ... putting life to work' (Lazzarato, 2004, p. 205; Lash and Urry, 1994, Chapter 10). But not all is about instrumental rationalisation: volunteering or participating in FlashMob events grants subjects affective and cultural citizenships that can be both localised, communal, and post-national. Where the politics of surveillance and control exclude, art offers the promise of inclusion and recognition. Worldmaking processes of this sort produce solid linkages between ethics and understandings of hope as the fabric of 'the ethical imagination', bringing questions of subjectivity and people's capacity for 'self-making'. Nor can such a utopia be actualised with conventional protest of the violent type, Rio 2016's artistic worldmakers suggest. Real hope does not always reside within conventional criticism of the power's shortcomings, it can also be found and affirmed outside of this framework of 'critique' (Moore, 2011), in culturally specific 'capacities' to 'aspire' via culture-work (Appadurai, 2013, p. 67; Appadurai, 2004), to alert to collective horizons of expectation (Kosseleck, 1985, p. 273) through ongoing productions of accounts of pasts and futures (Hirsch and Stewart, 2005, p. 236). Let us consider then how utopian worldmaking is engineered in Rio 2016's Ceremonies.

5   The Opening and Closing Ceremonies

Migration, nostalgia and the making of tourism mobilities

The Opening Ceremony

The 'Introduction' began with aerial images of the city of Rio de Janeiro in a music video, with Luiz Melodia singing '*Aquele Abraço*'. The song was written in the samba genre by Gilberto Gil during the military dictatorship, but its soft tunes, accompanied in the video with images of a sunny, buzzing Rio, were meant to induce nostalgia for an urban Olympic Eden. The lyrics contribute to the video's audio-visual travel, with concerted invocations of neighbourhoods, historic landmarks, samba schools and popular culture figures of Rio de Janeiro as a post-modern, soon-to-be global city. The display of local embodied traditions is infused with glimpses of Olympic sports, suggesting that Rio is also a collection of mobile urban formations, not fixed traditions. The touristic feel of the opening scene (waves crashing on Rio's shores) is transduced (Mackenzie, 2003), because it features as an evolving way of 'translating' knowledge claims about the past, the present and future of the city. The song's lyrics refer to Brazil's banal cultures, including the fans of the *Flamengo* football team, the popular television personality *Chacrinha*, the young girls of the *favelas*, the samba school of *Portela*, and the *Carnaval* street parade *Banda de Ipanema*. The song was written during times of political oppression by the soon-to-be self-exiled Gil. Shortly after his exile, Gil explained that this allowed him to capture the joy and happiness he had seen on the streets, which he had not felt for some time, as until his 1969 escape to Europe he was detained by the military regime. 'My intention was really, very simply, to give an embrace to the people of Rio ... It was a song of encountering, not leaving', he said. Personal memories are placed in the Olympic story at the service of a new transductive sequence, in which cinematic Rio figures in contradistinction to a hidden, immovable borderland. The city emerges as a liquid formation looking outwards, to other life-worlds and cultural articulations. The softness of the music, the brightness of the cinematic sequences of everyday life and the nostalgic tone of the lyrics sustain a bright affective atmosphere, pushing Brazil and Rio outwards, to the world (Thrift, 2004a, p. 64), thus cultivating global cultural relationality (Adey, 2008; Bissel, 2010).

A blended musical theme, featuring both samba and technologically enhanced classical instruments, accompanies the countdown to the opening. In line with the transductive cinematic preamble, the Ceremony is set as an exploratory journey of Rio's and Brazil's art-scenes in the world. But this search is also enframed by discourses of degrowth: the Ceremony's artistic performances were reportedly an homage paid to the spirit of *gambiarra*. Defined by the organisers as 'the Brazilian talent for making the most out of nothing' (McGowan, 6 August 2016), *gambiarra* features as Rio's very own impetus to enthusiasm (Hui, 2014), an alternative to conventional notions of 'resilience' under neoliberal globalisation. Evans and Sewell remind us that the media and popular culture, especially in the West, have absorbed the notion that we should have entrepreneurial Selves, 'that we must constantly be ready to retool ourselves in new opportunities, that seeking individual interest is natural, and that vast riches are the just reward for innovators' (Evans and Sewell, 2014, p. 63). Against an 'evotopian' (Hodgson, 1995) model of uncontrolled growth, Rio-Brazil's *gambiarra* looks to the creation of new, possibly brighter futures, with the help of native understandings of resilience.

Dimitrova-Savova (2009, p. 550), who uses the term 'heritage synaesthetics' in her study of UN-led artistic projects in the *favela* to describe 'the moving bodily practices that set the built environment alive and are a counterpart of heritage aesthetics, or the immobile quality usually ascribed to a historic site', provides the key to unlock uses of *gambiarra* in Rio 2016. An essential component of singing and dancing, *kinaesthesia* is constitutive of fusions of image-making with embodied, multisensory expressivity (Tzanelli, 2015c, p. 42). Against social scientific occulocentrism, *kinaesthesia* can also be applied to urban studies (De Certeau, 1988) and tourism theory (Crang and Franklin, 2001; Urry and Larsen, 2011). Making 'the best of what is available' is at least analogous to the globetrotting tourist rationale of adventure and a class- and status-free enactment of urban *flânerie* (Rojek, 1993, 1997) The *gambiarra* effect connects to positive *affects* that bring together centrifugal and centripetal movement in the Olympic city: on the one hand, as a creative enclave, the ceremonial stage engages localities' (including *favela* volunteers') creative potential, amplifying a sense of self-worth and recognition (Richards and Wilson, 2006); on the other, attending ceremonial performances induces in audiences (the Olympic guests) enthusiasm, energy and inner emotional action. Beyond this, as an immutable atmospheric 'thing', *gambiarra* connects local (Rio) to national histories of a pliable, rather than 'fixed' habitus, which can circulate more freely in the world as a unique property.

In the mega-event, a synecdochal connection of Rio to Brazil makes sense, given that not all members of its principal artistic contingent are *Cariocas*. Amongst the Ceremony's subtle references to federal connectivity we may count those on the sculptural properties of Brazilian design and specifically the work of Athos Bulcão. Featuring amongst the collaborators of the construction of Brasília and Oscar Niemeyer's projects, Bulcão's Marxist affiliation is also comparable with Gil's. The two together suggest a rejection of authoritarianism in favour of artistic freedom. But given that the Brazilian National Anthem, sang after the end of the segment, is inspired by the architectural forms of Oscar Niemeyer, they also provide a narrative of modern Brazilian identity. Thus, ceremonial renditions of Rio's development allow for varied ways of artistic expression as individualised, subcultural or national expressivity. Bulcão's European modernist influences complemented the Ceremony's tribute to indigenous geometry, African prints and Portuguese Arabic tin-glazed ceramic tilework (*Azulejos*), a functional (heat-retaining) architectural artform connected to the Ceremony's theme on sustainability. In fact, the ideals of peace and sustainability guided the 'Introduction's' on-stage transformation of the Greenpeace symbol's projection into a tree. We are not far from Calatrava's material discourse of environmentalism, which is now promoted from a national-urban perspective.

The 'Birth of Life' featured as protagonist the Amazon rainforest, followed by the birth of other forests that covered Brazil. This ecological network, which was represented by illuminated green strands orchestrated in dance by natives, was reminiscent of *Avatar's* (2009, dir. James Cameron) part-Brazilian inspired allegory of destruction of indigenous life-worlds and natural habitats by human militarism (Tzanelli, 2013a, 2015b). Much like environmental

Figure 5.1 Amazonian Brazilian Genesis: The Tree of Life
Source: Image by Sander van Ginkel, Flickr/Creative Commons Licensing.

philosophies centring on post-human ethics (Castree, 2005; Lorimer, 2010) and de-colonial transmodern manifestos (Dussel, 1995), the 'green network's' fine strands represented the Brazilian tree of life in its full complexity (Urry, 2005b, p. 3; Fraser *et al.*, 2005). Much like *Avatar's* elegiac narrative of human destruction, the green neural network's rhythms appear in the Ceremony to be disturbed by the arrival of the Portuguese people. We should not dismiss the fact that from the beginning of 'life', the Ceremony illustrated the formation of the indigenous peoples (represented by 72 dancers of the two major associations of the Parintins Festival, a popular annual celebration held in the Brazilian city of Parintins, Amazonas), thus intertwining nature with human nature in a post-human fashion, while *also allowing* Brazilians to claim an indigenous history of habitus genesis (Elias, 1978; Bourdieu, 1984).

This genesis is complicated in the succeeding sequences, where we watch the arrival of Europeans in caravels, the forced mobilities of enslaved Africans and the immigration of Arab and Japanese people. The representation of African labour in chains amidst a sea of dissolving green neurons flags the necessity to produce viable links between the *Social Contract* – the damage of which Dussel (1985) connects to the onset of modernity in colonisation and Mills (1994, 1998) associates with exclusions of black populations from ideas of 'human' (Tzanelli, 2016b) – and the *Natural Contract* (Serres, 1995) – the damage of the environment, which is consolidated by the onset of the Anthropocene. The sequence, which connects thematically to Meirelles'

Figure 5.2 The arrival of Japanese labour migrants in Brazil
Source: Image by Andy Miah, Flickr/Creative Commons Licensing.

documentary for the Museum of Tomorrow, outlines the ensuing fragmentation of the indigenous tree of life, but also its enrichment through successive migrations, paying tribute to the country's African, European and Asian heritages.

'Metropolis', the following segment, subsumes conceptions of indigenous 'life' under a visualised and highly technologised – given the use of on-stage projections of urbanity – discourse. The continuous God's eye view of the Ceremony, from which we, as distant viewers, apprehend Brazilian 'landscape', resembles that of a scientific expert's (Urry and Larsen, 2011, pp. 58–59), who speculates on the gigantic consequences of environmentally destructive urbanisation. Though verbally muted, the music theme allows for emotive speculation, transcending the idea of surveillance by a digital machine in which 'everyone is caught' (Foucault, 1980, p. 156). We watch dancers jumping from building to building – in reality, images projected onto the ceremonial stage – and heading to a back scene, on which we view the rise of a colourful urbanscape. In this urban façade the dancers-acrobats scale buildings under the rhythms of sound of the classic song '*Construção*' by Chico Buarque, which was created during the military dictatorship in Brazil, amid censorship and political prosecution. It was written by Buarque upon his return from Italy, where he had moved to avoid political prosecution. An elegy on the alienation of workers, the song narrates in interchangeable last words (which are *Proparoxitones*, 'as if they were pieces of a board game', according to Buarque) the last day of three building construction workers, who were killed in the course of their daily activities (Cavalcanti, October 2009). The ceremonial workers/acrobats rearrange illuminated cubes in an order outside the cityscape, but then they destroy the order. Then, the camera shifts focus from their task to a reproduction of a 14-bis plane, flown in real life 110 years earlier in the suburbs of Paris. The plane is boarded by an actor playing the Brazilian aeronautical inventor Santos-Dumont (1878–1932), who won the *Deutsch de la Meurthe* prize on 19 October 1901 on a flight that rounded the Eiffel Tower and proceeded to construct the heavier-than-air aircraft 14-bis. Known in Brazil as the 'father of aviation' and honoured in the Deodoro district of Rio, where a Museum of Aviation, Engineering and Brazilian History is based, Santos-Dumont's legacy also populates the mega-event's official website (Tzanelli, 2016c, p. 78). As the plane flew from Maracanã through Rio's main sights on the Stadium's mega-screens, audiences were immersed in Antônio Carlos Jobim's '*Samba do Avião*', a song he wrote for an Italian film, *Copacabana Palace* (1962), which was inspired by his love for airplanes and walks from Santos-Dumont airport (renamed in 1999 RIOgaleão – Aeroporto Internacional Tom Jobim) to Ipanema (Jobim, 2011).

The overall segment speaks about Brazilian modernity's relational birth with European technology that is not borrowed, but given to the alleged civilisational centre of the world by a pioneering Brazilian engineer. Thus, the segment's adoption of the cartographic eye (Weibel, 2011), the modern traveller's vision, is native and foreign at once. Where the construction of such a

Figure 5.3 Representations of urban Rio
Source: Image by Andy Miah, Flickr/Creative Commons Licensing.

'geometrics of space' would compensate for the colonisers' inability to map and gain access to indigenous territories and the native experience (Holton, 2005; Sloterdijk, 2009), Santos-Dumont's flight over the city introduces a different audio-visual *problématique*: that of the colonisation of urban life-worlds (Schutz and Luckmann, 1973, 1989; Habermas, 1989b). The segment's 'spherological poetics' (Sloterdijk, 2014) hint at Rio's submerged centre, turning Dumont's Euro-Brazilian imagineering on its head. The reshuffling of the ceremony's urbanscape also functions as critique of modernisation 'from within'. This is so, because it 'discloses' the practice of Haussmanisation guiding nineteenth-century Parisian cosmetic surgeries in working-class neigh-bourhoods that the bourgeoisie feared and the police could not penetrate (Harvey, 1985, p. 165; Scott, 1998, p. 62; Meade, 1997). Again, therefore, we see a fusion of ethics with the aesthetics of the spectacle to supersede silences about internal complexities guiding the relationship between modernity and coloniality (Herzfeld, 2002; Morana *et al.*, 2008; Dussel, 2013).

As the plane flew over Ipanema, 'Construção' was succeeded by 'The Girl from Ipanema', played by Daniel Jobim, Carlos Jobim's grandson. The legacy of the song also figured in the election by public vote of 'Vinicius' and 'Tom' as names for the Olympic and Paralympic mascots (Rio 2016 News, 14 December 2014). A world-wide 1960s hit, the song is a fusion of jazz with *bossa nova* composed by Antônio Carlos Jobim and Vinícius de Moraes. Originally a work-in-progress under the title '*Menina que Passa*' ('The Girl Who Passes By') for the musical comedy *Dirigível* (Blimp) by de Moraes and

Jobim, the song was inspired by then seventeen-year-old Heloísa Eneida Menezes Paes Pinto, who lived in Ipanema and had to buy cigarettes for her mother to the sound of 'wolf-whistles' (Castro, 2000, pp. 239–240). De Moraes once wrote that she was 'the paradigm of the young *Carioca*', a golden teenage girl mixing flower and mermaid, the feeling of youth that fades, 'a gift of life in its beautiful and melancholic constant ebb and flow' (Duggan, 7 February 2012).

Part of Brazil's macho cultural coding, the whistling, which denotes admiration for beauty, is updated in the Ceremony's casting of professional model Gisele Bündchen as 'The Girl'. In tandem, one must note that the creation of Olympic and Paralympic mascots Vinicius (a representation of different Brazilian animals with enhanced senses) and Tom (a fusion of plants found in Brazilian forests, apparently displaying *gambiarra* skills) (Rio 2016 News, 14 December 2014), obey two different principles: of ecological (acceptable to the IOC and global visitors) and animal-like, masculine *Carioca* consciousness (intelligible to natives). The unprocessed aspect of *Carioca hexis* (Bourdieu 1984) is thus in the Ceremony masculinised, as opposed to the city's feminine cosmopolitan *habitus*, which is befit for public display and admiration. We should not dismiss de Moraes' fixation on the 'golden' *Carioca* femininity of Heloísa, because it obeys the principles of Freyre's (1963) Brazilian *branqueamento*. The city of Rio has always been a charming landscape befit for *flâneurs* and tourists, as much as it has been marked by inequalities and harsh living conditions. The two realities constantly propel 'contradictory movements' in everyday life, casting urban walking as a 'coloured' class activity (de Certeau, 1988; Acerbi, 2014). Significantly, as the 'golden blonde' Bündchen completes her performance on stage, she smiles at the group of mostly black *funk* and *parkour* performers of the city-stage, extending her hands to them: only an 'educated' (Europeanised) and white desire can provide recognition to Rio's disenfranchised *favela* populations. Bündchen's communication with the city's other half plays on Lefebvre's (1979) notion of 'the right to the city', juxtaposing the *citadin* (urban inhabitant) to the *citoyenne* (real citizen), and highlighting the complexities involved in experiential space production (Acerbi, 2014, p. 100). Rio's cosmetic cosmopolitanism projects a eurhythmic atmosphere, fully harmonised with the requirements of economic and cultural globalisation (Lefebvre, 1992 [2015], p. 24; Nederveen Pieterse, 2006b).

The Bündchen/Heloise, who walked through Maracanã Stadium, following the curves that characterised Niemeyer's landmarks, such as the Pampulha Church and the Cathedral of Brasília, is a Brazilian, rather than mere *Carioca* figure, inscribed onto the country's urban palimpsests before and after 'The Girl from Ipanema'. So it is worth tracing earlier historical points at which the feminine education of desire appears in Brazil and how it is associated with practices of image-making and the body: the First Republican Era (1889–1930) would see the rise of 'a people's cinema' that the anarchist press regarded less as experimental art and more as a marriage between the camera's objectivity in narrative modes fostering a nationalist *posados de propaganda* (films with advertisements). As a commercial product, the First World War cinema allowed first-generation migrants to Brazil to achieve social mobility and assert their national affiliation (Conde, 2012, p. 116). With the intention of 'educating' spectators, such cinematic products discarded the previous socialist-unionist spirit of artistic activism and focused on ideas of inclusion in a rapidly transforming *Zona Sul*. This was Rio's commercial centre, now equipped with infrastructural facilities, tram lines, electricity, gas and sewage works, absent in the more populous *Zona Norte*. Simultaneously, Rio's transformation into a new European-style capital suggested the destruction of the *cortiços*, downtown dwellings largely populated by the new immigrant working classes. As socio-spatial restructuring was geared towards 'alien' population management (Foucault, 2007), new cultural fissures within the totality of immigrant community made an unpleasant appearance: whereas European immigrants (Portuguese, Spaniards and especially Italians) would soon be integrated into the phantasmagoric business industries of Rio (as film directors and actors), eventually overcoming xenophobic marginalisation and exclusion by the native upper classes, downtown former slaves, usually of black or *mulatto* descent, would remain consigned to the 'lower social orders'. The assistance that was provided to the nationalist and modernist national project formed a spectacular complexity of mobility characters, whereby European immigrants of first and subsequent generations stood as 'good' and productive subjects, whereas non-European immigrants from internal peripheries and the world's 'dark continent', former African slaves, became 'evil' and unproductive 'outlaws'.

Cinema's foreign ontological status contributed to the production of Rio's modernity in association with a native elite *en route* to transformation (Shohat and Stam, 1994, 2003). Where, initially, anarchist films of the Kropotkin mythopolitical range preached for the development of revolutionary consciousness even among the city's French-bred literati, journalists and intellectuals, new filmmaking trends, countering female seclusion in the private sphere, paved the way for the projection of feminine versions of urban *flânerie* and participation in the city's commons. Dark narrations of Rio's life through the tribulations of prostitutes or streetwalkers were replaced with the archetype of the New Woman, or *Melindrosa*. Placed in cityscapes – much like the Bündchen/Heloise's 'beautiful' walk in Niemayer's material curves – the *Melindrosa* symbolised contemporary landscape, 'fostering an imagery of constant body movement and urban mobility through multiple cultural sites' (Unruh, 2006, p. 15). Such representations of a feminised Rio reactivated a political ambivalence towards cultural materialism, now symbolised through feminine consumption and an air of freedom inducing anxiety about the future of the ideal middle-class 'Brazilian family'. European cinema invested in similar anxieties concerning the demise of family structures in the image of the *femme fatale*, an equally materialistic and rational calculator set to destroy men's social and economic credibility and honour in Euro-American cinematic imaginaries (Rich, 1995, p. 8; Maxfield, 1996; Wager, 1999). The progressive development of cinematographers' ease with the cinematic medium further fostered parallels between a feminised urban 'aesthetics of attraction', casting Brazilian modernity as ornamental copyism of foreign designs (Süssekind, 1997, p. 100).

Where spectacular technology gained ground in the city's make-up, art and social criticism began to question Rio's displacing engagement with Brazilian modernity. The city's 'out-of-placeness' in the federal national project interrogated the alignment of its modern landscape with Europe, thus 'marking a stark departure from the more dominant association of Brazilian modernity with the city of São Paulo' (Conde, 2012, p. 135). Paralleling, or even emulating European modernism's association with the feminine body as a mass cultural metaphor (Huyssen, 1987, p. 49; Kracauer, 1995), Rio's modernism invested in its *Melindrosa* to secure connection to humanity's great civilisational and cultural centres. Women in Rio began to conform to their allotted role as ornaments and projections of their families' status, acquiring more refinement in lifestyle shopping and greater worldliness to communicate the city's *febre mundanismo* (Conde, 2012, p. 136). The clear link between film and commerce in the years of the Republic also inserted the feminine figure in the new *posados de propaganda*, making the cinema screen a virtual extension of the *Cariocas'* desire for foreign lifestyles, products and living standards. The installation of this 'soft' imperial imaginary (Shohat and Stam, 1994, pp. 102–103) in Rio's phantasmagoric city produced its own Nemesis in the writings of its politically committed *cronistas* (journalists) and intellectuals, who saw in such developments the prostitution of *Carioca* culture and family values, and the destructive impact of exchange laws on the most intimate parts of life: 'home' (Simmel, 1971). A few decades fast-forward, late twentieth century's post-dictatorship landscape had changed borrowed form but not the form's content in Rio. The cultural coordinates had pluralised, with the need to look both eastwards, to the spectacular but civilized European core, for inspiration, and northwards, to Hollywood apparatus's soft power (Friedberg, 1993) and the strong arm of American militarism. Vargas' outreach policies of tourismification utilised the pliable feminine body image in marketisations of indigenous forms, such as samba, but rejected the idea of female emancipation at home.

It would be incorrect to argue that this militourist-like imaginary of consumption disappeared with Vargas: new states of emergency in consumption zones, such as those of the *favelas*, necessitated its renewal in policy centres of the post-dictatorship era (see Chapter 1). Lifestyle shopping of the Republican era is now creatively adapted, so as to allow Rio's *abertura* to accommodate the new popular trends of cosmetic surgery, holiday-making and recreational drug use (Sneed, 2008; Bell *et al.*, 2011; Botterill *et al.*, 2014). The tanned body – what is recognised as *morenidade* – is more socially valued than the white or black body (Pravaz, 2009, p. 91) because it conforms to a particular *Carioca* aesthetic, in which beauty is virtue and 'good shape' stands for a plausible feminine surface (ibid., p. 91). The power of the beautiful feminine body and the ideal of the emancipated *flâneuse* is such that Brazil's plastic surgery (*plástica*) has developed into a 'right' that has to be made accessible to the poor (*povão*). The 'democratisation' of *plástica* occurred during a period of rising economic inequality (1980s–1990s), when the term 'brazilianisation' became a synonym for savage capitalism. As Edmonds (2007) notes, 'fatal attractiveness' evolved in Brazilian recession contexts into a form of cultural capital, open to all, but also a mechanism of rejecting old patriarchal and authoritarian values.

The professionally accomplished Bündchen/Heloise is thus Brazil's new sculptural body: much like the late-1990s Brazilian cinematic allegorisations of femininity, she consolidates the fall of masculinity and the rise of female fecundity in cultural globalisation (Nagib, 2007, pp. 52–57); and much like post-modern Rio's atmospheric attunement to the world, she communicates a passion for creativity and connectivity (Hui, 2014). With arms open to the poor masses that now can achieve self-beautification, the ceremonial *Melindrosa* speaks the language of tourism: beaches connect to new technologies of the healthy, harmonious and beautiful body tourists can display in public and cosmetic industries market in new beautyscapes across the world as an attainable commodity (Holliday *et al.*, 2015), but the ceremonial *Carioca* can be a whitened class-bound and simultaneously classless native, as well as a cosmopolitan tourist. The fact that Bündchen can coexist on stage with embodied representations of the black and *moreno* (of African descent) body of *funkeiros* produces a metaphorical conception of social order for the nation as a tropical *mestiço* utopia (Pravaz, 2009, p. 84). The *moreno* body of the ceremonial cityscape displays a talent for intimacy and plasticity, especially in its feminised form (Freyre, 1974), in which it can incorporate and display samba and carnival performances (Pravaz, 2000, 2003). But the golden brown (almost *mulatto*, tanned black and hence Euro-Brazilian) body of spectacular Bündchen (known as *ficar pretto* or 'becoming tanned' as cultural capital), manufactured during the long *Carioca* months for the beach and the *Carnaval*, conforms to *corpolatria* (body worship) as ritual of auto-transformation (Pravaz, 2008). The overall segment debates true societal and cultural changes in Rio and Brazil, allegorising the host city's ability to change in increasingly globalised contexts – a true worldmaking statement. Hence, in the Ceremony, walking towards Gil and the 'tamed', colourful cityscape of pacification, Bündchen speaks the language of (bodily self)control and pronounced neoliberal market freedom.

Even if the body is a work in process we can never truly claim as exclusively our own (Butler, 2007), its performance attributes themselves (the way we literally move in the social world) can be turned into our own futural project. Without much heavy cinematic technology at their disposal, the ceremonial directors use the city's noetic and material bodies to muse over the new order of things, both liberating and restrictive for Rio's citizenry. Coupling the popular culture of the slum with the spectacular 'feminine' ethos of the city's globally networked cosmetic markets matches their sober statement that they would not use 'much technology' or blow the budget in such a difficult economic conjuncture for Brazil. This frugal *giambarra* ethos aligns with the ambivalence expressed by 1920s literati and *cronistas* towards the city's harmonisation with European capitalist structures. But if the Paris of the modernist consciousness was back then, or even now, that of order and beauty (Harvey, 2006), the Olympic Ceremony's refractions of post-modern Rio/ Paris are more prone to the chaotic complexities we associate with racialised subcultural style. The symbolic spatial separation of the dancers from the rest of the ceremonial stage/'urban space' signals inequality, casting the post-colonial city as a floating signifier in the capitalist era: a sort of 'third space' (Soja, 2008) or 'field domain' (Young, 2008), in which different forms of capital (embodied, virtual/digital, artistic and social) flow towards different channels, here bestowing glamour upon their holders and inserting the city into global governance circuits, there detracting from its 'prestige' (Larsen and Urry, 2008).

The following segment, 'Voices from the *Favela*', imagineers Rio's 'submerged centre' in a spectacular narrative of *samba* and *baile funk*. These music and dance styles, one with a long history and several stylistic transformations, the other very recent and hybrid, split the *favelas* as cultural 'sites' into two temporal axes in the ceremonial segment, legible to global visitors with little or elementary knowledge of local culture. The segment's narrative sits at a crucial crossroads for Rio and Brazil as a whole, between industrialisation and post-industrial mutations of capitalism that have accelerated ecological decline. As such, it reveals the *favela* as an urban site affecting conceptions of social-as-environmental decline, while cleverly *submerging* the origins of global capitalism: (Western) Europe. Both slums and slumming as a travel rite and a tourist niche on the one hand (Linke, 2012; Steinbrink *et al.*, 2012), and as the instigator of welfare concerns about the role of shantytown dwellers as social pollutants on the other (Stedman-Jones, 1971; Seaton, 2012; Vandana and Loftus, 2013; Tzanelli, 2015a), originate in European modernity. But it is also in European political thought and action, where we locate Romanticism as a nationalist trend, an artistic impetus and the origins of ecological consciousness (Urry, 1995). Today informing global calls to cosmopolitan solidarity (Beck, 2002a, 2007), a brand new Romantic ethic of care for the environment also incorporates the care for non-human, natural vulnerability. Thus, the segment opposes home-grown understandings of environmental racism, fostering human belonging in an ecological sphere in which humans are decentred – a statement not far from that which we encountered in Chapter 3 on the Museum of Tomorrow.

The segment included Brazilian samba recording artist Elza Soares, known for her first hit '*Mas que Nada*' (1963) and her election by BBC London as the singer of the millennium. Soares played '*O Canto de Ossanha*', a classic love song created by Baden Powell and Vinícius de Moraes that refers to the Orisha deity *Ossanha* worshipped in African and Afro-Brazilian religions such as *Candomblé* and *Umbanda*. The introduction of the song in the cere-mony celebrates Brazilian African roots and art: the Orisha deities of the Yoruba spiritual pantheon are part of a philosophy of *ashe* or life force, which is conveyed by all artforms, including the performative and the visual. *Ashe* is part of *iwa*, the nature of creativity perceptible only to those who have walked with the ancestors and can now claim tangible contact with them (Abiodun, 2001, p. 17). The song speaks of love mediated by an otherworldly being that does not sanction a reality based on spectacular display but on a multisensory and poly-aesthetic experience of the world based on blends of visual, verbal and musical performance 'associated with the ability *to amaze* and ... be unique and inimitable but in a traditional framework' (Tzanelli, 2016b, p. 103). Thus, 'love' and art are placed in the song in a phenomenological/metaphysical field, in which perception informs action (Lawal, 2001; Merleau-Ponty, 1962). Despite its African aesthetics, the song allows a visual *Carioca* landscape to be transferred to the cinematic medium with the help of home-grown stereotypes, such as those of the 'black rebel', the 'sexy *mulatta*' and the '*malandro*' or street hustler (Stam, 1997, pp. 333–336) – all those human characters set to distort human perception (on performativity and the black body see Tate, 2015).

There is a productive contradiction in the dancing sequences, which appears in every public performance of dance, but is exaggerated in cere-monial performance: the quest for an art of the body in action that exceeds the classic division of arts into plastic ('meant to produce images of bodies') and theatrical art ('placing the body at the service of a text to be interpreted' (Ranciére, 2013, p. 104)). Rio's samba dancers organised into schools have always worked at the interstices of this contradiction, as Vargas' regulation of social activities in *favela* artworlds and its touristified spaces imposed the display of a rigid grammar of bodily movements across space by *sambistas* that would soon become part of their ceremonial habitus (Shaw, 1999, p. 50; Davis, 2009, p. 13; Tzanelli, 2013a, pp. 112–113). The response of samba activists has been to render their bodies almost 'unlocatable' by turning them into an instrument fit to draw forms in space through movement. Hannam, Mostafanezdah and Rickly remind us that mobile materialities of heritage invite a consideration of geographical complexity of humans and non-humans 'that contingently enable people and things to move and to hold their shape as they transit across various regions, both physically and imaginatively' (2016, p. 9). The disciplinary forms of procession in *sambadromes* concealed the expression of the body's primordial rhythm from foreign onlookers, but amplified the release of inner energy, thanks to the development of stylistic contents, better compre-hended within and by other *sambistas*. Vargas' fixation upon the projection of *mestiçagem* as a positive Brazilian trait to respond to Europe-imported racism (Skidmore, 1993) would be responded to after the end of his regime with the rise of Brazilian filmmaking, in which black ethnic practices such as those of samba or *capoeira* would be elevated into ideal national types (Stam, 1997, pp. 333–336).

With the progressive global commoditisation of samba styles, this radical habitus moved, literally and figuratively, to new class and social sites. One of the most innovative aspects of the Olympic ceremonial team's worldmaking involved the proliferation of these 'geographies' of dance: this was achieved by placing the organised *sambistas'* dancing in the same performative centre as the *funkeiros'* art of movement, who nevertheless appeared to be better integrated into the stage's contemporary urbanscape. The Olympic ceremony accommodated music pieces, such as '*Rap da Felicidade*' sung by *funk* artist Ludmilla (born 1995, Rio de Janeiro, known as the MC Beyoncé). The eclipse of *sambistas* and the emergence of *funkeiros* parallel Dussel's (1995) speculations on the eclipse of the South American Other and the rise of Western modernist structures in the South Americas, only if we disregard the mobilisation of popular cultural artforms such as *funk* by the new urban/*favela* indigenes. Unhooking the *sambistas* from this symbolic urbanscape suggests their transformation into globally mobile objects, still barely comprehensible in their fluid unity by outsiders.

The rootedness of the *funkeiros'* performance is, nevertheless, also globally connected, thanks to their bodily fusions with the *parkour* movement. It is presented as a bundle of spatialised movements, forms that the painter's brush left on the canvas in two dimensions and the sculptor's knife fixed in immobile volumes (Ranciére, 2013, pp. 105–106, p. 157). After Ludmilla, rapper Marcelo D2 and singer Zeca Pagodinho simulated a duel of rhythms, with the latter performing '*Deixa a Vida Me Levar*'; then rappers Karol Conká and MC Sofia followed. The songs framed cultural performances that simulated conflicts as *maracatu*, a variety of genres originating in Afro-Brazilian traditions from the state of Pernambuco and incorporated into *Carnaval* styles (Crook, 2005; Conner, 2009), and *bumba-meu-boi*, a North and Northeastern Brazilian folk theatrical tradition that features in festivals and the *Carnaval*. Both genres connect to urban tourist cultures celebrating Brazilian *buen vivir* and joy in an adventurous fashion, so their ceremonial connection to *parkour* makes sense. This 'free-running' urban practice, which involves jumping, climbing and running over high urban structures in the urban landscape, invites participants to move playfully with and within places so as to experience excitement, fear or even release anger (Sheller, 2004; Saville, 2008; Merriman, 2015). In this segment, *favela* voices attain an image and an experiential dimension that connects them to Rio's brand as an exotic place, with a buoyant international visitor economy.

Contemporary *favelas* are spaces of disarray that ceremonial performance can only encapsulate in fragments. The most essential fragment is musical and embodied and comes under the name of *baile funk*. *Baile funk's* musical and bodily rhythms forge alternate utopias out of the everyday experience of violence and exclusion in the *favela* more explicitly than the samba genres, which have undergone a thorough civilised revamp in middle-class urban districts. Sneed's (2007, 2008) fieldwork in Rocinha proffers valuable glimpses into the city's contemporary rhythmopoetic changes with regards to the socio-political potential of alternative music scenes. Through his focus on *bailes funk*, he suggests that what new practices of extreme policing see in the *favelas'* new poetic trend as 'dangerous', has given life to creative articulations of belonging and being human in fusions of dangerousness, unbounded sexuality and mass culture. Sneed argues that, at the core of *funk* culture, there is a utopian impulse and the desire of *favelados* to be lifted out of scarcity, vulnerability and exclusion – to 'be transported to a place of abundance, power, and excitement through the experience of music' (Sneed, 2008, p. 60). The homological impetus between middle-class samba and working-class/ underclass *baile funk* produces a different type of imagineering, in which the uses of bodily technics (dance know-how) and musical technology (uses of digital and electronic instruments) would deny articulations of social imaginaries 'out of place' and critiques of non (*où* as in *u*-topia) places (*tópos* as in u-*topia*). Non-places are lodged in licit and formally sanctioned capitalist accumulation, zones of consumption produced by capitalist modes of social belonging. *Baile funk's* utopianism shares with the formalised non-places of samba consumption, because it does not belong to territorially situated governments: non-places do not contain organic forms of society, such as those associated with *favela* cultures (Augé, 2008, pp. 90–91). Testimony to this distinction is provided by the significance of *bailes de cominidade* (community dances) in the *favela*, which tend to be paid for and attended by heavily armed drug traffickers, but are also duly attended by locals and other *favelados* visitors (Sneed, 2008, p. 63).

Sneed's *favela* utopia, with its own makeshift imagineerings, recalls Paul Gilroy's (1993) elaborations on the ways African diasporic practices become musically articulated as moral, spiritual and political statements upon relocation in new territories, where host societies display varied degrees of hostility and racism towards newcomers. Gilroy, much like Fanon ([1958] 1970), emphasises the 'double consciousness' such hostility induces in diasporic subjects struggling for survival during their journeys. But he is uncompromisingly critical of the cultures of travel such subjects join in host societies as workers and prosumers. The clash between the Enlightenment principles of equality and liberty, on which the host society allegedly operates, and the collective experience of slavery, seem to overshadow all aspects of diasporic cultural life, which, according to Gilroy, finds expression in non-rationalist (non-Western) self-realisation in collective musical experiences. This argument, which has dominated the Anglo-Saxon cultural and political studies scene to date, is convincing up to a point. The association of utopian thinking with irrationality in emotionally charged action counters the organised nature of relevant protest in both Western and non-Western sites of resistance, including those of Rio's *favelas*. It also does not fully account for the rationality of emotion, and essentialises musical artwork. The inevitable suggestion is that, as is the case with other stereotyped artistic activities, which are seen as trivial feminine pursuits (Molotch, 2004), diasporic music aesthetics are considered irrational expressions of hurt befit for black people, especially men, and standing apart from Western technological rationalisation (on associations of technological labour with hegemonic masculinity see Connell, 1987, 1995).

Uncritical implementation of Gilroy's analysis would (dis)miss the historical remoteness of slavery in Rio's *favelas*, as well as their creative use in localised art-spaces; it also denies contemporary *favelados'* liberating ability to adapt new consumption styles and consumerist prerogatives of the middle- and upper-class range in their everyday life. Sneed (2007, 2008) notes, despite his use of Gilroy, that the economic constrictions in which *baile funk* consumers operate do not prevent them from adopting cultural codes from mainstream popular culture (including clothing and performing), or from welcoming (white) non-*favelados* into their parties. Most *bailes* play blocks of other styles of urban music, such as hip-hop, *pagode* or hard rock, and whatever class and racial connotations these styles might have is ignored (Sneed, 2008, p. 76). What is discussed as a form of 'resistance' to mainstream cultures of privilege and surveillance could, therefore, also be read as creative adaptation, a sort of aesthetic reflexivity 'from below' (Lash and Urry, 1994, pp. 49–50), asserting *favelados'* participation in glocalising processes of embodied and auratic *Brasilidade* (Brazilian-ness).

Such incipient globalisations and hybridisations also have other consequences. The differences between *baile funk* and 1960s and 1970s American or British *funk* cultures Sneed (2008) identifies, are based on music form and its so-called 'anthropophagic' styles (on *anthropofagia* see Chapter 1). The new *favelado* genre includes blends of electrofunk or Miami beats, a husky vocal delivery, frenetic samplings and sexualised dancing in the tradition of American hip-hop (Béhague, 2000; Lurie, 2001), with Brazilian instrumental interpretations of digitally enhanced lyrics and syncopated dance routines. But instead of considering this Brazilian 'mixing of melodic structures of national musical styles such as *axé*, capoeira, *forró*, and samba with features of international music, like R&B, techno, Miami bass, and hip-hop' (Sneed, 2008, pp. 60–61) as a copyist habit in legal terms (copyright theft), we should view it as a transcultural dialogue. Significantly, there is symmetry between *baile funkers'* denial of access to mainstream culture by regional and national cultures of surveillance and control (most *baile funk* songs do not enjoy widespread circulation, as is the case with their mainstream 'original' replicas) and mainstream, widely commercialised *baile funk* lyrics (routinely offensive, rejecting the social geography of Rio and the values assigned to rich neighbourhoods, hypersexualised and specific to slum experiences of dangerousness and suffering). There is also harmony between native Rio *funk* and foreign gangster and lowlife/subcultural music genres, both in terms of lyrics, performance and instrumental orchestration. Much like the pervasive outward-looking neoliberal turn of the city's institutional imagineerings, and much like the anthropophagic propensity displayed in other global-urban cultural industrial contexts (see Tzanelli, 2015a, Chapter 5 on Indian music genres), Rio's intimate *funkeiro* scenes develop thanks to their centrifugal cultural tendencies. Such non-institutionalised imagineering shares in form with the hypermobile ethos of cultural industrial production, in that it is prone to image-making, bodily adornment and performance – all of which lead to a proliferation of allegory (Tzanelli, 2013a, Chapter 2, 2008a). Here we may recall Benjamin's use of the term as a reference to 'the way a stable hierarchically ordered meaning is dissolved [so that] the allegory … points to kaleidoscopic fragments which resist any coherent notion of what it stands for' (Featherstone, 1991, p. 23). This replacement quality of meaning with signs (Lash and Urry, 1994) allows for the deep aestheticisation of everyday life in the big cities.

Finally, we cannot achieve a balanced account of Rio's ceremonial and everyday rhythmographies without an analysis of its *morro* cultures of creative violence, because the latter provide us with a crucial formative link between ethno-social morphogenesis (Archer 2010) and the new cosmetic cosmopolitan cultures of mobility (Nederveen Pieterse, 2006b; Sheller, 2014b). Although Sneed (2008, p. 71) considers *baile funk* as a sequestered culture, the prevalence of crime in *favelas* make his study applicable to Rio's social and cultural landscape at large. The socio-genesis of the city's *favelas* from slave enclaves and successive labour immigrations, acts as the anthropological equivalent of folk ethno-genesis. The illicit cultures of the mountains have provided different national imaginations with their own ambivalent 'wild' heroes, who informed centralised artistic narratives of belonging (Leoussi, 2004; Tzanelli, 2008b). Brazil's incomplete ethno-national integration and hurried globalisation necessitates a modified approach to this phenomenon of romanticising violence and streamlining into art-scenes – if anything, its strong cultural dimensions suggest that we transcend, but not dismiss the tradition of nationalism (Hannerz, 1990; Smith, 1990, 1995). In Rio's case, federalised administration and political localism are at odds with the *Cariocas'* strong attachment to the integrative project of *Brasilidade* – so much so, that as a *Citade Maravilhosa*, Rio displays the features of an autonomous formation in an island of urban singularities. The fact that samba and some of its musical variations are irrevocably connected to these violent topographic imaginaries, which are now intensely commoditised in tourist and mega-event contexts (Salazar, 2009, 2012, 2016; Salazar and Graburn, 2016), turns *Carioca favelarte* into a peculiar ethno-urban conduit of global communication, amenable to neoliberal profitable competition (Evans and Sewell, 2014).

Thus, the production of songs about *favela* gangsters known as *proibidâo* is the equivalent of the prohibitive mythistories we find in the folk cultures of European nations, which were subsequently 'disciplined' and beautified by the state and its organised academic and welfare institutions (Tzanelli, 2008b). The local ambivalence displayed towards *favela* gangsters, who are often construed as Robin Hood protectors of the poor in the face of the violence they spread, complies with the spirit of ethno-nationalist machismo and its global commoditisation in other music art-scenes. Notably, the spontaneous and honest communication of sexuality in *funk* performances and lyrics, which matches the new exhibitionist cultures of samba, has been dubbed *putaria*, 'in reference to activities associated with prostitutes, pejoratively referred to in Portuguese as *putas*' (Sneed, 2008, p. 74). Present in the ceremonial segment's female dance performances, twerking, or so-called '*tchan*', conforms to an intimate *Carioca* aesthetics of the ideal female body shape with small breasts and large buttocks – the body shape of women of African descent (Pravaz, 2009, p. 92). One may hypothesise here that the real social (class, racial) inequalities *funkeiro favelados* face in everyday life are presented, concealed and translated at once by and into gendered inequalities, conforming to the country's glamourised public cultures of mobility. Though in reality racial essentialisations play a pivotal role in Rio's cultural mobilities, their 'trafficking' across the nation and abroad are considered within localities with great ambivalence, as mechanisms of liberation from the state's gaze and subjection to a global gaze. The phenomenological mark of the 'stranger' in the city that traverses its domains and destabilises fixities of tradition (Bauman, 1991, p. 56), turns in *baile funk* into a being 'without a home', always 'multiplying masks and "false selves" … never completely true or completely false' (Kristeva, 1991, p. 8) – but always present in narratives of belonging.

The non-representational 'disclosure' of Rio's submerged centre in the Opening Ceremony suggests that formalised imagineerings, which are based on the principles of a more projective, 'second order' version of social reality, support informal *favela* imagineerings, which thrive on the principle of hope. The aim of such imagineerings is to re-make society on the principles of equality, thus bringing worldmaking home: to turn tourism (Hollinshead *et al.*, 2009) also into inner travel to one's own cultural centre. The utopian promise of a racial democracy, in which all races acquire a presence, shares much with the dream of discovering and inhabiting the ideal land of tourism, where all mobilities are recognised as equal (Henning, 2002; Ateljevic, 2008; Ateljevic *et al.*, 2013). This critical consideration of utopia in everyday performances of belonging gives back power to the powerless in paradoxical ways: it activates 'an intensely Brazilian space of hyper-*Brasilidade*, in all its racial openness, sensual playfulness, gregariousness, and merriment' (Sneed, 2008, pp. 77), ultimately producing more amenable conditions for the maintenance of local host–guest relations through the display of signs of beauty, love and culture; but it may not resolve social problems, to which now one can add the rise of a populist imaginary of traditionalist aesthetics, uncontrolled machismo and crime. Artistic utopias are always interpretative media, works in progress at the hands of deliberative democratic groups, from which we can exclude neither the *favelados* nor urban and national policy-makers.

Artistic technique allegorises social critique (Boltanski and Chiapello, 2004) as *krísis* (κρίσις) or aesthetic judgement, which conceals reflexive elaboration on contemporary crises destabilising human-nature ecosystemic complexes. This *krísis* is achieved by spectacular means with particular stylistic optics and colouration, present in Meirelles' *The Constant Gardener*'s (2005) lucid memory scenes and in the *City of God*'s gradual photological decline of the *favela*. Nagib (2007) and Diken and Laustsen (2008) discern three phases of narrative colouration in the *City of God*: the first is full of golden colours and light to denote innocence and a relaxed tempo; the second is painted in darker colours to allude to the *favela*'s violent disintegration; in the last period of drug wars, colours turn grey, and, 'ceasing to have any referent, violence becomes pure, naked violence' (Diken and Laustsen, 2008, p. 59). Notably, the Ceremony's 'moving cities' on the stage's earthly canvas are cold blue blocks plunged in darkness dressed in techno-tropic sounds that run into red and orange explosions: this is the coming of a very turbulent modernity, imposing rigid chiaroscuro rules on Brazilian cities' social fabric. It is as if the coldness of blue mobile city-blocks stands for a new order of things, in which biological nature (*zoē*) is separated from the political (*bíos*), and excluded from the body politic of the city (Agamben, 1998, p. 18). This darkness on the stage mediates the visuality of power as a 'secret sinister end' (Schmitt, 2003, p. 336; Urry, 2014, p. 8), prompting the ruler(s) to 'organise new security systems around himself [sic.] and to create new anterooms, corridors, and access to power' (Schmidt, 2003, p. 357).

If anything, the moving cities' dark hypermobility transforms them into the *favelas*' original political synecdoche. The virtual projections of 'cities' and their populations also resemble the critical narrative in *City of Men* (filmed in a pre-pacification Santa Marta), in which two young mailmen decide they can deliver mail better if streets have names and a map (Freeman, 2014, p. 17). The two cinematic characters' sign-posting and map-drawing is a technology attributed to state simplification and abstraction of complex reality (Scott, 1998, pp. 87–88). The virtuality of the performance also comes close to the uses of Google-mapping as a tool of visibility and real exposure of the *favelas* to the policing eye before their occupation by police patrols (Freeman, 2014, p. 18). But, instead of recreating areas of risk, the ceremonial segment suggests a free flow of bodies and emotions across 'blocks' of performance, each representing a region, a city and an atmosphere. These moving blocks also contest fixed practices of policing, as they remain in constant change, only enabling pleasurable 'intelligence' by global and local audiences. The *favelas*' ability to be hypermobile in global markets and immobile at home (Freire Medeiros, 2014), subjected to global tourist gazes but preserving their own intimate core in spite of such intrusions, proffers their absence as a sort of submerged global, rather than mere national urban core.

Google-like practices of mapping connect this segment to the following one on 'Climate Change' – only now, it is not the *favelas* that are placed under scrutiny, but whole global cities. A short video introduced the Anthropocene and human-made climate change. Featuring Ed Hawkins' visual spiral indicating rising global temperatures, with an animated projection of rising sea levels on places, including Amsterdam (host of the 1928 Games), Dubai, Lagos, Shanghai, Florida and the city of Rio de Janeiro itself, the segment emphasises the theme of human self-destruction. Narrated by Brazilian Academy Award-nominee actress Fernanda Montenegro and British Academy Award-winning actress Judi Dench, also reading from Carlos Drummond de Andrade's (born 1902, Minas Gerais; died 1987, Rio de Janeiro) modernist poem 'The Flower and the Nausea', the segment induces the same chilling effect we encountered in Meirelles' clip in the Museum of Tomorrow's entrance. Drummond de Andrade's poetry features themes such as loneliness, thus connecting to the great modernist poetic traditions of Europe that explore the onset of industrialisation in Romantic environmental tones (O'Brien, 2008, pp. 44–48). A black boy dressed in white walks on the cold blue stage amongst projected blocks to reach a sprouting flower – and we hear Dench's recitation:

> Promoting world peace is the basis of the Olympic spirit. Today there is an urgent need to also promote peace with the planet. Climate change and the depletion of natural resources need our attention and the Olympic Opening Ceremony is a wonderful opportunity to shed light on this subject. Brazil, with the largest forest and the largest reserve of biodiversity on the planet, is the right place for this message to be spread. It is not enough to stop harming the planet, it is time to begin healing it. This will be our Olympic message: Earthlings, let's replant, let's save the planet.
>
> Fagge *et al.*, 5 August 2016

And we watch the birth of meaning: corresponding to the Ceremony's animated 'Prologue' and the birth of the Amazonian Tree of Life, the flower's 'life' spreads across the stage in fine green threads. In this poetic event, it is not a white Conrad ploughing his way through the Amazonian 'heart of darkness', but an innocent black boy in white from the Tropics that bears testimony to the salvation of the memory of beauty, of spring. Like the European tradition of poetic modernism guiding T.S. Eliot's pen, the Olympic segment's harmonisation of local (Drummond de Andrade) and Western (Judi Dench) voices, warns that we must always remember what we did to our home planet, if we wish to be reborn (O'Brien, 2008, p. 47). But unlike the European modernist tradition, which provides no directions as to how to transcend the human-made (Great War) catastrophe, the Olympic segment points to the beginning of a solution: to avoid more wastage (degrowth's environmentalist philosophical core – Martinez-Alier, 2015) and to populate the planet with more nature.

In this segment we see a clearer connection of the country's colonial-come-military past (rife with historical incidents of deforestation, exploitation of local resources and the rise of consumer capitalism) to its present ecological problems and the imagineering of solidary, global futures. Moving beyond Euro- and Western-centric paradigms of modernity (Chakrabarty, 2000; Mignolo, 2000, 2002), the performance outlines a transmodern future, more inclusive of its negated alterities (represented by the black boy and the repressed urban nature), 'in a process of mutual creative fertilization' (Dussel, 1995, p. 76). As the segment's journey through the country's forests and local ecosystems ends with a panoramic view of Rio de Janeiro and the symbol of peace as a 'Tree of Life', Dench announces that each athlete will be provided in the ceremonial 'Parade' with a seed to plant. The 'Athletes' Forest for Rio de Janeiro' featured in these closing remarks as a symbolic beginning of our common future. With a panoramic perspective of Rio's urban stage, we hear the announcement of the athletic procession.

The 'Parade' was punctuated with a number of episodic 'events' that fit into the interrogation of global imaginaries of *dépense*, in agreement with the artistic ceremony: the first event included the Team of Refugee Athletes, who marched into the Stadium just ahead of the Brazilian team. The Team's athletes received a standing ovation from the crowd and an introduction by IOC President, Thomas Bach. He added that, by offering them a home in the Olympic Village, the IOC produced 'a symbol of hope for all the refugees in [the] world', making everyone better aware of the magnitude of the present crisis: 'These refugee athletes will show the world that, despite the unimaginable tragedies they have faced, anyone can contribute to society through their talent, skills and strength of the human spirit' (Meagher, 5 August 2016). Representing over 20 million displaced people from around the world, the

Figure 5.4 The boxes in which athletes place seeds
Source: Image by Sander van Ginkel, Flickr/Creative Commons Licensing.

Team was an IOC initiative that brought United Nations (UN) Secretary General Ban-Ki Moon to the Rio Olympics (Marans, 12 August 2016). The emphasis on humanitarianism in this gesture, openly supported by refugee athlete Yusra Mardini, injected into the ceremonial procession brighter colours, because it centred on the pursuit of hope. Mardini featured widely in the international press and the social media because of her and her sister's successful attempt to save the lives of 20 people, after jumping off their sinking dinghy into the Aegean Sea and pushing their boat to land (Saul, 5 August 2016).

Sewell (2008) hypothesises that the temporality of capitalism is composite, contradictory and hyper-eventful – an argument that merits modification if we consider the IOC's humanitarian initiative. The IOC is an unorthodox blend of ever-shifting capitalist networks, often at the service of old ideals: Olympic togetherness, meritocracy and equality. But capitalist prerogatives also negate such projects, leading to ethical clashes within hosting national polities and cultures, as well as international critique. The formation of the Refugee Team exemplifies capitalist responses to criticism of corporate indifference (Boltanski and Chiapello, 2004): as a gesture, it absorbs criticism and re-moulds it into ethically responsible action. As a mode of engagement with the future in the context of protracted displacement (Kleist and Jansen, 2016), the formation of this Olympic team suits the hyper-eventfulness of capitalism. Such positive intervention is certainly governed by 'humanitarian reason' as a principle under which 'moral sentiments enter the political sphere', as well as 'a way of governing this principle' (Fassin, 2013, p. 37; Hyndman, 2012). Fassin points out that the way people feel the obligation of saving strangers, thus granting them a gift of protracted life, is non-rational. Discarding the non-rationalist aspects of this initiative and casting the gesture as 'economic resourcefulness', would justify neither Mardini's courageous action nor the IOC's decision to grant it recognition. Practically and pragmatically, it takes extreme effort and resources to organise the support of a team that connects disparate but powerful and dangerous projects of political violence, potentially making the Olympiad and the particular mega-event a target.

An all-rationalist take fails intellectually in the consideration of the principle of hope as more than a strategy for media attention – as generative of action with a temporal sense of potential (Brun, 2015, 2016). If humanitarian reason pays more attention to the biological life of victims and the destitute, granting it with geopolitical coordinates (Fassin, 2012, p. 254), the Olympic initiative complements this with aspiration and emotion generative of a productive future for the refugee athletes. It helps to remember that, until the beginning of the twentieth century, the very idea of humanitarian aid remained bound to the alleviation of mainly suffering *male soldiers*, until as a consequence of two World Wars the definition was amended to include the care of children by organisations, such as the Children Fund. The 'neo-humanitarian' (Barnett, 2011) turn at the beginning of the Cold War, which split humanitarian action between the American capitalist ideal of global welfarism and the Soviet policy of supporting national liberation movements, did little to address gender or ethnic rights. Global governance organisations such as the United Nations (UN) and the World Health Organization (WHO) attempted to provide post-biopolitical definition of rights, by addressing the social construction of gender, but they clashed with national-institutional prerogatives based on sexism, racism and disablism (Cabanes, 2014). Hence, artistic-policy articulations of the Olympic Movement's 'right to the future' are not decorative in the 2016 Ceremonies: they highlight a need to think beyond old biopolitical frames that maintain a nationalist anti-globalisation ethic. Especially the shift from thanatourist imaginaries of war disaster to post-biopolitical utopias of professional mobility for women and non-white people projects a positive utopian aesthetic, much needed in the new age of disaster and crisis.

Brun (2016, p. 399) nicely frames this through Hannah Arendt's (1958) split between biological and biographical life, and through Simone de Beauvoir's ([1952] 1988) notion of 'immanence' and 'transcendence'. If biological life is repetitive, biographical life is, in the case of refugee athletes, an aspiration to betterment, a professional future and the ability to inspire the good through exemplary action. Biographical life is based on work, which allows for transcendence (as per de Beauvoir) and the production of future goals (Young, 2005, p. 138), thus granting the world with more durable positive structures. In the IOC's humanitarian initiative we find the seeds of a worldmaking project opposing crude capitalist imperatives. The project simultaneously enables refugees to transcend their biopolitical limitations, in which war and displacement trapped them, and to partake in the Olympiad's cine-tourist ethics of travel as subjects, rather than objects of the gaze. The principle of hope was also literally mediated after the end of the 'Athletes' Parade' with the award of the first Olympic Laurel to Kenyan runner and two-time Olympic champion Kipchoge Keino, who was accompanied by children flying 200 white kites shaped like doves. His contribution to education in his country featured in a short video filmed in the same sepia colours as those used in the *City of God*'s 'golden phase' of innocence. Significantly, his award was matched with images of children in Kenya inscribing messages of peace on kites: the synecdoche of peace-education-innocence-childhood-Africa countered critiques of ('First World') capitalist indifference in post-colonial contexts, turning the athlete (Kipchoge or Mardini likewise) from a misfortunate *Homo Sacer* (in Agamben's (1998) terms) or a humble *Homo Faber* (in Arendt's (1958) terms), into the new professional *Homo Mobilis*. The contribution of the two athletes to this professionalised 'human culture' is organised across gendered and racialised 'risk regimes' (Laurendeau, 2008) that produce different discourses of responsibility, along the lines of nation/education/mind (male) and globality/wild nature/the body (female). On a meta-level, however, the mega-event's broadcast representations of both athletes involve (technological) calibrations of human nature that middle-class, urbanites and guests can consume audio-visually (Pahl 1968, p. 271–273 in Olstead 2011, p. 89)

No Opening Olympic Ceremony is complete without the introduction of the Torch and the lighting of the Olympic Cauldron. Rio 2016's Cauldron was lit by Athens 2004 Marathon bronze medallist and recipient of the Pierre de Coubertin medal, Vanderlei Cordeiro de Lima (Lutz, 5 August 2016). Where in past mega-events the Torch's journey was the focus of social protests against the Games and human rights violations (Tzanelli, 2010), in Rio 2016 it featured a message embraced by most Brazilians. Adopting the strategy of social movements (MacAloon, 2006, pp. 28–29), the organisers focused on environmental protection and global warming, thus commissioning an Olympic Cauldron with a simpler form in comparison to past designs, which produced a smaller volume of flame and fewer emissions. The idea of inclusivity and conservation was widened, to produce an urban aesthetic amenable to the human right to inhabit social environments peacefully, regardless of class, status or race. This interpretative flexibility was achieved with the creation of a smaller sculpture for a second flame, for display in a plaza in front of the Candelária Church, a Baroque Catholic temple notorious for the murder of eight children by police on 23 July 1993. This public Cauldron was lit by Jorge Gomes, a 14-year-old runner who was adopted out of poverty and participated in Rio's *Vila Olímpica* programme (Brunhuber, 12 August 2016), providing access to sports training facilities to disadvantaged youth.

The second Cauldron attained a double meaning: for Brazilians and *Cariocas*, it was imbued with semi-religious significance, prompting remembrance of domestic violence against the homeless. There is a long history of helping the poor connected to the country's religious establishment as a humanitarian agent and to Vargas' very own populist political programme (Groppo, 2010, p. 129), so the Cauldron joined the city's and the country's ambivalent heritage. In this context, the city's internal other, the poor and often black populations, featured in relation to the imaginary of ecological disaster, speaking the language of political ecology. The second meaning of this *lieu de mémoire* (Nora, 1989) looked to another of Vargas' public innovations, the introduction of tourist mobilities, especially in Brazil's urban centres and its rebellious samba cultures (Tzanelli, 2013b, p. 112). The transformation of Afro-Brazilian heritage into tourist commodity matches the rationale of displaying biopolitical cleansing as disreputable heritage in the context of a globally mediated 'event' for the tourist gaze. Candelária's Cauldron is, thus, a 'dark spot', a site potentially performed to 'recreate a sense of historical reality' (Rojek, 1993, p. 147) and a thanatourist site of biopolitical magnanimity, like Ground Zero (Sather-Wagstaff, 2011).

The 'art' of the Torch and the Cauldron belong to American Anthony Howe, in whose work we identify elements of Calatrava's philosophy. Known for his large-scale kinetic sculptures that can be found in public spaces in Dubai, the United Arab Emirates, Southern California and New York City, Howe started his career with watercolour painting (Howe, 3 August 2016). For Rio 2016 his intent was to create a moving sculpture made up of

Figure 5.5 The Olympic Cauldron overseeing the Stadium
Source: Image by Andy Miah, Flickr/Creative Commons Licensing.

hundreds of spheres and plates organised concentrically around the Cauldron so as to amplify and reflect the light from it. 'My vision was to replicate the sun, using movement to mimic its pulsing energy and reflection of light,' explained the artist. 'I hope what people take away from the cauldron, the opening ceremonies, and the Rio games themselves is that there are no limits to what a human being can accomplish', he concluded (Brillon, 8 August 2016). Although the IOC gave Howe freedom to develop the Cauldron as he wanted, the agreed emphasis on solar energy reflected the overall theme of climate change of that Olympic Games. The Opening Ceremony's technical support setup was designed and constructed by British manufacturing and design firm Stage One, which was also in charge of installing a rigging system which allowed the aerial choreography of performers and scenery during the show (ibid.).

Weighing almost two tons and spanning 12 metres (40 feet) in diameter, the sculpture moves powerfully in the wind. Its connection to situated events, however, such as climate change and home-grown perceptions of 'terrorism' (the police attacked the youth in 1993 outside Candelária with such perceptions of public disturbance), generates hosting capacity, and an 'ability to relate' (Hui, 2014, pp. 172–173) through a multiplicity of intersecting mobilities of affect and history (Bærenholdt *et al.*, 2004). Again, the project's maker appears to be connected to cinematic art: Howe's work had previously been included in New York at Barneys, where Australian film auteur Baz Luhrmann and his costume designer wife Catharine Martin had delivered a four-window feat of 'Installation Art for the People' (Cascone, 8 August 2016). As part of the 'Truth' window display for 'Baz Dazzled', Howe's 'Beauty' kinetic sculptures and robot fireworks endlessly opening and closing (Davis, 19 December 2014) foretold his creation of the 2016 Cauldron. The suggestion of 'an evil hypnotist's wheel' (ibid.) in the design, followed Howe's play with red (fire), gold (steel) and black (night) in the Cauldron's display, which alluded to the work of the unconscious and to nature. But specifically the second Cauldron outside Candelária Church is nothing short of a pilgrimage akin to that offered by Calatrava's St Nicholas' Church in Ground Zero (see Chapter 3). We come full circle, from the materiality of architecture to the production of art in the mega-event's city, to consider the role of capitalist displays of 'death' (Korstanje, 2016b): currently, visitors to Candelária's Olympic Boulevard are delighted by the display of light and wind and photographed in front of the Cauldron (Guimarães, 9 August 2016). Local mourning has already given way to a festive atmosphere of educational-tourist potential. The collapse of some boundaries between art and everyday life, coupled with the *avant-gardiste* movement's use of art as a vehicle for public engagement (Zukin, 1982, 1988) transfer a very old political language into the new common spaces of tourism.

The Closing Ceremony

The prominence of dance and music in the recreation of a unique *Carioca* atmosphere was assigned to *Carnaval* veteran Rosa Magalhães (born 1947, Rio de Janeiro). The creative director is a Brazilian professor, artist and one of the most successful *Carioca* carnival designers, with five championships won since 1984, when the Sambadrome *Marquês de Sapucaí*, a downtown parade area of *Citade Nova*, was built by Niemeyer for samba schools to meet and compete (Da Redação, 19 December 2015). Her obvious connection to the city's post-authoritarian material heritage and Afro-Brazilian cultural capital, allows for a synecdoche to form between *Carioca* affective atmosphere and urban space, so as to 'reinscribe pleasure and desire in the urban project' (Lloyd, 2003, p. 94). Magalhães' ceremonial mission is, in short, to assert Rio de Janeiro's presence on a global urban map, with a powerful presentation of its affective brand (Löfgren, 2014). As Urry *et al.* (2016, p. 16) explain, 'in the neoliberal age of unbridled consumption' atmospheres function as a kind of silent language that can communicate ('engineer') simultaneously particular, largely symbolic, but also sensory, aspects of lifestyle or aesthetic impressions of the Self. But Rio's atmosphere is not ephemeral, as scholars suggested with regards to cultures of enthusiasm (Hui, 2014, p. 174) or airports as non-spaces of consumer capitalism (Urry *et al.*, 2016, p. 15 on the 'generic city'). *Carioca* atmospherics are based on Brazilian roots and routes of heritage and tradition (Clifford, 1992, 1997), as well as on their eventual mooring and indigenisation (Clifford, 2013). As we will see below, Magalhães' selection for the directorship of the Closing Ceremony marks a suggestive ideological transition from the discourses of frugality and degrowth, supported by some of the Opening event's (male) artistic contingent, to those of emotional and lifestyle plenitude, more amenable to Brazil's post-dictatorial, left-wing imaginary of *abertura*.

The Olympic Ceremony bridges the laws of calendrical time through artistic display of evenemential fragments that can insert the host into a global template of long duration. For Rio, there is no better way to 'fit into' a global sequence than a second introduction of Santos-Dumont's historic flight over Paris. An old film displaying the flight is projected, which cuts to a close-up shot of the actor playing Santos-Dumont. The actor checks his watch (rumoured to accompany the inventor during his flights), while we watch a colourful display of mechanical structures on the stage culminating in the ceremonial countdown. Thereafter, the stage is flooded with dancers in a celebration of the diversity of the country's flora, fauna and singing. The succession of the mechanical by the embodied and the natural produces the same palindromic movement we encountered in various segments of the Opening Ceremony and the mega-event's architectural and artistic displays. Rio is introduced as an urban form standing between nature and culture, which becomes worldly with the help of its music cultures (singers appear on stage). The ceremonial association between musical and lived time, a unique *Carioca* rhythm, both resembles and reassembles the bodies of the dancers into a cultural symphony (Lefebvre, [1992] 2015, pp. 73–74). In fact, the bodies produce various formations on stage, to represent Rio's iconic landmarks (approached from a Brazilian bird eye's view), such as the gentrified and tourismified district of Lapa, the statue of Christ the Redeemer and the Sugarloaf Mountain. The rhythmic movement of performers around a pulsating core projects a mediated centre akin to that analysed by Couldry (2000). Finally, the performers produce the Olympic Rings. In this fragment we deal with 'tourist marks' (MacCannell, 1989) and 'tourism imaginaries' (Salazar and Graburn, 2016), now evidently integrated into an increasingly globalised – and artistically 'radicalised' (Castoriadis, [1975] 1987) – *Carioca* imaginary. In this dialogical formation of Rio, tourism mobilities and the rule of Olympic hospitality take precedence (Getz, 2008, p. 405), making the city's 'form' and habitus.

Following the projection of atmospheric art-scenes, the next segment pays homage to the great Brazilian maestros. Martinho da Vila performed a rendition of the classic song '*Carinhoso*' by Pixinguinha, while images of the universe were projected on the ceremonial stage. A native *Carioca*, Pixinguinha (born Alfredo da Rocha Viana, Jr. 1897–1973) was a composer, arranger, flautist and saxophonist. He is considered one of the greatest Brazilian composers of popular music, known for his fusion of old *choro*, a nineteenth-century music genre, with contemporary jazz-like harmonies and Afro-Brazilian rhythms. He was one of the first Brazilian musicians and composers to take advantage of the new professional opportunities offered to musicians by the new technologies of radio broadcasting and studio recording at a time when Rio's elites were racially prejudiced. Originally associated with the lowlife cabarets of Lapa, then a red district, Pixinguinha's style was criticised for being corrupted by American jazz. His talent was eventually discovered by the wealthy Arnaldo Guinle, who sponsored his band's first European tour in 1921 and from Paris he would return to South America to visit Argentina on tours (Livingston-Isenhour and Garcia, 2005). The ceremonial performance of '*Carinhoso*' by Martinho da Vila, one of the main representatives of samba and *Música Popular Brasileira*, as well as a prominent figure of Afro-Brazilian questions and the Brazilian Communist Party (see Wikipedia, undated), hints at a temporal progression in race matters. The performance showcases the Afro-Brazilian contribution to Rio's culture in a moment of self-recognition as worthy to achieve what Dussel (1995, pp. 76–77) terms analectic solidarity between opposing terms (black/white, First/Third World, etc.). This performance alone looks at the 'popular' not as populist, but as the repressed side of Brazilian modernity that can 'emerge' only through performance, hence not directly as a social issue.

Yet, the 'issue' featured as the Closing Ceremony's core, given that da Vila's singing was immediately followed by the national anthem, sung by 26 children representing the 27 states, plus the federal district, on an animated formation of the Brazilian flag. The flagbearers of the Olympic teams were introduced on stage, followed by the athletes. In the centre of the arena and amidst a sea of colours and activity, samba singer Roberta Sá paid homage to legendary Carmen Miranda (born, Marco de Canaveses, Portugal 1909; died Beverly Hills, California, 1955), a Luso-Brazilian samba singer, dancer, Broadway actress, and film star, popular between the 1930s and the 1950s. Although Miranda's rise to fame fits into the refiguring of Brazilian nationalism during the regime of President Getúlio Vargas (Carvalho, 2013, p. 181), she is considered one of the precursors of *Tropicalismo*. Her rise to fame implicated her in President Roosevelt's 'Good Neighbor Policy', designed to strengthen links with Latin America and Europe, and she worked for several years during the Second World War with 20th Century Fox. In this context, Miranda was considered the 'goodwill ambassador' and promoter of intercontinental culture. In the ceremony, Miranda was impersonated as one of the most iconic Brazilian artists in a colourful skirt and a heavily ornamented fruit-headdress. She sang a rendition of '*Tico-Tico no Fubá*' ('Sparrow in the Cornmeal') a renowned Brazilian *choro* piece composed by Zequinha de Abreu in 1917. Not only was the song performed by Miranda onscreen in *Copacabana* (1947), it was featured in the '*Aquarela do Brasil*' segment of the Walt Disney animated film *Saludos Amigos* (1942) and in Woody Allen's comedy *Radio Days* (1987). The 'electronification' of memory (Urry, 1996, p. 63) that became a source of consternation for those who saw in technology the rise of commoditised amnesia (Holliday and Potts, 2012, p. 202), becomes here a way to remember in a global event not just a nationally significant figure, but a constellation of audio-visual industrial mobilities.

Miranda's global connectivity speaks volumes about the ambiguous status of artistic *Brasilidade*: her 'tutti-frutti' appearance image was much satirised and taken up as 'Camp' – so much so, that today the 'Carmen Miranda' persona is popular among drag performers (Carvalho, 2013, p. 181). For Veloso and other musicians contemplating a career abroad, Miranda helped transform the relationship between Brazilian musicians and American producers, so to think of her was 'to think about the complexity of this relationship' (Fey and Racine, 2000, p. 245). Indeed, the Latin American craze is considered responsible for the formation of the stereotype of the *Brazuca* or Brazilian US expatriate, to which Miranda's 'camp' personality contributed. It helps cross-referencing Miranda's 'Camp' with the 2014 FIFA World Cup's ceremonial display of Brazilian 'camp'; cinema and the presentation (in the same segment) of 'Adidas Brazuca' as the World Cup's ball – a name voted for by Brazilians and a local word that describes the Brazilian way of life (Tzanelli, 2015c, p. 91). For a culture that continues to treat sexual ambiguity with downright violence (Silva, 2014), this is significant. Veloso recognised in Miranda a simultaneous source of shame and pride, as her style managed to conquer white America, but intensified the gaze Brazilians began to cast on themselves as exotic, 'Negroid' commodities (ibid.). Miranda the 'camp' Brazilian is, thus, replete with associations of an effeminate and strangely black masculine Brazilian marginality, better exemplified in artistic mobilities. Holliday and Potts (2012) caution that, while 'Camp's' (as consciously fabricated 'bad taste') love of kitsch (unconsciously reproduced 'bad taste') is a way to celebrate denigrated taste from the position of the denigrated subject, it is also 'a way sending up the middle class pretentions of that group of aspirational working-class and middle-class people for whom respectability matt[ers] most' (ibid., p. 141). As an immediate neighbour to the new imperialist project of McDonaldisation (Ritzer, 2006) or Americanisation (Ickenberry, 2007), Brazil entertained all the benefits and faced all the problems cross-cultural fertilisation entails. Unlike Brazilian technology and high art, which have always retained strong links to Europe, Brazilian popular cultural art-scenes emerged in the twentieth and the twenty-first century primarily through hybridisations with American artforms.

This kind of hybridisation triggers problems of global recognition as a non-mimicking, 'original' and 'pure' cultural entity (Bhabha, 1990a, 1990b, 1990c, 1994), but also self-recognition as an autonomous one (Nederveen Pieterse, 2001). The glamorisation of ideas of mixing and *anthropofagia* in Brazilian art-scenes partook in what DaMatta (1995) saw as the tradition of choosing not to choose between several incompatible options, so as to create something new out of their contingent juxtaposition and mixing. The 'glue' or *goma* generating novelty out of diverse and often contradictory aesthetic principles, maintains 'a sense of an ambiguous temporal dimension and a continual, open-ended process, a circular stirring up of things, movement, and also an *adding* to without necessarily needing to take away anything' (Moehn, 2008, p. 167, emphasis in text). This take on hybridisation is certainly at odds with neat temporal progressions of cultural morphogenesis, so all Brazilian music and dance genres born out of contacts with the West are unique. But at the same time, the *goma* would prove to be a 'sticky' business for the new twentieth-century bourgeois professionals in the country, who had to adhere to the universalised principles of Western modernity, thus conducting their lives and labour 'in tangled relation to the middle class ideal' (Moehn, 2008, p. 169), while dealing with the realities of *abertura*, including hyperinflation and political corruption (Moehn, 2007). Hiding the native woes of an eternally postponed modernisation behind the dictum that 'Brazil is the country of the future', was not simply concomitant with the validation of a pluri-temporal experience in which race, gender and the body moved with frightening speed (DaMatta, 1995, p. 271; García Canclini, 1995). It also produced ambivalent affective atmospheres towards the dialogical others through which Brazilian culture would see itself (McCann, 2004, p. 224). Accordingly, any favourable comparisons with the United States began to wane past the 1960s in the heat of the black movement and its associations with activist intellectuals, allowing also for the emergence of critiques of the Brazilian nationalist myth of racial harmony – prominent in soul art-scenes (Bourdieu and Wacquant, 1999, pp. 41–43; Alberto, 2009, p. 6). Although, for a nation that based its self-image on traditional renditions of a 'gender order' (DaMatta, 1991 on gender and nation) accusations of 'Camp' create a third space, in which the subject (artist) and his/her (highly mobile) work have no clear identity (Molotch, 2004), they also make space for the creative display of agility, connectivity and cosmopolitanism.

New media scenes negotiate this problematic cosmopolitan togetherness in the Olympic 'event'. Immediately after a firework display, popular Sound-Cloud and YouTube Norwegian electronic tropical music producer Kygo and singer-songwriter Julia Michaels (born Julia Carin Cavazos, Iowa, 1993) performed 'Carry Me' as part of a segment that promoted the new Olympic Channel service launching after the Games (*Billboard Staff*, 16 August 2016). The nationality of both artists is superseded by their mobile musical profile, featuring Olympic industrial human capital as a highly mobile human family beyond race, gender, class and the like (Tzanelli, 2015a, Chapter 2). Since the mid-twentieth century, various Olympic ceremonial shows have been including conceptions of racial, ethnic and gendered harmony to ensure national 'arrogation': the claim of national values as unchanged while being subjected to amenable reinterpretations (Tomlinson, 1996). The paucity of scholarly studies of ceremonial rituals and their overwhelmingly racial, ethnic and gendered allegories of belonging also reproduced this silencing of 'arrogating discourses' (for exceptions see Hogan, 2003). Such studies are eye-opening: in Mexico 1968 the ceremonial script centred on the host's ability to deliver an honourable Games with little investment, and to discharge its mission to represent the 'Third World' with *sombreros* and a suspect socialist representation of peasantry marching alongside the working classes to the future (Brewster and Brewster, 2006). A *de facto* ethnic and gendered discourse on development also featured in the Sydney 2000 Opening Ceremony, where ethnic and gendered hierarchies were negotiated as national allegories (Hogan, 2003; Housel, 2007). A fusion of Mexico 1968 and Sydney 2000's post-colonial performances of ethnic and gendered national identity featured in the Athens 2004 Opening Ceremony, with an emphasis on Greece's 'forgotten' contribution to European civilisation (Tzanelli, 2004, 2008c). Beijing 2008's ceremonial configuration of Chinese national identity as a 'displaced' gendered and ethnic agent in the 'birth' and 'evolution' of Western European civilisation, who returns to claim a central place in human history (Tzanelli, 2010), matched previous worldmaking techniques. At the other end, London 2012's technologised identity bespoke of nationalist valorisation (see Tzanelli, 2013a on the notion of *tornadóros* as an ideal type of the technical working man).

The shift from gendered and ethnic or racialised representations to seamless cosmopolitan mobilities is not tackled in Rio 2016's segment by the ceremonial directors, *stricto sensu*. The segment is meant to promote the launching of the Olympic Channel as a Pan-human venture, so the short clip on the Stadium's big screens depicts different human types (races and cultures) dancing, superimposed onto Rio's magnificent seascape. But the accommodation of this event into *Carioca* mega-event contexts would, unavoidably, activate multi-temporal processes, especially given the Ceremony's organisation by a Tropicalist team. At the heart of Oswald de Andrade's 1928 *Manifesto Antropofago* stood the native idea of cannibalism as a way to absorb the enemies' strengths (Andrade, 1999). Andrade and the Tropicalists suggested selective consumption of 'First World' cultural models and advanced technologies 'in the creation of a "technified natural man"' and an innovative, mixed national culture that would be suitable for export to the First World' (Moehn, 2008, p. 162). The introduction of the Olympic Channel and, through it, of various human 'types' (including the *Cariocas*), is a step further: not only does it reject the folklorisation of Brazilian underdevelopment in globalised times (Perrone and Dunn, 2001), it legalises and masculinises Brazil's, rather than Rio's, insertion into global post-modernities – a variation of the Kantian aesthetically informed model of cosmopolitan belonging (Lash and Urry, 1994, Chapter 3).

The emphasis on landscape is succeeded by 'The Art of the People', in which we watch the ground-breaking discovery of cave painting in the archaeologically important National Park of the Serra da Capivara in the state of Piau. The rock paintings, which depict wild animals and human figures, are incorporated into complex scenes involving hunting, supernatural beings, sexual activity, skirmishing and dancing. Specialists date the rock art to between 25,000 and 36,000 years ago, thus challenging the widely held view that the Americas were first colonised from the North, via the Bering Straits at around 10,000 BC (Nash, undated). The projection of cave paintings is replaced with indigenous choreography and music, as dancers form various geometric shapes on a red-and-ochre coloured stage emulating the colour of rock art. The overall segment signifies the indigenous origins of *téchne*, suggesting that it can be connected to contemporary technologies, such as those of digitised music and TV or Internet broadcasting (Gallope, 2011, pp. 48–49) in a schema countering circular conceptions of capitalist time. Thus, ideas of the 'gift' of civilisation (Tzanelli, 2004) acquire a rationale akin to that of native *Ubuntu* philosophy (Romano, 2015). Such cosmopolitan togetherness and connectivity also guides the following reflecting theme, in which the audience is invited to remember and mourn lost people.

The stage is flooded with blue darkness and words such as souvenir and *sodade* (nostalgia) appear and fade. The poet Arnaldo Antunes is reading aloud his poem '*Saudade*', which speaks of the embodiment of memory (*The New York Times*, 21 August 2016), while its words are projected onto the stage. The segment commemorates, amongst other events, the death of Stefan Henze, a former Olympian and current German kayak women's team coach, after a crash near the Olympic Park (BBC Sports, 15 August 2016). The visual composite that emanates from a 'centre' (a lantern at the centre of the Stadium) resembles the experiential journey of dark heritage tourists, who are often invited to occupy a liminal space between consumption and commemorative rituals during their journeys (Biran *et al.*, 2011; Graburn, 2012). The digital projection of ideational memoryscapes on the stage produces the darkest type of tourist as a third-order (cinematic) journey (Kaelber, 2007). Remembering from a distance features as an experiential journey to sites of memory that are both personal and collective (Urry, 2004, p. 209; Nora, 1989; Huyssen, 1995) – a trope belonging simultaneously to European and Brazilian high modernism (Gibbons, 2007). The two segments problematise set discourses of origins in the making of our world from two often contrasting perspectives: the embodied, biological and material on the one hand, and the cultural, phenomenological and civilisational on the other. In this blend, *Carioca* nature is imagineered through variations of human action in technical and technological (art)styles.

This Euro-Brazilian fusion is disrupted with the illumination of the stage, on which new dancers and a singer narrate the contribution of Portuguese and African cultures to the Brazilian tradition of lace-making. The singer musically enframes the rotating dancers with '*Mulher Rendeira*', a piece representing the Brazilian *sertão* as a feminised margin. According to the Ceremony's organisers, the oldest people claim that the song 'was composed by the "King of Cangaço", Lampião [a bandit], inspired by his grandmother, a celebrated lace-maker' (*The New York Times*, 21 August 2016). The feminisation of heritage, which is both musical and craft-orientated (*Mulher Rendeira* is the lace-maker), positions ceremonial imagineering (led by female artist Magalhães) as a third-order, artistic activity (Tzanelli, 2011, Chapter 6). As is the case with the romanticisation of contemporary *baile funk's* gangsters, *cangaceiros* (social bandits) from the late nineteenth-century poverty-stricken Brazilian Northeast would spread terror by looting, raiding and kidnapping, thus disrupting state order. Yet, the same bandits would come to occupy a special place in both popular and state-instituted imaginations featuring *sertão* traditions. Lampião's song portrays the memory of craft, as preserved in Brazil's anomic networks, hence the nation's, rather just a city's cultural intimacy (Herzfeld, 2005).

This synecdoche appeals to a systemic organisation of rural and urban life-worlds, in ways emulating processes of invisible colonisation or 'crypto-colonialism' (Habermas, 1989b; Herzfeld, 2002), but with interpretative twists not accounted for in systemic theory. The city enmeshes and reworks rural imaginaries and the national centre appropriates different federal urban imaginaries for purposes of self-presentation to global guests, but the strategy is not devoid of emotional investment exceeding motivation, as Habermas (1989a) would contend. The song's early lyrics feature an interlocutor requesting that the lace-maker teaches them 'to make lace/and I will teach you to make love' (or 'teach you to flirt') (Rhythm and Roots, undated). They present the figure of the lace-maker as part of a technological assemblage that partook in Brazilian *phylogenesis* (racial birth) through a superimposition of the mechanosphere onto the biosphere (Guattari, 2001, p. 42). The idea of lace-making as both a technological prosthesis and an embodied know-how craft reinforces Latour's (1993) dictum that we have never been modern (Tzanelli, 2016b, p. 120). Simultaneously, the use of craft knowledge as an initiation into sexual rituals contributes to the consolidation of *Carioca*-as-Brazilian atmospherics: while 'sweetening' tourist transaction (the 'lace' is an auratic souvenir and lace-making is a folklore experience for guests – Hume, 2013), it ratifies the *Cariocas'* self-recognition as embodied hosts offering with emotion.

Even though the segment is integrated into a progressive story of Brazilian self-realisation, whereby 'old' traditions simply fed into national *branquea-mento,* bodily movements assume a life of their own, inviting audiences to re-code versions of the primordial Brazilian body. The experience of stage perfor-mance invites a proto-scientific method of comprehension (ceremonial gazing) that prioritises experience (Turner, 1996; Schilling, 2003). At the same time, the project of transmodern comprehension is streamlined into a narrative opposing masculine/muscular power, which is valorised in Western philoso-phies of domination (Sawicki, 1991; McNay, 1992; Dussel, 1996). At all times, we observe the display of rhythms through and on acting (dancing) bodies, which conceives of the world, hence *introduces a perspective* by sensible-aesthetic means (Lefebvre, [1992] 2015, p. 26). The ceremonial display of Brazilian mobilities fuses notions of the 'secret' (those belonging to memory, recollection and the body) with the 'public' (those we find in celebrations) and the 'fictional' (those we know as 'habitus'). Because Rio's ceremonial atmo-sphere 'hinge[s] on the presence of an experiencing subject through which atmosphere is conceptualised and analysed' (Sørensen, 2015, p. 64), we cannot ignore the presence of the onlooker, the mega-event guest. The Cere-mony's black primordial and/or feminine Brazil bears the potential to restore our faith in pilgrimage enactments that post-modernity's speedy rhythms destroyed (Bauman, 1996, p. 8). This return to slow time reinstitutes pilgrim-age as a vector for the gazers, allowing them to structure an eternal Brazilian space (of heritage), if only for a few hours.

The last performance showcases dance scenes bringing to life clay dolls, common in Northeastern Brazil. The figurines are performed by members of *Grupo Corpo*, which has toured four continents with their mix of ballet and contemporary choreography infused with Brazilian styles of dance (Flanagan, 2016). The dolls come to life to '*Asa Branca*', which is the music of the 'King of *Baião*' (a rhythm originating in Bahia) Luiz Gonzaga. The song, written in 1947 by Luiz Gonzaga and Humberto Teixeira, speaks of the migration of the 'white wing' – a literal translation of the song's title referring to the *pica-zuro* pigeon, a Brazilian species – that leaves the *sertão*, when it becomes completely arid. The song's hero, unable to make a living, must leave his lady-love Rosinha, with a promise to return. To create this metaphor for exile and longing (*saudade*) for homecoming, the song's creators collected oral tradi-tions from Serra da Borborema, in Pernambuco. The song's metaphor of the 'white wing' entertained global popularity, further bolstered by Veloso's recording of Gonzaga and Teixeira's work in London in 1971 and Raul Seixas' recording of Elvis Presley's 'Blue Moon of Kentucky' (Angelo, 2009). The choreographer for the clay doll dancers, who performed a mix of ballet and *forró*, a popular dance from Northeast Brazil (*The New York Times*, 21 August 2016), reportedly hoped to reference clay's history as an early human tool and a source of creation (Flanagan, 2016). Thus, the dance routine comes to symbolise the plasticity of the human body (Dewsbury, 2011), reflected through dance moves of professional migrants. The segment's tem-poral framing points to a territory-bound (Northeastern *sertão*) progression from amateur to professional labour and from immobile vagabondage to mobile tourism. The performance is followed by a celebration of clay on the arena by a larger group of dancers dressed as clay dolls. Significantly, the seg-ment concludes with an on-screen introduction of the Victory Ceremony for the Marathon, thus suggesting a connection between mobility and bodily plasticity in the Olympic now, rather than narrow Brazilian context. This silently trans-fers audiences back to the discourse of hope and human betterment we encountered in the introduction to the Refugee Team.

The transition from the cultures of a *Homo Faber* to those of *Homo Mobilis* is completed with the introduction of the four newly elected members of the IOC Athletes' Commission: fencer Britta Heidemann (Germany), table tennis player Ryu Seung-min (South Korea), swimmer Dániel Gyurta (Hun-gary) and pole vaulter Yelena Isinbayeva (Russia). Applause for the con-tribution of volunteers follows, with twice Latin Grammy-awarded Pernambucan Lenine's (born Recife, 1959) song '*Jack Soul Brasileiro*'. Thereafter, the Olympic flag was handed over by Rio de Janeiro Mayor Eduardo Paes to IOC President Thomas Bach, who then handed it over to Tokyo Governor Yuriko Koike. We are now facing a four-year interlude before the next mega-event stop.

6   Tokyo 2020

Urban amnesia and the technoromantic spirit of capitalism

Imaginative future-making in the Olympic project

Every prospective Olympic host departs on a developmental journey with multiple stops, profitable avenues, turning points and deadlocks. Tokyo is not an exception to this rule: the city won the bid to host the Olympic Games on 7 September 2013 at the 125th IOC Session in Buenos Aires, thus marking a significant passage from the IOC's uncompromising decision to grant the hosting of such mega-events to South American cities/countries. Japan, which had lost the 2016 bid to Rio, cannot be placed among 'developing nations'; on the contrary, it is a world player in the international economic arena. Tokyo had previously hosted the 1964 Summer Olympics, which would serve in terms of infrastructural development as a starting point. On 3 August 2016 it was reported that the IOC had approved the addition of five sports to the programme of the 2020 Olympics, including the return of baseball and soft-ball, and the introduction of youth-oriented events such as skateboarding and surfing (ESPN, 4 August 2016). Despite the March 2011 earthquake and tsunami, which affected much of eastern Japan, the determination to 'bring back the Olympics' (Reuters, 15 July 2011), in the words of Japanese Olympic Committee (JOC) Chief Tsunekazu Takeda, led to Tokyo's election for the 2020 mega-event.

On the economic front, the 2020 host's developmental programme placed emphasis on the amplification of aerial passages and rail routes within, to and from the city: plans were laid to increase slot capacity at both Haneda and Narita International Airports by easing airspace restrictions, and to create a new, privately funded 400-billion yen railway line, linking both airports through an expansion of Tokyo Station, so as to reduce travel time from Tokyo Station to Haneda and Narita. The JOC, headed by former Prime Minister Yoshiro Mori, confirmed in 2012 that the National Olympic Stadium in Tokyo would receive a $1 billion upgrade and full-scale reconstruction for the 2019 Rugby World Cup and the 2020 Olympics, but in 2015 it was confirmed that the design of this project would be led by Kengo Kuma at a higher cost (Himmer, 17 July 2015). So far, planning was managed by both the city and the Japanese centre, with an eye to capitalising on Tokyo 1964's legacy potential: of the 33 venues, several were previously used for the 1964 Summer Olympics and some will be located within the central business area of Tokyo, northwest of the Olympic Village. In this respect, the JOC's commitment to sustainability – the goal is to ensure Tokyo 2020 is the most eco-friendly Olympic Games – which will focus on both venue-reuse and cost-efficient solutions of the city's climate, is supported by the artifice of technology as a tool of leisure. Of course, much like creativity, sustainability is open to interpretation, involving things such as urban anti-sprawl, smart growth (Barnett, 2007; Glaeser, 2012), green urbanism based on energy-saving architecture (Lehmann, 2011) and innovative design (Jensen, 2014), or automobile efficiency (Urry, 2007, 2011). Several of these interpretations made their way into Tokyo 2020's planning: 20 venues will be located in the vicinity of Tokyo Bay, southeast of the Olympic Village, predominantly on Ariake, Odaiba and the surrounding artificial islands (Joy, 23 September 2016). Well-founded rumours suggested that, despite any use of traditional costumes, music or design, Tokyo 2020 will be a high-tech spectacle, consolidating a clash between the old Japan of temples and samurais with the new of urban architectural and technological mobilities. Simultaneously, Tokyo 2020's *oeconomie artificialem* is geared towards the delivery of a safe mega-event, for the benefit of the growing touristic masses in the city.

If we follow Amin and Thrift's (2002) argument, such consumption practices are placed under the strategy of urban and regional economic development, where 'the impact of the imagination and fantasy becomes [sic.] a major part of the conduct of business ... to [be] turned into profit' (2002, p. 125). But this over-rationalised thesis omits examining the cultural coordinates of imagination: its cosmological pathways and roots. As the analysis of Rio 2016 ceremonies manifests in Chapter 5, the host's cosmological mobilities and immobilities often feed the script of artistic ceremonial imaginaries. Social analysis must account for the coexistence of an ethno-national 'inside' with a transnational, if not generalised global 'outside' imaginary, enclosed in artistic worldmakings of this kind, offering valuable insight into glocalisation (Robertson, 1992, 1995) and cultural mobilities beyond the national borderlands (Schein, 2000; Sheller, 2003, 2004; Sebro, 2016). If we adhere to a Dascalian (Dascal, 1987) conception of synecdochical development, 'technology' as a worldmaking process is always implanted with intentionalities we find in bodies, intellects, machines and emotions, not the 'impersonal market forces' of political theory (see Chapter 2).

The 2016 Handover to Tokyo 2020 bears testimony to such synecdochical (dis)connectivities between the glocal logic of material developmental projects and embodied art. The following section grants Tokyo's mega-event project depth: it considers the city's and the country's philosophical basis of artistic creativity, especially with regard to its famous arts of *manga* and *anime.* This analysis is intertwined with Japan's and Tokyo's engagement with other nations and cultures diachronically. The following Chapter draws on this combined cultural and politico-economic profile to 'read' the Ceremonial

Handover as an artistic statement, replete with philosophical and politico-economic meaning. Such philosophical scripts are rooted in the development of ancient Japanese cultures of travel, which, in contemporary popular cultural contexts appeal not to esoteric pilgrims, but to everyday practices of association in the city.

Provincialised cosmopolitanisms and cosmobilities: Japan in constant transition

The Japanese experience of modernity is nothing short of the mega-event's split between an artificial and an imaginative economy, behind which we find contextual adaptations of Olympic ecumenism to ideological demands of post-colonial nationalism (for elaborations on mega-events and modernity see Roche, 2000; on post-colonial nationalism see Chatterjee, 1986, 1993). Even further in the background, we meet pre-national, ethnic cultural divisions between a real, a phenomenal and a noumenal universe, all three of which would spatialise historical time to achieve a degree of cross-cultural comprehension. Under rival conditions between modern Western European, and later also American transatlantic domination, and regional (what counts in Japan as 'domestic') Chinese cross-fertilisation, the Japanese experience of development and mobility through time and space would – *could only* – be 'mapped' (*á la* Sloterdijk, 2014) as a dialogue. This prescriptive dialogue took place between reality and *Realpolitik* on the one hand, and ideality and collective psychic experience on the other.

The nature of this predicament has always been cultural through and through, in that it gestured towards ways of being in the natural, the phenomenal and the scientific/rational worlds (Remmling, 1961, p. 24; Geertz, 2000, pp. 154–156; Marcus, 2011, pp. 136–18). Graburn's (2012, pp. 50–51) meticulous elaboration on the persistence in contemporary Japanese culture of a split between 'outer' touristic travels, performed by the body across concrete geographical terrains, and 'inner' exploratory journeys of one's intimate Self, will guide the analysis of the 2016 Ceremonial Handover. For the moment, it is worth stressing that the modern (colonised, post-colonised and nationalised) collective Japanese psyche has been displaying all the symptoms of a split between a so-called *tatemae*, a public self-image, and a *honne*, an intimate experiential Self; and that the two Selves commenced their lives as rival ontologies based on epistemological splits between the mobile, scientific spirit of Western European Enlightenment and the Eastern artistic spirit of a Chinese-inspired Japan. This ancient split is being negotiated in contemporary capitalist contexts by means of what we may call Japanese 'acculturation' into Western discourses and performances of individualism (Boltanski and Chiapello, 2004, p. 20, pp. 25–26). This negotiation allows for the emergence of a third, individual Self which is fully aligned with capitalist development (Katagiri, 2013). The third Self grants the two other Selves a cosmopolitan veneer that we associate with cultures of capitalist mobility not devoid of justice or morality (Swain, 2009). A preliminary focus on this Chinese-inspired Japanese Self helps to situate temporally and spatially the significance of *anime* as Japanese animation for Tokyo 2020's ceremonial performance in Maracanã; explain why its directors and organisers harmonised their projective means with Rio's narratives of degrowth and post-Foucaultian biopolitics; and think critically about Tokyo's passage through post-modernity as a 'worlded city' engaging in the 'art of being global' (Ong, 2011, p. 3).

An introduction to globalising imperatives and realities of Japanese cultural cosmobilities has to be filtered through cultural-sociological and religious-philosophical debates on two controversial Japanese art-forms: *manga* and *anime*. Neither of them stands apart from nation-formation, so it is worth mobilising Hutchinson's (2005) suggestion that nations enclose 'zones of conflict' prompted by the coexistence and occasional amalgamation of modern and traditional voices, and the bloody conflicts these may eventually induce. Contemporary Japanese identity was conditioned by several centuries of 'ethnic overlaying' (Hutchinson, 2004). A high concentration of ethnic memories in layers of experience would be streamlined into Japan's globally now disseminated popular culture. I do not wish to surgically separate conceptions of 'folk' from notions of 'popular culture': not only do the former inform the latter's contemporary form, they spill into populist uses of both as nostalgic national 'artefacts' or heritage. Katagiri (2013, p. 139) purports a four-stage development of Japanese post-war society: the ideal (late 1940s to 1960s, encompassing debates upon democracy and socialism), the dream (1960s to 1970s, encompassing rampant consumerism and development), the fiction (from the 1970s to the 1980s, corresponding to advanced consumerism) and that of fragmentation (from around 1990, corresponding to globalisation). The stages, which produce a teleological schema of development akin to that of Western modernity, are roughly followed in what I discuss below, but with an emphasis on unities and ruptures between social and cultural (art)forms, because my focus is primarily aesthetic. On this, we may note that contemporary clashes between notions of 'heritage' as Japanese national property on the one hand, and individual freedom and autonomy on the other, reflected divides between public and private realms early on, so any study of nationalism or national identity may be regarded as a taboo because of its alleged anti-globalising ethos. Stranded between public and private realms, the Japanese individual engages in endless dramatisations of this conflict that often recycle this four-stage movement in popular culture.

Studies of nation-formation prove of use here, because folk and popular imaginations continue to be informed by linguistic modality (Smith, 1999). Tze-Yue (2010) provides several observations on the role of language – what I consider more appropriately as the *cultural conditioning of articulation* (Tzanelli, 2015a, Chapters 1, 2; see also Anderson, 2006) – in the development of Japanese indigenous art and culture through time. For her, the issue lies with representation and the immediacy of communication, which for Japan would rest on the hierarchical qualification of mind, soul and body. Following Kristeva's (1984) understanding of holistic subjective social articulation, Tze-Yue notes that the modern linguistic revolution in Japan reduced bodily functions, rhythms and energies to the semiotic realm, when they should function as inseparable from subjectivity. Her observations mirror the conundrums of identity produced by Afro-Brazilian encounter with Western European modes of being and knowing (Tzanelli, 2015c), which we can also detect in other colonial contexts (on African cultures see Tzanelli, 2016b).

Because Tze-Yue concentrates on a visual medium (*anime*), she turns to Merleau-Ponty's other-than-linguistic – but still visual – forms of communication, such as painting. Significantly, she singles out Merleau-Ponty's discussion of the prevalence of silence in pictorial art as a sign leading us back to 'the vague life of colours' (1964, p. 45): as an act, *to not speak* leaves several possibilities of interpretation open, only if one does not know where to look and what to interpret. Merleau-Ponty's observation certainly connects to Mannheim's preoccupation with the interpretative connection between the whole and the parts as extrinsic or intrinsic properties (Mannheim, [1922–24] 1980; Longhurst, 1989). Through elaborations based on various other thinkers she concludes that, especially in a Japanese indigenous thought filtered through Chinese Zen-Buddhist cosmology, the oblique aspects of language are brought to the fore in particular artistic performances, in what she recognises as *anime's* predecessors: the highly stylised *nō* theatre and the Japanese puppet theatre (*bunraku*). Past Tze-Yue's analysis, one may note that what binds animate and inanimate performance in theatre is the knowing unnaturalness of movement, which is based on the non-realist, religious epistemology of both aforementioned art-forms. In agreement with Tze-Yue (2010, p. 100), one may note that the stiffness and slowness of movement in *nō* and *bunraku,* as well as their emphasis on non-representation (the 'innate psychological state of character' (ibid.)), outline East Asian theatrical stylists as the seemingly inactive art of *ma* – the very 'science of time and space' (ibid., 34) guiding late twentieth-century *anime* storytelling in the established Japanese film industry. In conclusion, two of Japan's ancient theatrical traditions to which we trace the origins of *manga-anime* are conspicuous manifestations of the inner Japanese Self or *honne* (Napier, 2007).

At this point, one may build a bridge between the country's artistic-cosmological and socio-political rhythms to access the formation of a recognisable Japanese geopolitical vision. Building a bridge is important, because of strategic continuities and evident ruptures: if *nō* and *bunraku* are now seen as 'heritage arts', the country's safeguarding or expulsion of religious forms is part of an ongoing search for a coherent national Self. *Anime's* emphasis on the silent breath and inner state of the protagonist, which punctuates emotion, follows in the steps of Japanese twentieth-century history, which, as is the case with most of its post-Meiji Restoration (1880s) experience, is marked by technological experimentation and an accompanying military propaganda, always endorsed from 'outside' (Europe, the US) (Dower, 1999; Allison, 2004). It is not surprising that *anime* was integrated into Japan's rising urban cultural industries after the Second World War, when the genre had to cope with imposed pressures to expand economically while ameliorating ideological edges in the country's involvement with imperialism, xenophobia and genocidal nationalism. The way forward was to embrace popular cultural policies siding with the economic gains of the American McWorld (*á la* Barber, 2003, 2010), not to linger on past traumas and traditions. Both as an international political programme and as a travel/touristic style, the Japanese *tatemae* connected to the Western *oeconomie artificialem*, which had mutated as a militourist industry in previously conquered parts of the world. Much like its primordial alter ego that we locate in its Chinese-born cultural/linguistic heritage, the inner artistic Japanese Self (of the exploratory *honne*), would be populated with contradictory and highly creative emotions.

In the political realm, such emotions married with a hunger for international recognition by economic achievement to renegotiate Japan's anti-American spirit of jingoistic nationalism. After the Second World War defeat and the country's serving as a militourist outpost catering for American soldiers' pleasure, a historiographical clash, akin to that of the German *Historikerstreit* (Habermas, 1989a), between scholars reiterating the victimisation of the country in the hands of Western Powers and those condemning the self-denial of its implication in its post-war condition (Goto-Jones, 2009, pp. 80–81), led to further national demoralisation. The defeat and humiliation Japan experienced in the hands of American policy-makers after the war gave rise to *Nihonjinron* (cultural nationalism), which negotiated the ideology of *wakon yōsai* (Japanese spirit and Western technology). An essentialised assumption that the Japanese people are both culturally and racially homogeneous, and that the West is corrupt and unworthy of respect, but in possession of technological features with which Japan has to catch up, if not surpass (Sugimoto, 2006, pp. 479–480), merged. After all, Japan's post-war rise was because the country was the greatest beneficiary of American Cold War policy (Iwabuchi, 2008, p. 547). The contradictory ethics of *Nihonjinron*, which were based on the conflict between two imaginary opponents, the 'West' and 'Japan' (Iwabuchi, 1994), had multiple consequences for Japanese culture and society: they honed the nation's competitive capitalist spirit and produced the second greatest world economy, validated the merits of a culture of overwork, but also suggested that, turning one's back on competitors is not a forward-looking attitude (Delanty, 2003). This is the point at which we can locate the rise of the individual Self in Japanese culture, a subjectivised identity that, in the plane of politics, would guide separation from American imperialism, borrowing from American forms and, most significantly, a fusion of regional collaboration with territorial competition.

The rise of the individual Self followed a similar path only up to point. After the end of the Cold War and the collapse of the Eastern Bloc, Japan's accelerated growth began to slow down. In the dawn of the twenty-first century, national commentators started talking about a 'decade of loss' (*ushinawareta jûnen*), and the widening gap between haves and have nots, especially in the country's biggest cities, became more apparent. Pessimism deepened in the country's mediated representations and became more wide-spread in public opinion, where we can now even detect negative conceptions of globalisation (Iwabuchi, 2008, p. 548). Concerted policy responses included processes of city branding and the marketing of new 'cool' Japanese urban cultures to bolster transnational media collaboration (ibid.). At the same time, emphasis on instilling Japanese traditions in schoolchildren and exces-sive celebration of international success in sports completed the institution of a cultural programme of 'banal nationalism' (Billig, 1995). Seeds of this pro-gramme were present in the official recognition of *nisshôki* (Rising Sun Flag) and *kimigayo* (national anthem) in 1999 by Prime Minister Obuchi; former Prime Minister Koizumi's visit to Yakusuni shrine and attempts to reform the 'un-Japanese' Fundamental Law of Education to provide patriotism classes; and Prime Minister Shinzō Abe's involvement in providing historically revi-sionist school textbooks and pushing the revision of Article 9 to legitimate Japanese rearmament (Goto-Jones, 2009, p. 133). The airbrushing of Japanese war atrocities combined with a rise of cultural industries, such as (domestic and international) tourism and film, promises to lift Japan out of its post-war deadlocks and to bring its urban project to a happy conclusion.

And yet, the argument that contemporary Japan has been displaying a schizophrenic attitude of victimisation-with-aggressiveness should be requali-fied: the hard political potential of *ressentiment* as a policy of militarised nationalist domination over rivals, which has led nations to bloodshed in other parts of the world (Greenfeld, 1990, 1992; Tzanelli, 2011), has been calibrated into a soft expansionist policy in Japan, following the rules of cul-tural globalisation (Tomlinson, 2007). This cultural globalising script sticks close to the *oeconomie imaginationis* as a revisionist programme focusing on emotional and aesthetic education. To make it more specific to this analysis: Tokyo's imaginative discourse in the Handover Ceremony both underpins a dream-like, secondary revisionist discourse (see Gourgouris, 1996 on Castor-iadis' notion of the 'radical imaginary') of contemporary Japanese identity and radically revises its historically resentful basis. Such complementary ways of dealing with the past set the artistic Japanese vision apart from other Asian examples. There is no better comparison to trace in the Olympic domain of the arts than that provided by ceremonial performances in Beijing 2008. Narrating Chinese national identity as a 'displaced' agent in the 'birth' and 'evolution' of Western European civilisation, who returns to claim a central place in human history, Beijing 2008's artistic production sketched con-temporary Chinese *honne*-like *ressentiment* towards the West that can 'do' technology better – indeed, has been the global cradle of technologies (Tzanelli, 2010).

Such instances can place art next to technology as a means of violence, even though the former does not supplant the latter's objectives in direct ways. Of course, Tokyo's encounters with the consequences of *oeconomie artificialem* follow international patterns: the city's growing international migrant labour and racial intermarriage (of which it claims the highest percentage in the country) is met with suspicion, bolstering public discourses of securitisation and surveillance. Institutional racism, violently directed especially against Chinese migrants, can be found in the city's administrative top, with Tokyo Governor Ishihara Shintaro making racist comments in 2000 in public (Morris-Suzuki, 2003). Discourses of surveillance also find increasing public support after the infamous sarin gas attack on Tokyo underground by the religious sect *Aum Shinrikyō* (20 March 1995), which killed 12 people and injured more than 12,000 (Sawai, 2013, p. 204; Metraux, 1995; Cameron, 1999). As Ito and Suzuki (2013, pp. 116–117) aptly note, since the sarin attack and the Hanshin-Awaji Earthquake in the 1990s, the realisation that both man-made and environmental risks make Japan a less safe country increased the focus on sub-political action in social movements and volunteering campaigns. Twenty-first century Japan is a textbook case of Beck's (1992) 'risk society', which, in recent years forged a discourse of 'solidarity by anxiety' we recognise even the 2016 Handover's narrative of Japanese culture.

Still, even though Japan had to embrace the artifice of Western technology, the game of global recognition would be won in the domain of *oeconomie imaginationis*. The globalised genre of *manga* and *anime* could allow for profitable *and* healing manipulations of memory, curving sustainable paths to the future (Klein, 2000). The nationalist slogan *kokusaika* (internationalisation) was embraced by the government and Japanese companies alike before in the 1980s, when Japan was recognised as an economically powerful nation-state (Kondo, 1997). As was the case with other parts of the world, policies of internationalisation in the country centred on multi-scalar, post-national urban networking (Harvey, 1989; Hubbard and Hall, 1998; Cochrane, 2011). Today, Japan's main cities act as major financial articulations and creative industrial hubs, despite the post-1980s' burst economic bubble. Cross-border partnerships and cooperation between Japanese cities and non-Western countries are also proliferating among multinational corporations with continuous US intervention. The Americanisation of Japanese *anime* series, such as Pokémon, by USA Nintendo, may be removing their cultural specificity (Iwabuchi, 2004, 2008) but assists in Japanese economic expansion.

Especially for Tokyo, which displayed the highest concentration of creative industries in the country early on, at first Japan's double 'opening up' to US and regional Asian markets seemed to meet primarily the needs of national development (Richards, 2011; Baker and Ruming, 2014; Lederman, 2015). If 'brand nationalism' (Urry, 2003, p. 107) placed Japan in the economic world order, a careful designing of Tokyo's urban branding was absolutely essential in the face of competition with urban heritage spots, such as Kyoto. The capital of temple pilgrimage, Kyoto attracts many tourists every year, but such tourism is overwhelmingly domestic in nature (Graburn, 1983, 2004). To compete with long-standing tourism-pilgrimage trends, Tokyo's experience economy has also embraced the 'serial reproduction' of consumption-led strategies, involving 'landscape cloning' and non-place 'making' (Richards and Wilson, 2006; Smith, 2007; Richards, 2014). But where in other world urban formations 'non-place making' erases entrenched urban landscapes, in Tokyo the rise of the 'Fantasy City' of technological and virtual artifice recalls the production of Japanese rural Arcadias (Hannigan, 2007), as much as it might lead to the 'reduction' of the city's alleged 'urban authenticity' (Hannigan, 1998; Hoffman *et al.*, 2003; Zukin, 2010).

Tokyo brands itself along the lines of the Japanese individual Self, a travelling culture that may borrow from an ancient Kyoto-sponsored pilgrim *honne*, but which nevertheless considers novel, centrifugal (*á la* Cohen (1979)) possibilities. We must look back to Tokyo's indigenous virtual craft to explain this bipolar tendency: the pronounced rejection of Japan's shared linguistic/cultural background with China (both nations are *kanji*: they use Chinese characters) in *anime* seems to conform to Tokyo's cultural rhythms, because it breaks with old traditions of religious travel pilgrimage. Quite apart from that, Tokyo may be attracting domestic pilgrimage tourists, but a growing tourist niche is to be found in truly 'placeless' cinematic hits, such as *Lost in Translation* (2003, dir. Sofia Coppola) filmed there. The Japanese National Tourist Organisation's campaign to bolster international visits to the filmed sites in Tokyo (Iwabuchi, 2008, p. 551) works towards urban image-building, which breaks with tradition and embraces Americanisation with a Japanese twist (the film's treatment of Tokyo as a generic city was widely criticised even as racist). The general regard of Japanese post-war schizophrenia seems to be undergoing a hermeneutic calibration in Tokyo's policies of urban branding, which are more amenable to displays of cultural hybridisation with the erstwhile 'enemy' (Nederveen Pieterse, 2006a).

We may even consider Tokyo's new collective Self as the cultural reflection of so-called 'contents tourism'. Much like the simulatory nature of cinematic tourism in other parts of the world (Tzanelli, 2007, Chapter 3), where movies were filmed and generated tourist performances of cinematic scripts by global fans, 'contents tourism' designates popular cultural simulations of fictional events. Such 'events' may stem from traditional 'scripts' (religious mythological or folkloric), or may be just the 'scripts' of popular literature (*manga* and *anime*, TV and Internet drama) (Nishikawa *et al.*, 2015). Most of such folkloric – soon transformed to post-modern – worldmakings point to popular cults and creative beliefs disseminated on the Internet by Japanese youth cultures, such as those held by young computer 'geeks' (*otaku*). And it is important to note that 'contents tourism' is nothing other than a popular rendition of Japanese post-modern transformationalism in terms of globalisation theory: it renders *otaku* consumer recognition of a double-layer epochal structure, 'clearly distinguish[ing] between *the surface outer layer within which dwell simulacra*, i.e. works, and *the inner deep layer within which dwells the database*, i.e. the settings' (Azuma, 2009, p. 33, emphasis in text).

These tendencies and styles, both policy and popular, appeal to conceptions of cultural borrowing and re-morphing into something new – hence, they resemble what we encountered in Brazilian *anthropofagia*. Tokyo's 'anthropophagic' tendencies can be detected in its erection of post-modern buildings and entertainment parks for the post-tourist gaze (Ritzer and Liska, 1997; Gottdiener, 1997). As others have repeatedly noted (Vattimo, 1988; Nederveen Pieterse, 1998, 2004, 2009; Delanty, 2003), the intimacy and agential flair of Western encounters with other forms of synchronisation informs Asian understanding of cultural adaptation in Japan's case. The city's post-modern architectural morphogenesis presupposes the design of what Urry (2007, p. 266) calls 'place reflexivity', as a 'set of disciplines, procedures and criteria that enable each place to monitor, evaluate and develop its "potential" within the emerging patterns of global travel'. On the one hand, Tokyo's redesign as a global phantasmagoric city invites accusations of 'palimpsestic violence' (Huyssen, 2000, 2003) as the erasure of socio-historical context and the separation of material development from social milieus and everyday practices (Albrow, 1997, pp. 50–54; Dürrschmidt, 1997, pp. 56–58; Iwabuchi, 2008, p. 554; Eade, 2000). On the other, not only does its simulating potential produce and reproduce its global brand as a virtual post-modern metropolis (Sassen and Roost, 1999, p. 143; MacCannell, 2011), it matches the centrifugal cultural spirit of its indigenous *anime* industry (Lury, 2004; Tze-Yue, 2010). These two arguments coexist in the 2016 Handover Ceremony, in which Tokyo's 'digital utopia' can both assert the return to the world of arts and crafts and the rise of sustainable community living in harmony with nature, and point to the dangers of hyper-mobility and the demise of rooted sociality and tradition. The clash is resolved in hard realistic and artistic/ceremonial contexts alike in the face of human-made and natural disasters that afflicted Japan in the present century: the Great East Japan Earthquake and the ensuing tsunami disaster (Pilling, 2014, pp. 3–15).

Now it becomes more evident why we will not find a response in the 2016 Handover to Tokyo 2020 matching exactly that of Beijing 2008's in London 2012. Though, I argue, the manipulative potential of Western technology as an amnesiac agent (Huyssen, 1995) is present in ways compatible with the global rise of virtual travel utopias, subtle references to Japan's soft cultural policies and a respect towards cultural connectivity in the face of a lingering degrowth, foster a cosmopolitan analytic (Delanty, 2009, 2011). This *selective* cosmopolitan analytic should not be dissociated from the Tokyo 2020 artistic performances' 'submerged urban centre': a polyphonic, multicultural and multi-ethnic Japanese 'nature', which has been under constant homogenising pressure by the state at least since the mid-twentieth century (Siddle, 2008; Fish, 2008). This 'culture' – or rather, *cultures* – does not apply exclusively to new migrations but enmeshes the Japanese city's new youth cultures, which often react to memorial obstinacy with retreat from the commons and travel into their new individualised *honne*. The same culture manifests in transformations in the built environment: it has been noted that the nostalgic search for authentic marginality amongst rural and mountain communities and cultures amidst the country's rush to industrialisation and militarisation (Ivy,

1995; Graburn, 2015) has, more recently, transfigured into the restoration of architectural heritage and the construction of simulacra of European communities for touristic performances, habitation and sustainable development of previously abandoned (after the war) rural areas (Hendry, 2000, p. 19; Favell, 2015a, pp. 150–151).

Akin to nationalist serialisation of indigenous culture and 'way of life', such projects took off in the context of post-Cold War reconstruction of Japanese identity and post-Fordist urban transformation. Such projects often match the 'structurally nostalgic' resurrections of ethno-nationalist habitus and way of living in European post-war contexts (Bauman, 2001; Herzfeld, 2005), with an eye to bolstering creativity at best (Wojan *et al.*, 2007; Bell and Jayne, 2010; Stolarick *et al.*, 2010) and a hint of fascistic ideology at worst. But the fact that the Handover to Tokyo 2020 took place under the auspices of a conservative administration seems to have affected its artistic ceremonial narrative in ambivalent and contradictory ways: the 'on-stage story' ignored both the prospective Japanese host's unquestionable contemporary ethnic diversity and any domestic calls to return to its ostensible roots. As I proceed to explain, the ceremony's *anime-manga* introduction and acrobatic dance routines sustain a centrifugal gaze that moves the city away from 'old' Japan's socio-cultural centre (Cohen, 1979) and into global policy sites of consumption.

Associated with histories of Japanese migration, the effects of rootless travel mobilities and present concerns shared by international polities, such as failing sustainability, Tokyo 2020's programmatic statement focuses on ideas of the neoliberal creative city (Gowan, 2003; Evans and Sewell, 2014). But this creative city image is not necessarily identical to Western ones, in that, at least in 2016 ceremonial artwork, it is based on the exposition of a Japanese subconscious in the country's consciousness – a dream-like process of representation and simulation advanced by filmmaking referents (Kashimura, 2013). Salazar (2016, p. 5), who contends that mega-events are major sites and sources of cultural imagination and urban exposure gestures towards this observation but opts for an instrumental analysis of their spectacular economies, as cash-generating machines. Let us follow his rationale for a while: the 'modish' urban imaginary treats Tokyo in a romantic techno-Orientalist manner (Yoshimoto, 1989; Morley and Robbins, 1995; Ueno, 2002) only when it looks to *Japanese* traditions that grant its *anime-manga* framing national historical depth. The post-modern city of Tokyo itself is depicted as a rootless product of globalisation, a receptacle of mobilities of labour, technology, arts and money – representations we could associate with other developed cities (Sassen, 2001) – only for the eyes of less literate visitors. Yet, as I proceed to argue, Tokyo 2020's globetrotting atmosphere of the generic phantasmagoric city and its mediatised cosmopolitan gaze that inspects 'from afar' (Szerszynski and Urry, 2006) is challenged by an inner gaze operating on a cognitive and emotional plane but shared via technology. Non-Japanese Olympic audiences inhabit the non-spaces of Tokyo (for comparisons see

Andranovich's (2016, p. 57) analysis of Los Angeles in the context of post-1984 Olympic development); yet, as is the case with Rio de Janeiro's segmented logic of representation, if their inspecting mode persists, they may find out that Tokyo's concrete reality 'intertwines' and 'tangles' its places of memory (*lieux de memoire* – Nora, 1989) with its proliferating non-places (Augé, 2008, pp. 86–87).

Mergers and clashes between virtual and cinematic technologies of *anime*, with a romantic travel gaze that inspects the city as a repository of ethnic memory produce Tokyo's neoliberal 'techno-romantic spirit' (Coyne, 1999): a spirit akin to that of rooted Japanese national identity, now producing global flows of ideas, products and images (Ueno, 2002). We must be cautious however: Tokyo 2020's technoromanticism appeals, in a peculiar post-Platonic style, to the 'real world', which is for younger generations the world of the digit (akin to Plato's world of Ideas as absolute reality beyond materialism). It is only on this non-material, but thoroughly real for Japanese subjects, plane that, as citizens, they can be whole again, part of a community existing beyond that of the 'nation' as a sort of cosmopolitan *ecstasis* or extension to hyper-reality (see Coyne's (1999, pp. 50–52, pp. 54–55) notion of 'technoromantic holism' and Sawai's (2013, p. 209) analysis of young people's 'romantic cynicism' in Japan as analogous to nationalist obedience). The next Chapter's analysis suggests that we read the Ceremony's 'frames of *anime*' (Tze-Yue, 2010) by placing the Weberian rules of 'elective affinity' (Weber, 1985) in post-religious contexts of global consumption (Campbell, 1987). The expulsion of indigenous art to the semiotic realm (Kristeva, 1984) by Zen-Buddhism, hence Japanese ancient heritage, activated contemporary *anime's* centrifugal movement, first toward secular-nationalist ideologies and later into global creative industrial markets. Where Tokyo 2020's old *honne* displays the properties of resentful creativity in the valorising race to the top of international urban hierarchy, its new individual artistic/crafty Self explores the liberating, utopian possibilities of alternate digital realities.

On the outside, the *tatemae* morphs digital narratives of Tokyo and reveals that the prospective mega-event's worldmaking imperative is to energise global movements of labour, ideas, artefacts and culture (Richards, 2014, p. 133). On the outside, the ceremonial narrative crafts the archetype of the 'romantic tourist', an involved imagineer, activist and world traveller, able to enhance the host city's global profile. This felicitous professional update of the old Grand Tourist as an artistic-cum-bureaucratic explorer of the exotic connects to the beginnings of tourism in the consolidation of tourist spots by artists, scholars, scientists and intellectuals at first, for international elites, before being taken up by popular narratives and can help identify the impact of new players as they progressively enter the tourist scene (Gravari-Barbas and Graburn 2012, p. 4). This 'romantic tourist' transfigures Urry's (2002b) ideal tourist type, but with an intentionality transcending that of personal leisure and even 'tourism' as such. Upon this transcendence, contemporary Tokyo's new individualistic *honne* makes a shy appearance to question the

Ceremony's otherwise exotic atmospherics: the romantic tourist of Tokyo that remembers is in fact the digital bureaucratic worker of a brutal capitalist system born out of Japan's international race to the top. We are back to regimes of governmentality: although contemporary managerial practices seek to assert the workers' subjective freedom, thus 'doing away' with the carceral solitude in which workers would find themselves in factories, they promote a sort of monastic solitude in its place, akin to that of the romantic tourist's individualist ethos. This solitude is disrupted by the romantic tourist/ mega-event worker, through their participation in global networks, but also a more general strategy of 'opening up' to opportunities for connectivity, cooperation and co-creation (Tarde [1899] 2003, p. 199, p. 201). Though a worker, the city's *technoromantic* tourist is also an agent in a position to liberate themselves from this disciplinary apparatus, because of their ability to make new worlds outside work infinitesimally and not exclusively for the benefit of the city-firm (e.g. Lazzarato, 2004). Far from being a successful society of control, Tokyo and Japan as a whole constantly negotiate their relationship with the colonisation of power by money and financial networks, which are implicated in the production of the mega-event in search of self-growth (Dascal, 1987, p. 11). Money may be a force of mind, an infinite virtuality aspiring towards actualisation, but the groups of experts involved in its production and circulation remain responsible for public opinion modulation in virtual and terrestrial spaces.

The directors for the Handover were Hiroshi Sasaki (creative supervisor), Ringo Sheena (creative supervisor and music director), Mikiko Mizuno (choreographer and stage director) and Kaoru Sugano (creative director). Sasaki is known as an innovative artist and director of various events, ranging from the Tokyo International Film Festival to advertising campaigns for leading telecommunication companies and airline industries. His attempt to enlist the support of companies and celebrities to join the reconstruction campaign after the 2011 Great East Japan Earthquake received public attention. Award-winning singer and film and *Kabuki* (Japanese dance drama) songwriter Sheena is known for her theme song for the NHK programmes featuring the 2014 FIFA World Cup. Owner of ELEVENPLAY dance company, Mikiko is a choreographer and stage director for the famous popular group Perfume. She has also choreographed several theatre productions, TV commercials and PR videos and is renowned for her innovative work, in which she tries to incorporate multisensory stimuli. Sugano is an international award-winning creative director in the fields of advertising, design and arts, specialising in technology and expression, who was previously involved in the Tokyo 2020 Olympic bid video presentations and in Bjork's and Eno's video projects (for individual profiles see Tokyo 2020, undated). All four principal directors have a background in art of non-representational nature, which fits Japanese cosmological pasts and international futures of mobility alike (*Advertimes*, 22 August 2016). Much like the Rio 2016 Opening and Closing Ceremonies, the Handover's choreomobile arrangement was managed by a group of imagineers set to narrate the projective host's worlds. Acting as both a 'worlding' statement (Ong, 2011) that places Tokyo amongst other world cities, and a phenomenal composition of new Japanese urban rhythms, the Handover provided glimpses at Tokyo 2020's *oeconomie imaginationis*.

One may argue that the Handover's artistic ceremonial project communicates with Tokyo's 'radical imaginary' (Castoriadis, [1975] 1987) that seeks to expand art as business outside the confines of the nation-state and into an international Olympic event. In this respect, the Handover to Tokyo follows the workings of a conservative 'evotopian' or evolutionary utopian (Hodgson, 1995) composition of ideological (neoliberal) nature (Mannheim, [1929] 1968). This composition translates Japanese 'dark histories' into rootless landscapes, ready to participate in individually tailored journeys. But in phenomenological terms, this practice of 'mind-walking' (Ingold, 2010), the noetic movements the creative artists perform, to follow and construct the meanings of the Ceremony, communicates with the reflexive attitude of the Japanese exploratory tourist (Graburn, 2012). This ideal-typical exploratory subject moves across urban surfaces, while representing them to mega-event visitors, thus inducing pleasure to them. However, upon this transitional communicative phase, the Ceremony crosses the boundary separating ideology from utopia to become integrated into a vision of the future. In this vision, Tokyo – or Japan as its urban synecdoche – overcomes cultural isolation to achieve togetherness in an international community. By following the script of its overwhelmingly popular 'contents tourism', which is also seen as the only way of engaging the young *hikikomori* (self-imposed recluses) with some form of civil society driven by popular cultural interests, the Handover places Tokyo's future world(s) in digital utopian frames. Such fames are based on notions of giving and receiving in communal and universal, transnational frames, with the help of artistic technological creativity. Tokyo 2020's gift to the world is thus not a resentfully displayed spectacle, but an ennobling gesture of connective potential, set to battle dark pasts and create good futures.

7 The Handover Ceremony
Digital gift economies in a global city

In the opening segment, 'Kimigayo', the Japanese national anthem was sung and the flag of Japan was projected onto the Stadium, while another flag was raised on the flagpole. A projected red circle on the Stadium symbolised the Japanese flag's Rising Sun. Twenty performers in white costumes, with illuminated hems, appear in the closing red circle's periphery, moving toward the centre of the stadium as the circle closes to form the *Hinomaru* or Japanese national flag. Inspired by the art of *origami* paper folding, which originates in the Edo period (1603–1867), the robotic performers' costumes included headpieces and corsets handmade by students and volunteers. They ride personal mobility scooters developed in Japan that allow drivers to manipulate movement, by shifting their body's gravity. With intention to transform a flat square sheet of paper into a finished sculpture through folding and sculpting techniques, traditional Japanese *origami* was contrasted with the Chinese craft of *Kirigami*, which involves the use of cuts, glue or markings on the paper. Sculpting and giving shape to things without adhesive materials promotes a naturalist conception of art, untainted by technologies we find in Western thought. Note, however, how the narrative is 'enframed' by Japan's globally mediated national symbol, which confirms the country's association with Western and European political philosophies of nation-building: not only does the national flag emerge as a technologically endorsed 'way of being' in the segment, one of Japan's originary *Téchnes* (the ancient art of making *origami*) literally clothes its subsequent technicity. Technicity refers here to the general properties of technology as human (electronic and material) prosthesis, which is represented by the robots (Gallope, 2011, pp. 48–49; Frabetti, 2011, pp. 14–15). Japan and Tokyo as its synecdoche appear through the technological 'reframing' of *origami* with such an aura of factuality, that they both seem 'uniquely realistic' and unquestionable in their singularity (Geertz, 1973, p. 90). The introduction is nothing short of what media and tourism theorists would associate with a 'mediated centre', a cultural core irreducible to its individual properties and standing for a coherent identity (Cohen, 1979; Couldry, 2003).

This gesture towards tradition is, however, immediately replaced by one towards modernity and contemporary world cultures. 'Arigato from Japan' produces concentric ripples to reach distant centres of governance and disaster management, with a performance featuring young people in formations spelling a message of gratitude in Japanese and other languages. The performance included a total of 10,000 students from three prefectures (Iwate, Miyagi and Fukushima), as well as schools from Tokyo conducting Olympic and Paralympic educational initiatives towards 2020. It also featured an onstage projected presentation of human formations of the word to signify gratitude for the support Japan received for the Great East Japan Earthquake; the hospitality received by Japanese athletes, artists and others during the Rio 2016 Summer Olympics; and Tokyo's selection to host the next mega-event in 2020 (*Advertimes*, 22 August 2016). The makers of the Ceremonial Handover noted that the Japanese *Arigato* and its Brazilian equivalent, *obrigado*, are syntactically similar – 'somewhat uncanny, as Rio and Tokyo are cities on the opposite sides of the globe' (Tokyo 2020, undated). Perhaps the geographical commentary stood for more than physical distance, given the two cities' contrasting economic position on global urban scales; in any case, both words' root is traced in Portuguese, therefore in the past colonial mobilities the two cities share.

This shared transmodern articulation of historical fragments that, in Tokyo's case, 'piece together' belonging in a greater-than-the-national whole, points to the Japanese notion of *kyosei* (cosmopolitanism) – the Western and European equivalent of participation in a global community, while recognising difference (Sugimoto, 2012; Delanty, 2014). We could identify intentionality in this display of *Kyosei* in the ways it connects compassion (intimate, localised and immediate) to the global politics of pity (disembedded, distant and globalised) (Arendt, 1963; Boltanski, 1999). In any case, we deal with a specific artistic – but centrally endorsed – interpretation of *dépense* as a way to humanise loss and ritualise excess waste (Romano, 2015, p. 87). The segment equalises humanitarian support as gift-giving with an expressive ritual of gratitude: *Shishutsu* (支出), as cost and as disbursement, suggests a process of (re)distribution, a transnational cultural *potlach* through which the social regenerates beyond national borders (Mauss, 1954; Bataille, [1949] 1988). It is the human-made (by educated young generations) *Arigato*, Japan's future community, that delivers the message of hope – a community that remembers to pay its debts.

The Handover's visualisation and musicalisation of gratitude point to 'articulation' as multisensory, cross-cultural communication, but again with the help of varieties of (bodily, digital and cinematic) technology (Tzanelli, 2015a, p. xx, pp. 30–31). The segment's musical presentation ('Anthem Outro'), was arranged by award-nominated film music composer Jun Miyake (born 1958, Kyoto). Known for his ability to fuse seemingly disparate elements in his compositions, Miyake represents new Japan's cultural hybridity. Notably, the prominence of cultural work in his musical arrangement for the Handover 'fades out' together with the image of the flag on the Stadium to thank those who aided the country during the 2011 Tōhoku earthquake and tsunami. This musical worldmaking (Straw's (1991) original rendition of 'articulation') reminds us that, as much as world cities are 'products of voyages and circulation of daily movements', their audio-visual articulations can always invoke nostalgia for solidarity, belonging or safety – the 'things' that 'glue' together humans in utopian scenarios (Samuels *et al.*, 2010, p. 336; Gray, 2007; Sakakeeny, 2010). One may even argue that the Handover's solidary performance attends to the trauma inflicted onto the collective Japanese psyche by modernity and individualisation as alienation from communal support (see Ito and Suzuki, 2013, pp. 128–129 on Japanese individualisation as the coming of Beck's 'second modernity').

Miyaki's nomination for his composition for *Pina* (dir. Tim Wenders), a 2011 German 3D surreal documentary film about the contemporary dance choreographer Pina Bausch (IMDB, 2016) that premiered out of competition at the 61st Berlin International Film Festival, fits into the Ceremony's transitional narrative. The cinematic spectacle's display of 'bodies in motion' on set-pieces, bracketed by solo and duo performances set in the wilds of the cityscape, articulates the 'episodic' nature of the ceremonial fragment as an ethno-national *bricolage* embedded in a global city. If we consider this *bricolage* as constitutive of the interstitial emergence of the city in global capitalist networks only (Sassen, 2001, 2006; Soja, 2008), then we may miss the discursive excess of its fabulist aspects. Far from merely rendering spatialised urban narratives to a 'fable' (Soja, 2006, pp. xvi–xvii) for commoditisation purposes, the *bricolage* operates as a way to reinterpret heritage in Tokyo's represented built environment. In fact, the way in which this segment links to the introduction of the 2020 sports programme in 'Tokyo is Warming Up' is an exercise in urban *flânerie*, in which common people and athletes both gaze (at Japanese landscapes) and are gazed upon (as objects integrated in Japanese landscapes). The presentation of an 'active' Tokyo is not unique in the Olympic chronicles, if we consider Los Angeles' 'framing' of sports and youth as an Olympic gift to Californian culture (Andranovich, 2016, pp. 62–63)

The 'neat and streamlined' form of Tokyo supported by the Handover's directors (see Tokyo 2020, undated) obeys specific morphogenetic principles. These principles re-implant the ceremonial gaze into urban atmospheres that we associate with mega-event tourism (Getz, 2008). In the first few seconds of the segment 'Tokyo is Warming Up', we are raced through long shots of the city at night and its busy streets during the morning rush hours. A young athletic *flâneuse* akin to Rio's beautiful *Melindrosa* opens the sequence in acrobatic spins and contemporary music outside Shibuya Station. Shibuya is a district where Japanese teenagers 'like to parade their fashions' (Pilling, 2014, p. 188), so the young *flâneuse*'s presence is meant to communicate the city's subcultural streaming into 'micro-masses' connected to office environments. The flexible *moga*, as the contemporary Japanese *Melindrosa* is called, stands for a whole feminised culture on the basis of consumerist excess and identity-building on accumulation of stylised haircuts, expensive, especially European clothing and profitable dating with older men (Goto-Jones, 2009,

p. 118). It is as if we meet in this persona *malandro's* feminine counterpart: a calculative tour guide ready to relieve foreign onlookers (mega-event tourists) of their wallets (Iwabuchi, 2002). Notably, the female acrobat conforms to *anime* aesthetics and their sexualisation in Japanese sociospheres: the *moga's* adolescent appearance and school-like uniform appeals to a variety of home and international audiences, including male *Otaku* and middle-aged men. Her sharp look and fast bodily *Hexis* counter the cultures of Japanese self-control we associate with 'gentle relations', a technique of expression celebrating intersubjective identity-making and social sensitivity towards the other (Katagiri, 2013, pp. 154–156). In fact, given the omnipresence of *Moe* (burning passion, affection) in the assessment of female *Anime* personas as fixation upon a particular character feature (e.g. glasses, clothing, etc. – see Miho, 2015, p. 122), it may not be incorrect to associate digital projections of femininity with commodity fetishism in Japanese globalisation contexts. The segment's *moga* herself is, therefore, a peculiar post-feminist character not averse to subordination as role-playing, while embracing individualism and choice as empowering tools (Dales and Bulbeck, 2013, pp. 159–160) – all performances traditionally attributed to middle-class white men (Newmahr, 2011, p. 684, p. 690; Laurendeau and Shahara, 2008). This is Tokyo's and urban Japan's definition of an emerging aesthetic of 'hipster cool', which can also stand for a universal example of urban shabby *chic* (Dávila, 2012, p. 136; Lederman, 2015, pp. 49–51).

The *moga's* acrobatics commence in Shibuya's so-called 'Scramble Crossing', where various intersections meet and which people use as a meeting point. One of Tokyo's significant landmarks, the Crossing has featured in movies and television shows, which take place in Tokyo, such as *Lost in Translation* (2003, dir. Sofia Coppola), *The Fast and the Furious: Tokyo Drift* (2006, dir. Justin Lin), *Resident Evil: Afterlife* (2010, dir. Paul W.S. Anderson) and *Retribution* (2012, dir. Paul W.S. Anderson), as well as on domestic and international news broadcasts (Glionna, 23 May 2011). Audiences are provided with a 'taster' of the city's cinematic tourist landmarks, allowing space for 'creative performativity' in which, although the overall event (the movie's episode) is staged, its unfolding as tourism 'is entirely immanent, and resistant to representational signification' (Cloke, 2006, p. 105). Although most cinematic or film tourism commences as a visitation of filmed sites (Hudson and Ritchie, 2006; Macionis and Sparks, 2009; Beeton, 2006, 2010; Croy, 2010), the unique experiential connection – the visitor's 'living in the moment' – evades representation by the tourist industry as such (Thrift, 2007). Shibuya is an example of the symbolic economy of the spectacle, 'a "cultural" space connecting tourism, consumption and style of life' (Zukin, 1995, p. 83; Richards, 2011, p. 1229), but its meaning is left open to global audiences touring the 'site' with *moga's* help.

Athletes appear to perform their athletic craft over Tokyo's landmarks, with their dark histories overlaid by tourismification: Tokyo Station is a hypermobile urban spot, also associated with two assassination attempts on

Japanese prime ministers. In 1921, Takashi Hara was stabbed to death by an ultra-rightist in front of the south wing as he arrived to board a train for Kyoto, and in 1930 Osachi Hamaguchi was shot in the same spot by a rightist (Goto-Jones, 2009, p. 77). Against such unpleasant memories, Tokyo's presentation of creative 'hotspots' is organised around ethnic enclaves (Shaw, 2007) and creative precincts (Hee *et al.*, 2009) in brightest colours, with great success. Asakusa, another mediated landmark in the segment, is an ancient entertainment district (an old *Geisha* area) from the Edo period, which is famous for the *Sensō-ji*, a Buddhist temple snuggling amongst other temples, the oldest amusement park in Japan (*Hanayashiki*), its catering for older Japanese film tourists and its frequent *Matsuri* (*Shinto* festivals). The area also hosts the annual Brazilian samba festival and boasts significant Brazilian presence in the local community as the base of the Association of Samba Schools of Asakusa (UnmissableJAPAN.com, undated). As another ceremonial highlight, the Odaiba area, which features an artificial island and will host some sports in 2020 across the Rainbow Bridge from central Tokyo, originates in the construction of six island fortresses in 1853 by Egawa Hidetatsu for the Tokugawa shogunate in order to protect Edo from attack by sea. The primary threat in Odaiba (*Daiba*: cannon batteries placed on the islands) was Commodore Matthew Perry's Black Ships, the arrival of which would alter Japanese history and set the country on a course to modernisation (Gluck, 1985; Wilson, 1992). The area's rejuvenation in the 1990s is connected to its redevelopment as a tourist and leisure zone, with several large hotels and shopping malls. This was assisted by the improvement of transportation links in the first decade of the twentieth-first century, which allowed several large companies, including Fuji Television, to move their headquarters to the island. The island is, therefore, a relic of the country's old imported militourist logic, now integrated into the forthcoming mega-event's *oeconomie artificialem*, but with a calculative touch of imagination.

All in all, we can conclude that Tokyo 2020's introduction to the festive city, which 'Loves Sport', as a large banner declares in the segment's video presentation, embraces compassion, surveillance, control and entertainment, all at once. Where Urry (2007, p. 57) identifies four modes of mobility (*flânerie*, tourist consumerism, connoisseurship and virtual commercial travel), we could add a fifth, based on the gaze of pity, the *distant looking into* disaster zones (Boltanski, 1999). But instead of setting this gaze against the other four, we can place all of them in several possible combinations, making room in clearly identifiable heritage landscapes, now replete with affect. Such interweaving of urban rhythms produces urban ecologies not as fixed systems but as relational creations in constant flux. Tokyo as an urban form has always been lodged between these apparently opposing types of mobile constellations (Cresswell, 2001) – one centring on self-gratification and carefree enjoyment, the other on responsibility and self-control – because of its turbulent movement through time. The tourist landmarks of the segment have also been terrorist hotspots and wartime stations, thus intertwining in the biographies of the city life and death. The spokespersons of Tokyo 2020's *oeconomie imaginationis* silence death in favour of pleasure and consumption, thus replicating what Reijnders (2009) saw as the transformation of guilty landscapes (concentration camps and murder locations) into thanatourist destinations.

In the segment, athletes pass a red ball (a symbol of the relay from Rio to Tokyo) between them. Popular *anime* and *manga* characters Captain Tsubasa, Doraemon, Pac-Man, Hello Kitty and Super Mario also participate in this game of fast transfer. The cultural 'odorlessness' (Iwabuchi, 2002, p. 27) of the fictional characters, their *mukokusei* (lacking clearly identifiable Japanese national, racial, or ethic markers – Brown, 2005, p. 7) is thus complemented with a strong ethno-national statement made by the featured Japanese athletes. The two groups of game participants work towards creative combinations of a profitable fictional world, a 'fantasyscape' or 'alternate reality' (Napier, 2005, p. 293) of globalisation *and* an ethnically original life-world, that of civic participation and nationalisation (Smith, 1995). At the same time, the 'biographical life' (Arendt, 1958) of Japanese athletes, their participation in Olympic cosmopolitanism, hints at a raging debate in *anime* Japanese science fiction on the 'creolisation' of Japanese subjectivity (Tatsumi, 2007, p. 256) that allows for globalism to be imagined 'as multi-odoured and decentered from bounded spaces' (Allison, 2008, p. 110; Azuma, 2009). Ultimately, the 'many faces *of anime*' (Fennell *et al.*, 2012, p. 443) appeal to reflect the contemporary decentred cultures of urban Japan, in which young populations seek ways to enjoy alternate forms of leisure, not dictated by rigid tradition and nationalist heritage.

The ceremonial segment is also representative of the alternative cinematic tourists of the mind (those 'travelling the interior' (*Naimen*), where reality is projected – Muro 1974 in Graburn, 2012, p. 56): the *Otaku* young men, stereotyped as obsessively interested in particular topics, frequently 'anti-social' in habits and engaging in activities including computer games, *anime* or *manga* they collect in vast numbers or in 'cosplay' reconstructions of their favourite characters (Goto-Jones, 2009, pp. 118–119). Drawing on Kojéve's reading of Hegelian 'phenomenology of spirit', Azuma (2009) sees in the rise of the *otaku* cult the collapse of Japanese culture into a sort of pointless animalism, a non-aspirational economy pronouncing the 'end of history' in the neoliberal era of consumerism (Fukuyama, 1992). Although this trend connects to the *Bundan* (loose groups) of early twentieth-century writers, who consciously sought to separate themselves from the Japanese intelligentsia and city life (Graburn, 2012, p. 64), the emergence of a *Hikikomori* ('acute social withdrawal') generation in the 1990s (male adolescents refusing to leave their bedrooms, failing to update their education or attract girls and even beating up their parents) coincided with the *Otaku* phenomenon.

Yet, we may even recognise in the *Otaku* Bauman's (1996) pilgrim as a rootless individual, always on the move, and always hungry for meaning-making. The *Otaku* phenomenon can also be considered as an alternative to the 'grown-up' Japanese escapism to the countryside, which involves physical mobility. If we consider Maruyama's (Katagiri, 2013, pp. 142–145) notion of 'individualisation', we could respectively identify the two groups as privatised and centrifugal on the one hand, and atomised, centripetal and subordinate to authorities and the cultural centre on the other. Generally, however, the privatised *Otaku* phenomenon may be far from a psychological malaise – as others noted (Furlong, 2008), acute withdrawal often represents an anomic response to a situation, where tradition no longer provides adequate clues to appropriate behaviour. Hence, the *Otaku Hikikomori* youth bears the potential to turn into an anomic tourist neo-tribe (Maffesoli, 1996), with an interest in Japanese commons and future life-worlds (on tourism and anomie as social facts see Dann, 1977, 2002; on Maruyama's self-governing democratisation as 'individualisation' see Katagiri, 2013, p. 144, p. 149). As a popular subculture that has been growing since the 1970s to become a buoyant market in the 2000s, it is the equivalent of Brazilian literary and musical anarchism that informed Rio 2016's Opening and Closing Ceremonies. Making their cultural mark through engagement with 'girl's novels', and displaying all the characteristics associated with *manga* sentimentalism – something that has also grown into a cult in the anti-war *anime* creations of Miyazake (Tze-Yue, 2010, pp. 129–132) – the *Otaku* subculture forms a synecdoche with the very soft entrepreneurial atmosphere of contemporary Japanese identity and travel subjectivities. The 'softness' and 'gentleness' of such cultural archetypes, which allegedly promoted digital remoteness, given *Otaku* techno-philia, is, in fact, on a par with what Asano (2013, pp. 190–192) sees in *Wangiri* (the practice of one ring on the mobile, followed by hanging up/cut, to signal connectivity), as 'full-time intimate community'. Against the critical tone of older generations in Japan, at least *manga*'s professionalised inward-looking 'form' is also selectively extrovert and intersubjective, therefore homologous to the so-called '*Haiku* travel', a purposive internal movement across the surface of a geographic interior (*Naimen*) that can expose one's 'bare self' (*Honne*) (Graburn, 2012, p. 65).

The ceremony's *anime* frame is simultaneously internal and external to Japanese self-narration, enabling a particular form of animation, and maintaining a unique relationship with realism and filmic space. Where live action cinema is characterised by movement into depth, *anime* uses 'multipanel animation'. The difference between the two techniques is phenomenally homologous to the difference between European understandings of technology and travel as organised physical mobility across time and space (Lash and Urry, 1994; Urry, 2002) and Japanese notions of popular cultural or pilgrimage travel of one's inner surface beyond set temporal limits. *Anime*'s multipanel animation is based on flat layers that account for 'depth' (akin to the aforementioned '*Haiku* travel'): each of them 'reveals' a reality, which is succeeded by another one, lying at the bottom of the pile (LaMarre, 2009). Hence, the exploratory travel into Japanese urban spaces in the segment is deceptively conventional, where *anime* sequences are involved: proof of this is Doraemon's collaboration with Super Mario to drill a 'hole in the ground' that cuts time

travel from Tokyo to Rio short, and delivers Abe/Super Mario on the ceremonial stage. This 'animatic' form of mobility that defies temporal laws,
allows the spectator (the mega-event's 'cinematic tourist') to inspect the ceremonial presentation's series of panels as 'picture postcards' of Tokyo (Foltete
and Litot, 2015), before the end of the segment – a neat transition from
indigenous to global technics in a very short amount of time. At the same
time, it suggests that *anime* may not be adhering to a mono-logical production of reality (that of national identity, for example) but is inherently *irreal*: it
can accommodate conflicting truths and bring them in unison in statements
corresponding with one of many possible worlds (Goodman, 1978, pp. 109–116;
Goodman, 1984, pp. 30–44). *Anime* is a worldmaking tool befit for a globally
broadcast Ceremony.

It has been suggested that Japanese *anime* and *manga* products enclose
Japan as a 'signifier' for a particular 'fantasy-ware' reproduced from other
countries (Allison, 2008, p. 107). If so, Abe/Super Mario is far from an
odourless statement – on the contrary, he is an elaboration of the country's
'soft power' that, free of physical violence, can spread beyond military borders (Nye, 2004, 2008). Tokyo/Japan's soft power is mediated in the segment
through a subtle reference to the fast everyday rhythms surrounding cultures
of work, including long-distance commuting (Edensor, 2011, 2014). But there
is also an 'infrapolitical' flair in Abe's appearance in the show, hard to miss:
not only does the segment's *anime* 'comedy travel' allow Japanese subjects to
ridicule both themselves and the state in a theatrical reversal of roles
(Findlen, 1998, p. 249; Herzfeld, 2005, p. 14), it successfully frames civil
society, by enabling reconstructions of situated sociality in global spaces of
communication. Such uses of political ridicule emerge in situations of vulnerability to allow afflicted subjects to 'blow off' some steam in safe ways (Obadare,
2009). In the chaotic urban spaces of Tokyo, only simulacra of sociality can
retrieve notions of communal belonging. Here *Otaku* rituals of cosplay and
purposive inner travel acquire a new dimension, as mediators of political
and social role-playing people cannot enact in real spaces of interaction. The
carnivalesque atmospherics of Abe's 'travel' in Mario's green tube and pop-
ping out in the centre of Maracanã's stage reveal – that is, *expose* – Japan's
ontological-political centre as mere human 'stuff' that our *Honne* selves share
in a silently agreed social contract (Žižek, 1999). Abe's appearance in the
Ceremony is an extraordinary activity. Ceremonially, it had a precedent in
London 2012, with Queen Elizabeth II's interaction with a quintessentially
British fictional hero, James Bond, and her alleged parachuting from a
helicopter into the Stadium (Tzanelli, 2013b, pp. 52–53).

Infrapolitical statements also enclose realities, as is the case with Abe's
contents tourism on the ceremonial screen. The horrific reality hidden in
Abe's performance rests with Japanese work cultures. His *anime*-cinematic
and finally on-stage appearance as a stressed businessman, jumping from cars
into airplanes to meet deadlines, are unambiguous references to one of post-
war Japan's most enduring social ailments: *Karōshi* or death by overwork.

Invented as a term in the late 1970s to describe the increasing number of people in their prime years suffering from fatal strokes, heart attacks and mental health illness attributed to overwork, *karōshi* would evolve into an acute social problem in the late-1980s Bubble Economy. Japan's global economic ascendance after the Second World War defeat and capitulation to US economic styles acted as a compensatory mechanism for an 'emasculated' nation increasingly calling for a return to traditions associated with right-wing politics (Goto-Jones, 2009, p. 117). Super Mario seems in this comic depiction of a very black reality to be the narrator of a contemporary evolutionary utopian fable. Forged on the super-fast mould of American work structures, Japan's post-war cultural dream hides the depletion of mixed and informal economies by corporate ethics from the public gaze (on 'evotopia' see Hodgson, 1995). The connection of America's new corporate 'MacWorlds' to Japan's contemporary social pathologies is, in fact, exemplified by the elevation of actual suicide sites in Japan into tourist attractions. Their capital value hinges on their simulation potential, as is the case with similar spots across Europe and the USA that 'milk the macabre' (Dann, 1998, p. 15; Rojek, 1993). The phenomenon is not far from the conundrum of kitschification of memory and tragedy in safe ways, invoking melancholia (Sharpley and Stone, 2009; Stone, 2013a, 2013b). Comparable to the notion of the *memento mori* of European Romanticism, the Japanese novelists' popularisation of death as a beautiful, if terminal experience, finds new fertile ground in the connection of *karōshi* cultures of work to death-sites. For example, the Tōjinbō Cliffs, which were popularised by famous writers such as Takami Jun, Kyoshi Takahama and Toyoko Kamsaki, became popular suicide spots and the locus of a dark tourist industry, which today entertains popularity mostly amongst domestic tourists (Boomachine, 6 March 2013; Mauger *et al.*, 2016).

The association of places of death with celebrity has been discussed by scholars in relation to travel motives and the perceived value of the 'dark spot' (Rojek, 1993; Lee *et al.*, 2008; Lundberg and Lexhagen, 2012). But if such sites can be potentially performed to 'recreate a sense of historical reality' (Rojek, 1993, p. 147), they can also be re-staged within ceremonial allusions of a moribund nature (on tourist performances see Bærenholdt *et al.*, 2004). On the ceremonial stage, the working *karōjisatsu* man, who is prone to commit suicide because of mental stress, is taken through two processes: first, as a celebrity joke, Super Mario/Abe becomes integrated into capitalist somnambulism (Castoriadis, [1975] 1987) as a thana-capitalist spectacle himself (Korstanje, 2016b). The second process communicates with a national mythopoetics, whereby Mario/Abe as a man, who looks after the enlarged Japanese national family, simply tends to his masculine responsibilities. The gendering of responsibility in Japanese culture and its social consequences, including long-hour work and illness (Dasgupta, 2005), recasts the traditional Western 'heterosexual matrix' as an inviolable ethno-national norm in performative ways (Butler, 2007). This engenders understandings of the 'edge' in Japanese edgework, while also associating hegemonic notions of gender identity with particular spaces of the city as a lively financescape (Olstead, 2011, p. 89–90). Hence, the ceremonial stage activates multiple strategic mergers of *tatemae* with *honne* to simultaneously satisfy the more ignorant foreign gaze and the domestic public gaze that is constantly monitoring the politician's behaviour (known as *Seken*).

Urry *et al.* (2016) elaborate through the work of Böhme (1993) and others on the ways 'the generability of atmospheres' helps in staging work: 'commodities, politics, firms, and entire cities are staged. The self-staging of people is also an essential aspect of the everyday world' (Löw, 2008, p. 45 in Urry *et al.* 2016, p. 18). Abe as the stage's respectable *Homo Mobilis* almost inevitably invites connections in the minds of the Japanese public with the figure of the businessman-salaryman, the most frequent *karōshi* victim because of his after-hours work-related socialising and the drinking parties (*Nomikai*) he attends to network within and without the company (Hiyama and Yoshihara, 2008). The demand for 'networking' with powerful officials and bosses is shared with other Asian cultures, such as the Chinese, in which building up one's 'social capital' has produced, in more recent decades, *Karōshi*'s Chinese sibling: *ghuolaosi* (Osburg, 2013). With statistical publications by the Japanese Ministry of Labour from 1987 and comparable International Labour Organization (ILO) monitoring, *karōshi* triggered the 'freeter' movement among younger generations in Japan, which involves trying out different jobs and part-time employment, so as to decide on their own potential (Dasgupta, 2005, p. 171). Abe's professional cinematic profile is, however, very different to this reaction, hinting at dissonance and an artistic critique of Japan's 'canonical generation' (Ben Ze'ev and Lomsky-Feder, 2009). Thus, the segment acts as a speculum pushed into Japan's national/cultural body, to diagnose problems of fixity on bad pasts (for cross-cultural comparisons see Tzanelli, 2011). Accounting for contemporary Japan's 'social morphogenesis' (younger generations using structured power to overcome its traps) and potential 'morphostasis' ('freeters' embracing canonical values or pushed into overwork) (Zeuner, 1999, p. 80), the segment allows audiences to envisage escapes from reality while reality is shaped before their eyes in utopian or dystopian (*anime*) terms (Naylor and Helford, 2014). The overall story outlines a post-growth artistic imaginary: it performatively interrogates the nature of potential agents in Japanese social transformations, as well as the elements (work-share, work reduction and leisure) the agents utilise in their revolution (labour flows). Super Mario's story is nothing short of a dip into Japan's bio-economic rhythms to investigate its problematic societal metabolism (Şorman, 2015, p. 42).

Problematisations of Japan's social metabolism do not harm cultural communication in the segment, on the contrary, they adhere to a cosmopolitan imaginary that 'does not devalue the other culture as "inferior" or "less developed"' (Iwabuchi, 2008, p. 546). Rather, a spatialised difference is explicated by situating two or more cultural interlocutors in the Stadium 'on the same temporal level in the late modern capitalist world' (ibid.) If the Super

Mario/Abe segment is so transparent, it is because many from the audience can share the event of the worker's death in silence (see Cohnitz and Rossberg (2016) on Goodman's 'mereology'). Yet, as explained above, *anime*'s irrealist position allows the narrative to assume different, even conflicting vantage points. This is why Abe the romantic tourist-bureaucrat effortlessly gives way in the ceremony to a *bricolage* staging the nation for global audiences. As contemporary notions of structured work time give way to an undefined temporal development of Japanese *Ethnies*, the Olympic consumer can relax and enjoy again – for, if the following dance and performance routines achieve something, it is more towards the production of affective atmospheres within spaces, an 'organization of distraction … [to] reinscribe pleasure and desire in the urban project' (Lloyd, 2003, p. 94).

'Sport Technology' does precisely that: through animated projection of movements and images representing 33 sports and 50 dancers in the field, it narrates developments in sport selection in the Olympic Games. Japanese augmented reality technology makes athletes swoop down through the air in a presentation of individual sports by techniques of zooming in and out of focus, field rotating and planar shooting. It is as if the mega-event's cinematic viewer has assumed the technological position of a camera dolly, moving around the field to provide different angles of vision. Tze-Yue (2010, pp. 99–100) makes some interesting observations on the stiff movement of *anime* characters as derivative of *Nō* and *Kyōgen* stage-acting (*Nōgaku*). This stiffness, which corresponds to the two genres' stylised performance to reflect the character's inner psychological state, is evident in the slow and elaborate movement of the animated athletes of the segment. The presentation's austere tone clashes with the slapstick humour of the previous section, which came closer to the so-called *manga eiga*, a popular comics-influenced cinematic genre commonly used in advertising. Unlike this 'foreign' product, the presentation of sports comes closer to the Chinese-influenced stylistics of art film (*kaiga eiga*) (ibid., p. 102), suggesting the forthcoming Olympics will be a fully Japanese experience, with heritage stylistics. Yet, such stylistics are replete with global communicative potential in a tourist-like fashion, if we consider that *manga-anime* also connects to the contemporary wandering street artists of the *Shōwa* era, who would create stories with picture-cards in open-air theatres for the country's proto-tourists (Tsurumi, 1987, p. 33).

The pace picks up with acrobatics and dancing by a group of Aomori University gymnasts, who move around, through and in between illuminated frames. Aomori's four-time award-winning team of rhythmic gymnasts at the All-Japan National Championship, in which the competitors include corporate teams, connects to the birth of Japanese male rhythmic gymnastics sixty years ago through combinations of elements of gymnastic traditions from Sweden, Denmark and Germany (Otake, 17 August 2013). Sponsored and produced by renowned fashion designer Issey Miyake, and working with US-based choreographer Daniel Ezralow for the Opening Ceremony of the 2014 Sochi Winter Olympics, the Tōhoku Aomori team achieved international recognition. The professionalisation of this once female-dominated sport for men in a region bleeding in human populations to other parts of the country, is already a developmental initiative: the team now participates, like most artistic and athletic groups, around the world, but especially in European events, where male rhythmic gymnastics is an established sport. Miyake, who says his thoughts have been with the Tōhoku region, following the Great East Japan Earthquake, saw in 2013 in the vibrant young athletes 'a ray of hope for the future emanating from Aomori' (Nippon.com, 23 October 2013). Aomori's ceremonial performance, which foretold Japan's gold medal in artistic gymnastics at the Rio 2016 Olympics (Mirás, 8 August 2016), took place on a stage and the Stadium's screens, onto which audiences saw images of gymnasts at work. Again, therefore, Tokyo 2020's narrative focused on blends of cognitive/emotional technics, technology and embodied *téchne*. Enacted literally (the Stadium was flooded in darkness) and metaphorically (as a cognitive, emotional and physical effort) as a dark journey, the segment allowed for connections between arts and sport (Tzanelli, 2013b).

The return to displays of ethnic uniqueness engineered by the bodies of a dance group, counters the consumerist 'common difference' of transnational image and cultural flows in the city (Wilk, 1995 in Iwabuchi 2008, p. 546). Mikiko's imagineering of the segment also drew on past experience from collaborations with Rizomatiks, a Japanese company dedicated to creating large-scale commercial and artistic projects using both arts and technology. Past uses of drones and projection mapping (otherwise known as 'video mapping' and 'spatial augmented reality'), a technology used to turn objects, often irregularly shaped, into a display surface for video projection (Valentine, 20 May 2014), informed the Ceremony's presentation of sports. For once, the use of militarised technology is placed at the service of art, transforming surveillance tools from *oeconomie artificialem* into creative flows, ready to be streamlined into the *oeconomie imaginationis*. The synecdochical arrangement of human bodies and imaging with music placed all three in the position of 'signs' (*semeia*), available to participate in the articulation of the city and the nation (Tzanelli, 2015a, p. 31). Where the 'Super Mario' narrative physicalised and animated Japan's power at once, the Amori performance reminded viewers of the inherent polygenesis of sociality, which manifests in the form of assemblages or multiple competing social compositions such as those of the mobile artists (Tonkonoff, 2013, p. 277). The overall 'semiotechnological arrangement' (Langlois, 2012), of bodies as 'words' and groups and technologies as 'sentences', symbolised the multiple mobilities enclosed in an Olympic city.

Mobility is part of Tokyo's geographical biography, which effortlessly intertwines an aquatic landscape with liquid post-modern living, as the following segment, 'The City of Waterways', suggests. The city flourished in ancient and modern times thanks to its waterways and rivers, which allowed natural passages for trade and intercultural contact to grow, as was the case with several Mediterranean cities and island civilisations in the past (Braudel,

1996). Another panoramic view of the city at night in deep blue, with Sumida River and the Rainbow Bridge as centrepieces, allows for a second inspection of natural and industrial touristic sites on the stage. The segment presents mobility as Tokyo's 'centre' – not a physical but a cultural and intellectual construct, ordering the place's symbolic values and beliefs, and structuring its activities and roles of persons within networks of local, national and global institutions (Shils, 1975). However, the Bridge and the River's magnificent view and glamourised presence also allude to a significant absence from the Handover's performances, which is automatically spotted only by 'knowing insiders': the *mura* (village), the Japanese equivalent of Brazil's *sertão*. It is estimated that there are between one and three million *Burakumin*, the descendants of a caste-like 'untouchable' class known as *eta* in feudal times (Gordon, 2009, p. 65; Pilling, 2014, p. 49). The idea that Japan is mono-cultural and exclusively middle class, which conforms to the idealised image of the *Nihonjin-ron* literature, erases the presence of ethnic minorities, such as the Okinawans and the Ainu, from the country's ethno-demographic profile (Weiner, ed., 2008; Sugimoto, 2003). Scattered descendants of Ainu hunter-gatherers in the northern part of the island of Hokkaido, who speak a language distinct from the Japanese and are more fair-skinned, still exist, but the state does not recognise them. The 2000 report produced by a Commission on 'Japan's Goals in the 21st Century' under Prime Minister Obuchi, stressed the apparent 'population thinning' dangers of a country that is hostile towards minority cultures and immigration, and promotes homogeneity over egalitarianism and equity (Goto-Jones, 2009, p. 142).

The ceremony's absent *mura* is very present in the nightmares of a society that for some has lost its way to the future. Today Japan's very own symbolic and physical hinterland, which lives in less accessible areas, leaving the great bulk of its population to squeeze in overcrowded urban areas, the *mura* margin is constantly being redeemed in the recreational realm, in such mundane activities as those of fishing, boating, camping and skiing (Graburn, 2015). The exoticisation of minority cultures for recreation is nothing peculiarly Japanese, of course, but a universal occurrence in cultural industries such as film and tourism – and in this respect, not 'advertising' such cultures in a mega-event could also be read as a refusal to objectify them. As part of the 1980s 'Exotic Japan' programme, national automobility systems and travel companies had set to educate urbanites about the nation's wild hinterland (Ivy, 1995), whereas in more recent decades, government programmes consolidated the *Furusato* (old home town) and *Mura Okoshi* (village revitalisation) movements (Graburn, 1995a, 1995b) in the steps of the, familiar by now, Italian *cittaslow*. If such references seem to be irrelevant in the analysis of the Ceremonial Handover, we may just focus on the musical superimposition of nostalgia onto the dark blue cityscape in Maracanã to reconsider: the contrast between the chorus' mourning tone and the moving image's super-fast traffic lights suggests a loss (of nature) one can only retrieve through organised leisure activities, such as mega-event tourism.

But on stage, 'nature' is definitely superseded by 'culture' in the innovative human and technological formations of the next segment, 'The City of Festivals'. Heartbeat-like handclaps open a combination of three dances, *Omotenashi No Mai* (hospitality dance), *Ōendan no Mai* (cheering squad dance, an essential aspect of sports events) and *Arigato no Mai* (thank-you dance), in which performers dressed in colourful stylish costumes alternate between slow and elaborate and fast and flexible moves. Some dancers arrange illuminated frames around a pedestal, on which another group of performers wave 'Tokyo 2020' banners. The frames gather at the centre to form Tokyo 2020's Olympic emblem in 45 rectangular cubes, projected on big screens from above, to symbolise the concept of 'Unity in Diversity' (Tokyo 2020, undated, p. 7). The sequence, which brings together ideas of hospitality, applause and reciprocity, projects 'openness' onto a global, mega-event template (Lashley, 2007; Lashley and Morrison, Eds, 2000). It highlights how the directors exercise an emic reselection and reproduction of narratives from specific cultural cosmologies to 'make' tourism – what Hollinshead (1998) discusses as a spectacular 'fantasmatics'. The colourful costumes and the elaborate dance also hint at a *Kabuki* influence in the segment, which is Mikiko's specialism. *Kabuki* drama, today enlisted as UNESCO-recognised intangible heritage (see UNESCO, 2008), is said to originate in riverside performances of Kyoto prostitutes, but the genre's 'acculturation' into early twentieth-century Japanese mores was seen as an alignment of Japanese with Western codes (Pilling, 2014, pp. 68–69).

Kabuki's meaning ('to lean' or 'to be out of the ordinary'), designated *Kabuki* as an *avant-garde* type of theatre early on – a normative interpretation of extraordinariness, given the genre's connection to sexually suggestive themes and the fact that its performers were exclusively male and often available for prostitution (Louis, 2002). But in a Japan *en route* to modernisation, artistic, theatrical coding communicated with social transformations of intimacy, in recognition of the fact that *honne/tatemae* divides, cannot accommodate liberal freedom. Mannheim's ([1936] 1968, pp. 219–221) elaboration on Chilean hostility towards earthly achievements of a more fundamental struggle achievable only in *kairos*, in contradistinction with liberal relocations of ecstasy from the soul into the body, also reflect modern Japanese problematisations of this divide. Early on, 'disreputable' art used the body in Japanese entertainment to articulate such non-representational experiences. *Kabuki*'s insertion into twenty-first century art-scenes thus 'encodes' changes in sexual values and practices and the relocation of sexual intimacy in the marketplace (Featherstone, 1991b; Giddens, 1992; Beck and Beck-Gernshein, 1995; Plummer, 1995; Bernstein, 2001; Bauman, 2003). A post-Enlightenment (Mannheim, [1936] 1968, pp. 35–36) fracturing of the unitary 'Self' exposed *tatemae* to technocratic and conformist domains of human action, but also opened up new avenues of exploration and experimentation, especially for younger generations in Japan, which pioneered techno-romantic escapism and the dramatisation of individuality (Elliott,

2013, p. 136). Note that in the widely popular socio-philosophy of the Akira Asada type, propagated in *Toso – Ron: Sukizo Kizzu no Boken* (*On Escape: Adventures of the Schizo Kids*, 1984), *Toso* stands for both 'escape' and a homonym for 'struggle' (Sawai, 2013, p. 201) – a pair we often find in bipolar debates on thanatourism as a way to consume suffering in carefree ways (Rojek, 1993; Korstanje and Ivanov, 2012; Tzanelli, 2016a) and/or enact heritage pilgrimage (Mowatt and Chancellor, 2011). The recent popularisation of *Otaku*-style DIY cultures, and the *moga*-style consumerist exposition of the body, form paradoxical homologies with *Kabuki* as the once art of the gutter twenty-first century art-scenes would recognise as 'cool'. Once more, we note a convergence of sexual intimacy with hospitality in the Handover, blurring the border between disinterested reciprocity and rationalised exchange.

On stage, the dancers' in-line formations around a 'centre' – a pedestal on which cheerleaders wave Tokyo 2020's banner – possibly stands as a reference to *Hanamichi* ('flower path'), a walkway, which extends into the audience and via which dramatic *Kabuki* entrances and exits are made. Yet, the dancers' movement is circular rather than linear, highlighting Tokyo's festival centre instead. The illumination of performance is also musical: contemporary 'big band' jazz tunes ('*Bōenkyō no Soto no Keshiki (Pasaisaje)*' 'View Outside of the Telescope' by Sheena Ringo) are filtered through the style of six-time Grammy Award winner Burt Freeman Bacharach (born 1928), an American composer, songwriter, record producer, pianist and singer. The over-poweringly instrumental song composition was originally made by Ringo for Hideki Noda's 2012 stage play *Egg* (Uchida, 26 May 2014). Bacharach's preference for background in jazz harmony, with striking syncopated rhythmic patterns, irregular phrasing, frequent modulation, and odd, changing meters (also fitting the needs of filmmaking, in which he was regularly involved as composer), accentuated the 'theatrical' performance of the Olympic segment's dancers, also bringing Ringo's composition closer to urban neo-*noir* filmic traditions. Evidently, the overall segment pulls together the expertise of different artists for the production of a creative narrative. This is a segment signalling the transformation of discourses of urban festivalisation and cultural heritage tourism into discourses about network or knowledge society (Bærenholdt and Haldrup, 2006; Larsen and Urry, 2008; Richards, 2010, 2014).

The same enthusiastic atmosphere (Florida, 2002; Hui, 2014) is carried through to the concluding segment, 'Grand Finale', which is framed musically by Ringo's self-same composition. A sculpture modelled after Tokyo Sky Tree, one of Tokyo's latest landmarks, emerges from Super Mario's pipe. The sculpture foregrounds Mount Fuji's shape and Tokyo's cityscape silhouette with Tokyo Tower, the Rainbow Bridge and the Tokyo Metropolitan Government Buildings. The blue colouration of shapes refers to Japan's national colour, blue, but also to Sky Tree's neo-futurist exterior lattice, which is painted with a colour officially called 'Skytree White', an original colour based on a bluish white traditional Japanese colour called *Aijiro* (de Vivo, 8 August 2012). Significantly, the 'shadowgraph' (what the formation of shadows on the stage refers to), which originates in the Edo Period (1603–1867), is designated by the artistic directors as a 'popular' form of art (Tokyo 2020, undated, p. 7). Much like Beijing 2008's emphasis on calligraphy as an ancient Chinese art (Tzanelli, 2010), Tokyo 2020's Handover emphasised the originality of an indigenous form of popular culture. But it is also hard to miss that the representation of Tokyo's Sky Tree on stage (its erection as a phallic symbol) is antithetically symmetrical to the feminine, tube-like form of the Museum of Tomorrow. It is as if Abe, the nation's patriarch, is made genetically by the city's 'architectural control', a mode of sociation specific to Japanese society, in which people maintain their freedom on the surface layer but further down, in depth, they are prey to a surveillance system that integrates them into the urban environment (Sawai, 2013, p. 212).

In agreement with feminist suggestions that the 'woman' is only seen, in de Beauvoir's terms (2007, p. 356), as both 'herself and her negation, a kingdom and a place of exile', pure nature, Abe's architectural enclosing into Tokyo's cityscape reveals the ugly biopolitics of gender-making, because it associates the 'man' with culture. So, if we connect the slapstick delivery of Abe to Maracanã to the fact that Japanese society still has a long way to go on women's rights (Pilling, 2014, pp. 205–209; Ehara, 2013, pp. 166–167, pp. 168–169), we are left with another embarrassing infrapolitical statement by the ceremonial directors in a true 'rite of passage' fashion for Tokyo, the soon-to-be Olympic partner in mega-event development (MacAloon, 2006). The Abe/Mario 'delivery', in pure biological terms, obeys a nostalgic discourse of 'Camp', from consciously reminiscing while also expunging unpleasant moments (Holliday and Potts, 2012, p. 72). The finale summarises representations of the city's heritage as 'popular' in line with a Western imaginary of growth, distinct from the nation's Chinese *kanji* past, but also from modern Western cultural formations. This way, the Olympic staging of national and urban self-narration by Tokyo creates long-lasting brands of emotional appeal, so as to integrate a culturally specific milieu into a global one (Albrow *et al.*, 1997, pp. 30–31; Lury, 2004). As the ceremony's performers are lined across the shadow cityscape with the cubes, the idea of the city as an extension of its human capital acquires a novel dimension: it is not ideas or architecture, but a creative assemblage that makes Tokyo – and this is what will welcome Olympic visitors to Japan in four years' time.

Bowing and extending their bodies in postures that recall the stiffness of *anime* cinema, the performers insert ethno-national character into glocal cultural industrial governance, ultimately *animating* Tokyo 2020's 'experience economy' (Pine and Gilmore, 1999). The subtle reference to animation/*anime* is significant: as a broadcasting, restaurant and observation tower in Sumida, Tokyo, the tallest structure in Japan, the tallest tower in the world and the second tallest structure in the world after the Burj Khalifa (829.8 m/2,722 ft) (Yamamoto, 22 May 2012), the neo-futurist Sky Tree currently posits as the equivalent of Beijing 2008's Bird's Nest Stadium, London 2012's 'ArcelorMittal Orbit' (Tzanelli, 2013b, pp. 73–77) and Rio 2016's Museum of Tomorrow (see Chapter 3). In fact, the transformation of Super Mario's green tube, from which Abe emerged in a previous segment, into the stage's 'Tower' clearly connects the two Olympic hosts' (Rio and Tokyo) developmental projects in atmospheric 'heritage attraction' terms (Bonn *et al.*, 2007).

The 'link' is meant, however, as more than a suspicion of urban competition, or a propagation of links between policy-making models in administrative terms (Luckman *et al.*, 2009). It is, above all, a statement on cosmopolitan togetherness and sharing in creativity and heritage that goes at least as far back as the historical human flows from Japan into Brazil. The grand finale's focus on the regeneration of meaning also has strong audio-visual dimensions, which the two countries and Olympic hosts share as heritage in music and the moving image (on urban image-making see Lynch, 1960 and Colomb, 2013). Oscillating between the social affordances of bodies and souls as more-than psychological 'traits' (Alampay, 2009; Germann Molz, 2012; Germann Molz and Paris, 2015) and traditions of technological 'enframing' imported from the West and Europe, the overall Handover's narrative shares more in atmospheric depth than meets the eye, so to speak. Hence, Tokyo 2020's urban morphogenetic parable can be 'read' as a continuation of Rio's formulaic development, now standing between the need for touristic contact as worldmaking and the phantom of degrowth.

8 Conclusion

Dark journeys and hopeful futures

> True genesis is not at the beginning *but at the end*, and it starts to begin only when society and existence become radical, i.e. *grasp their roots*.
>
> (Bloch, 1986, p. 1376)

Heritage interpretation *redux*: evotopianism and the war of worlds

We are reminded that, despite their community-building aspirations, mega-events are almost always 'disruptive media events', because they involve 'intensely mediatised public rituals interrupting everyday routines across the globe' (Van den Broucke *et al.*, 2016, p. 166). But in a world that constantly remakes itself through merged DIY and professional recordings of reality fragments or multiple realities, such disruptions extend beyond the mega-event's three-week span. The struggle of domination over 'interpretation' (ibid., p. 168) is often lost before it commences, because of the proliferation of audience-viewing and apprehending of the recorded 'event'. On the other hand, as much as mega-events are fleeting experiences for visitors/guests, or contractual incidents in a lifetime of movement for their professional labour, it is good to remember their structural permanence as imaginaries of aspiration for the host and its localities (Müller, 2016). The very act of sight-seeing hosts as people and as land – today amplified with the introduction of new media – moves human subjects systematically 'into a position of adjacency to the symbolic order' (MacCannell, 2012, p. 186), and this enforces a direct encounter with the symbolic world. However, the host's symbolic worlds are organised around tacit territorial frames with their own social and cultural borders and divisions (Rumford, 2006). These real worlds encroach upon one's desire to play the tourist for a day, the disengaged artist or the impartial director, suggesting that the represented picturesque or spectacular of the city or the village – two primary meaning-making frames in mega-event contexts – encourage a morality of effort and solitude (MacCannell, 2011).

At first, it is peculiar to speak of 'solitude' in such a crowded human universe, but new media platforms facilitate just that: the search for meaning in a fragmented world (Bauman, 1998), to ameliorate the loss of authenticity with lifestyle mobilities of the tourist type (Strausberg, 2011). Post-modern pil-grimages of the audio-visual machine go hand-in-hand these days with physical tourist movement, in a circular journey that takes us from a starting-point we call 'home' to other places or non-places, then back to where we started, alleg-edly with more knowledge about other places, ideas and people. And yet, it is also possible that our subjection to a *tórnos*, a wheel of circular movement (as any 'tourism' from home to holiday land and then back implies), leaves us with the same knowledge we had before about ourselves as humans engaging in *peregrinatio*, as lonely *perigrini*, foreigners, exiles or strangers (Bauman, 1991; Smith, 1992; Theobald, 1998; Tzanelli, 2013b). Such peregrinations enabled by audio-visual machines may both amplify this feeling of distance from one's core and activate one's empathy, bringing them closer to other worlds in need. The Olympic holiday is such a case in point, with YouTube hosting various 'incidents' of tourist compassion that take place before, during and after the Olympic event. YouTube is, we may say, an 'unregulated diary' of such backstage developments to formalised eventisation: a co-created 'travel book' telling us good and bad stories about the making of worlds in hosting ter-ritories, available to anyone with a computer and an Internet connection. A few suggestive relevant clips will commence this Chapter's concluding remarks in the form of alternate reality propositions or 'worlds'. Consider the following:

Reality 1

Several DIY and international, especially Western, channels and newspapers reported attempts in various *favelas* to extinguish the Torch, while designated athletes were performing their usual Olympic pilgrimage through poor townships (see for example Reuters and Thornhill, 28 June 2016; Complex News, 15 July 2016; Gomes, 3 August 2016). There were arrests of these 'deviants' by police.

Reality 2

A video narrates the way in which a 'hero's welcome' was extended to Brazi-lian Judo gold medallist Rafaela Silva while visiting *City of God*, her former *favela* home. A black woman exclaims on camera how proud she is of Silva's achievement, and wishes that one of her five children will also make her proud in a similar way one day. 'She fought and suffered for it', the inter-viewee concludes, and a male reporter adds how Silva had to endure racism and discrimination in her struggle to be recognised and even face dis-qualification because of allegations that she cheated in her sport (France 24 English, 24 August 2016).

Reality 3

The same channel that reported about Silva's 'homecoming', also released on YouTube a video examining the tourist boom in *Babilonia*. This small *favela*, which is five minutes away from *Copa Cabaña*, has been receiving foreign visitors ever since its pacification in 2009. 'It is chaotic but organised', says a French tourist, who did not expect to find a cheerful and colourful place where he stayed for the duration of his holiday with friends. Hostel owners say that the Olympic Games have allowed them to increase prices and 'keep the local economy going', so foreign tourism works 'to the benefit of the entire community' (France 24 English, 12 August 2016).

Reality 4

A video 'exposes' the things Olympic organisers do not want guests to see, with a special focus on *favela* displacements and evictions in *Vila Autodromo*. We are granted a 'look' into the ways bulldozers demolish the last of the *favela* homes near the main Olympic Stadium, displacing hundreds of locals; a view of ruined walls, on which graffiti ('Apartheid', 'Sociospatial Justice') points fingers at the administrative machine's inhuman approach; an inspection of a short interview with a spokesperson from Amnesty International, who confirms the authorities' aggressive approach towards the local families; and a 'close-up' of particular *favela* residents mourning the loss of their homes. Critics believe 'officials are embarrassed by the slums, and want to keep them out of sight of tourists in Rio for the Olympic Games' (Trends Now, 3 August 2016).

Some of these 'worldviews' (*á la* Mannheim, [1936] 1968) or 'world versions' (*á la* Goodman, 1978) reject the argument that mega-events might also exorcise phantoms of militarism while invoking their operational logic: technology. But it is worth remembering that artistic-technological irrealism, which here seems to strike a technocratic chord (Rose, 1999), produces melodies in the service of *oeconomie artificialem*, regardless of what its artistic makers think. At the same time, the four realities might remain fixated upon an agreed viewpoint: outside these tragic or difficult frames of life, for us, as tourist snoopers, the Olympic world is our oyster. We can replay these tragedies like movies in 'thana-capitalism's' (Korstanje, 2016b) vast global auditorium, become upset, but then also have the luxury to forget. The technocratic eye manages to intrude into such versions of the world, excluding all other perspectives in favour of 'pure' political commitment. The 'right to privacy' (Benhabib, 1992, p. 112), now subsumed by industrial image-making in the service of capitalist network interests, including those of the Olympic city and nation, seems to proliferate Holocaust-like denials across the 'developing' and 'Third' worlds. Here *oeconomie artificialem* rears its ugliest face: as Bauman (1989) explained, the tragedy of the Holocaust should be attributed to the bureaucratic rationalisation of history. A combination of classification of humans into worthy and unworthy 'species' with the concerted exercise of forgetting and 'eye-closing' to different growth opportunities, allowed for the elimination of those identified as 'defective'. Thinking of the Olympic mega-event as a travelling culture, with enough history of violence and forgetting, immediately suggests an analogical application of bureaucratic failure in host mega-event territories. The Americas and other subaltern world territories were invented as negations of modernity from the very beginning, after all, so why not erase their contribution to human diversity altogether (Dussel, 1995, p. 19; Mignolo, 2000, p. 50)?

And yet, there are infinite worlds out there to consider, prompting us to reboot, accelerate our skills of perception and re-focus: fast-tracking to the Opening and Closing Ceremonies of Rio 2016 and the Handover to Tokyo 2020, we are confronted with local volunteers and athletes happy 'to be part of it' and to have a job; artists and directors who tell stories full of hope and about good futures; and global guests/audiences pleased to offer their stipend to the movement and applaud natives for their efforts. Fast-tracking to *Porto Maravilha* we see revamped sites, where abandonment and crime reigned, and another technological narrative of a better tomorrow, of the possibility to sustain a human and natural home, full of fecundity and joy.

The different worlds take positions of confrontation, ready to clash in an ultimate battle over definition, for or against capitalist phantasmagoria. Yet, both camps use similar tools in their narrative of utopias, or their absence and negation thereof: where the attempt to extinguish the Flame pays attention to 'ordinary affects' (Stewart, 2007) as expressions of a preference to live differently and be 'otherwise' (Povinelli, 2012), narratives of inclusion and recognition through sport also promise utopia as both negation and affirmation, 'ideally giving rise to that "third thing" that Bloch believed was out of reach from architecture' (Coleman, 2013, p. 162). Mega-event imagineering is thus allegedly revealed as both a response to the absence of a beautiful and inclusive civic order and its causal malady, in a movement endlessly repeating the failures of capitalist machinations.

Elaborating on Foucault's model of subjection, Hollinshead (1999) notes changes in the Western model of civic humanism, with new equilibria emerging in the living systems of cultural, political or administrative exclusion, to produce a new model of social life '*based no longer on inherited ties of sovereignty/ obedience, but on the emanative and reflective impulse of domination/subjugation that is carried by and within the governing invitation*' (1999, p. 16, emphasis in text; Taylor, 1986, p. 101). Hollinshead's framing of knowledge/ power linked to domination/subjugation foretells the certainty of victimisation (there are no certain or visible masters but there is always a victim), refusing to acknowledge the creative possibles subjected (non)citizens can use to their own interests. And we need not connect such future-orientated actions exclusively to rational motivations without emotion: what matters here is that the cage scholars such as Hollinshead or Bauman and Lyon (2012) identify in their work has its escape routes. Although everyday life, which is subsumed by Olympic industries, might figure as 'colonised' by capitalism in pessimistic accounts, in reality it always forms a site of resistance, because the banal and the ordinary shields it from the totalising reach of the system (Jameson, 1995, p. 265; Gardiner, 2004, pp. 229–230; Coleman, 2013: 156). Even with cameras on site the human body can perform dance routines puzzling to the digital warden.

Let us follow this dark path for a while, however, because discarding it may also be unwise (there will be space in the following section to reconsider our artistic imagineers' utopian contribution in detail). Thinking of the Olympic mega-event as a travelling culture, with enough history of violence and for-getting, immediately suggests an analogical application of bureaucratic failure in mega-event host territories. As explained in Chapter 1, the Olympic Games are imbued with multi-scalar effervescence of temporal reasoning (Kleist and Jansen, 2016, p. 381), fostering 'regimes of anticipation' (Zeitlyn, 2015, p. 390) conditioned by past events and futures, including remembered hopes and fears. This means that the actual mega-event industries, which specific Olym-pic hosts and their partners come to form, ought to operate as mobility apparatuses. The role of these apparatuses is to shift in practical terms futures from the domain of fate to the realm of action potential and from individual or local base to collective human action (Harvey, 2000; Adam, 2010). In the case of Rio, where the colonial and authoritarian pasts cast a heavy shadow over the present, old frameworks of modernist progress acquire a temporal reasoning that reanimates as future possibilities and 'hopes' (Jansen and Löfving, 2009; Berlant, 2011; Bryant, 2016). Similar urban possibilities might emerge in oppressive sites in Tokyo, where migrant and native labour face a lifetime in the cages of discrimination or unequal work. The presence of societal hope, this collective vision of meaningful and dignified social life within an urban polity, is connected to the ability to maintain the possibility of upward social mobility, but with well-being possibilities in sight (Hage, 2003, p. 13). Yet, the mega-event's objectives and aims highlight an uneven distribution of this possibility to give meaning to life, hence to participate in collective ways of governing desires and hopes for the future. Technocracy intrudes again in one's best dreams, turning them into nightmares.

The problem entails a disconnection between societal hopes, artistic cri-tiques and relations of attachment 'to compromised conditions of possibility'; as a result, the realisation of a better life is deemed to be impossible to attain (Berlant, 2011, pp. 2–3). The blocked social mobility of certain populations in Rio's 'Olympic City' replays unpleasant violent scripts of exclusion, based on the impossibility of hope nested in movement (Hage, 2003). It is, by now, a global secret that Rio as a post-modern urban formation has also included in restrictive regimes of mobility the *favelas*, to protect the mega-city's global consumers, thus ensuring a peculiar absence of societal hope from them in favour of their futural top-down development (see Salazar and Glick Schiller, 2014 on 'regimes of mobility'). The replacement of seemingly disorganised regimes of local socialities with externally imposed political ecological sys-tems of 'regeneration' has not allowed time for ensured investment in spec-ulative transitional planning for these communities. This simply means that, though *favela* regenerations may not be evil or inessential *per se*, their 'upgrading' in the absence of citizen welfare, which fits well with neoliberal modes of governance and privatisation (Greenhouse, 2010), did not allow space for the emergence of resilience mechanisms, nor did it consider the damaging effects of hopelessness in reproductions of 'internal terrorisms' (Korstanje *et al.*, 2014).

I consider with some degree of suspicion the very notion of 'resilience', as individually oriented responsibility for the realisation of the 'good life', which is written in big block letters all over the mega-event's ceremonial and architectural artwork. In Rio's case, this can act in favour of neoliberal evotopianism by merely activating the Darwinian socialist models of the Republican era, so much in line with Lula's aspiring *abertura* policies (on social Darwinism in unionised socialism see Conde, 2012, p. 107). Resilience may revolve around a desire for continuity and re-establishment of past values (Ringel, 2014 in Kleist and Jansen, 2016, p. 384), but not for the better – and this would also apply to the *favelados'* pleas to be left alone to get on with their lives as before. For positive change to occur, empathy has to inspect problems and arrive at durable solutions (Boltanski, 1999) – not by mobilising the fascistic tools of surveillance, but by creating an environment in which *the affected party can articulate positive action for themselves.* At the same time, the discourse of socio-cultural adaptability to economic crises fits nicely with materialist utopias as an imperfect, contingent process (e.g. see Levitas, 2013b), only to strengthen neoliberal social insensitivity. Worse, it may dress up deep-seated problems, such as racism or sexism, into inequality instances with no historical depth merely linked to capitalist 'glitches', such as class inequities (Goldberg, 1993, p. 69). Note that the same social suicidal tendencies may apply to Japanese life prospects in the city, with migrant workers staying hidden from public sight and young native workers sacrificing their souls to the altar of work. As we now move from one Olympic city to the next, the notion of empathy merits redefinition, in light not just of difference, but also of commonalities across sites of human activity. Now we can juxtapose and assess the function of economies of artifice and imagination – for, as I proceed to explain, where the first harden structural possibilities the latter *might* create inclusive utopias based on different forms of movement.

Imaginaries of movement and the right to stay put

I will treat the statement that, unlike YouTube users, distinguished mega-event labour, such as ceremonial directors and eponymous artists, enjoy a better life than township populations or anonymous workers in the Olympic city as potential truism. As stated in Chapter 2, we must take on board the exilic profile of some of them in Rio's case, or the structural constrictions under which they operate in Tokyo's case, to relativise conceptions of privilege and inequality. I do not challenge social problems with this statement, because they are real. My focus nevertheless is not reality frames and measurements of this type, but what distinguished mega-event art contributes to the Olympic project as a compassionate mobile culture, its representational and utopian work. Constrictive notions of the 'romantic tourist' as an obedient mega-event worker in the service of the 'Olympic firm's' technoromanticism (see Chapters 6 and 7), may lead us to the self-same problems as those we find in accounts of methodological nationalism. Such labour both advertises ethno-national cultures and highlights their potential beyond discourses of nation-formation or jingoism. It is my contention that the mega-event's choreomobile artistic network lodges its project in the complexities of any official attempts 'to organise [its] activities, beliefs and unofficial resistance to the power of those who claim to know what is right and good' (Eade, 1992, p. 31). These powerful constituencies may not be concrete establishments in the Olympic city or the nation, but reside in those repositories of memory associated with the host's heritage lifespan as this is constructed by its 'imagined community' (Anderson, 2006).

Let me explain more by likening mega-event art to both exilic worldmaking (in Hannah Arendt's (1958) terms) and to secular, even post-modern pilgrimage (in Collins-Kreiner (2010), Tzanelli (2013a) and Goodman's (1978) irrealist worldmaking terms). Arendt's notion of artistic worldmaking allows us to consider the nature of artistic exile as more than a political institutional consequence: artists consider modernity – and post-modernity – as both sites of desolation and freedom (McGowan, 2011), thus seeing all humans as both potentially disembedded and free to act on the world. Arendt's worldmaking is the making of a Baumanesque pilgrim, who can detect the detrimental effects of carelessness towards fellow humans and their earthly home. In this respect, mega-event artistic worldmakings are creative pilgrimages that reclaim one's right to be free at 'home'. The group of narrative experts that create pilgrimages for the big screen, in architectural formations and in the Olympic Stadium, transcend conventional biopolitics (*á la* Foucault, 2007), because they prioritise narrativity with (auto)biographical depth in their work. This understanding of biopolitics, which is akin to Arendt's (1958) conception of political life as participation in the city's commons, is seen in this study as the ability and skill of artists to produce utopias of social cohesion and cross-cultural communication. The ability of these experts to imagine new forms of social bonding that can allow the Olympic city to act as a magnet for creativity and innovative urban design is well recognised in academic literature (Frey, 2009; Richards, 2011, 2014). However, their distinctive mobilisation of technology, not as mere instrumental tool of ordering, but a creative comportment of irrealist worldmaking, highlights a basic difference between economies of artifice and imagination.

Similarly, Richards (2014, p. 136) has noted a homological link between creative tourism and Richard Sennett's elaborations in the *Craftsman* (2008) and *Together* (2012). Both studies explore the development of human skills and ways of shaping one's social relations *and* physical environment. 'Nature' perceived as purpose-free is transformed by the technology of labour into culture, which fuels the dreams of *Hominem Faber*, allowing them to engineer the future. This necessitates an optimistic nihilism that can only be born out of experience of failures or successes, which can be used then in other contexts: it is this Blochian *docta spes*, or 'educated hope' (Zimmerman, 2013, p. 247) that transforms the *Homo Faber* of organic imagineering into a *Homo Mobilis* of mechanical imagineering, who is thus also a *Homo Mundis*. In this respect, 'reclaiming home' can easily include utopian scenarios of rebuilding homes for humanity, instead of a particular nation or city – a phenomenon I placed in all three Olympic Ceremonies of the present study under the rubric of cosmopolitanism. These days, mega-events are never 'pure' heritage events – if there is such a thing as primordial authenticity and purity in tangible and intangible heritage. The Olympic city and the host culture as a whole are co-created, updated by contemporary cultural interactions with multiple 'others', who peregrinate them audio-visually and terrestrially. But when ethno-national memories begin to dissolve, merge and fuse with global concoctions, we are left with gaps. For Bloch, by clinging onto golden visions or nightmares of a non-existing past, we may even meet our historical entelechy in fascism (Thompson, 2013, p. 16). Technology manufactures new phantoms or ideal types, more durable and functionally orientated towards future problem-solving than the old ones. Here we may also find the production of visions about the 'end of times' or 'history', which have plagued the artistic imagination for centuries (Kermode, 2000). What is new and increasingly more recurring in Olympic mega-event art and architecture is the underlining of contemporary global imaginaries by a synecdochical connection between environmental (climate change) and social (wars, militarist violence, racism) catastrophisms. Philosophies of catastrophism, present in policy frameworks and contexts, prompt debates on positive or practical action. But what about their aesthetic core?

Artistic imagineers hold agential power in the battle of the worlds, because they participate in the audio-visual arrangement of the mega-event's overlapping ecologies: a physical ecology of movement, a symbolic one marked by struggle and competition over definitions, and a media ecology overlaying the previous two (Vannini *et al.*, 2009, p. 466). If we follow Berlant (1997) and Bauman (2000), then we have to conclude that, because media ecologies have been overtaken by a politics of confessional intimacy and shaming, mega-event mediatisations suffer from a withdrawal from the public sphere as a justice-making sphere, and by a concentration on marketable intimacies of cosmetic nature, akin to the 'nip-and-tuck' ethos of Brazilian feminine middle classness. Brazilian *docta spes* has taught the 'knowing' native to act as an essentialised female being to achieve mobility, where an equally essentialised black male being, allegedly uneducated in desire, stays fixed in *favela* territories. On top of this, not only do we have to account for the proliferation of public and private spheres in our neoliberal era, 'the public has become overextended into affairs that ought to be the concern of private sector interests' (Sheller and Urry, 2003, p. 109). The impoverishment of the public sphere(s) by voyeurism in compassionate surveillance's stead, and the global feminisation of public–private divides, which hold immense power in the case of post-colonial and post-imperial national cultures such as Brazil and Japan, do not assist in the eradication of memorial ghosts; they just allow for their malignant transmutation into resentment and hatred, then unleashed upon the weak and powerful others in physical and symbolic ways, respectively.

In this 'schematisation' (Stiegler, 2011) of world mobilities, their bureaucratic rationalisation as 'spectacles', Olympic art is assigned with the job to remember, forget and manipulate the past for educational purposes, while all mega-event artists are *also* subjected to critiques of worthless labour and expenditure by the critics of neoliberal commoditisation. Stranded between the rock of their 'effeminate' public identity as insensitive spenders of public money and the hard place of a personal commitment to fair and just art-making, we watch them either succumb to conservative pontifications of degrowth or reproduce the ascetic spirit of contemporary self-development for mass consumption. In some cases, the situated identity of artistic imagineers as affluent tourists is even set against imagined fixed ideals of native culture, which, as scholars have argued, often end up being nothing more than a mirror image of Eurocentric constructions of primordial, underdeveloped difference (see Appiah (1997) on Afrocentric and Eurocentric constructions of race). As *baile funk* utopias teach us, the *favelados* are anything but uneducated in desire, so we would do better to attribute their retrogressive behaviour to unequal opportunities.

These ideological immobilities also communicate with broader reactions. Specifically, we must address in mega-event management and elsewhere, in industrial image-making of the host, the recurring conflict of tourism, travel and leisure, with imaginaries of degrowth and local cultural sustainability. Here maladies of ideational and practical nature come together, blocking utopian imagination and planning in equal steads. Established tourism theorists (Swain, 2009; MacCannell, 2011) have repeatedly stressed that the ethical basis of tourism rests in furthering human understanding and cross-cultural communication. Yet, currently, much like other industries based on production-consumption chains (Ateljevic, 2000), tourism imaginaries of justice cannot provide effective mechanisms of *dépense*: travelling contributes to environmental pollution, community change and structural reorganisation not always beneficial for the hosts. Capitalism's growth-orientated form of action promotes the expansion of servile capacity in host societies and thus also the fear of their impending metabolic collapse in the future (Romano, 2015, p. 88). The most sustained critique of this twin process comes from degrowthers, who preach on putting an end to mobility and growth or treat mobility as unfair capital (Carter, 2016, pp. 23–24, pp. 28–29 on mega-events in particular), while also associating development with unfreedom. Here the coin has two sides: because of its basis in catastrophism, the act of acknowledging degrowth also brews potentially anti-globalising trends, promoting introspective communal collaboration against global cross-fertilisation and mobility in the event of scarcity. Degrowth as a political and cultural blue-print is the enemy of transmodern future-making, the project of political, economic, ecological, erotic, pedagogical and religious liberation – what Dussel (1995, pp. 75–76) calls an 'analectic *incorporative* solidarity between center/periphery, man/woman, different races, different ethnic groups, different classes, civilisation/nature, Western culture/Third World cultures'. I would also add the grey spaces between such binarisms, because they too can become targets as spaces of difference.

Ironically, the ghost of scarcity and the treatment of potential risks as 'real' play into the hands of neoliberal ideology. It is not coincidental that classical degrowthers have little to say about culture as an autonomous field of human activity, thus discarding the significance of devising new collective rituals of *dépense* in public. The very idea of making as artistic creativity underwent a similar economy-based analysis in tourism studies, leading to considerations of tourism as a potentially destructive force for native cultures (Bruner, 1989; Hugher, 1989; Cohen, 1995). But the institution of mega-events and their adjacent tourist industries as such are not evil; it is their operative agents and contexts that we must potentially consider as such. As Boltanski and Chia-pello (2004, pp. 28–30, p. 42) have explained, in some cases, capitalism is coerced by strong criticism into incorporating the very values in whose name it was criticised, thus assuming a positive role in the correction of justice-making mechanisms. The system's most fundamental failure is its current inability to dissociate liberation and justice-making from mobility *at all times*, also enabling human communities to enjoy a good life in their cultural and natural habitats uninterrupted by its artificial 'events'. The key to a better collective and individual future rests with the preservation and expansion of the *oeconomie imaginationis*, in which art constantly and experimentally produces new futural worlds free of the necessity or pressure of rootless movement but also amenable to difference.

Any such 'project' merits additional caution, because it might even replicate the bureaucratic conundrums of history in the realm of contemporary artistic creativity. The transformation of 'public sphere' into a 'public screen' (Sheller and Urry, 2003, p. 118) often does not grant silenced populations a voice; alternatively, it may allow media constituencies to produce a radically altered voice on their behalf and in the service of the 'capillaries of power' (Foucault 1995 in Salmond 2010, p. 99). Especially in contemporary Olympic mega-events, thana-capitalist failure rests with a particular type of politics subsuming the malleable and ever-changing memory magma we know as 'popular culture' as a 'possible', a mere product in the hands of managers of populations and their fortunes (Lazzarato, 2004). Popular culture is slowly but surely asphyxiated in claustrophobic interstices between populism in necropolitics. There is no way to survive trapped between populist imperatives in hosting cities, which concentrate on art's use-value for crowd manipulation, and traditional necropolitics (Mbembe, 2003), coerced uprootings from 'home' of all kinds, including censorship and slavery displacements, which produce resentful memory repositories for exiled communities. This is the bread and butter of populist strategy, which may allegedly enframe *volonté générale*, the general will of the *hoi polloi* (Aslanidis, 2016), in reproductions of the past, hence in ultra-conservative utopias (Mannheim, [1936] 1968).

Environmental racism is the latest offspring of such histories, which poison world cultures. The poisoning does not always take effect by means of forgetting by affluent groups, but *also excessive remembering* by the affected communities, which often choose to die in street riots and protests instead of living as refuse. Such nihilistic self-sacrifice does not enable transmodern ethics to actualise in the subaltern's self-discovery of innocence and sacrifice in the altar of neoliberal post-modernisation (Dussel, 1995, p. 76). But also, by asking ceremonial art to simply fit into a box of remembering or forgetting in the front stages of collective performance, when the mega-event's hosting culture is so malleable and ever-changing, curtails its changing nature. Broadcast globally every four years, such deaths would forget that younger generations hold the key to hopeful futural scenarios. Novel ways of dreaming, creating and associating in the Olympic city should, therefore, acquire a stronger voice in the stead of tired repetitions of tradition, but such a voice should also not suppress the speculation on old generational mistakes and tragedies altogether. Economies of imagination can become effective economies of *dépense*, which do not just perform and sing the past in ceremonial pageantries, but make sustainable future worlds in every mega-city's multiple rhythms.

References

Abiodun, R. (2001) African aesthetics. *Journal of Aesthetic Education*, 35(4): 15–23.

Acerbi, P. (2014) 'A long poem of walking': Flâneurs, vendors, and chronicles of post-abolition Rio de Janeiro. *Journal of Urban History*, 40(1): 97–115.

Adam, B. (2010) History of the future: Paradoxes and challenges. *Rethinking History* 14(3): 361–378.

Adam, B. and Groves, C. (2011) Futures tended: Care and future-oriented responsibility. *Bulletin of Science, Technology & Society* 31(1): 17–27.

Adey, P. (2006) If mobility is everything then it is nothing: Towards a relational politics of (im)mobilities. *Mobilities*, 1(1): 75–94.

Adey, P. (2008) Airports, mobility and the calculative architecture of affective control. *Geoforum*, 38: 438–451.

Adey, P. (2010) *Mobility*. London: Routledge.

Adorno, T. and Horkheimer, M. (1991) *The Dialectic of Enlightenment*. New York: Continuum.

Advertimes (2016). Hiroshi Sasaki, Kaoru Sugano, Ringo Shiina and MIKIKO work together for Tokyo's performance at Rio Closing Ceremony (in Japanese). 22 August. Available at: www.advertimes.com/20160822/article232304/ [accessed: 5 December 2016].

Agamben, G. (1998) *Homo Sacer*. Stanford, CA: Stanford University Press.

Alampay, E. (ed.), (2009) *Living the Information Society in Asia*. Singapore: Institute of Southeast Asian Studies.

Alberto, P.L. (2009) When Rio was black: Soul music, national culture, and the politics of racial comparison in the 1970s Brazil. *Hispanic American Historical Review*, 89(1): 3–39.

Albertsen, N. and Diken, B. (2003) Artworks' networks – field, system or mediators? Department of Sociology On-line Papers. Available at: http://comp.lancs.ac.uk/sociology.soc105bd.html [accessed: 30 March 2012].

Albrow, M. (1997) Travelling beyond local cultures: socioscapes in a global city. In: J. Eade (ed.), *Living the Global City*. London: Routledge, pp. 7–55.

Albrow, M., Eade, J., Dürrschmidt, J. and Washbourne, N. (1997) The impact of globalization on sociological concepts: Community, culture and milieu. In: J. Eade (ed.), *Living the Global City*. London: Routledge, pp. 20–36.

Alexander, J.C. (2006) Cultural pragmatics: Social performance between ritual and strategy. In: J.C. Alexander, B. Giesen and J.L. Mast (eds), *Social Performance, Symbolic Action, Cultural Pragmatics and Ritual*. Cambridge: Cambridge University Press, pp. 29–90.

Alexander, J.C. (2008) Iconic consciousness in art and life: Surface/depth beginning with Giacometti's Standing Woman. *Theory, Culture & Society*, 25(5): 1–19.

Alexander, J.C. (2010) Iconic consciousness and the material feeling of meaning. *Thesis Eleven*, 103(1): 10–25.

Alexander, J.C. (2011) Clifford Geertz and the strong program: Human sciences and cultural sociology. In: J.C. Alexander, P. Smith and M. Norton (eds), *Interpreting Clifford Geertz*. New York: Palgrave Macmillan, pp. 55–64.

Alexander, J.C., Eyerman, R., Giesen, B., Smelser, N.J. and Sztompka, P. (2004) *Cultural Trauma and Collective Identity*. Berkeley: University of California Press.

Alexander, J.C. and Smith, P. (2001) The strong program in cultural theory: Elements of structural hermeneutics. In: J. Turner (ed.), *The Handbook of Sociological Theory*. New York: Kluwer, pp. 135–150.

Allison, A. (2008) The attractions of the J-Wave for American youth. In: W. Yasushi and D.L. McConnell (eds), *Soft Power Superpowers*. Armonk, NY: East Gate, pp. 99–110.

Allison, G. (2004) *Japan's Postwar History*, 2nd edn. Ithaca, NY: Cornell University Press.

Almandoz, A. (2003) The emergence of modern town planning in Latin America. Finnish Research Seminar on Latin America, Helsinki, 22 May. Available at: www.helsinki.fi/aluejakulttuurintutkimus/tutkimus/xaman/articulos/2003_01/almandoz.html [accessed: 11 September 2016].

Amin, A. and Thrift, N. (2002) *Cities*. Cambridge: Polity.

Amoore, L. (2013) *The Politics of Possibility*. Durham, NC: Duke University Press.

Anderson, B. (2006) *Imagined Communities*, 2nd edn. London: Verso.

Anderson, B. (2009) Affective atmospheres. *Emotion, Space and Society*, 2: 77–81.

Anderson, B. (2013) *Us and Them?* Oxford: Oxford University Press.

Anderson, T.T. (2011) Complicating Heidegger and the truth in architecture. *Journal of Aesthetics and Art Criticism*, 69(1): 69–79.

Anderson, T. and Leal, D. (2001) *Free Market Environmentalism*. New York: St Martin's Press.

Andrade, O. (1999) The cannibalist manifesto. *Third Text*, 46: 92–96.

Andranovich, G. (2016) Olympic City Los Angeles: An exploration of the urban imaginary. In: N.B. Salazar, C. Timmerman, J. Wets, L. Gama Gato and S. Van den Broucke (eds), *Mega-Event Mobilities*. Abingdon: Routledge, pp. 52–68.

Angelo, A. (2009) As 100 maiores músicas Brasileiras – 'Asa Branca'. *Rolling Stone Brasil*. Available at: http://rollingstone.uol.com.br/listas/100-maiores-musicas-brasileiras/asa-branca/ [accessed: 11 December 2016].

Appadurai, A. (2004) The capacity to aspire: Culture and the terms of recognition. In: V. Rao and M. Walton (eds), *Culture and Public Action*. Palo Alto, CA: Stanford University Press, pp. 59–84.

Appadurai, A. (2013) *The Future as Cultural Fact*. London: Verso.

Appiah, K.A. ([1991] 2009) Is the post- in postmodernism the post- in postcolonial? *Critical Enquiry*, 17(2): 336–357.

Appiah, K.A. (1997) Europe upside down: Fallacies of the new Afrocentrism. In: R.R. Grinker and C.B. Steiner (eds), *Perspectives on Africa*. London: Blackwell, pp. 728–731.

Appiah, K.A. (2006) *Cosmopolitanism*. New York: W.W. Norton & Co.

Aravamudan, S. (1999) *Tropicopolitans*. Durham, NC: Duke University Press.

Archdaily (2013). Santiago Calatrava: The metamorphosis of space. 5 December. Available at: http://www.archdaily.com/454797/santiago-calatrava-the-metamorphosis-of-space/ [accessed: 7 September 2016].

Archer, M. (1995) *Realist Social Theory*. Cambridge: Cambridge University Press.

Archer, M. (2010) Morphogenesis versus structuration: On combining structure and action. *The British Journal of Sociology*, 61(s1): 225–252.

Architecture Week (2004). Calatrava's Classical Greek. 20 October. Available at: www. architectureweek.com/2004/1020/design_1-2.html [accessed: 7 September 2016].

Arcilla, P. (2015). Santiago Calatrava's City of Arts and Sciences stars in Disney's 'Tomorrowland'. *Archdaily*, 23 May. Available at: http://www.archdaily.com/633527/santiago-calatrava-s-city-of-arts-and-sciences-stars-in-disney-s-tomorrowland?ad_medium=widget&ad_name=recommendation [accessed: 7 September 2016].

Ardener, E. (1989) *The Voice of Prophecy and Other Essays*. Oxford: Basil Blackwell.

Argyrou, V. (2005) *The Logic of Environmentalism*. Oxford: Berghahn.

Arendt, H. (1958) *The Human Condition*, 2nd edn. Chicago, IL: University of Chicago Press.

Arendt, H. (1963) *On Revolution*. New York: Viking Press.

Arendt, H. (1968) *Between Past and Future*. New York: Penguin Books.

Arendt, H. (2007) *The Promise of Politics*. New York: Schocken Books.

Arias-Maldonado, M. (2007) An imaginary solution? The green defence of deliberative democracy. *Environmental Values*, 16: 233–252.

Arnold, D. (2005) Virtual tourism – a niche in cultural heritage. In: M. Novelli (ed.), *Niche Tourism*. Oxford: Elsevier Butterworth-Heinemann, pp. 223–231.

Asano, T. (2013) Network, community and culture. In: A. Elliott, M. Katagiri and A. Sawai (eds), *Routledge Companion to Contemporary Japanese Social Theory*. New York: Routledge, pp. 179–195.

Aslanidis, P. (2016) Is populism an ideology? Refutation and a new perspective. *Political Studies*, 64(1S): 88–104.

Ateljevic, I. (2000) Circuits of tourism: Stepping beyond the 'production/consumption' dichotomy. *Tourism Geographies*, 2(4): 369–388.

Ateljevic, I. (2008) Transmodernity: Remaking our (tourism) world? In: J. Tribe (ed.), *Philosophical Issues in Tourism*. Bristol and Toronto: Channel View Publications, pp. 278–300.

Ateljevic, I., Morgan, N. and Pritchard, A. (2013) *The Critical Turn in Tourism Studies*. Abingdon: Routledge.

Augé, M. (2008) *Non-Places*. London and New York: Verso.

Azuma, H. (2009) *Otaku*. Minneapolis, MN: University of Minnesota Press.

Badiou, A. (2013) *Rhapsody for the Theatre*. London: Verso.

Bærenholdt, J.O. (2013) Governmobility: The powers of mobility. *Mobilities*, 8(1), pp. 20–34.

Bærenholdt, J.O. and Haldrup, M. (2006) Mobile networks and place making in cultural tourism staging: Viking ships and rock music in Roskilde. *European and Urban Regional Studies*, 13(3): 209–224.

Bærenholdt, J.O., Haldrup, M., Larsen, J. and Urry, J. (2004) *Performing Tourist Places*. Aldershot: Ashgate.

Baker, T. and Ruming, K. (2014) Making 'Global Sydney': Spatial imaginaries, worlding and strategic plans. *International Journal of Urban and Regional Research*, 39(1): 62–78.

Bal, M. (2003) Visual essentialism and the object of visual culture. *Journal of Visual Culture*, 2(1): 5–32.

Bal, M. (2006) *The Mieke Bal Reader*. Chicago, IL: University of Chicago Press.

Balch, O. (2016). Funding problems hit plan to clean Rio's polluted waterways ahead of Olympics. *The Guardian*, 1 February. Available at: https://www.theguardian.com/ sustainable-business/2016/feb/01/funding-problems-hit-plan-clean-rios-polluted-wate rways-olympics [accessed: 5 September 2016].

Baldacchino, G. (2010) *Island Enclaves*. Montreal: McGill-Queen's University Press.

Balibar, E. (1991) Citizen subject. In: E. Cadava, P. Connor and J. Nancy (eds), *Who Comes After the Subject?* New York: Routledge, pp. 33–57.

Barber, B. (2003) *Jihad versus McWorld*. London: Corgi Books.

Barber, B. (2010) Terrorism and the new democratic realism. In: G. Ritzer and Z. Atalay (eds), *Readings in Globalization*. Oxford: Wiley Blackwell.

Barbosa, L.N. (1995) The Brazilian jeitinho: An exercise in national identity. In: D.J. Hess and R. DaMatta (eds), *The Brazilian Puzzle*. New York: Columbia University Press, pp. 35–48.

Barke, M., Escasany, T. and O'Hare, G. (2001) Samba: A metaphor for Rio's favelas? *Cities*, 8(4): 259–270.

Barnett, J. (2007) *Smart Growth in a Changing World*. Chicago, IL: APA Planners Press.

Barnett, M. (2011) *Empire of Humanity*. Ithaca, NY: Cornell University Press.

Barry, A. and Thrift, N. (2007) Gabriel Tarde: Imitation, invention and economy. *Economy and Society*, 36(4): 509–525.

Bataille, G. ([1949] 1988) *The Accursed Share*, vol. I. London: Urzone.

Bauman, Z. (1988) *Freedom*. Minnesota: University of Minnesota Press.

Bauman, Z. (1989) *Modernity and the Holocaust*. Cambridge: Polity.

Bauman, Z. (1991) *Modernity and Ambivalence*. Cambridge: Polity.

Bauman, Z. (1996) *Tourists and Vagabonds*. Institut für Höhere Studien (IHS), Wien, Abt. Politikwissenschaft 30, pp. 7–15. Available at: http://nbn-resolving.de/urn:nbn: de:0168-ssoar-266870 [accessed: 13 September 2016].

Bauman, Z. (1997) *Modernity and its Discontents*. Cambridge: Polity.

Bauman, Z. (1998) *Globalization*. New York: Columbia University Press.

Bauman, Z. (2000) *Liquid Modernity*. Cambridge: Polity.

Bauman, Z. (2001) *Community*. Cambridge: Polity.

Bauman, Z. (2003) *Liquid Love*. Cambridge: Polity.

Bauman, Z. and Lyon, D. (2013) *Liquid Surveillance*. Cambridge: Polity.

BBC Sports (29 January 2016). Zika virus: Olympic venues to be inspected daily before and during Games. Available at: www.bbc.co.uk/sport/olympics/35444254 [accessed: 19 October 2016].

BBC Sports (15 August 2016). Stefan Henze: Germany canoe slalom coach dies following car crash. Available at: www.bbc.co.uk/sport/olympics/37090353 [accessed: 10 November 2016].

Beard, J.L. (2007) *The Political Economy of Desire*. New York: Glasshouse.

Beaverstock, J.V., Derudder, B., Faulconbridge, J.R. and Witlox, F. (2009) International business travel: Some explorations. *Geografiska Annaler*, 91: 193–202.

Beck, U. (1992) *Risk Society*. London: Sage.

Beck, U. (1999) *Individualization*. London: Sage.

Beck, U. (2002a). The cosmopolitan society and its enemies. *Theory, Culture & Society*, 19(1–2): 17–44.

Beck, U. (2002b). The terrorist threat: World risk society revisited. *Theory, Culture & Society*, 19(4): 25–56.

Beck, U. (2006) Living in the world risk society. *Economy and Society*, 35(3): 329–345.

Beck, U. (2007) The cosmopolitan condition: Why methodological nationalism fails. *Theory, Culture & Society*, 24(7–8): 286–290.

Beck, U. (2009) *World at Risk*. Cambridge: Polity.

Beck, U. and Beck-Gernsheim, E. (1995) *The Normal Chaos of Love*. Cambridge: Polity.

Beck, U., Giddens, A. and Lash, S. (1994) *Reflexive Modernization*. Cambridge: Polity.

Becker, H. (1982) *Art Worlds*. Berkeley: University of California Press.

Beek, W. and Schmidt, A. (eds), (2012) *African Hosts and their Guests*. New York: James Currey.

Beeton, S. (2005) *Film-induced Tourism*. Toronto: Channel View.

Beeton, S. (2006) Understanding film-induced tourism. *Tourism Analysis*, 11: 181–188.

Beeton, S. (2010) The advance of film tourism. *Tourism and Hospitality: Planning and Development*, 7: 1–6.

Béhague, G. (2000) Afro-Brazilian traditions. In: D.A. Olsen and D.E. Sheehy (eds), *The Garland Handbook of Latin American Music*. New York: Garland Publishing, pp. 272–287.

Bell, D. (1976) *The Cultural Contradictions of Capitalism*. New York: Basic Books.

Bell, B. and Wakeford, K. (eds), (2008) *Expanding Architecture*. New York: Metropolis.

Bell, C. and Lyall, J. (2002) *The Accelerated Sublime*. Westport, CT: Praeger.

Bell, D. and Jayne, M. (2010) The creative countryside: Policy and practice in the UK rural cultural economy. *Journal of Rural Studies*, 26: 209–218.

Bell, D., Holliday, R., Jones, M., Probyn, E. and Sanchez-Taylor, J. (2011) Bikinis and bandages: An itinerary for cosmetic surgery tourism. *Tourist Studies*, 11(2), pp. 139–155.

Ben-Ze'ev, E. and Lomsky-Feder, E. (2009) The canonical generation: Trapped between personal and national memories. *Sociology*, 43(6): 1047–1066.

Benhabib, S. (1992) *Situating the Self*. New York: Routledge.

Benhabib, S. (1996) *The Reluctant Modernism of Hannah Arendt*. London: Sage.

Berger, P. and Luckmann, T. (1966) *The Social Construction of Reality*. New York: Doubleday.

Berking, H. (1999) *Sociology of Giving*. London: Sage.

Berlant, L. (1997) *The Queen of American Goes to Washington City*. Durham, NC: Duke University Press.

Berlant, L. (2011) *Cruel Optimism*. Durham, NC: Duke University Press.

Berman, M. (1982) *All that is Solid Melts into Air*. New York: Simon and Schuster.

Bernal, Y. (2016). Rio's official blames financial troubles for pollution woes, *Phys.org*, 29 June. Available at: http://phys.org/news/2016-06-rio-blames-financial-pollution-woes. html [accessed: 5 September 2016].

Bernstein, E. (2001) The meaning of the purchase: Desire, demand and the commerce of sex. *Ethnography*, 2(3): 389–420.

Bertman, S. (1998) *Hyperculture*. Westport, CT: Praeger.

Bhabha, H.K. (1990a). DissemiNation. In: H.K. Bhabha (ed.), *Nation and Narration*. New York: Routledge, pp. 291–322.

Bhabha, H.K. (1990b). Narrating the nation. In: H.K. Bhabha (ed.), *Nation and Narration*. New York: Routledge, pp. 1–7.

Bhabha, H.K. (1990c). The Other Question: Difference, discrimination and the discourse of colonialism. In: R. Ferguson, M. Gevr, T.T. Min-Ha and C. West (eds), *Out There*. Cambridge, MA: MIT, pp. 71–87.

Bhabha, H.K. (1994) *The Location of Culture*. London and New York: Routledge.

Bigo, D. (2006) Globalized (in)security: The field and the ban-opticon. In: D. Bigo and A. Tsoukala (eds), *Illiberal Practices of Liberal Regimes*. Paris: L'Harmattan, pp. 10–48.

Billboard Staff (2016). Kygo to perform at Rio Olympics Closing Ceremony. 16 August. Available at: http://www.billboard.com/articles/news/dance/7476054/kygo-rio-olympics-closing-ceremony [accessed: 10 November 2016].

Billig, M. (1995) *Banal Nationalism*. London: Sage.

Biran, A., Poria, Y. and Oren, G. (2011) Sought experience at dark heritage sites. *Annals of Tourism Research*, 38(3): 820–841.

Birnie, P., Boyle, A. and Redgwell, C. (2009) *International Law and the Environment*. Oxford: Oxford University Press.

Birtchnell, T. and Urry, J. (2012) Fabricating futures and the movement of objects. *Mobilities*, 8(3): 1–18.

Bissel, D. (2010) Passenger mobilities: Affective atmospheres and the sociality of public transport. *Environment and Planning D: Society and Space*, 28: 270–289.

Black, D. and Van der Westhuizen, J. (2004) The allure of global games for 'semi-peripheral' polities and spaces: A research agenda. *Third World Quarterly*, 25(7): 1195–1214.

Bleecker, J. and Knowlton, J. (2006) Locative media: A brief bibliography and taxonomy of GPS-enabled locative media. *Leonardo: Electronic Almanac*, 14(3). Available at: www.leoalmanac.org/wp-content/uploads/2012/07/Locative-Media-A-Brief-Bibliography-And-Taxonomy-Of-Gps-Enabled-Locative-Media-Vol-14-No-3-July-2006-Leonardo-Electronic-Almanac.pdf [accessed: 19 September 2016].

Bligh, M., Casad, B., Grotto, A. and Schlehofer, M. (2011) Navigating public prejudices: The impact of media and attitudes on high-profile female political leaders. *Sex Roles*, 65(1–2): 69–82.

Bloch, E. (1986) *The Principle of Hope*, vol. II. Cambridge, MA: MIT.

Bloch, E. (1988) *The Utopian Function of Art and Literature*. Cambridge, MA: MIT.

Bloomberg (2015) Rio Olympics ceremony to cost 10% of London's lavish event open, 22 September. Available at: www.bloomberg.com/news/articles/2015-09-22/rio-olympics-ceremony-to-cost-10-of-london-s-lavish-event-open [accessed: 20 October 2016].

Boes, K., Buhalis, D. and Inversini, A. (2015) Conceptualising smart tourism destination dimensions. In: *Information and Communication Technologies in Tourism 2015*. Lugano: Springer, pp. 391–403.

Bohm, D. (1980) *Wholeness and the Implicate Order*. London: Routledge and Kegan Paul.

Böhme, G. (1993) Atmosphere as the fundamental concept of a new aesthetics. *Thesis Eleven*, 36: 113–126.

Böhme, G. (1995) *Atmosphere*. Frankfurt: Suhrkamp.

Bollens, S. (2007) *Cities, Nationalism, and Democratization*. New York: Routledge.

Boltanski, L. (1999) *Distant Suffering*. New York: Cambridge University Press.

Boltanski, L. (2012) *Love and Justice as Competences*. Cambridge: Polity.

Boltanski, L. and Chiapello, E. (2004) *The New Sprit of Capitalism*. London: Verso.

Boltanski, L. and Thévenot, L. (2006) *On Justification*. Princeton, NJ: Princeton University Press.

Bonn, M.A., Joseph-Matthews, S.M., Dai, M., Hayes, S. and Cave, J. (2007) Heritage/cultural attraction atmospheres: Creating the right environment for the heritage/cultural visitor. *Journal of Travel Research*, 45(3): 345–354.

Boomachine (6 March 2013). SAVING 10,000 – Winning a war on suicide in Japan – 自殺者1万人を救う戦い. Available at: www.youtube.com/watch?v=oo0SHLxc2d0 [accessed: 6 April 2017].

Born, G. (2010) The social and the aesthetic: For a post-Bourdieusian theory of cultural production. *Cultural Sociology*, 4(2): 171–208.

Born, G. and Hesmondhalgh, D. (eds) (2000) *Western Music and its Others*. Chicago, IL: University of California Press.

Botterill, D., Seixas, R.D.C.S. and Hoeffel, J.L. (2014) Tourism and transgression: Resort development, crime and the drug economy. *Tourism Planning and Development*, 11(1): 27–41.

Bourdieu, P. (1977) *Outline of a Theory of Practice*. Cambridge: Cambridge University Press.

Bourdieu, P. (1984) *Distinction*. Cambridge, MA: Harvard University Press.

Bourdieu, P. (1990) *In Other Words*. Stanford, CA: Stanford University Press

Bourdieu, P. (1993) *The Field of Cultural Production*. Oxford: Polity.

Bourdieu, P. (1997) Selections from the logic of practice. In: P. Bourdieu, *The Logic of the Gift*. London: Routledge, pp. 190–230.

Bourdieu, P. (1998) *Practical Reason*. Cambridge: Polity.

Bourdieu, P. and Darbel, A. (1990) *The Love of Art*. Stanford, CA: Stanford University Press.

Bourdieu, P. and Wacquant, L.J.D. (eds), (1992) *An Invitation to Reflexive Sociology*. Chicago, IL: University of Chicago Press.

Boyle, P. and Haggerty, K.D. (2009) Spectacular security: Mega-events and the security complex. *International Political Sociology*, 3(3): 257–274.

Braathen, E., Mascarenhas, G. and Sørbøe, C.M. (2015) A 'city of exception'? Rio de Janeiro and the disputed social legacy of the 2014 and 2016 sports mega-events. In: V. Viehoff and G. Poynter (eds), *Mega-Event Cities*. Aldershot: Ashgate, pp. 261–270.

Braidotti, R. (2013) *The Posthuman*. Cambridge: Polity.

Braudel, F. (1996) *The Mediterranean and the Mediterranean World in the Age of Philip II*, vol. II. Chicago, IL: University of California Press.

Brenner, N. (2004) *New State Spaces*. Oxford: Oxford University Press.

Brewster, C. and Brewster, K. (2006) Mexico City 1968: Sombreros and skyscrapers. In: A. Tomlinson and C. Young (eds), *National Identity and Global Sports Events*. New York: SUNY, pp. 99–116.

Brillon, J. (2016). Diminutive Rio 2016 cauldron complemented by massive kinetic sculpture. *Dezeen Magazine*, 8 August. Available at: www.dezeen.com/2016/08/08/rio-2016-cauldron-massive-kinetic-sculpture-anthony-howe/ [accessed: 8 November 2016].

Brown, S.T. (2005) Screening anime. In: S.T. Brown (ed.), *Cinema Anime*. New York: Palgrave Macmillan, pp. 1–19.

Brun, C. (2015) Active waiting and changing hopes: Toward a time perspective on protracted displacement. *Social Analysis*, 59(1): 19–37.

Brun, C. (2016) There is no future in humanitarianism: Emergency, temporality and protracted displacement. *History and Anthropology*, 27(4): 393–410.

Bruner, E.M. (1989) Tourism, creativity and authenticity. *Studies in Symbolic Interaction*, 10: 109–114.

Brunhuber, K. (2016). Formerly homeless boy who lit Olympic cauldron now has 'beautiful life'. 12 August. Available at: http://www.cbc.ca/news/world/rio-olympics-boy-who-lit-cauldron-1.3716398 [accessed: 8 December 2016].

Bryans, P., Cunningham, R. and Mavin, S. (2010) Fed-up with Blair's babes, Gordon's gals, Cameron's cuties, Nick's nymphets. *Gender in Management*, 25(7), pp. 550–569.

Bryant, R. (2016) On critical times: Return, repetition, and the uncanny present. *History and Anthropology*, 27(1): 19–31.

Buhler, J., Neumayer, D. and Deemer, R. (2009) *Hearing the Movies*. New York: Oxford University Press.

Burawoy, M. (1989) Two methods in search of science: Skocpol versus Trotsky. *Theory & Society*, 18: 765–805.

Burton-Carvajal, J. (2000) South American cinema. In: J. Hill and P. Church Gibson (eds), *Film Studies*. Oxford: Oxford University Press, pp. 194–202.

Buscema, C. (2011) The harvest of Dionysus: Mobility/Proximity, indigenous migrants and relational machines. In: G. Pellegrino (ed.), *The Politics of Proximity*. Aldershot: Ashgate, pp. 43–60.

Büscher, M., Liegl, M. and Thomas, V. (2014) Collective intelligence in crises. In: V. Maltese, M. Rovatsos, A. Nijholt and J. Stewart (eds), *Social Collective Intelligence*. Cham: Springer, pp. 243–266.

Büscher, M., Kerasidou, X., Liegl, M., Petersen, K. (2016) Digital urbanism in crises. In: R. Kitchin and S.Y. Perng (eds), *Code and the City*. London and New York: Routledge, pp. 163–177.

Butler, J. (1993) *Bodies that Matter*. London: Routledge.

Butler, J. (1997) *The Psychic Life of Power*. Stanford, CA: Stanford University Press.

Butler, J. (2007) *Gender Trouble*, 2nd edn. London: Routledge.

Butler, J. (2009) *Frames of War*. London: Verso.

Butler, N. (2015). Rio 2015 promise 'original' Olympic Opening Ceremony despite low budget. Inside the Games, 23 September. Available at: www.insidethegames.biz/arti cles/1030407/rio-2016-promise-original-olympic-opening-ceremony-despite-low-budget [accessed: 20 October 2016].

Cabanes, B. (2014) *The Great War and the Origins of Humanitarianism, 1918–1924*. Cambridge: Cambridge University Press.

Caffyn, A. (2012) Advocating and implementing slow tourism. *Tourism Recreation Research*, 37(1): 77–80.

Caldeira, T. (2000) *City of Walls*. London: Routledge.

Călinescu, M. (1987) *Five Faces of Modernity*. Durham, NC: Duke University Press.

Cameron, G. (1999) Multi-track microproliferation: Lessons from Aum Shinrikyo and Al Qaida. *Studies in Conflict and Terrorism*, 22(4): 277–309.

Campbell, C. (1987) *The Protestant Ethic and the Spirit of Modern Consumerism*. Oxford: Basil Blackwell.

Campbell, J. (2008) *The Hero with a Thousand Faces*. Novato, CA: New World.

Cantor-Navas, J. (2016). Rio Olympics: Anitta, Ceatano Veloso, Gilberto Gil to perform at Olympic ceremony. *Billboard*, 15 July. Available at: www.billboard.com/a rticles/columns/latin/7438960/rio-olympics-anitta-caetano-veloso-gilberto-gil [accessed: 20 October 2016].

Capra, P. (1996) *The Web of Life*. London: Harper Collins.

Cardoso, F.H. and Faletto, D. (1979) *Dependency and Development in Latin America*. Berkeley: University of California Press.

Carter, N. (2007) *The Politics of the Environment*. Cambridge: Cambridge University Press.

Carter, P. (2010) *Road to Botany Bay*. Minneapolis, MN: University of Minnesota Press.

Carter, P. (2013) *Meeting Place*. Minneapolis, MN: University of Minnesota Press.

Carter, P. (2015) *Places Made After Their Stories*. Nedlands, WA: UWA Publishing.

Carter, T.F. (2016) Pulling back the curtain: On mobility and labour migration in the production of mega-events. In: N.B. Salazar, C. Timmerman, J. Wets, L. Gama Gato and S. Van den Broucke (eds), *Mega-Event Mobilities*. Abingdon: Routledge, pp. 16–32.

Carvalho, B. (2013) *Porous City*. Liverpool: Liverpool University Press.

Cascone, S. (2016). Two-ton sculpture mesmerizes crowd at Olympic Torch lighting Ceremony. *Artnet News*, 8 August. Available at: https://news.artnet.com/art-world/a nthony-howe-kinetic-sculpture-olympic-flame-339013 [accessed: 9 November 2016].

Castells, M. (1996) *The Rise of the Network Society*. Oxford: Blackwell.

Castells, M. (2004) Informationalism, networks and the network society: A theoretical blueprint. In: M. Castells (ed.), *The Network Society*. Cheltenham: Edward Elgar, pp. 3–45.

Castells, M. (2009) *Communication Power*. Oxford: Oxford University Press.

Castoriadis, C. ([1975] 1987) *The Imaginary Institution of Society*. Cambridge, MA: Cambridge University Press.

Castree, N. (2005) *Nature*. London: Routledge.

Castro, R. (2000) *Bossa Nova: The Story of the Brazilian Music That Seduced the World*. San Francisco, CA: A Cappella.

Cavalcanti, M. (2016) Rio's Olympic ruins. Open Democracy, 21 August. Available at: www.opendemocracy.net/mariana-cavalcanti/rio-s-olympic-ruins [accessed: 19 October 2016].

Cavalcanti, P. (2009) Construção. *Rolling Stone Brasil*, Edição 37(1), October. Available at: http://rollingstone.uol.com.br/edicao/37/noticia-3939#imagem0 [accessed: 1 November 2001].

Chaban, M. (2014). The canvas and creativity drive renowned architect Santiago Calatrava's structures. *New York Daily News*, 21 March. Available at: www.nydaily news.com/life-style/real-estate/santiago-calatrava-works-art-article-1.1728805 [accessed: 7 September 2016].

Chakrabarty, D. (2000) *Provincializing Europe*. Princeton, NJ: Princeton University Press.

Chatterjee, P. (1986) *Nationalist Thought and the Colonial World*. Minneapolis, MN: University of Minnesota Press.

Chatterjee, P. (1993) *The Nation and its Fragments*. Princeton, NJ: Princeton University Press.

Chion, M. (1994) *Audio-Vision*. New York: Columbia University Press.

Chown, M. (2007) *The Never-Ending Days of Being Dead*. London: Faber & Faber.

Clarke, J. (2010) After neo-liberalism? Markets, states, and the reinvention of public welfare. *Cultural Studies*, 24(3): 375–394.

Clifford, J. (1992) Travelling cultures. In: L. Grossberg, C. Nelson and P. Treichler (eds), *Cultural Studies*. New York: Routledge, pp. 96–116.

Clifford, J. (1997) *Routes*. Cambridge, MA: Harvard University Press.

Clifford, J. (2013) *Returns*. Cambridge, MA: Harvard University Press.

Cloke, P. (2006) Rurality and creative nature-culture connections. In: H. Clout (ed.), *Contemporary Rural Geographies*. London: Routledge, pp. 96–110.

Close, P., Askew, D. and Xin, X. (2006) *The Beijing Olympiad*. London: Routledge.

CNN (2003). Brazil's Gilberto Gil, minister of cool. 1 September. Available at: http://edition.cnn.com/2003/WORLD/americas/09/01/brazil.people.gil.reut/ [accessed: 23 October 2016].

Coaffee, J. (2009) *Terrorism, Risk and the Global City*. Farnham: Ashgate.

Cochrane, A. (2011) Making up global urban policies. In: G. Bridge and S. Watson (eds), *The New Blackwell Companion to the City*. Oxford: Blackwell, pp. 738–746.

Cohen, E.H. (1975) Review A World of Strangers by Lyn Hofland, 1973. *American Journal of Sociology*, 80(4): 1024–1026.

Cohen, E.H. (1979) A phenomenology of tourist experiences. *Sociology*, 13(2): 179–201.

Cohen, E.H. (1995) Touristic craft ribbon development in Thailand. *Tourism Management*, 16(3): 225–235.

Cohen, E.H. (2011) Educational dark tourism in populo site: The Holocaust Museum in Jerusalem, *Annals of Tourism Research*, 38(1): 193–209.

Cohen, S. (2005) Screaming at the moptops: Convergences between tourism and popular music. In: D. Crouch, R. Jackson and F. Thompson (eds), *The Media and the Tourist Imagination*. New York: Routledge, pp. 76–91.

Cohnitz, D. and Rossberg, M. (2016) Nelson Goodman. *The Stanford Encyclopedia of Philosophy* (Spring 2016 Edition, ed. by Edward N. Zalta). Available at: http://plato.stanford.edu/archives/spr2016/entries/goodman/ [accessed: 27 April 2016].

Coleman, N. (2005) *Utopias and Architecture*. Abingdon: Routledge.

Coleman, N. (2013) 'Building in empty spaces': Is architecture a 'degenerate utopia'? *The Journal of Architecture*, 18(2): 135–166.

Collins-Kreiner, N. (2010) Researching pilgrimage: Continuity and transformations. *Annals of Tourism Research*, 37(2): 440–456.

Colomb, C. (2013) *Staging the New Berlin*. London: Routledge.

Complex News (2016). Man tries to put out Olympic Torch with fire Extinguisher. *YouTube*, 15 July. Available at: www.youtube.com/watch?v=6C5SaKLsb4c [accessed: 22 January 2017].

Conde, M. (2012) *Consuming Visions*. Charlottesville: University of Virginia Press.

Conduru, R. (2004) Tropical tectonics. In: A. Forti and E. Andreoli (eds), *Brazil's Modern Architecture*. Munich: Phaidon.

Connell, J. and Gibson, C. (2004) World music: Deterritorialising place and identity, *Progress in Human Geography*, 28(3): 342–361.

Connell, R.W. (1987) *Gender and Power*. Stanford, CA: Stanford University Press.

Connell, R.W. (1995) *Masculinities*. Berkeley, CA: University of California Press.

Conner, R. (2009) *Brazilian Blackface: Maracatu clearance and the Politics of Participation*. Master's thesis, University of California, Riverside.

Corrêa, C. and Kitano, C. (2015) Gamification in tourism: The Brazil Quest game. National Council for Scientific and Technological Development. Available at: www.academia.edu/11058323/Gamification_in_Tourism_Analysis_of_Brazil_Quest_Game [accessed: 19 September 2016].

Cornelissen, S. (2010) The geopolitics of global aspiration: Sport mega-events and emerging powers. *International Journal of the History of Sport*, 25(16): 3008–3025.

Cosgrove, D. and Jackson, P. (1987) New directions in culture geography. *Area*, 19: 95–101.

Couldry, N. (2000) *The Place of Media Power*. London: Routledge.

Couldry, N. (2003) *Media Rituals*. New York: Routledge.

Couldry, N. (2012) *Media, Society, World*. Cambridge: Polity.

Cowan, J.K. (1990) *Dance and the Body Politic in Northern Greece*. Princeton, NJ: Princeton University Press.

Coyne, R. (1999) *Technoromanticism*. Boston, MA: MIT.

Crang, M. and Franklin, A. (2001) The trouble with tourism and travel theory. *Tourist Studies*, 1(1): 5–22.

Cresswell, T. (2001) The production of mobilities. *New Formations*, 43(1): 11–25.

Cresswell, T. (2006) *On the Move*. London: Routledge.

Cresswell, T. (2010) Towards a politics of mobility. *Environment and Planning D*, 28(1): 17–31.

Cresswell, T. (2016) Black moves: Movements in the history of African-American mobilities. *Transfers*, 6(1): 12–25.

Cresswell, T. and Merriman, P. (2001) *Choreographies of Mobilities*. Aldershot: Ashgate.

Crook, L. (2005) *Brazilian Music*. Santa Barbara, CA: ABC-CLIO.

Crossley, N. (2002) Global anti-corporate struggle: A preliminary analysis. *British Journal of Sociology*, 53(4): 667–691.

Crossley, N. (2003) From reproduction to transformation: social movement fields and the radical habitus. *Theory, Culture & Society*, 20(6): 43–68.

Croy, G.W. (2010) Planning for film tourism: Active destination image management. *Tourism and Hospitality Planning & Development*, 7(1): 21–23.

Crutzen, P.J. (2002) Geology of mankind. *Nature*, 415(86/87): 23.

Crutzen, P.J. and Stoermer, E.F. (2000) The Anthropocene. *Global Change Newsletter*, 41: 17–18.

Currah, A. (2007) Managing creativity: The tensions between commodities and gifts in a digital networked environment. *Economy and Society*, 36(3): 467–494.

Curran, J.P. (2011) *Media and Democracy*. London: Routledge.

Czeglédy, A.P. (2003) The words and things of Ernest Gellner. *Social Evolution & History*, 2(2): 6–33.

D'Alisa, G., Kallis, G. and DeMaria, F. (2015) From austerity to dépense. In: G. D'Alisa, F. DeMaria and G. Kallis (eds), *Degrowth*. New York: Routledge, pp. 215–220.

Da Redação (2015). Rio 2016: Rosa Magalhães deve comandar encerramento. 19 December. Available at: http://esporte.band.uol.com.br/rio-2016/noticia/100000772124/rio-2016-rosa-magalhaes-deve-comandar-encerramento.html?mobile=true [accessed: 9 December 2015].

Dales, L. and Bulbeck, C. (2013) From feminism to postfeminism in forty years? In: A. Elliott, M. Katagiri and A. Sawai (eds), *Routledge Companion to Contemporary Japanese Social Theory*. New York: Routledge, pp. 158–161.

DaMatta, R. (1991) *Carnivals, Rogues, and Heroes*. Notre Dame, IN: University of Notre Dame Press.

DaMatta, R. (1995) For an anthropology of the Brazilian tradition – or 'A virtude esta no Meio'. In: D.J. Hess and R. DaMatta (eds), *The Brazilian Puzzle*. New York: Columbia University Press, pp. 270–291.

Dann, G.M.S. (1977) Anomie, ego-enhancement and tourism. *Annals of Tourism Research*, 4(4): 184–194.

Dann, G.M.S. (1996) *The Language of Tourism*. Wallingford: CABI.

Dann, G.M.S. (1998) The dark side of tourism. *Etudes et Rapports*. Aix-en-Provence: Centre International de Reserches et d'Etudes Touristiques, L(14): 1–31.

Dann, G.M.S. (2002) The tourist as a metaphor of the social world. In: G.M.S. Dann (ed.), *The Tourist as a Metaphor of the Social World*. Wallingford: CABI, pp. 1–18.

Dann, G.M.S. and Seaton, A.V. (2001) Slavery, contested heritage and thanatourism. In: G.M.S. Dann and A.V. Seaton (eds), *Slavery, Contested Heritage and Thanatourism*. New York: Haworth Hospitality Press, pp. 1–29.

Dascal, M. (1987) *Leibniz*. Amsterdam: John Benjamin's.

Dasgupta, R. (2005) *Salarymen Doing Straight*. New York: Routledge.

Dávila, A. (2012) *Culture Works*. New York: New York University Press.

Davis, B. (2014). Baz Luhrmann's Christmas Nightmare at Barneys. *Artnet News*, 19 December. Available at: https://news.artnet.com/opinion/baz-luhrmanns-christmas-nightmare-at-barneys-198831 [accessed: 9 December 2016].

Davis, D.J. (2009) *White Face, Black Mask*. Ann Arbor: Michigan State University Press.

Davis, M. (1990) *City of Quartz*. London: Verso.

Davis, M. (2006) *Planet of Slums*. London: Verso.

Davis, M. and Monk, D.M. (2007) *Evils Paradises*. New York: The New Press.

Dayrell, C. and Urry, J. (2015) Mediating climate politics: The surprising case of Brazil. *European Journal of Social Theory*, 18(3): 257–273.

De Beauvoir, S. ([1952] 1988) *Second Sex*. London: Cape.

De Beauvoir, S. (2007) The independent woman. In: S. During (ed.), *The Cultural Studies Reader*. Abingdon: Routledge, pp. 337–357.

De Certeau, M. (1988) *The Practice of Everyday Life*. Berkeley: University of California Press.

De Visser, R.O. and McDonnell, E.J. (2013) 'Man points': Masculine capital and young men's health. *Health Psychology*, 32(1): 5–14.

De Vivo, D. (2012). Tokyo Sky Tree: The world's tallest broadcasting tower. *Megalopolis Now*, 8 August. Available at: https://megalopolisnow.com/2012/08/08/tokyo-sky-tree-the-worlds-tallest-broadcasting-tower/ [accessed: 15 December 2016].

Debord, G. (1995) *Society and the Spectacle*. New York: Zone.

Degen, M. (2004) Barcelona's Games: The Olympics, urban design, and global tourism. In: M. Sheller and J. Urry (eds), *Tourism Mobilities*. London: Routledge, pp. 131–142.

Del Chiappa, G. and Baggio, R. (2015) Knowledge transfer in smart tourism destinations: Analyzing the effects of a network structure. *Journal of Destination Marketing and Management*, 4(3): 145–150.

Delanty, G. (2003) Consumption, modernity and Japanese cultural identity: The limits of Americanization? In: U. Beck, N. Sznaider and R. Winter (eds), *Global America*. Liverpool: Liverpool University Press, pp. 114–133.

Delanty, G. (2009) *The Cosmopolitan Imagination*. Cambridge: Cambridge University Press.

Delanty, G. (2011) Cultural diversity, democracy and the prospects of cosmopolitanism: A theory of cultural encounters. *British Journal of Sociology*, 62(4): 633–656.

Delanty, G. (2014) Not all is lost in translation: World varieties of cosmopolitanism. *Cultural Sociology*, 8(4): 374–391.

Deleuze, G. and Guattari, F. (1988) *A Thousand Plateaus*. London: Athlone.

Denzin, N.K. and Lincoln, Y.S. (1998) *Collecting and Interpreting Qualitative Material*. London: Sage.

Derrida, J. (1976) *Of Grammatology*. Baltimore, MD: John Hopkins University Press.

Derrida, J. (1994) *Spectres of Marx*. New York: Routledge.

Derrida, J. and Dufourmantelle, A. (2000) *Of Hospitality*. Stanford, CA: Stanford University Press.

Deslandes, A. and King, D. (2006) Autonomous activism and the global justice movement: Aesthetic reflexivity in practice. *Journal of Sociology*, 42(3): 310–327.

Dewsbury, J.D. (2011) The Deleuze-Guattarian assemblage: Plastic habits. *Area*, 43(2): 148–153.

Dezeen Magazine (2015). Calatrava's City of Arts and Sciences is 'insane' and 'amazing' says George Clooney. 21 May. Available at: www.dezeen.com/2015/05/21/cala trava-city-of-arts-sciences-valencia-tomorrowland-george-clooney-brad-bird/ [accessed: 7 September 2016].

Dezeen Magazine (2015). Museum of Tomorrow by Santiago Calatrava opens in Rio de Janeiro. 17 December. Available at: www.dezeen.com/2015/12/17/science-museum -of-tomorrow-santiago-calatrava-opens-rio-de-janeiro-brazil/ [accessed: 15 September 2016].

Dickinson, J.E. and Lumsdon, L.M. (2010) *Slow Travel and Tourism*. London: Earthscan.

Dickinson, J.E. and Peters, P. (2014) Time, tourism consumption and sustainable development. *International Journal of Tourism Research*, 16(1): 11–21.

Diken, B. and Laustsen, C.B. (2008) *Sociology through the Projector*. London: Routledge.

DiMaggio, P. (1987) Classification in art. *American Sociological Review*, 52(4): 440–455.

DiMaggio, P. (1992) Cultural boundaries and structural change: The extension of the high culture model to theatre, opera and dance, 1900–1940. In: M. Lamont and M. Fournier (eds), *Cultivating Differences*. Chicago, IL: University of Chicago Press, pp. 21–57.

Dimitrova Savova, N. (2009) Heritage kinaesthetics: Local constructivism and UNESCO's intangible-tangible politics at a favela museum. *Anthropological Quarterly*, 82(2): 547–585.

Donald, J. (1999) *Imagining the Modern City*. London: Athlone Press.

Donald, S.H. and Gammack, J.G. (2007) *Tourism and the Branded City*. Farnham: Ashgate.

Donnelly, P. (2004) Sport and risk culture. In: K. Young (ed.), *Sporting Bodies, Damaged Selves*. Oxford: Elsevier, pp. 29–57.

Douglas, I., Hodgson, R. and Lawson, N. (2002) Industry, environment and health through 200 years in Manchester. *Ecological Economics*, 41(2): 235–255.

Dower, J. (1999) *Embracing Defeat*. London: W.W. Norton.

Dryzek, J. (2000) *Deliberative Democracy and Beyond*. Oxford: Oxford University Press.

Dryzek, J. (2005) *The Politics of the Earth*. Oxford: Oxford University Press.

Duggan, B. (2012) An Ode to Heloísa, 7 February. Available at: www.latinamerica ncoalition.org/blog/31/An-Ode-to-Heloisa [accessed: 2 November 2016].

Duncan, J. (1999) Dis-orientation: On the shock of the familiar in a far-away place. In: J. Duncan and D. Gregory (eds), *Writes of Passage*. London: Routledge, pp. 161–179.

Dunn, C. (2001) *Brutality Garden*. Chapel Hill: University of North Carolina Press.

Dürrschmidt, J. (1997) The delinking of locale and milieu. In: J. Eade (ed.), *Living the Global City*. London: Routledge, pp. 56–72.

Dussel, E. (1985) *Philosophy of Liberation*. New York: Orbis.

Dussel, E. (1995) *The Invention of the Americas*. New York: Continuum.

Dussel, E. (1996) *The Underside of Modernity*. Atlantic Highlands, NJ: Humanities Press.

Dussel, E. (2013) *Ethics of Liberation in the Age of Globalization and Exclusion*. Durham, NC: Duke University Press.

Eade, J. (1992) Pilgrimage and tourism at Lourdes, France. *Annals of Tourism Research*, 19(1): 18–32.

Eade, J. (2000) *Placing London*. New York: Berghahn.

Eade, J. and Mele, C. (2002) Understanding the city. In: J. Eade and C. Mele (eds), *Understanding the City*. Malden, MA: Blackwell, pp. 1–24.

Eckersley, R. (2000) Deliberative democracy, ecological representation and risk: Towards a democracy of the affected. In: M. Saward (ed.), *Democratic Innovation*. London: Routledge, pp. 117–132.

Eckersley, R. (2004) *The Green State*. Cambridge, MA: MIT Press.

Edensor, T. (2005) Mediating William Wallace: Audio-visual technologies in tourism. In: D. Crouch, R. Jackson and F. Thompson (eds), *The Media and the Tourist Imagination*. New York: Routledge, pp. 105–118.

Edensor, T. (2010) *Choreographies of Rhythm*. Aldershot: Ashgate.

Edensor, T. (2011) Commuter: Mobility, rhythm, commuting. In: T. Cresswell and P. Merriman (eds), *Geographies of Mobilities*. Farnham: Ashgate, pp. 189–204.

Edensor, T. (2014) Rhythm and arrhythmia. In: P. Adey (ed.), *The Routledge Handbook of Mobilities*. London and New York: Routledge, pp. 163–171.

Edmonds, A. (2007) 'The poor have the right to be beautiful': Cosmetic surgery in neoliberal Brazil. *Journal of the Royal Anthropological Institute*, 13(2): 363–381.

Ehara, Y. (2013) Japanese feminist social theory and gender equality. In: A. Elliott, M. Katagiri and A. Sawai (eds), *Routledge Companion to Contemporary Japanese Social Theory*. New York: Routledge, pp. 162–175.

Ehlers, E., Moss, C. and Krafft, T. (2006) *Earth System Science in the Anthropocene*. Berlin: Springer Science.

Ekeli, K. (2007) Green constitutionalism: The constitutional protection of future generations. *Ratio Juris*, 20(3): 378–401.

Elias, N. (1978) *The Civilising Process, vol. I: The History of Manners*. Oxford: Blackwell.

Elias, N. (1982) *The Civilising Process, vol. II: State Formation and Civilisation*. Oxford: Blackwell.

Elliott, A. (2013) Prelude: The three selves in Japanese society. In: A. Elliott, M. Katagiri and A. Sawai (eds), *Routledge Companion to Contemporary Japanese Social Theory*. New York: Routledge, pp. 135–138.

Elliott, L. (2004) *The Global Politics of the Environment*. Basingstoke: Palgrave Macmillan.

Elmer, G. (2010) Locative networking: Finding and being found. *Aether*, 5A(March): 18–26.

Erlmann, V. (1999) *Music, Modernity and the Global Imagination*. Oxford: Oxford University Press.

Erlmann, V. (2004) But what of the ethnographic ear? Anthropology, sound and the senses. In: V. Erlmann (ed.), *Hearing Cultures*. Oxford: Berg, pp. 1–20.

Escobar, A. (1995) *Encountering Development*. Princeton, NJ: Princeton University Press.

Escobar, A. (2015) Development, critiques of. In: G. D'Alisa, F. DeMaria and G. Kallis (eds), *Degrowth*. New York and London: Routledge, pp. 29–32.

Esping-Andersen, G. (1994) Welfare state and the economy. In: N.J. Smelser and R. Swedberg (eds), *The Handbook of Economic Sociology*. Princeton, NJ: Princeton University Press, pp. 711–732.

ESPN (2016). IOC approves addition of five sports for 2020 Tokyo Olympics. 4 August. Available at: www.espn.com/olympics/story/_/id/17211614/ioc-approves-addition-five-sports-2020-tokyo-olympics [accessed: 8 December 2016].

Evans, P.B. and Sewell, W.H. Jr. (2014) The neoliberal era: Ideology, policy and social effects. In: P. Hall and M. Lamont (eds), *Social Resilience in the Neoliberal Era.* Cambridge: Cambridge University Press, pp. 35–68.

Fagge, N., Bhatia, S., Ashford, B. and Styles, R. (2016) Brazil ignites the samba spirit! Rio Olympics is off with a bang but only after opening ceremony with empty seats, climate change lectures and ugly protests outside. *Daily Mail*, 5 August. Available at: www.dailymail.co.uk/new/article-3726239/Rio-Olympics-Opening-Ceremony-begin-heavy-security-presence.html [accessed: 27 June 2017].

Fanon, F. ([1958] 1970) *Black Skin, White Masks.* London: Paladin.

Fassin, D. (2012) *Humanitarian Reason.* Berkeley: University of California Press.

Fassin, D. (2013) The predicament of humanitarianism. *Qui Parle: Critical Humanities and Social Sciences*, 22(1): 33–48.

Favell, A. (2015a) Echigo-Tsumari and the art of the possible: The Fram Kitagawa philosophy in theory and practice. In: F. Kitagawa (ed.), *Art Place Japan.* New York: Princeton Architectural Press, pp. 143–173.

Favell, A. (2015b) *Immigration, Integration and Mobility.* Colchester: ECPR Press.

Favell, A., Feldblum, M. and Smith, M.P. (2007) The human face of global mobility: A research agenda. *Society*, 44(2): 25–55.

Fayos-Solá, E., Marín, C. and Jafari, J. (2014) Astrotourism: No requiem for meaningful travel. *Pasos*, 12(4): 663–671.

Featherstone, M. (1991) *Consumer Culture and Postmodernism.* London, Thousand Oaks, CA and New Delhi: Sage.

Fennell, D., Liberato, A.S.Q., Hayden, B. and Fujino, Y. (2012) Consuming anime. *Television & New Media*, 14(5): 440–456.

Fey, I.E. and Racin, K. (2000) *Strange Pilgrimages.* London: Rowman & Littlefield.

Fincher, R., Jacobs, J.M. and Anderson, K. (2002) Rescripting cities with difference. In: J. Eade and C. Mele (eds), *Understanding the City.* Malden, MA: Blackwell, pp. 27–48.

Findlen, P. (1998) Between carnival and lent: The scientific revolutions at the margins of culture. *Configurations*, 6(2): 243–267.

Fish, R.A. (2008) 'Mixed-blood' Japanese: A consideration of race and purity in Japan. In: M. Weiner, (ed.), *Japan's Minorities.* London: Routledge, pp. 40–58.

Flanagan, M. (2016) Reactions to the red costume dance at the Closing Ceremony show love for Brazil's culture. Romper. Available at: www.romper.com/p/reactions-to-the-red-costume-dance-at-the-closing-ceremony-show-love-for-brazils-culture-16825 [accessed: 11 November 2016].

Florida, R. (2002) *The Rise of the Creative Class.* New York: Basic Books.

Flynn, D. and Soto, A. (2016). Record Brazil protests put Rousseff's future in doubt. 14 March. Available at: www.reuters.com/article/us-brazil-rousseff-protests-idUSKCN0WF0IX [accessed: 19 October 2016].

Foltete, J.-C. and Litot, J.B. (2015) Scenic postcards as objects for spatial analysis of tourist regions. *Tourism Management*, 49: 17–28.

Fontes, M., Videira, P. and Calapez, T. (2013) The impact of long-term scientific mobility on the creation of persistent knowledge networks. *Mobilities*, 8(3): 440–465.

Ford, H. and Geiger, R.S. (2012) 'Writing up rather than writing down': Becoming Wikipedia literate. *WikiSym*, August: 27–29.

Ford, H. and Wajcman, J. (2016) 'Anyone can edit', not everyone does: Wikipedia and the gender gap. *Social Studies of Science*, pp. 1–16, LSE Research Online.

Available at: http://eprints.lse.ac.uk/68675/1/Wajcman_Anyone%20can.pdf [accessed: 24 March 2017].

Foster, S.L. (2008) Movements contagion: The kinaesthetic impact of performance. In: T. Davis (ed.), *The Cambridge Companion to Performance Studies*. Cambridge: Cambridge University Press, pp. 46–56.

Foster, S.L. (2009) *Worlding Dance*. Basingstoke: Palgrave Macmillan.

Foster, S.L. (2010) *Choreographing Empathy*. Abingdon: Routledge.

Foucault, M. (1976) *The Birth of the Clinic*. London: Tavistock.

Foucault, M. (1979) *Discipline and Punish*. New York: Vintage.

Foucault, M. (1980) *Power/Knowledge*. New York: Harvester Press.

Foucault, M. (1988) Technologies of the Self. In: L.H.H. Martin, H. Guttman and P.H. Hutton (eds), *Technologies of the Self*. Amherst: University of Massachusetts Press, pp. 16–49.

Foucault, M. (1997a) *The Archaeology of Knowledge*. London: Routledge.

Foucault, M. (1997b) The birth of biopolitics. In: P. Rabinow (ed.), *Michel Foucault*. New York: New Press, pp. 73–85.

Foucault, M. (1998) *The History of Sexuality, vol. I: The Will to Knowledge*. London: Penguin.

Foucault, M. (2007) *Security, Territory and Population*. Basingstoke: Palgrave Macmillan.

Foucault, M. (2010) *The Birth of Biopolitics*. London: Palgrave Macmillan.

Frabetti, F. (2011) Rethinking the digital humanities in the context of originary technicity. *Culture Machine*, 12: unpaginated. Available at: www.culturemachine.net/index.php/cm/article/download/431/461 [accessed: 12 September 2014].

France 24 English (2016). Rio Olympics: 'Slum tourism' spreads in favelas during Olympic Games. 12 August. Available at: www.youtube.com/watch?v=d7hop2GHBio [accessed: 7 April 2017].

France 24 English (2016). Rio 2016: Brazilian gold medalist Rafaela Silva given a hero's welcome visiting former favela home. 24 August. Available at: www.youtube.com/watch?v=RCA6EOG8wD4 [accessed: 22 January 2017].

Franklin, A. (2004) Tourism as an ordering: Towards a new ontology of tourism. *Tourist Studies*, 4(3): 277–301.

Franko Aas, K. (2007) Analysing a world in motion: Global flows meet criminology of the other. *Theoretical Criminology*, 11(2): 283–303.

Fraser, M., Kember, S. and Lury, C. (eds), (2005) Inventive life: Approaches to the New Vitalism. *Theory, Culture & Society*, 22(1): 1–14.

Freeman, J. (2014) Raising the flag over Rio de Janeiro's favelas: Citizenship and social control in the Olympic city. *Journal of Latin American Geography*, 13(1): 7–38.

Freire Medeiros, B. (2014) *Touring Poverty*. Abingdon: Routledge.

Freudendal-Pedersen, M. (2015) Whose commons are mobilities spaces? – The case of Copenhagen's cyclists. *ACME*, 14(2): 598–621.

Freudendal-Pedersen, M., Hannam, K. and Kesselring, S. (2016) Applied mobilities, transitions and opportunities. *Applied Mobilities*, 1(1): 1–9.

Frey, O. (2009) Creativity of places as a source of cultural tourism. In: G. Maciocco and S. Serreli (eds), *Enhancing the City*. Heidelberg: Springer, pp. 135–154.

Freyre, G. (1963) *The Mansions and the Shanties*. New York: Knopf.

Freyre, G. (1974) *The Gilberto Freyre Reader*. New York: Knopf.

Friedberg, A. (1993) *Window Shopping*. Berkeley, CA: University of California Press.

Fukuyama, F. (1992) *The End of History and the Last Man*. New York: Free Press.

Fullagar, S., Wilson, E. and Markwell, K. (2012) Starting slow: Slow mobilities and experiences. In: S. Fullagar, K. Markwell and E. Wilson (eds), *Slow Tourism*. Bristol: Channel View, pp. 1–11.

Fuller, G. (2009) Store-Forward. In: S. Cwerner, S. Kesselring, J. Urry (eds), *Aeromobilities*. London: Routledge, pp. 63–76.

Fuller, S. (2008) *Dissent over Descent*. Cambridge: Icon.

Fuller, S. (2012) The art of being human: A project for general philosophy of science. *Journal of General Philosophy of Science*, 43: 113–123.

Fullerton, L. and Ettema, J. (2014) Ways of worldmaking in Wikipedia: Reality, legitimacy and collaborative knowledge-making. *Media, Culture & Society*, 36(2): 183–199.

Furlong, A. (2008) The Japanese hikikomori phenomenon: Acute social withdrawal among young people. *The Sociological Review*, 56(2): 309–325.

Furuto, A. (2012). Santiago Calatrava: The 'Quest for Movement' exhibition. *Archdaily*, 2 July. Available at: www.archdaily.com/248664/santiago-calatrava-the-quest-for-movement-exhibition/ [accessed: 7 September 2016].

Fussey, P. and Coaffee, J. (2012) Balancing local and global security leitmotifs: Counter-terrorism and the spectacle of sporting mega-events. *International Review for the Sociology of Sport*, 47(3): 268–285.

Gallope, M. (2011) Technicity, consciousness and musical objects. In: M. Clarke and D. Clarke (eds), *Music and Consciousness*. Oxford: Oxford University Press, pp. 47–64.

Galloway, A. (2010) Locating media futures in the present – Or how to map emergent associations & expectations. *Aether*, 5A(March): 27–36.

García Canclini, N. (1995) *Hybrid Cultures*. Minneapolis, MN: University of Minnesota Press.

Gardiner, M. (2004) Everyday utopianism: Lefebvre and his critics. *Cultural Studies*, 8(3): 228–254.

Geertz, C. (1973) *The Interpretation of Cultures*. New York: Basic Books.

Geertz, C. (2000) *Available Light*. Princeton, NJ: Princeton University Press.

Gehl, J. (2010) *Cities for People*. Washington, DC: Island Press.

Germann Molz, J. (2009) Representing pace in tourism mobilities: Staycations, slow travel and the amazing race. *Journal of Tourism and Cultural Change*, 7(4): 270–286.

Germann Molz, J. (2012) *Travel Connections*. Abingdon: Routledge.

Germann Molz, J. and Gibson, S. (eds), (2007) *Mobilizing Hospitality*. Aldershot: Ashgate.

Germann Molz, J. and Paris, C.M. (2015) The social affordances of flashpacking: Exploring the mobility nexus of travel and communication. *Mobilities*, 10(2): 173–192.

Getz, D. (2008) Event tourism: Definition, evolution, and research. *Tourism Management*, 29: 403–428.

Gibbons, J. (2007) *Contemporary Art and Memory*. London: I.B. Tauris.

Gibson, O. (2014). Rio 2016 Olympic preparations damned as 'worst ever' by IOC. *The Guardian*, 29 April. Available at: www.theguardian.com/sport/2014/apr/29/rio-2016-olympic-preparations-worst-ever-ioc [accessed: 19 October 2016].

Gibson, S. (2006) A seat with a view: Tourism, immobility and the cinematic travel guide. *Tourist Studies*, 6(1): 157–178.

Giddens, A. (1979) *Central Problems in Social Theory*. London: Macmillan.

Giddens, A. (1984) *The Constitution of Society*. Cambridge: Polity.

Giddens, A. (1985) *A Contemporary Critique of Historical Materialism*, vol. II. Cambridge: Polity.

Giddens, A. (1990) *The Consequences of Modernity*. Cambridge: Polity.

Giddens, A. (1991) *Modernity and Self-Identity*. Cambridge: Polity.

Giddens, A. (1992) *The Transformation of Intimacy*. Cambridge: Polity.

Giddens, A. (1994) Living in a post-traditional society. In: U. Beck, A. Giddens and S. Lash (eds), *Reflexive Modernization*. Cambridge: Polity, pp. 56–109.

Giddens, A. (2002) *Runaway World*. London: Profile Books.

Giddens, A. (2009) *The Politics of Climate Change*. Cambridge: Polity.

Gilroy, Paul (1993) *The Black Atlantic*. Cambridge, MA: Harvard University Press.

Girginov, V. (2016) Leveraging the Olympic Games: Universal and local imaginaries and mobilities. In: N.B. Salazar, C. Timmerman, J. Wets, L. Gama Gato and S. Van den Broucke (eds), *Mega-Event Mobilities*. Abingdon: Routledge, pp. 145–164.

Giulianotti, R. and Klauser, F. (2010) Security governance and post mega-events: Toward an interdisciplinary research agenda. *Journal of Sport and Social Issues*, 34(1): 49–61.

Giulianotti, R. and Klauser, F. (2012) Sport mega-events and terrorism: A critical analysis. *International Review for the Sociology of Sport*, 47(3): 307–323.

Giulianotti, R., Armstrong, G., Hales, G. and Hobbs, D. (2015) Global sport mega-events and the politics of mobility: The case of the London 2012 Olympics. *British Journal of Sociology*, 66(1): 118–140.

Glaeser, E., (2012) *Triumph of the City*. New York: Penguin.

Glionna, J.M. (2011). Japan's orderly Shibuya Scramble. *Los Angeles Times*, 23 May. Available at: http://articles.latimes.com/2011/may/23/world/la-fg-japan-intersection-2011 0523 [accessed: 11 December 2016].

Gluck, C. (1985) *Japan's Modern Myths*. Princeton, NJ: Princeton University Press.

Goffman, E. (1974) *Frame Analysis*. London: Penguin.

Goldberg, T. (1993) *Racist Culture*. Oxford and Cambridge, MA: Blackwell.

Goldfarb, J.C. (2012) *Political Culture*. Cambridge: Polity Press.

Gomes, W. (2016). Man trying to erase 2016 Olympic torch with water and lime high of a house. 3 August. Available at: www.youtube.com/watch?v=_XU7mrWdfxs [accessed: 22 January 2017].

Goodman, N. (1951) *The Structure of Appearance*, 3rd edn. Boston, MA: Reidel.

Goodman, N. (1978) *Ways of Worldmaking*. Indianapolis, IN: Hackett.

Goodman, N. (1984) *Of Mind and Other Matters*. Cambridge, MA: Harvard University Press.

Gordon, A. (2009) *A Modern History of Japan*, 2nd edn. Oxford: Oxford University Press.

Gosling, J. and Case, P. (2013) Social dreaming and ecocentric ethics: Sources of non-rational insight in the face of climate change catastrophe. *Organization*, 20(5): 705–721.

Goto-Jones, C. (2009) *Modern Japan*. Oxford: Oxford University Press.

Gottdiener, M. (1997) *The Theming of America*. Boulder, CO: Westview Press.

Gourgouris, S. (1996) *Dream Nation*. Stanford, CA: Stanford University Press.

Gowan, P. (2003) The new liberal cosmopolitanism. In: D. Archibugi (ed.), *Debating Cosmopolitics*. London: Verso, pp. 51–66.

Graburn, N.N.H. (1983) *To Pray, Pay and Play*. Aix en-Provence: Centre des Hautes Etudes Touristiques.

Graburn, N.H.H. (1995a) The past in the present in Japan: Nostalgia and neo-traditionalism in contemporary Japanese tourism. In: R.W. Butler and D.G. Pearce (eds), *Changes in Tourism*. London: Routledge, pp. 47–70.

Graburn, N.H.H. (1995b) Tourism, modernity and nostalgia. In: A. Ahmed and C. Shore (eds), *The Future of Anthropology*. London: Athlone Press, pp. 158–178.

Graburn, N.H.H. (2004) The Kyoto tax strike: Buddhism, shinto and tourism in Japan. In: E. Badone and S.R. Roseman (eds), *Intersecting Journeys*. Chicago, IL: University of Illinois, pp. 125–139.

Graburn, N.H.H. (2012) The dark is on the inside: The honne of Japanese exploratory tourists. In: D. Picard and M. Robinson (eds), *Emotion in Motion*. Farnham: Ashgate, pp. 49–71.

Graburn, N.H.H. (2015) Reconstructing tradition: Tourism and modernity in China and Japan. International Conference on Cultural Heritage (August). Seongnam, Seoul: Academy of Korean Studies.

Graham, S. (2010) *Cities Under Siege*. London: Verso.

Gravari-Barbas, M. and Graburn, N. (2012) Tourist imaginaries. *Via@ – International Interdisciplinary Review of Tourism*, 1(1). Available at: http://www.viatourismreview.net/Editorial1_EN.php [accessed: 1 December 2016].

Gray, L.E. (2007) Memories of the empire, mythologies of the soul: Fado performance and the shaping of saudade. *Ethnomusicology*, 53(1): 106–130.

Greenfeld, L. (1990) The formation of the Russian national identity: The role of status insecurity and ressentiment. *Comparative Studies in Society and History*, 32(3): 549–591.

Greenfeld, L. (1992) *Nationalism*. Cambridge, MA: Harvard University Press.

Greenhouse, C.J. (2010) *Ethnographies of Neoliberalism*. Philadelphia: University of Pennsylvania Press.

Gretzel, U., Werthner, H., Koo, C. and Lamsfus, C. (2015) Conceptual foundations for understanding smart tourism ecosystems. *Computers in Human Behavior*, 50: 558–563.

Groppo, A. (2010) *The Two Princes, Juan D. Perón and Getulio Vargas*. Villa María: Eduvim.

Grosz, E. (2005) *Time Travels*. Durham, NC: Duke University Press.

Guattari, F. (2001) Machinic heterogenesis. In: D. Trend (ed.), *Reading Digital Culture*. Malden, MA: Blackwell, pp. 38–51.

Gudeman, S. (1986) *Economics as Culture*. London: Routledge Kegan Paul.

Gudeman, S. (2001) *The Anthropology of Economy*. Malden, MA: Blackwell.

Gudeman, S. (2008) *Economy's Tension*. New York: Berghahn.

Gudeman, S. (2015) Piketty and Anthropology. *Anthropological Forum*, 25(1): 66–83.

Guffey, E.E. (2006) *Retro*. London: Reaktion.

Guffey, E.E. (2014) Crafting yesterday's tomorrows: Retro-futurism, steampunk and making in the twenty-first century. *Journal of Modern Craft*, 7(3): 249–266.

Guimarães, S.P. (2016). A star is born: Olympic Cauldron becomes downtown Rio's latest must-see attraction. *Rio 2016 News*, 9 August. Available at: www.rio2016.com/en/news/a-star-is-born-olympic-cauldron-becomes-downtown-rio-s-latest-must-see-attraction [accessed: 9 November 2016].

Guiver, J. and McGrath, P. (2016) Slow tourism: Exploring the discourses. *DosAlgarves: A Multidisciplinary Journal*, 27: 11–34.

Guttman, A. (2006) Berlin 1936: The most controversial Olympics. In: A. Tomlinson and C. Young (eds), *National Identity and Global Sports Events*. New York: SUNY, pp. 65–82.

Gwerner, S. (2009) Introducing aeromobilities. In: S. Gwerner, S. Kesselring and J. Urry (eds), *Aeromobilities*. Abingdon: Routledge.

Haas, P. (1992) Knowledge, power and international policy coordination. *International Organization*, 46(1): 1–35.

Habermas, J. (1987) *The Philosophical Discourse of Modernity*. Cambridge, MA: MIT Press.

Habermas, J. (1989a). *The New Conservatism*. Cambridge, MA: MIT Press.

Habermas, J. (1989b). *The Theory of Communicative Action, vol. II: Lifeworld and System*. Boston, MA: Beacon Press.

Hage, G. (2003) *Against Paranoid Nationalism*. Annandale: Pluto Press & Merlin.

Hall, C.M. (2009) Degrowing tourism: Décroissance, sustainable consumption and steady-state tourism. *Anatolia*, 20(1): 46–61.

Hall, D. (2005) Transport tourism – travelling through heritage and contemporary recreation. In: M Novelli (ed.), *Niche Tourism*. Oxford: Elsevier Butterworth-Heinemann, pp. 89–100.

Halstead, B. (1989) Patterns of decay and dissolution. *The New Scientist*, December: 23–30, pp. 75–77.

Hannam, K. (2006) Tourism and development III: Performances, performativities and mobilities. *Progress in Development Studies*, 6(3): 243–249.

Hannam, K., Mostafanezhad, M. and Rickly, J. (2016) *Event Mobilities*. London: Routledge.

Hannam, K., Sheller, M. and Urry, J. (2006) Mobilities, immobilities and moorings. *Mobilities*, 1(1): 1–22.

Hannerz, U. (1990) Cosmopolitans and locals in world culture. *Theory, Culture & Society*, 7(2): 237–251.

Hannigan, J. (1998) *Fantasy City*. London: Routledge.

Hannigan, J. (2007) From fantasy city to creative city. In: G. Richards and J. Wilson (eds), *Tourism, Creativity and Development*. London: Routledge, pp. 48–56.

Hardt, M. and Negri, A. (2000) *Empire*. Cambridge, MA: Harvard University Press.

Hardt, M. and Negri, A. (2004) *Multitude*. New York: Penguin.

Harper, T.J. ([1977] 2001) Afterword. In: J. Tanizaki, *In Praise of Shadows*. London: Vintage, pp. 65–73.

Harvey, D. (1985) *Consciousness and the Urban Experience*. Baltimore, MD: John Hopkins University Press.

Harvey, D. (1989) From managerialism to entrepreneuralism: The transformation of urban governance in late capitalism. *Geografiska Annaler*, 71(1): 3–17.

Harvey, D. (2000) *Spaces of Hope*. Berkeley, CA: University of Berkeley Press.

Harvey, D. (2006) *Paris, Capital of Modernity*. New York: Routledge.

Hasson, S. (2002) The syntax of Jerusalem: Urban morphology, culture, and power. In: J. Eade and C. Mele (eds), *Understanding the City*. Malden, MA: Blackwell, pp. 278–304.

Hays, K.M. (1998) Fredric Jameson's 'Architecture and the critique of ideology'. In: K.M. Hays (ed.), *Architecture Theory Since 1968*. Cambridge, MA: MIT.

Hee, L., Schroepfer, T., Nanxi, S. and Ze, L. (2009) From post-industrial landscape to creative precincts: Emergent spaces in Chinese cities. *International Development Planning Review*, 30(3): 249–266.

Heidegger, M. (1967) *Being and Time*. Oxford: Blackwell.

Heidegger, M. (1975) The origin of the work of art. In: *Poetry, Language, Thought*. New York: Harper Colophon.

Heidegger, M. (1993) *Basic Writings*. San Francisco, CA: Harper Collins.

Heilbroner, R. (1974) *An Inquiry into the Human Prospect*. New York: Norton.

Held, D. (2003) Cosmopolitanism: Globalisation tamed? *Review of International Studies,* 29(4): 465–480.

Held, D. (2004) *Global Covenant.* Cambridge: Polity.

Held, D., Roger, C. and Nag, E.M. (2013) Controlling the Amazon: Brazil's evolving response to climate change. In: D. Held, C. Roger and E.M. Nag (eds), *Climate Governance in the Developing World.* Cambridge: Polity.

Hendry, J. (2000) *The Orient Strikes Back.* Oxford and New York: Berg.

Henning, C. (2002) Tourism: Enacting modern myths. In: G.M.S. Dann (ed.), *The Tourist as a Metaphor of the Social World.* Wallingford: CABI, pp. 169–188.

Herzfeld, M. (2002) The absent presence: Discourses of crypto-colonialism. *South Atlantic Quarterly,* 101(4): 899–926.

Herzfeld, M. (2005) *Cultural Intimacy,* 2nd edn. New York: Routledge.

Herzfeld, M. (2006) Spatial cleansing: Monumental vacuity and the idea of the West. *Journal of Material Culture,* 1(1–2): 127–149.

Herzfeld, M. (2008) The ethnographer as theorist. In: M. Mazower (ed.), *Networks of Power in Modern Greece.* London: Hurst, pp. 147–168.

Herzfeld, M. (2016) *The Siege of Spirits.* Chicago, IL: University of Chicago Press.

Hesmondhalgh, D. (2007) *The Cultural Industries.* 2nd edn. London: Sage.

Heynen, H. (1999) *Architecture and Modernity.* Cambridge, MA: MIT.

Hiller, H.H. (2006) Post-event outcomes and the post-modern turn: The Olympics and urban transformation. *European Sports Management Quarterly,* 6(4): 317–332.

Hiller, H.H. (2016) Sport mega-events as mega-projects: Interaction effects and local mobilities. In: N.B. Salazar, C. Timmerman, J. Wets, L. Gama Gato and S. Van den Broucke (eds), *Mega-Event Mobilities.* Abingdon: Routledge, pp. 128–144.

Himmer, A. (2015). Japan rips up 2020 Olympic stadium plans to start anew. 17 July. Available at: http://sports.yahoo.com/news/japan-pm-orders-full-review-2020-olymp ic-stadium-070207621–spt.html [accessed: 5 April 2017].

Hirsch, E. and Stewart, C. (2005) Ethnographies of historicity. *History and Anthropology,* 16(3): 261–274.

Hiyama, T. and Yoshihara, M. (2008) New occupational threats to Japanese physicians: Karoshi (death due to overwork) and karojisatsu (suicide due to overwork). *Occupational and Environmental Medicine,* 65(6): 428–429.

Hochschild, A. (1979) Emotion work, feeling rules, and social structure. *American Journal of Sociology,* 85: 551–575.

Hochschild, A. (1983) *The Managed Heart.* Berkeley: University of California Press.

Hodgson, G.M. (1995) The political economy of utopia. *Review of Social Economy,* 53(2): 195–214.

Hoffman, L.M., Fainstein, S.S. and Judd, D.R. (2003) *Cities and Visitors.* London: Blackwell.

Hofland, L.H. (1973) *A World of Strangers.* New York: Basic Books.

Hogan, J. (2003) Staging the nation: Gendered and ethnicized discourses of national identity in Olympic Opening Ceremonies. *Journal of Sport and Social Issues,* 27(2): 100–123.

Holdnak, A. and Holland, S.M. (1996) Edu-tourism: Vacationing to learn. *Parks and Recreation,* 31(9): 72–75.

Holliday, R.and Potts, T. (2012) *Kitsch!* Manchester: Manchester University Press.

Holliday, R., Bell, D., Jones, M., Hardy, K., Hunter, E., Proby, E. and Sanchez Taylor, J. (2015) Beautiful face, beautiful place: Relational geographies and gender in cosmetic surgery tourism websites. *Gender, Place & Culture,* 22(1): 90–106.

Hollinshead, K. (1998) Disney and commodity aesthetics: A critique of Fjellman's analysis of 'distory' and the 'historicide' of the past. *Current Issues in Tourism*, 1(1): 58–119.

Hollinshead, K. (1999) Surveillance of the worlds of tourism: Foucault and the eye of power. *Tourism Management*, 20(1): 7–23.

Hollinshead, K. (2004) Tourism and the new sense: Worldmaking and the enunciative value of tourism. In: M.C. Hall and H. Tucker (eds), *Tourism and Postcolonialism*. London: Routledge, pp. 25–42.

Hollinshead, K. (2009) The 'worldmaking' prodigy of tourism: The reach and power of tourism in the dynamics of change and transformation. *Tourism Analysis*, 14(1): 139–152.

Hollinshead, K., Ateljevic, I. and Ali, N. (2009) Worldmaking agency – worldmaking authority: The sovereign constitutive role of tourism. *Tourism Geographies*, 11(4): 427–443.

Holton, R. (2005) The inclusion of the non-European world in international society, 1870–1920: Evidence from global networks. *Global Networks*, 5(3): 239–259.

Holton, R. (2008) *Global Networks*. Basingstoke: Palgrave Macmillan.

Homer-Dixon, T. (2006) *The Upside of Down*. London: Souvenir.

Honoré, C. (2005) *In Praise of Slow*. London: Orion Books.

Horne, J. (1992) *The Intelligent Tourist*. MacMahon's Point: Margaret Gee Holdings.

Horne, J. and Manzenreiter, W. (2006) *Sports Mega-Events*. London: Blackwell.

Horne, J. and Manzenreiter, W. (2016) The production of the spectacle: Conceptualising labour and global sports mega-events. In: N.B. Salazar, C. Timmerman, J. Wets, L. Gama Gato and S. Van den Broucke (eds), *Mega-Event Mobilities*. Abingdon: Routledge, pp. 33–51.

Housel, T.H. (2007) Australian nationalism and globalization: Narratives of the nation in the 2000 Sydney Olympics' Opening Ceremony. *Critical Studies in Media Communication*, 24(5): 446–461.

Howard, C. (2012) Speeding up and slowing down: Pilgrimage and slow travel through time. In: S. Fullagar, K. Markwell and E. Wilson (eds), *Slow Tourism*. Bristol: Channel View, pp. 11–24.

Howe, A. (2016). American kinetic wind-sculptor, Anthony Howe, kicking off the Rio 2016 Olympics in dramatic fashion with one-of-a-kind Olympic Cauldron. *R Newswire*, 3 August. Available at: www.prnewswire.com/news-releases/american-kine tic-wind-sculptor-anthony-howe-kicking-off-the-rio-2016-olympics-in-dramatic-fashion-with-one-of-a-kind-olympic-cauldron-300308490.html [accessed: 8 November 2016].

Hubbard, P. and Hall, T. (1998) The entrepreneurial city and the 'new urban politics'. In: T. Hall and P. Hubbard (eds), *The Entrepreneurial City*. Chichester: John Wiley and Sons, pp. 1–27.

Hudson, S. and Ritchie, J.R.B. (2006) Promoting destinations via film tourism: An empirical identification of initiatives. *Journal of Travel Research*, 44(3): 387–396.

Hugher, H.L. (1989) Tourism and the arts: A potentially destructive relationship? *Tourism Management*, 10(2): 97–99.

Hui, A. (2014) Enthusiasm. In: P. Adey, D. Bissell, K. Hannam and P. Merriman (eds), *The Routledge Handbook of Mobilities*. New York: Routledge, pp. 172–182.

Hume, D.L. (2013) *Tourism Art and Souvenirs*. London: Routledge.

Hutchinson, J. (2004) Myth against myth: The nation as ethnic overlay. In: M. Guibernaeu and J. Hutchinson (eds), *History and National Destiny*. Oxford: Blackwell, pp. 109–124.

Hutchinson, J. (2005) *Nations as Zones of Conflict*. London: Sage.

Huyssen, A. (1987) *After the Great Divide.* Bloomington, IN: Indiana University Press.
Huyssen, A. (1995) *Twilight Memories.* London: Routledge.
Huyssen, A. (2000) Present pasts: Media, politics, amnesia. *Public Culture,* 12(1), pp. 21–38.
Huyssen, A. (2003) *Present Pasts.* Stanford, CA: Stanford University Press.
Hyndman, J. (2012) The geopolitics of migration and mobility. *Geopolitics,* 17(2): 243–255.
Ickenberry, G. J. (2007) Globalization as American hegemony. In: D. Held and A. McGrew (eds), *Globalization Theory.* Cambridge: Polity, pp. 41–61.
IMDB (undated) Andrucha Waddington. Available at: www.imdb.com/name/nm 0905343/bio?ref_=nm_ov_bio_sm [accessed: 23 October 2016].
IMDB (undated) Fernando Meirelles. Available at: www.imdb.com/name/nm0576987/ [accessed: 20 March 2017].
IMDB (2013) Tropicália (2012), dir. M. Machado. 5 July. Available at: www.imdb. com/title/tt1497880/ [accessed: 23 October 2016].
IMDB (2016) Pina Bausch. Available at: www.imdb.com/name/nm0062471/ [4 July 2017].
Inglis, D. (2014) Cosmopolitans and cosmopolitanism: Between and beyond sociology and political philosophy. *Journal of Sociology,* 50(2): 99–114.
Ingold, T. (2008) When ANT meets SPIDER: Social theory for anthropods. In: C. Knappett and L. Malafouris (eds), *Material Agency.* New York: Springer, pp. 209–216.
Ingold, T. (2010) Ways of mind-walking: Reading, writing, painting. *Visual Studies,* 25 (1): 15–23.
Ingold, T. (2012) The perception of user-producer. In: W. Gunn and J. Donovan (eds), *Design and Ethnography.* Farnham: Ashgate, pp. 19–33.
Ito, M. and Suzuki, M. (2013) Acceptance of Beck's theory in Japan: From environmental risks to individualization. In: A. Elliott, M. Katagiri and A. Sawai (eds), *Routledge Companion to Contemporary Japanese Social Theory.* New York: Routledge, pp. 114–131.
Ivy, M. (1995) *Discourses of the Vanishing.* Chicago, IL: University of Chicago Press.
Iwabuchi, K. (1994) Complicit exoticism: Japan and its Other. *Continuum,* 8(2): 48–82.
Iwabuchi, K. (2002) *Recentering Globalization.* Durham, NC: Duke University Press.
Iwabuchi, K. (2004) How 'Japanese' is Pokémon? In: J. Tobin (ed.), *Pikachu's Global Adventure.* Durham, NC: Duke University Press, pp. 53–79.
Iwabuchi, K. (2008) Lost in TransNation: Tokyo and the urban imaginary in the era of globalization. *Inter-Asia Cultural Studies,* 9(4): 543–556.
Jacobs, J. ([1961] 1992) *The Death and Life of Great American Cities.* New York: Random House.
Jacobs, K. (2014). Santiago Calatrava: The world's most hated architect? *Fastcodesign,* 18 December. Available at: www.fastcodesign.com/3039658/santiago-calatrava-the-worlds-most-hated-architect [accessed: 8 September 2016].
Jaguaribe, B. and Hetherington, K. (2004) Favela tours: Indistinct and mapless representations. In: M. Sheller and J. Urry (eds), *Tourism Mobilities.* London: Routledge, pp. 155–166.
Jameson, F. (1985) Architecture and the critique of ideology. In: J. Ockman (ed.), *Architecture, Criticism, Ideology.* Princeton, NJ: Princeton Architectural Press, pp. 51–87.
Jameson, F. (1995) Is space political? In: C.C. Davidson (ed.), *Anyplace.* Cambridge, MA: MIT, pp. 192–205.
Jansen, S. and Löfving, S. (eds), (2009) *Struggles for Home.* Oxford: Berghahn.

Jay, M. (1986) The empire of the gaze: Foucault and the denigration of vision in twentieth-century French thought. In:M. Foucault and D. Couzens Hoy (eds), *Foucault: A Critical Reader.* Oxford, Blackwell.

Jay, M. (1993) *Downcast Eyes.* Berkeley, CA: University of California Press.

Jensen, A. (2011) Mobility, space and power: On the multiplicities of seeing mobility. *Mobilities,* 6(2): 255–271.

Jensen, O.B. (2013) *Staging Mobilities.* London: Routledge.

Jensen, O.B. (2014) *Designing Mobilities.* London: Routledge.

Jensen, O.B.Ditte Bendix, L. and Wind, S. (2016) Mobilities design – towards a research agenda for applied mobilities research. *Applied Mobilities,* 1(1): 26–42.

Jensen, O.B. and Freudendal-Pedersen, M. (2012) Utopias of mobilities. In: M. Hviid Jacobsen and K. Tester (eds), *Utopia.* Farnham: Ashgate, pp. 197–218.

Jessop, B. (2002) The political economy of scale. In: Perkmann, M. and Sum, N.-L. (eds), *Globalization, Regionalization, and Cross-Border Regions.* Basingstoke: Palgrave Macmillan pp. 25–49.

Jobim, H. (2011) *Antonio Carlos Jobim.* Montclair, NJ: Hal Leonard.

Johnson, P. (1991) *The Birth of the Modern.* London: Phoenix.

Joy, A. (2016). In focus: A look at Tokyo 2020 Summer Olympics. The Culture Tip. 23 September. Available at: https://theculturetrip.com/asia/japan/articles/in-focus-a-look-at-tokyo-2020-summer-olympics/ [accessed: 8 December 2016].

Kaelber, L. (2007) A memorial as virtual traumascape: Darkest tourism in 3D and cyberspace to the gas chambers of Auschwitz. *e-Review of Tourism Research* (eRTR), 5(2): 24–33. Available at: http://ertr.tamu.edu [accessed: 10 February 2015].

Kaldor, M. (2003) *Global Civil Society.* Cambridge: Polity.

Kaplan, A. (1999) *The Developing of Capacity.* Cape Town: Community Development Resource Association.

Kashimura, A. (2013) Japanese psychoanalysis: Deciphering the Japanese unconsciousness and supporting the Japanese subject. In: A. Elliott, M. Katagiri and A. Sawai (eds), *Routledge Companion to Contemporary Japanese Social Theory.* New York: Routledge, pp. 67–89.

Kassabian, A. (2000) *Hearing Film.* London: Routledge.

Katagiri, M. (2013) The three selves in Japanese society: Individualized, privatized and psychologized selves. In: A. Elliott, M. Katagiri and A. Sawai (eds), *Routledge Companion to Contemporary Japanese Social Theory.* New York: Routledge, pp. 139–157.

Kennett, C. and de Moragas, M. (2006) Barcelona 1992: Evaluating the Olympic legacy. In: A. Tomlinson and C. Young (eds), *National Identity and Global Sports Events.* New York: SUNY, pp. 177–196.

Kermode, F. (2000) *The Sense of Ending.* New York: Oxford University Press.

Kesselring, S. (2009) Global transfer points: The making of airports in the mobile risk society. In: S. Gwerner, S. Kesselring and J. Urry (eds), *Aeromobilities.* London: Routledge, pp. 39–60.

Kesselring, S. (2016) Planning in motion: The new politics of mobility in Munich. In: P. Pucci and M. Galleoni (eds), *Understanding Mobilities for Designing Contemporary Cities.* Cham: Springer, pp. 67–85.

Khazan, O. (2016) What happens when there's sewage in the water? *The Atlantic,* 31 March. Available at: www.theatlantic.com/health/archive/2016/03/what-happens-when-theres-sewage-in-the-water/476013/ [accessed: 19 October 2016].

Kim, S. (2015) Interdisciplinary approaches and methods for sustainable transformation and innovation. *Sustainability,* 7(4): 3977–3983.

Kirschenblatt-Gimblett, B. (1997) *Destination Cultures*. Berkeley, CA: University of California Press.

Klauser, F. (2008) Spatial articulations of surveillance at the FIFA World Cup 2006 in Germany. In: K.F. Aas, H.O. Gundhus and H.M. Lomell (eds), *Technologies of Insecurity*. London: Routledge, pp. 61–80.

Klauser, F. (2011a) The exemplification of 'fan zones': Mediating mechanisms in the reproduction of best practices for security and branding at Euro 2008. *Urban Studies*, 48(15): 3203–3219.

Klauser, F. (2011b) Interpretative flexibility of the event-city: Security, branding and urban entrepreneurialism at the European Football Championships 2008. *International Journal of Urban and Regional Research*, 36(5): 1039–1052.

Klein, K. (2000) On the emergence of memory in historical discourse. *Representations*, 69(Winter): 127–153.

Kleist, N. and Jansen, S. (2016) Hope over time: Crisis, immobility and future-making. *History and Anthropology*, 27(4): 373–392.

Kondo, S. (1997) *About Face: Performing Race in Fashion and Theatre*. New York: Routledge.

Korstanje, M.E. (2014) Heritage that hurts: Tourists in the memoryscapes of September 11. *Journal of Heritage Tourism*, DOI: 10.1080/1743873X.2014.888816.

Korstanje, M.E. (2015) *A Difficult World*. New York: Nova Science Publishers.

Korstanje, M.E. (2016a) The ethical borders of slum tourism in the mobile capitalism: A conceptual discussion. *Revista de Turismo*, 21: 22–32.

Korstanje, M.E. (2016b) *The Rise of Thana-Capitalism and Tourism*. Abingdon: Routledge.

Korstanje, M. and Ivanov, S. (2012) Tourism as a form of new psychological resilience: The inception of dark tourism. *Cultur: Revista de Cultura e Turismo*, 6(4): 56–71.

Korstanje, M., Tzanelli, R.and Clayton, A. (2014)Brazilian World Cup 2014, terrorism, tourism and social conflict. *Event Management*, 18(4): 487–491.

Kosseleck, R. (1985) *Futures Past*. New York: Columbia University Press.

Kracauer, S. (1995) *The Mass Ornament*. Cambridge, MA: Harvard University Press.

Kracauer, S. ([1960] 1997) *Theory of Film*. Princeton, NJ: Princeton University Press.

Kristeva, J. (1984) *Revolution in Poetic Language*. New York: Columbia University Press.

Kristeva, J. (1991) *Strangers to Ourselves*. New York: Columbia University Press.

Kurosawa, F. (2004) A cosmopolitanism from below: Alternative globalisation and the creation of solidarity without bounds. *Archives Européenes de Sociologique*, 45(2): 133–255.

Lakatos, I. (1976) *Proofs and Refutations*. Cambridge: Cambridge University Press.

LaMarre, T. (2009) *The Anime Machine*. Minneapolis, MN: University of Minnesota Press.

Lamsfus, C. and Alzua-Sorzabal, A. (2013) Theoretical framework for a tourism internet of things: Smart destinations. *TourGUNE Journal of Tourism and Human Mobility*: 15–21.

Lamsfus, C., Martín, D., Alzua-Sorzabal, A. and Torres-Manzanera, E. (2015) Smart tourism destinations: An extended conception of smart cities focusing on human mobility. In: *Information and Communication Technologies in Tourism 2015*. New York: Springer International Publishing, pp. 363–375.

Lanfant, F.M. (1995) International tourism, internationalization and the challenge to identity. In: M.F. Lanfant, J.B. Allock and E.M. Bruner (eds), *International Tourism*. London: Sage, pp. 24–43.

Langlois, G. (2012) Meaning, semiotechnologies and participatory media. *Culture Machine*, 12, unpaginated. Available at: www.culturemachine.net/index.php/cm/article/viewDownloadInterstitial/437/467 [accessed: 10 February 2013].

Lara, F.L. (2011) Incomplete utopias: Embedded inequalities in Brazilian modern architecture. *Architectural Research Quarterly*, 15(2): 131–138.

Larsen, J. and Urry, J. (2008) Networking in mobile societies. In: J.O. Baerenholdt, B. Granås and S. Kesserling (eds), *Mobility and Place*. Aldershot: Ashgate, pp. 89–101.

Lasch, C. (1991) *The Culture of Narcissism*. New York: W.W. Norton & Co.

Lash, S. (1988) Discourse of figure? Postmodernism as a regime of signification. *Theory, Culture & Society*, 5(2–3): 311–336.

Lash, S. and Urry, J. (1994) *Economies of Signs and Space*. London: Sage.

Lashley, C. (2007) Studying hospitality: Beyond the envelope. *International Journal of Tourism and Hospitality Research*, 1(3): 185–188.

Lashley, C., and Morrison, A. (eds), (2000) *In Search of Hospitality*. Oxford: Butterworth-Heinemann.

Latour, B. (1987) *Science in Action*. Cambridge, MA: Harvard University Press.

Latour, B. (1990) Drawing things together. In: M. Lynch and S. Woolgar (eds), *Representations in Scientific Practice*. Cambridge, MA: MIT, pp. 19–68.

Latour, B. (1993) *We Have Never Been Modern*. New York: Harvester Wheatsheaf.

Latour, B. (1999) On recalling ANT. In: J. Law and J. Hassard (eds), *Actor Network Theory and After*. Oxford: Blackwell, pp. 15–25.

Latour, B. (2005) *Reassembling the Social*. Oxford: Oxford University Press.

Latour, B., Maugin, P. and Teil, G. (1992) A note on socio-technical graphs. *Social Studies on Science*, 22(1): 33–57.

Latour, B. and Woolgar, S. (1986) *Laboratory Life*. Princeton, NJ: Princeton University Press.

Law, J. (2004) *After Method*. London and New York: Routledge.

Laurendeau, J. (2008) Gendered risk regimes: A theoretical consideration of edgework and gender. *Sociology of Sport Journal*, 25: 293–309.

Laurendeau, J. and Shahara, N. (2008) Women could be every bit as good as guys: Reproductive and resistant agency in two 'action' sports. *Journal of Sports and Social Issues*, 32: 24–47.

Lawal, B. (2001) Àwòrán: Representing the self and its metaphysical Other in Yoruba art. *The Art Bulletin*, 83(3): 498–526.

Lawrence, W.G. (2003) Social dreaming as sustained thinking. *Human Relations*, 56(5): 609–662.

Lazarin, M. (2008) Modernism: Heidegger's 'The Origin of the Work of Art', *Journal of Ryukoku University*, 472: 46–64.

Lazzarato, M. (2004) From capital-labor to capital-life. *Ephemera Theory Multitude*, 4(3): 187–208.

Lazzarato, M. (2015) Neoliberalism, the financial crisis and the end of the liberal state. *Theory, Culture & Society*, 32(7–8): 67–83.

Leahy, T. (2008) Discussion of 'global warming and sociology'. *Current Sociology*, 56(3): 475–484.

Leakey, R. and Lewin, R. (1995) *The Sixth Extinction*. London: Widenfeld and Nicolson.

Lear, J. (2006) *Radical Hope*. Cambridge, MA: Cambridge University Press.

LeBaron, E. (2014) Reimagining the geography of the favelas: Pacification, tourism and transformation in Complexo Do Alemao, Rio de Janeiro. *Tourism Review International*, 18(4): 269–282.

Lederman, J. (2015) Urban fads and consensual fictions: Creative, sustainable and competitive city policies in Buenos Aires. *City & Community*, 14(1): 47–67.

Lee, S., Scott, D. and Kim, H. (2008) Celebrity fan involvement and destination perceptions. *Annals of Tourism Research*, 35(3): 809–832.

Leeds, E. (1996) Cocaine and parallel polities in the Brazilian urban periphery: Constraints on local-level democratization. *Latin American Research Review*, 31(3): 47–83.

Lefebvre, H. (1979) Space: Social product and use value. In: J.W. Friedberg (ed.), *Critical Sociology*. New York: Irvington Publishers.

Lefebvre, H. (1991) *The Production of Space*. Oxford and Cambridge, MA: Basil Blackwell.

Lefebvre, H. ([1992] 2015) *Rhythmanalysis*. London: Bloomsbury.

Lehmann, S. (2011) *Principles of Green Urbanism*. London: Earthscan.

Lennon, J. and Foley, M. (2000) *Dark Tourism*. London: Continuum.

Lenskyj, H.J. (2008) *Olympic Industry Resistance*. Albany, NY: SUNY.

Leoussi, A. (2004) The ethno-cultural roots of national art. In: M. Guibernaeu and J. Hutchinson (eds), *History and National Destiny*. Oxford: Blackwell, pp. 143–159.

Leteen, L. (2012) What is 'Critique of Worldmaking'? Nelson Goodman's conception of philosophy. *Enrahonar: Quaderns de Filosofia*, 49: 29–40.

Leung, M.W.H. (2013) 'Read ten thousand books, walk ten thousand miles': Geographical mobility and capital accumulation among Chinese scholars. *Transactions of the Institute of British Geographers*, 38(2): 311–324.

Levitas, R. (2013a). Singing summons the existence of the fountain: Bloch, music and utopia. In: P. Thompson and S. Žižek (eds), *The Privatization of Hope*. Durham, NC: Duke University Press, pp. 219–245.

Levitas, R. (2013b). *Utopia*. London: Palgrave Macmillan.

Lincoln, Y.S. and Guba, E.G. (1985) *Naturalistic Enquiry*. Thousand Oaks, CA: Sage.

Linke, U. (2012) Mobile imaginaries, portable signs: The global consumption of iconic representation of slum life. *Tourism Geographies*, 14(2): 294–319.

Lins, P. (1997) *City of God*. London: Bloomsbury.

Lister, R. (1997) *Citizenship*. London: Macmillan.

Livingston-Isenhour, T.E. and Garcia, T.G. (2005) *Choro*. Indianapolis: Indiana University Press.

Lloyd, J. (2003) Airport technology, travel, and consumption. *Space and Culture*, 6(2): 93–109.

Löfgren, O. (2014) Urban atmospheres as brandscapes and lived experiences. *Place Branding and Public Diplomacy*, 10(4): 255–266.

Lomholt, I. (2016). Museum of Tomorrow Rio de Janeiro. *E-Architect*, 15 July. Available at: www.e-architect.co.uk/brazil/museum-tomorrow-rio [accessed: 11 September 2016].

Longhurst, B. (1989) *Karl Mannheim and the Contemporary Sociology of Knowledge*. New York: St Martin's Press.

Lorimer, J. (2010) Elephants as companion species: The lively biogeographies of Asian elephant conservation in Sri Lanka. *Transactions of the Institute of British Geographers*, 35(4): 491–506.

Louis, F. (2002) *Japan Encyclopedia*. Cambridge, MA: Harvard University Press.

Lowenthal, D. (1985) *The Past is a Foreign Country.* Cambridge: Cambridge University Press.

Luckman, S., Gibson, C. and Lea, T. (2009) Mosquitoes in the mix: How transferable is creative city thinking? *Singapore Journal of Tropical Geography*, 30(1): 70–85.

Lundberg, C. and Lexhagen, M. (2012) Bitten by the Twilight Saga: From pop culture consumer to pop culture tourist. In: R. Sharpley and P.R. Stone (eds), *Contemporary Tourist Experience*. Abingdon: Routledge, pp. 147–164.

Lurie, S. (2001) Funk and hip-hop transculture: Cultural conciliation and racial identification in the 'Divided City'. In *Brazil 2001: A Revisionary History of Brazilian Literature and Culture*, 4(5): 643–659. Fall River, MA: RPI Press.

Lury, C. (2004) *Brands*. London: Sage.

Lutz, T. (2016). Rio Olympics 2016: Opening ceremony kickstarts the Games – as it happened. *The Guardian*, 5 August. Available at: www.theguardian.com/sport/live/2016/aug/05/olympics-opening-ceremony-rio-2016-live [accessed: 8 November 2016].

Luxembourg, R. (1998) *Reform or Revolution?* London, Chicago, IL and Melbourne: Revolutionary Classics.

Lynch, K. (1960) *The Image of the City*. Cambridge, MA: MIT and Harvard University Press.

Lynch, P., Germann Molz, J., McIntosch, A., Lugosi, P. and Lashley, C. (2011) 'Theorizing hospitality', *Hospitality & Society*, 1(1): 3–24.

Lyng, S. (2005) *Edgework*. New York: Routledge.

Lyotard, F. (1984) *The Postmodern Condition*. Manchester: Manchester University Press.

Maasen, S. and Weingart, P. (2000) *Metaphors and the Dynamics of Knowledge*. London: Routledge.

MacAloon, J. (2006) The theory of spectacle: Reviewing Olympic ethnography. In: A. Tomlinson and C. Young (eds), *National Identity and Global Sports Events*. New York: SUNY, pp. 15–39.

MacCannell, D. (1989) *The Tourist*. London: Macmillan.

MacCannell, D. (2011) *The Ethics of Sightseeing*. Berkeley: University of California Press.

MacCannell, D. (2012) On the ethical stake in tourism research. *Tourism Geographies*, 14(1): 183–194.

Macedo, S. (2009) The vertical cityscape in São Paulo: The influence of modernism in urban Brazil. In: V. Del Rio and W. Sambiedda (eds), *Beyond Brasília*. Gainesville: University of Florida Press.

Macionis, N. and Sparks, B. (2009) Film tourism: An incidental experience. *Tourism Review International*, 13(2): 93–102.

Mackenzie, A. (2002) *Transductions*. London: Continuum.

Mackenzie, A. (2003) Transduction: Invention, innovation and collective life. Available at: www.lancaster.ac.uk/staff/mackenza/papers/transduction.pdf [accessed: 25 September 2016].

MacKenzie, D. (1996) *Knowing Machines*. Cambridge, MA: MIT Press.

Maffesoli, M. (1996) *The Time of the Tribes*. London: Sage.

Malthus, T. (1798) *Essay on the Principle of Population as it Affects the Future Improvement of Society*. London: St Paul's Churchyard.

Mannheim, K. ([1922–1924] 1980) *Structures of Thinking*. London: Routledge & Kegan Paul.

Mannheim, K. ([1929] 1993) *From Karl Mannheim*. New Brunswick, NJ: Transactions.

Mannheim, K. ([1936] 1968) *Ideology and Utopia*. New York: Harcourt, Brace & World.

Maoz, D. (2006) The mutual gaze. *Annals of Tourism Research*, 33(1): 221–239.

Marans, D. (2016). Team Refugees gets standing ovation at Olympics Opening Ceremony. *Huffington Post*, 12 August. Available at: www.huffingtonpost.com/entry/team-refu gees-standing-ovation_us_57a5e29ee4b056bad215af5f [accessed: 8 November 2016].

Marcus, G.E. (2011) Geertz's legacy before the modes of cultural analysis of his time: Speculative notes and queries in remembrance. In: J.C. Alexander, P. Smith and M. Norton (eds), *Interpreting Clifford Geertz*. New York: Palgrave Macmillan, pp. 131–144.

Marcuse, H. (1955) *Eros and Civilization*. New York: Beacon Press.

Marcuse, H. (1986) *One-Dimensional Man*. London: Ark.

Marin, L. (2016) *Utopics*. Secaucus, NJ: Springer.

Martin, R. (1999) Globalization? The dependencies of a question. *Social Text*, 17(3): 1–14.

Martinez-Alier, J. (2015) Environmentalism, currents of. In: G. D'Alisa, F. DeMaria and G. Kallis (eds), *Degrowth*. New York and London: Routledge, pp. 37–40.

Martin-Jones, D. (2013) The Dardenne Brothers encounter Enrique Dussel: Ethics, Eurocentrism and a philosophy for world cinemas. In: M. Monteiro, G. Giucci and N. Besner (eds), *Além dos Limites* (*Beyond the Limits*). Rio de Janeiro: State University of Rio de Janeiro Press, pp. 71–105.

Massey, D. (2005) *For Space*. London: Sage.

Mauger, L., Remael, S. and Phalen, B. (2016) *The Vanished*. New York: Sky Pony Press.

Mauss, M. (1954) *The Gift*. London: Free Press.

Maxfield, J.F. (1996) *The Fatal Woman*. London: Associated University Press.

Mbembe, A. (2003) Necropolitics. *Public Culture*, 15(1): 11–40.

McCann, B. (2004) *Hello, Hello Brazil*. Durham, NC: Duke University Press.

McCann, E. (2011) Urban policy mobilities and global circuits of knowledge: Toward a research agenda. *Annals of Association of American Geographers*, 10(1): 107–130.

McCann, E. and Ward, K. (2010) Relationality/territoriality: Toward a conceptualization of cities in the world. *Geoforum*, 41: 175–184.

McFarland, T. (1981) *Romanticism and the Forms of Ruin*. Princeton, NJ: Princeton University Press.

McGowan, C. and Pessanha, R. (1998) *The Brazilian Sound*. Philadelphia, PA: Temple University Press.

McGowan, J. (2011) Ways of worldmaking: Hannah Arendt and E.L. Doctorowa respond to modernity. *College Literature*, 38(1): 150–175.

McGowan, T. (2016). Opening Ceremony: 'Rio is ready to make history' as Olympic Games begin. *CNN*, 6 August. Available at: http://edition.cnn.com/2016/08/05/sport/ opening-ceremony-rio-2016-olympic-games/ [accessed: 28 October 2016].

McKee, R. (1999) *Story*. London: Methuen.

McNay, L. (1992) *Foucault and Feminism*. Oxford: Blackwell.

Meade, T.A. (1997) *'Civilizing' Rio*. University Park, PA: The Pennsylvania State University Press.

Meagher, G. (2016). From helplessness to hope: Inspirational tales of the Refugee Olympic Team. *The Guardian*, 5 August. Available at: www.theguardian.com/sport/ 2016/aug/05/helplessness-rio-hope-olympic-refugee-team [accessed: 8 November 2016].

Merleau-Ponty, M. (1962) *Phenomenology of Perception*. London: Routledge and Kegan Paul.

Merleau-Ponty, M. (1964) *Signs*. Evanston, IL: Northwestern University Press.

Merleau-Ponty, M. (1965) *The Structure of Behaviour*. London: Methuen.

Merleau-Ponty, M. (1968) *The Visible and the Invisible*. Evanston, IL: Northwestern University Press.

Merriman, P. (2005) Driving places: Marc Augé, non-places, and the geographies of England's M1 motorway. In: M. Featherstone, N.J. Thrift and J. Urry (eds), *Automobilities*. London: Sage, pp. 145–168.

Merriman, P. (2015) Mobilities I: Departures. *Progress in Human Geography*, 39(1): 87–95.

Metraux, D.A. (1995) Religious terrorism in Japan: The fatal appeal of Aum Shinrikyo. *Asian Survey*, 35(12): 1140–1154.

Michael, M. (1996) *Constructing Identities*. London: Sage.

Mignolo, W.D. (2000) *Local Histories/Global Designs*. Princeton, NJ: Princeton University Press.

Mignolo, W.D. (2002) The enduring enchantment (or the epistemic privilege of modernity and where to go from here). *The South Atlantic Quarterly*, 101(4): 927–954.

Miho, A. (2015) The construction of discourses on otaku: The history of subcultures from 1983 to 2005. In: P.W. Galbraith, T.H. Kam, B.-O. Kamm and C. Gerteis (eds), *Debating Otaku in Contemporary Japan*. London and New York: Bloomsbury, pp. 105–128.

Miller, P. and Rose, N. (2010) *Governing the Present*. Cambridge: Polity.

Millington, R. and Darnell, S.C. (2014) Constructing and contesting the Olympics online: The internet, Rio 2016 and the politics of Brazilian development. *International Review for the Sociology of Sport*, 49(2): 190–210.

Mills, C.W. (1994) Non-Cartesian sums: Philosophy and the African-American experience. *Teaching Philosophy*, 17(3): 223–243.

Mills, C.W. (1998) *Blackness Visible*. Ithaca, NY: Cornell University Press.

Mirás (2016). Japan take gold in Rio 2016 team artistic gymnastics, Russia edge China for silver. 8 August. Available at: www.rio2016.com/en/news/Japan-take-gold-in-Rio-2016-team-artistic-gymnastics [accessed: 13 December 2016].

Mittelman, H. (2004) Ideologies and the globalisation agenda. In: M.B. Steger (ed.), *Rethinking Globalism*. Lanham, MD: Rowman & Littlefield, pp. 15–26.

Moehn, F. (2007) Music, citizenship and violence in postdictatorship Brazil. *Latin American Music Review*, 28(2): 180–219.

Moehn, F. (2008) Music, mixing and modernity in Rio de Janeiro. *Ethnomusicology Forum*, 17(2): 165–202.

Moffitt, B. (2014) How to perform crisis: A model for understanding the key role of crisis in contemporary populism. *Government and Opposition*, 50(2): 189–217.

Molotch, H. (2004) How art works: Form and function in the stuff of life. In: R. Friedland and J. Mohr (eds), *Matters of Culture*. Cambridge: Cambridge University Press, pp. 341–377.

Montalbán, M.V. (1992) *Barcelonas*. London: Verso.

Moore, H. (2011) *Still Life*. Cambridge: Polity.

Morana, M., Dussel, E. and Jágueri, C. (2008) *Coloniality at Large*. Durham, NC: Duke University Press.

Morley, J. (2014) Diversity, dynamics and domestic energy demand: A study of variation in cooking, comfort and computing. PhD Thesis. Lancaster University.

Morley, D. and Robbins, K. (1995) *Spaces of Identity.* London: Routledge.

Morris-Suzuki, T. (2003) Immigration and citizenship in contemporary Japan. In: J. Maswood, J. Graham and H. Mayajima (eds), *Japan.* London: Routledge Curzon, pp. 163–178.

Mosedale, J. (2012) Diverse economies and alternative economic practices in tourism. In: I. Ateljevic, N. Morgan and A. Pritchard (eds), *The Critical Turn in Tourism Studies.* London: Routledge, pp. 94–107.

Mowatt, R. and Chancellor, C.H. (2011) Visiting death and life: dark tourism and slave castles. *Annals of Tourism Research,* 38(4): 410–434.

Mudde, C. and Kaltwasser, R. (2013) Exclusionary vs. inclusionary populism: Comparing contemporary Europe and Latin America. *Government and Opposition,* 48(2): 147–174.

Muldoon, J. (2016) Arendtian principles. *Political Studies,* 64(1S): 121–135.

Müller, J.W. (2014) 'The people must be extracted from within the people': Reflections on populism. *Constellations,* 21(4): 483–493.

Müller, M. (2016) Mobilities and mega-events: Four challenges, one warning. In: N.B. Salazar, C. Timmerman, J. Wets, L. Gama Gato and S. Van den Broucke (eds), *Mega-Event Mobilities.* Abingdon: Routledge, pp. 179–186.

Mulvey, L. (2006) Visual pleasure and narrative cinema. In: M.G. Durham and D.M. Kellner (eds), *Media and Cultural Studies.* Oxford: Blackwell, pp. 342–352.

Murdock, J. (2010). Calatrava's 'Museum of Tomorrow' to showcase a greener future for Rio. *Architectural Record,* 4 October. Available at: www.architecturalrecord.com/articles/5358-calatrava-s-quot-museum-of-tomorrow-quot-to-showcase-a-greener-future-for-rio [accessed: 15 September 2016].

Nadler, R. (2016) Plug & play places: Subjective standardization of places in multi-local lifeworlds. In: P. Pucci and M. Colleoni (eds), *Understanding Mobilities for Designing Contemporary Cities.* Cham: Springer International, pp. 109–128.

Nagib, L. (2007) *Brazil on Screen.* London and New York: I.B. Tauris.

Nagib, L. (2011) *World Cinema and the Ethics of Realism.* New York: Continuum.

Nairn, T. (1997) *Faces of Nationalism.* London: Verso.

Napier, S.J. (2005) *Anime.* New York: Palgrave Macmillan.

Napier, S.J. (2007) *From Impressionism to Anime.* New York: Palgrave Macmillan.

Nash, G. (undated). The rock art of Serra da Capivara: America's oldest art? Available at: www.bradshawfoundation.com/south_america/serra_da_capivara/ [accessed: 10 November 2016].

Natanson, M. (1986) *Anonymity.* Bloomington: Indiana University Press.

Naylor, A. and Helford, E.R. (2014) Science fiction anime: National, nationless, transnational, post/colonial. *Science Fiction Film and Television,* 7(3): 309–314.

Nederveen Pieterse, J. (1998) Hybrid modernities: Mélange modernities in Asia. *Sociological Analysis,* 1(3): 75–86.

Nederveen Pieterse, J. (2001) Hybridity, so what? The anti-hybridity backlash and the riddles of recognition. *Theory, Culture & Society,* 18(2–3): 219–245.

Nederveen Pieterse, J. (2004) *Globalization and Culture.* Lanham, MD: Rowman & Littlefield.

Nederveen Pieterse, J. (2006a) Globalization as hybridization. In: M.G. Durham and D. Kellner (eds), *Media and Cultural Studies.* Malden, MA: Blackwell, pp. 658–680.

Nederveen Pieterse, J. (2006b) Emancipatory cosmopolitanism: Towards an agenda. *Development and Change,* 37(6): 1247–1257.

Nederveen Pieterse, J. (2009) Multipolarity means thinking plural: Modernities. *Protosociology*, 26(1): 19–35.

Nederveen Pieterse, J. (2010) *Development Theory*. Los Angeles, CA: Sage.

Nederveen Pieterse, J. and Parekh, B. (1995) Shifting imaginaries: Decolonization, internal decolonization, postcoloniality. In: J. Nederveen Pieterse and B. Parekh (eds), *The Decolonization of Imagination*. London: Zed, pp. 1–19.

Neeley, K.A. (2001) *Mary Somerville*. Cambridge: Cambridge University Press.

Negri, A. (1998) *Exil*. Paris: Éditions Mille.

Negruşa, A.L., Toader, V., Soficǎ, A., Tutunea, M.F. and Rus, R.V. (2015) Exploring gamification techniques and applications for sustainable tourism. *Sustainability*, 7(8): 11160–11189.

Newmahr, S. (2011) Chaos, order and collaboration: Toward a feminist conceptualization of edgework. *Journal of Contemporary Ethnography*, 40(6): 682–712.

Nicolini, D. (2009) Zooming in and out: Studying practices by switching theoretical lenses and trailing connections. *Organization Studies*, 30(12): 1391–1418.

Nicolis, G. (1995) *Introduction to Non-Linear Science*. Cambridge: Cambridge University Press.

Nicolson, M.H. (1997) *Mountain Gloom and Mountain Glory*. Seattle: University of Washington Press.

Nippon.com (23 October 2013). Men's rhythmic gymnastics: A Japan original. Available at: http://www.nippon.com/en/views/b02402/ [accessed: 13 December 2016].

Nisbet, R. (1969) *Social Change and History*. Oxford: Oxford University Press.

Nishikawa, K., Seaton, P. and Yamamura, T. (eds), (2015) *The Theory and Practice of Contents Tourism*. Sapporo: Hokkaido University.

Nora, P. (1989) Between memory and history: *Les lieux de mémoire*. *Representations*, 26(2): 7–25.

Norum, R. and Mostafanezhad, M. (2016) 'A chronopolitics of tourism', *Geoforum*, 77(3): 157–160.

Nye, J.S. Jr. (2004) *Soft Power*. New York: Public Affairs.

Nye, J.S. Jr. (2008) Foreword. In: W. Yasushi and D.L. McConell (eds), *Soft Power Superpowers*. Armonk, NY: East Gate, pp. ix–xiv.

O'Brien, M. (2008) *A Crisis of Waste?* New York: Routledge.

O'Dwyer, C. (2004) Tropic knights and Hula belles: War and tourism in the South Pacific. *Journal for Cultural Research*, 8(1): 33–50.

O'Gorman, K. (2007) Dimensions of hospitality: Exploring ancient and classical origins. In: C. Lashley, P. Lynch and A. Morrison (eds), *Hospitality*. Oxford: Elsevier, pp. 17–33.

Obadare, E. (2009) On the uses of ridicule: Humour, 'infrapolitics' and civil society in Nigeria. *African Affairs*, 108(431): 241–261.

Obrador-Pons, P., Crang, M. and Travlou, P. (2009) *Cultures of Mass Tourism*. Farnham: Ashgate.

Odih, P. (1999) Gendered time in the age of deconstruction. *Time and Society*, 8(1): 9–38.

Ohmae, K. (1990) *The Borderless World*. London: Collins.

Olsen, D. (1986) *The City as a Work of Art*. New Haven, CT: Yale University Press.

Olstead, R. (2011) Gender, space and fear: A study of women's edgework. *Emotion, Space and Society*, 4, pp. 86–94.

Olympic.org (2016). Decision of the IOC Executive Board concerning the participation of Russian athletes in the Olympic Games Rio 2016. 24 July. Available at:

www.olympic.org/news/decision-of-the-ioc-executive-board-concerning-the-participa
tion-of-russian-athletes-in-the-olympic-games-rio-2016 [accessed: 19 October 2016].

Olympic.org (2016). Olympic channel to launch on 21 August 2016. 27 July. Available
at: www.olympic.org/news/olympic-channel-to-launch-on-21-august-2016 [accessed:
19 October 2016].

Ong, A. (2011) Worlding cities, or the art of being global. In: A. Roy and A. Ong
(eds), *Worlding Cities*. Malden, MA: Blackwell.

Ortiz, R. (2000) Popular culture, modernity and nation. In: V. Schelling (ed.), *Through
the Kaleidoscope*. London: Verso, pp. 127–147.

Osburg, J. (2013) *Anxious Wealth*. Stanford, CA: Stanford University Press.

Otake (2013) Image-flip for male rhythmic gymnasts. *Japan Times*, 17 August. Available
at: www.japantimes.co.jp/life/2013/08/17/general/image-flip-for-male-rhythmic-gym
nasts/#.WEVKY7KLTcs [accessed: 13 December 2016].

Ousby, I. (2002) *The Englishman's England*. London: Pimlico.

Paolucci, G. (1998) Time shattered: The postindustrial city and women's temporal
experience. *Time & Society*, 7(2–3): 265–281.

Parkhurst Ferguson, P. (1994) The flâneur on and off the streets of Paris. In: K. Tester
(ed.), *The Flâneur*. London: Routledge, pp. 22–42.

Paulson, S. (2015) Political ecology. In: G. D'Alisa, F. DeMaria and G. Kallis (eds),
Degrowth. New York and London: Routledge, pp. 45–48.

Perlman, J.E. (1976) *The Myth of Marginality*. Berkeley: University of California
Press.

Perlman, J.E. (2010) *Favela*. New York: Oxford University Press.

Piketty, T. (2014) *Class in the Twenty-First Century*. Cambridge, MA: Harvard
University Press.

Pilling, D. (2014) *Bending Adversity*. London and New York: Penguin.

Pine, B.J. and Gilmore, J. (1999) *The Experience Economy*. Cambridge, MA: Harvard
Business School.

Pink, S. (2008) Mobilising visual ethnography: Making routes, making place and
making images. *Qualitative Research*, 9(3). Available at: www.qualitative-research.
net/index.php/fqs/article/view/1166/2575 [accessed: 29 June 2016].

Pink, S., Horst, H., Postill, J., Hjorth, L., Lewis, T. and Tacchi, J. (2015) *Digital
Ethnography*. London: Sage.

Piore, M.J. and Sabel, C.F. (1984) *The Second Industrial Divide*. New York: Basic
Books.

Plummer, K. (1995) *Telling Sexual Stories*. London: Routledge.

Polanyi, M. (1966) *The Tacit Dimension*. New York: Doubleday.

Popper, K. (1959) *The Logic of Scientific Discovery*. London: Hutchinson.

Povinelli, E.A. (2012) The will to be otherwise/The effort of endurance. *South Atlantic
Quarterly*, 111(3): 453–475.

Pravaz, N. (2000) Imagining Brazil: Seduction, samba and the mulatta's body.
Canadian Women's Studies, 20(2): 48–55.

Pravaz, N. (2003) Brazilian mulatrice: Performing race, gender and the nation. *Journal
of Latin American Anthropology*, 8(1): 116–147.

Pravaz, N. (2008) Samba, Carnaval and the myth of 'racial democracy' in Rio de
Janeiro. *Identities*, 15(1): 80–102.

Pravaz, N. (2009) The tan from Ipanema: Freyre, morenidade, and the cult of the body
in Rio de Janeiro. *Canadian Journal of Latin American and Caribbean Studies*, 34(67):
79–104.

Prigogine, I. (1997) *The End of Certainty.* New York: Free Press.

Putnam, H. (1996) Reflections on Goodman's Ways of Worldmaking. In: J. McCormick (ed.), *Starmaking.* Cambridge, MA: MIT, pp. 107–124.

Raiskin, J.L. (1996) *Snow on the Cane Fields.* Minneapolis, MN: University of Minnesota Press.

Ramose, M.B. (1999) *African Philosophy through Ubuntu.* Harare: Mond Books.

Ramose, M.B. (2015) Ubuntu. In: G. D'Alisa, F. DeMaria and G. Kallis (eds), *Degrowth.* New York and London: Routledge, pp. 212–214.

Rancière, J. (2004) *The Politics of Aesthetics.* London: Bloomsbury.

Rancière, J. (2011) *The Emancipated Spectator.* London: Verso.

Rancière, J. (2013) *Aesthesis.* London: Verso.

Reijnders, S. (2009) Watching the detectives: Inside the guilty landscapes of Inspector Morse, Baantjer and Wallander. *European Journal of Communication,* 24(2): 165–281.

Religion & Ethics (9 September 2005). Saint Nicholas Greek Orthodox Church. Available at: www.pbs.org/wnet/religionandethics/?p=9457 [accessed: 7 September 2016].

Remmling, G.W. (1961) Karl Mannheim: Revision of an intellectual portrait. *Social Forces,* 40(1): 23–30.

Reuters (15 July 2011). Olympics – Tokyo tiptoes into 2020 bid race. Available at: www.reuters.com/article/olympics-tokyo-bid-idUSL3E7IF1XH20110715 [accessed: 8 December 2016].

Reuters and Thornhill, T. (2016). Moment man attempts to douse Olympic torch by throwing a bucket of water over it as passes through his town. *The Daily Mail.* 28 June. Available at: www.dailymail.co.uk/news/article-3662424/Man-arrested-Brazil-a ttempt-douse-Olympic-torch.html [accessed: 22 January 2017].

Rhythm and Roots (undated). Mulher Rendeira – 'A versão autentica'. Available at: http:// rhythmandrootsblog.com/2010/12/13/mulher-rendeira-a-versao-autentica/ [accessed: 10 November 2016].

Rich, A. (2001) *Arts of the Possible.* New York and London: W.W. Norton.

Rich, R.B. (1995) Dumb lugs and femme fatales. *Sight and Sound,* 5(11), pp 6–11.

Richards, G. (2010) *Leisure in the Network Society.* Tilburg: Tilburg University Press. Available at: www.academia.edu/1271795/Leisure_in_the_Network_Society?auto= download [accessed: 15 December 2016].

Richards, G. (2011) Creativity and tourism: The state of the art. *Annals of Tourism Research,* 38(4): 1225–1253.

Richards, G. (2014) Creativity and tourism in the city. *Current Issues in Tourism,* 17(2): 119–144.

Richards, G. and Wilson, J. (2006) Developing creativity in tourist experiences: A solution to the serial production of culture? *Tourism Management,* 27(6): 1209–1223.

Ricoeur, P. (1984–1988) *Time and Narrative,* vols I–III. New York: Columbia University Press.

Rifkin, J. (2014) *The Zero Marginal Cost Society.* Basingstoke: Palgrave Macmillan.

Rio 2016 Olympic Wiki (undated). Rio 2016 – Biggest sporting event on the planet! Available at: http://rio2016olympicswiki.com/about-rio-2016-summer-olympics/ [accessed: 19 October 2016].

Rio 2016 News (2014) Rio 2016 Olympic and Paralympic mascots named Vinicius and Tom by public vote, 14 December. Available at: www.rio2016.com/en/news/rio-2016-o lympic-and-paralympic-mascots-named-vinicius-and-tom-by-public-vote [accessed: 2 November 2016].

Rio 2016 News (2015) Is it a spaceship? No it's the Museum of Tomorrow, new symbol of the 2016 Olympic host city, 18 December. Available at: www.rio2016.com/en/news/is-it-a-spaceship-no-it-s-the-museum-of-tomorrow-new-symbol-of-the-2016-olympic-host-city [accessed: 23 August 2016].

Rio 2016 News (2016) Rio 2016 following World Health Organization advice on zica alert, 2 February. Available at: www.rio2016.com/en/news/rio-2016-following-world-health-organisation-advice-on-zica-alert [accessed: 25 September 2016].

Rio 2016 News (2016) Opening ceremony choreographer promises masterpiece of dance and passion, 16 June. Available at: www.rio2016.com/en/news/opening-ceremony-choreographer-promises-masterpiece-of-dance-and-passion [accessed: 24 October 2016].

Ritzer, G. (2006) Globalization and McDonaldization. In: G. Ritzer (ed.), *McDonaldization*. London: Sage.

Ritzer, G. and A. Liska (1997) 'McDisneyization' and 'post-tourism': Contemporary perspectives on contemporary tourism. In: C. Rojek and J. Urry (eds), *Touring Cultures*. London and New York: Routledge, pp. 96–112.

Roberts, J. (2011) *Environmental Policy*. Abingdon: Routledge.

Roberts, K. (2004) *The Leisure Industries*. London: Palgrave.

Robertson, J. (2005) *The Case for the Enlightenment*. Cambridge: Cambridge University Press.

Robertson, R. (1992) *Glocalization*. London: Sage.

Robertson, R. (1995) Glocalization: Time-space and homogeneity-heterogeneity. In: M. Featherstone, S. Lash and R. Robertson (eds), *Global Modernities*. London: Sage, pp. 133–152.

Robinson, J. (2002) Global and world cities: A view from off the map. *International Journal of Urban and Regional Research*, 26(3): 531–554.

Robinson, J. (2011) Travels of urban neoliberalism: Taking stock of the internationalization of urban theory. *Urban Geography*, 32(8): 1087–1109.

Robinson, M. and Picard, D. (eds), (2009) *The Framed World*. Farnham: Ashgate.

Robinson, M. and Robertson, S. (2014) Challenging the field: Bourdieu and men's health. *Social Theory & Health*, 12(4): 339–360.

Roche, M. (2000) *Mega Events & Modernity*. New York: Routledge.

Roche, M. (2002) The Olympics and 'global citizenship'. *Citizenship Studies*, 6(2): 165–181.

Rojek, C. (1993) *Ways of Escape*. Basingstoke: Macmillan.

Rojek, C. (1997) Indexing, dragging and the social construction of tourist sights. In: C. Rojek and J. Urry (eds), *Touring Cultures*. London: Routledge, pp. 52–74.

Rojek, C. (2010) *The Labour of Leisure*. London: Sage.

Romano, O. (2014) *The Sociology of Knowledge in a Time of Crises*. London and New York: Routledge.

Romano, O. (2015) Dépense. In: G. D'Alisa, F. DeMaria and G. Kallis (eds), *Degrowth*. New York and London: Routledge, pp. 86–89.

Rose, N. (1999) *Powers of Freedom*. Cambridge: Cambridge University Press.

Roy, A. (2011) Postcolonial urbanism: Speed, hysteria, mass dreams. In: A. Roy and A. Ong (eds), (2011) *Worlding Cities*. Malden, MA: Blackwell.

Roy, A. and Ong, A. (eds) (2011) *Worlding Cities*. Malden, MA: Blackwell.

Ruggiero, V. (2000) New social movements and the 'Centi Sociali' in Milan. *Sociological Review*, 48(2): 167–185.

Rumford, C. (2006) Theorizing borders. *European Journal of Social Theory*, 9(2): 155–170.

Rutheiser, C. (1996) *Imagineering Atlanta*. New York: Verso.

Sachs, A. (2006) *The Humboldt Current*. New York: Penguin.

Sahlins, M. (1972) *Stone Age Economics*. Chicago, IL: Aldine.

Sahlins, M. (1976) *Culture and Practical Reason*. Chicago, IL: University of Chicago Press.

Sahlins, M. (2013) On the culture of material value and the cosmography of riches. *HAU: Journal of Ethnographic Theory*, 3(2): 161–195.

Sakakeeny, M. (2010) 'Under the bridge': An orientation of soundscapes to New Orleans. *Ethnomusicology*, 54(1): 1–27.

Salazar, N.B. (2009) Imaged or imagined? Cultural representations and the 'tourismification' of peoples and places. *Cashiers d'Études Africaines*, 49(1–2): 49–71.

Salazar, N.B. (2012) Tourism imaginaries: A conceptual approach. *Annals of Tourism Research*, 39(2): 863–882.

Salazar, N.B. (2016) Introduction: Exposing sports mega-events through a mobilities lens. In: N.B. Salazar, C. Timmerman, J. Wets, L. Gama Gato and S. Van den Broucke (eds), *Mega-Event Mobilities*. Abingdon: Routledge, pp. 1–15.

Salazar, N.B. and Glick Schiller, N. (eds), (2014) *Regimes of Mobility*. London: Routledge.

Salazar, N.B. and Graburn, N.H.H. (2016) Towards an anthropology of tourism imaginaries. In: N.B. Salazar and N.H.H. Graburn (eds), *Tourism Imaginaries*. Oxford: Berghahn, pp. 1–30.

Salmond, M. (2010) The power of momentary communities: Locative media and (in)formal protest. *Aether*, 5A(March): 90–100.

Samuels, D.W., Maintjes, L., Ochoa, A.M. and Porcello, T. (2010) Soundscapes: Toward a sounded anthropology. *Annual Review of Anthropology*, 39: 329–345.

Sánchez Taylor, J. (2000) Tourism and 'embodied' commodities: Sex tourism in the Caribbean. In: S. Clift and S. Carter (eds), *Tourism and Sex*. London and New York: Pinter, pp. 168–178.

Santiago Calatrava Biography (undated). in *Encyclopedia of World Biography*. Available at: http://www.notablebiographies.com/newsmakers2/2005-A-Fi/Calatrava-Santiago.html [accessed: 6 September 2016].

Sassen, S. (2001) *The Global City*. Princeton, NJ: Princeton University Press.

Sassen, S. (2006) *Territory, Authority, Rights*. Princeton, NJ: Princeton University Press.

Sassen, S. (2014) *Expulsions*. Cambridge, MA: Belknap Press.

Sassen, S. and Roost, F. (1999) The city: Strategic site for the global entertainment industry. In: D. Judd and S. Fainstein (eds), *The Tourist City*. New Haven, CT: Yale University Press, pp. 143–154.

Sather-Wagstaff, J. (2011) *Heritage that Hurts*. Walnut Creek, CA: Left Coast Press.

Saul, H. (2016). Yusra Mardini: Olympic Syrian refugee who swam for three hours in sea to push sinking boat carrying 20 to safety. *The Independent*, 5 August. Available at: www.independent.co.uk/news/people/yusra-mardini-rio-2016-olympics-womens-swimming-the-syrian-refugee-competing-in-the-olympics-who-a7173546.html [accessed: 8 November 2016].

Saville, S.J. (2008) Playing with fear: Parkour and the mobility of emotion. *Social & Cultural Geography*, 9(8): 891–914.

Sawai, A. (2013) Postmodernity. In: A. Elliott, M. Katagiri and A. Sawai (eds), *Routledge Companion to Contemporary Japanese Social Theory*. New York: Routledge, pp. 200–220.

Sawicki, J. (1991) *Disciplining Foucault*. London: Routledge.

Scarros, K. (2014). Hagia Sophia spirit abound in Calatrava's St. Nicholas Ground Zero Church design. *The National Herald*, 8 March. Available at: www.thenationalherald.com/39510/?doing_wp_cron=1473255594.8782870769500732421875 [accessed: 7 September 2016].

Schama, S. (1996) *Landscape and Memory*. London: Fontana Press.

Schein, L. (2002) Mapping Hmong media in diasporic space. In: F. Ginsburh, L. Abu-Lughod and B. Larkins (eds), *Media Worlds*. Berkeley, CA: University of California Press, pp. 229–244.

Schilling, C. (2003) *The Body and Social Theory*. London: Sage.

Schmitt, C. (2001) *State, Movement, People*. Corvallis, OR: Plutarch Press.

Schmitt, C. (2003) *The Nomos of the Earth in the International Law of Jus Publicum Europaeum*. New York: Telos.

Schutz, A. and Luckmann, T. (1973) *The Structures of the Lifeworld*, vol. I. Evanston, IL: Northwestern University Press.

Schutz, A. and Luckmann, T. (1989) *The Structure of the Lifeworld*, vol. II. Evanston, IL: Northwestern University Press.

Scott, A. (2010) Cultural economy and the creative field of the city. *Geografiska Annaler, B*, 92(2): 115–130.

Scott, D. (2004) *Conscripts of Modernity*. Durham, NC: University Press.

Scott, J. (1998) *Seeing Like a State*. New Haven, CT: Yale University Press.

Scranton, R. (2015) *Learning How to Die in the Anthropocene*. San Francisco, CA: City Lights Media.

Seaton, A.V. (1996) Guided by the dark: From thanatopsis to thanatourism. *International Journal of Heritage Studies*, 2(4): 234–244.

Seaton, T. (2012) Wanting to live with common people … ? The literary evolution of slumming. In: F. Frenzel, K. Koens and M. Steinbrink (eds), *Slum Tourism*. London: Routledge, pp. 21–48.

Sebro, T.H. (2016) Necromobility/choreomobility: Dance, death and displacement in the Thai-Burma border-zone. In: K. Hannam, M. Mostafanezhad and J. Rickly (eds), *Event Mobilities*. London: Routledge, pp. 95–108.

Segal, D. (2015). Petrobras oil scandal leaves Brazilians lamenting a lost dream. *The New York Times*, 7 August. Available at: www.nytimes.com/2015/08/09/business/international/effects-of-petrobras-scandal-leave-brazilians-lamenting-a-lost-dream.html?_r=0 [accessed: 19 October 2016].

Segawa, H. (1994) The essentials of Brazilian modernism. *Design Book Review*, 32/33, pp. 64–68.

Selwyn, T. (1999) *The Tourist Image*. Chichester: Wiley.

Sennett, R. (2008) *The Craftsman*. London: Penguin.

Sennett, R. (2012) *Together*. New Haven, CT: Yale University Press.

Serres, M. (1995) *The Natural Contract*. Ann Arbor: University of Michigan Press.

Sewell, W. (1990) Three temporalities: Toward a sociology of the event. CSST Working CRSO Working Paper #58 Paper #448.

Sewell, W.H. Jr. (2008) The temporalities of capitalism. *Socio-Economic Review*, 6(3): 517–537.

Sharpley, R. and Stone, P. (2009) Representing the macabre: Interpretation, kitschification and authenticity. In: R. Sharpley and P.R. Stone (eds), *The Darker Side of Travel*. Bristol: Channel View Publications, pp. 109–128.

Shaw, L. (1999) *The Social History of the Brazilian Samba*. Aldershot: Ashgate.

Shaw, S.J. (2007) Ethnic quarters in the cosmopolitan-creative city. In: G. Richards and J. Wilson (eds), *Tourism, Creativity and Development*. London: Routledge, pp. 189–200.

Sheller, M. (2003) *Consuming the Caribbean*. New York: Routledge.

Sheller, M. (2004) Demobilizing and remobilizing Caribbean paradise. In: M. Sheller and J. Urry (eds), *Tourism Mobilities*. London: Routledge, pp. 13–21.

Sheller, M. (2008) Always turned on: Atlantic City as America's accursed share. In: A. Cronin and K. Hetherington (eds), *Consuming the Entrepreneurial City*. London: Routledge, pp. 107–121.

Sheller, M. (2013) The islanding effect: Post-disaster mobility systems and humanitarian logistics in Haiti. *Cultural Geographies*, 20(2): 185–204.

Sheller, M. (2014a) Sociology after the mobilities turn. In: P. Adey, D. Bissell, K. Hannam, P. Merriman and M. Sheller (eds), *The Routledge Handbook of Mobilities*. New York: Routledge, pp. 45–54.

Sheller, M. (2014b) The new mobilities paradigm for a live sociology. *Current Sociology*, 62(6): 789–811.

Sheller, M. and Urry, J. (2003) Mobile transformations of 'public' and 'private' life. *Theory, Culture & Society*, 20(3): 107–125.

Sheller, M. and Urry, J. (2016) Mobilizing the new mobilities paradigm. *Applied Mobilities*, 1(1): 10–25.

Shields, R. (2003) *The Virtual*. London: Routledge.

Shils, E. (1975) *Center and Periphery*. Chicago, IL: University of Chicago Press.

Shohat, E. and Stam, R. (1994) *Unthinking Eurocentrism*. New York: Routledge.

Shohat, E. and Stam, R. (2003) *Multiculturalism, Postcoloniality and Transnational Media*. New Brunswick, NJ: Rutgers University Press.

Shove, E., Pantzar, M. and Watson, M. (2012) *The Dynamics of Social Practice*. London: Sage.

Siddle, R.M. (2008) The Ainu: Indigenous people of Japan. In: M. Weiner (ed.), *Japan's Minorities*. London: Routledge, pp. 21–39.

Sider, L. (ed.), (2003) *Soundscape*. London: Wallflower Press.

Silva, M.L. (2014) Queer sex vignettes from a Brazilian favela: An ethnographic striptease. *Ethnography*, 16(2): 223–239.

Simmel, G. (1971) *On Individuality and Social Forms*. Chicago, IL: University of Chicago Press.

Simoni, V. (2008) Shifting power: The destabilisation of asymmetries in the realm of tourism in Cuba. *Tsantsa*, 13: 89–97.

Simoni, V. (2013) Intimate stereotypes: The vicissitudes of being Caliente in touristic Cuba. *Civilizations*, 61(2): 181–198.

Simoni, V. (2015) *Tourism and Informal Encounters*. New York: Berghahn.

Sirigos, D. (2014). Hagia Sophia spirit abound in Calatrava's St. Nicholas Ground Zero Church design. *The National Herald*, 8 March. Available at: www.thenationalherald.com/39510/?doing_wp_cron=1473255594.8782870769500732421875 [accessed: 7 September 2016].

Skidmore, T. (1993) *Black into White*. New York: Oxford University Press.

Sloterdijk, P. (2009) Geometry in the colossal: The project of metaphysical globalization. *Environment and Planning D: Society and Space*, 27(1): 29–40.

Sloterdijk, P. (2014) *Globes: Macrospherology, vol. II: Spheres*. Cambridge, MA: MIT.

Smith, A.D. (1990) Towards a global culture? *Theory, Culture & Society*, 7(2): 171–191.

Smith, A.D. (1995) *Nations and Nationalism in a Global Era*. Cambridge: Polity .

Smith, A.D. (1999) *Myths and Memories of the Nation*. Oxford: Oxford University Press.

Smith, M. (2009) Ego-tripping without ethics or idea(l)s? In: J. Tribe (ed.), *Philosophical Issues in Tourism*. Bristol: Channel View Publications, pp. 261–277.

Smith, M.K. (2007) Space, place and placelessness in the culturally regenerated city. In: G. Richards (ed.), *Cultural Tourism*. Haworth: Binghamton, pp. 91–112.

Smith, V.L. (1992) The quest in guest. *Annals of Tourism Research*, 19(1): 1–17.

Sneed, P. (2007) Bandidos de Cristo: Representations of the power of criminal factions in Rio's proibidão funk. *Latin American Music Review*, 28(1): 220–241.

Sneed, P. (2008) Favela utopias: The bailes funk in Rio's crisis of social exclusion and violence. *Latin American Research Review*, 43(2): 57–79.

Soares, L.E. (2016) *Rio de Janeiro*. London: Allen Lane/Penguin.

Soares, L.E. (2016). After the party: Rio wakes up to an Olympic hangover. *The Guardian*, 21 August. Available at: www.theguardian.com/books/2016/aug/21/rio-2016-olympic-games-brazil-legacy-party?CMP=share_btn_link [accessed: 19 September 2016].

Soja, E.W. (2006) Cityscapes as cityscapes. In: C. Linder (ed.), *Urban Spaces as Cityscapes*. New York: Routledge, pp. xv–xviii.

Soja, E.W. (2008) Third space: Toward a new consciousness of space and spatiality. In: K. Ikas and G. Wagner (eds), *Communicating in the Third Space*. London: Routledge, pp. 49–61.

Sontag, S. (2013) *Essays of the 1960s & 70s*. New York: The Library of America.

Sørensen, T.F. (2015) More than a feeling. *Emotions, Space and Society*, 15(4): 64–73.

Şorman, A.H. (2015) Metabolism, societal. In: G. D'Alisa, F. DeMaria and G. Kallis (Eds), *Degrowth*. New York and London: Routledge, pp. 41–44.

Stam, R. (1997) *Tropical Multiculturalism*. Durham, NC: Duke University Press.

Stedman-Jones, G. (1971) *Outcast London*. Oxford: Oxford University Press.

Steel, P. (2016). Museum of Tomorrow comes to Glasgow 2016. 23 August. Available at: www.museumsassociation.org/news/23082016-museum-of-tomorrow-comes-to-glasgow-2016 [accessed: 27 March 2017].

Steger, M.B. (2008) *The Rise of the Global Imaginary*. Oxford: Oxford University Press.

Stein, M. (2004) The critical period of disasters: Insights from sense-making and psychoanalytic theory. *Human Relations*, 57(10): 1243–1261.

Steinbrink, M., Frenzel, F. and Koens, K. (2012) Development and globalization of a new trend in tourism. In: F. Frenzel, K. Koens and M. Steinbrink (eds), *Slum Tourism*. London: Routledge, pp. 1–18.

Stewart, K. (2011) *Ordinary Affects*. Durham, NC: Duke University Press.

Stewart, K. (2011) Atmospheric attunements. *Environment and Planning D: Society & Space*, 29(3): 445–453.

Stiegler, B. (2011) *Technics and Time, vol. III: Cinematic Time and the Question of Malaise*. Stanford, CA: Stanford University Press.

Still, J. (2010) *Derrida and Hospitality*. Edinburgh: Edinburgh University Press.

Stolarick, K., Denstendt, M., Donald, B. and Spencer, G. (2010) Creativity, tourism and economic development in a rural context: The case of Prince Edward County. *Journal of Rural Community Development*, 5(1–2): 238–254.

Stone, P.R. (2013a) Dark tourism scholarship: A critical review. *Journal of Tourism, Culture and Hospitality Research*, 7(3): 307–318.

Stone, P.R. (2013b) Deviance, dark tourism and 'dark leisure': Towards a (re)configuration of morality and the taboo in secular society. In: S. Elkington and S. Gammon (eds), *Contemporary Perspectives in Leisure*. Abingdon: Routledge, pp. 54–64.

Strange, S. (1996) *The Retreat of the State*. Cambridge: Cambridge University Press.

Strausberg, M. (2011) *Religion and Tourism*. London: Routledge.

Straw, W. (1991) Systems of articulation, logics of change: communities and scenes in popular music. *Cultural Studies*, 5(3): 368–388.

Sugimoto, Y. (2003) *An Introduction to Japanese Society*, 2nd edn. Port Melbourne: Cambridge University Press.

Sugimoto, Y. (2006) Nation and nationalism in contemporary Japan. In: G. Delanty and K. Kumar (eds), *The SAGE Handbook of Nations and Nationalism*. London: Sage, pp. 473–487.

Sugimoto, Y. (2012) Kyosei: Japan's cosmopolitanism. In Delanty, G. (ed.), *Routledge Handbook of Cosmopolitanism Studies*. London: Routledge, pp. 452–462.

Süssekind, F. (1997) *Cinematograph of Words*. Stanford, CA: Stanford University Press.

Swain, M. (2009) The cosmopolitan hope of tourism: Critical action and worldmaking vistas. *Tourism Geographies*, 11(4): 505–525.

Swindler, A. (1986) Culture in action: Symbols and strategies. *American Sociological Review*, 51(2): 273–286.

Szerszynski, B. and Urry, J. (2006) Visuality, mobility and the cosmopolitan: Inhabiting the world from afar. *British Journal of Sociology*, 57(1): 113–131.

Tanizaki, J. ([1997] 2001) *In Praise of Shadows*. London: Vintage.

Tarde, G. ([1890] 2001) *The Laws of Imitation*. New York: Henry Holt & Co.

Tarde, G. ([1899] 2003) *The Transformations of Power*. Paris: Seuil.

Tate, S.A. (2007) Black beauty: Shade, hair and anti-racist aesthetics. *Ethnic and Racial Studies*, 30(2): 300–319.

Tate, S.A. (2009) *Black Beauty*. Aldershot: Ashgate.

Tate, S.A. (2015) Performativity and 'raced' bodies. In: K. Murji and J. Solomos (eds), *Theories of Race and Ethnicity*. Cambridge: Cambridge University Press, pp. 180–197.

Tatsumi, T. (2007) Afterword. In: C. Bolton, J. Csicsery-Ronay and T. Tatsumi (eds), *Robot Ghosts and Wired Dreams*. Minneapolis: University of Minnesota Press, pp. 250–259.

Taylor, C. (1986) Foucault on freedom and truth. In: D.C. Hoy (ed.), *Foucault*. Oxford: Blackwell, pp. 69–102.

Taylor, C. ([1987] 1995) *Philosophical Arguments*. Cambridge, MA: Harvard University Press.

The Associated Press (2015). Rio Olympics organisers: Opening ceremony will be cheap. 22 September. Available at: www.cbc.ca/sports/rio-olympics-organizers-op ening-ceremony-will-be-cheap-1.3239309 [accessed: 26 October 2015].

The New York Times (2016) Highlights from the Rio Olympics Closing Ceremony, 21 August. Available at: www.nytimes.com/interactive/2016/08/21/sports/olympics/rio-closing-ceremony-live.html [accessed: 10 November 2016].

Theobald, W.F. (1998) The meaning, scope and measurement of travel and tourism. In: W.F. Theobald (ed.), *Global Tourism*, 2nd edn. Oxford: Butterworth Heinemann, pp. 3–21.

Thompson, F. (2005) Journeying in the Third World: From Third Cinema to tourist cinema? In: D. Crouch, R. Jackson and F. Thompson (eds), *The Media and the Tourist Imagination*. New York: Routledge, pp. 215–229.

Thompson, P. (2013) Introduction: The privatization of hope and the crisis of negation. In: P. Thompson and S. Žižek (eds), *The Privatization of Hope*. Durham, NC: Duke University Press, pp. 1–20.

Thrift, N. (1999) The place of complexity. *Theory, Culture & Society*, 16(3): 31–70.

Thrift, N. (2004a) Intensities of feeling: Towards a spatial politics of affect. *Geografika Annaler B*, 86(1): 57–78.

Thrift, N. (2004b) Movement-space: The changing domain of thinking resulting from the development of new kinds of spatial awareness. *Economy & Society*, 33(4): 582–604.

Thrift, N. (2007) *Non-Representational Theory*. London: Routledge.

Tilly, C. (1964) *The Vendee*. Cambridge, MA: Harvard University Press.

Tilly, C. (1984) *Big Structures, Large Processes, Huge Comparisons*. New York: Russell Sage Foundation.

Timms, J. (2016) The relay of mega-event activism: Why global organising bodies need to be targeted. In: N.B. Salazar, C. Timmerman, J. Wets, L. Gama Gato and S. Van den Broucke (eds), *Mega-Event Mobilities*. Abingdon: Routledge, pp. 108–127.

Tokyo 2020 (undated). Flag handover guide. Available at: https://tokyo2020.jp/en/sp ecial/rio-to-tokyo/olympic-flaghandover/olympic-flaghandoverguide.pdf [accessed: 8 December 2016].

Tomlinson, A. (1996) Olympic spectacle: Opening ceremonies and some paradoxes of globalization. *Media Culture & Society*, 18(4): 583–602.

Tomlinson, A. and Young, C. (eds), (2006) *National Identity and Global Sports Events*. New York: SUNY.

Tomlinson, J. (2007) Cultural globalization. In: G. Ritzer (ed.), *The Blackwell Companion to Globalization*. Oxford: Blackwell.

Tonkonoff, S. (2013) A new social physic: The sociology of Gabriel Tarde and its legacy. *Current Sociology*, 61(3): 267–282.

Toohey, K. and Veal, A.J. (2000) *The Olympic Games*. New York: CABI.

Trends Now (2016). Inside Rio's favelas – Truth of Rio Olympics 2016 – Brazil cover up. 3 August. Available at: https://www.youtube.com/watch?v=EPEPsLAvxsA [accessed: 22 January 2017].

Tsurumi, S. (1987) *A Cultural History of Japan, 1945–1980*. London: KPI.

Tully, S. (2013). Is 'Tomorrowland' movie tied to Disneyland area? 28 January. Available at: www.ocregister.com/news/movie-409540-disney-tomorrowland.html [accessed: 5 September 2016].

Turner, B.S. (1996) *The Body and Society*. London: Sage.

Tyfield, D. and Urry, J. (2014) Special issue: Energy and society. *Theory, Culture & Society*, 31: 1–226.

Tzanelli, R. (2004) Giving gifts (and then taking them back): Identity, reciprocity and symbolic power in the context of Athens 2004. *The Journal of Cultural Research*, 8(4): 425–446.

Tzanelli, R. (2007) *The Cinematic Tourist*. London and New York: Routledge.

Tzanelli, R. (2008a) Cultural intimations and the commodification of culture: Sign industries as makers of the 'public sphere'. *The Global Studies Journal*, 1(3): 1–10.

Tzanelli, R. (2008b) *Nation-Building and Identity in Europe*. Basingstoke: Palgrave-Macmillan.

Tzanelli, R. (2008c) The nation has two voices: Diforia and performativity in Athens 2004. *European Journal of Cultural Studies*, 11(4): 489–508.

Tzanelli, R. (2010) Mediating cosmopolitanism: Crafting an allegorical imperative through Beijing 2008. *International Review of Sociology*, 20(2): 215–241.

Tzanelli, R. (2011) *Cosmopolitan Memory in Europe's 'Backwaters'*. Abingdon: Routledge.

Tzanelli, R. (2013a) *Heritage in the Digital Era*. London: Routledge.

Tzanelli, R. (2013b) *Olympic Ceremonialism and the Performance of National Character*. Basingstoke: Palgrave Macmillan.

Tzanelli, R. (2015a) *Mobility, Modernity and the Slum*. Abingdon: Routledge.

Tzanelli, R. (2015b) On Avatar's (2009) touring semiotechnologies: From cinematic utopias to Chinese heritage tourism. *Tourism Analysis*, 20(3): 269–282

Tzanelli, R. (2015c) *Socio-Cultural Mobility and Mega-Events*. Abingdon: Routledge.

Tzanelli, R. (2016a) Dark tourism and digital gift economies: Some epistemological notes. In: M.E. Korstanje (ed.), *Terrorism in a Global Village*. New York: Nova Publishers, pp. 105–134.

Tzanelli, R. (2016b) *Thanatourism and Cinematic Representations of Risk*. Abingdon: Routledge.

Tzanelli, R. (2016c) Virtual mega-event imaginaries and worldmaking imperatives in Rio 2016. In: N.B. Salazar, C. Timmerman, J. Wets, L. Gama Gato and S. Van den Broucke (eds), *Mega-Event Mobilities*. Abingdon: Routledge, pp. 69–89.

Tze-Yue, H.G. (2010) *Frames of Anime*. Hong Kong: Hong Kong University Press.

Tzionis, A. (1999) *Santiago Calatrava*. Toronto: Universe.

Uchida, M. (2014) 椎名林檎単独インタビュー [Ringo Sheena solo interview], 26 May. Available at: https://web.archive.org/web/20140527051300/http://natalie.mu/music/pp/sheenaringo02/page/6 [accessed: 15 December 2016].

Ueno, T. (2002) Japanimation and techno-Orientalism. In: B. Grenville (ed.), *The Uncanny*. Vancouver: Arsenal Pulp Publications, pp. 223–231.

UNEP/UNWTO (2005) Making tourism more sustainable: A Guide for policy makers. Available at: www.unep.fr/shared/publications/pdf/DTIx0592Xpa-Tourism PolicyEN.pdf [accessed: 16 October 2016].

UNESCO (2008) Kabuki theatre, Japan: Inscribed in 2008 (3.COM) on the Representative List of the Intangible Cultural Heritage of Humanity (originally proclaimed in 2005). Available at: www.unesco.org/culture/ich/en/RL/kabuki-theatre-00163 [accessed: 15 December 2016].

UnmissableJAPAN.com (undated). Asakusa Samba Carnival. Available at: http://www.unmissablejapan.com/events/asakusa-samba-carnival [accessed: 11 December 2016].

Unruh, V. (2006) *Performing Women and Modern Literary Culture in Latin America*. Austin: University of Texas Press.

Urry, J. (1990) *The Tourist Gaze*. London and New Delhi: Sage.

Urry, J. (1995) *Consuming Places*. London: Routledge.

Urry, J. (1996) How societies remember the past. In: S. MacDonald and G. Fyfe (eds), *Theorizing Museums*. Oxford: Blackwell, pp. 45–63.

Urry, J. (2002a) The global complexities of September the 11th. *Theory, Culture & Society*, 19(4): 57–69.

Urry, J. (2002b) *The Tourist Gaze*, 2nd edn. London: Sage.

Urry, J. (2003) *Global Complexity*. Cambridge: Polity.

Urry, J. (2004) Death in Venice. In: M. Sheller and J. Urry (eds), *Tourism Mobilities*. London and New York: Routledge, pp. 205–215.

Urry, J. (2005a) The complexities of the global. *Theory, Culture and Society*, 22(5): 235–254.

Urry, J. (2005b) The complexity turn. *Theory, Culture & Society*, 22(5): 1–14.

Urry, J. (2007) *Mobilities*. Cambridge: Polity.

Urry, J. (2008) The London Olympics and global competition: On the move. *Twenty First Century Society*, 3(3): 289–293.

Urry, J. (2010) Consuming the planet to excess. *Theory, Culture & Society*, 27(2–3): 191–212.

Urry, J. (2011) *Climate Change and Society*. Cambridge: Polity.

Urry, J. (2013) *Societies Beyond Oil*. London: Zed.

Urry, J. (2014) *Offshoring*. Cambridge: Polity.

Urry, J. and Larsen, J. (2011) *The Tourist Gaze 3.0*. London: Sage.

Urry, J., Elliott, A., Radford, B. and Pitt, N. (2016) Globalisations utopia? On airport atmospherics. *Emotion, Space and Society*, 16: 13–20.

Valentine, B. (2014). Dancing with drones. Hyperallergic (Dance Education). 20 May. Available at: http://hyperallergic.com/127496/dancing-with-drones/ [accessed: 13 December 2016].

Van den Broucke, S., Timmerman, C., Vandervoordt, R. and Gama Gato, L. (2016) An agenda for future mega-event research. In: N.B. Salazar, C. Timmerman, J. Wets, L. Gama Gato and S. Van den Broucke (eds), *Mega-Event Mobilities*. Abingdon: Routledge, pp. 165–178.

Vandana, D. and Loftus, A. (2013) Speculating on slums: Infrastructural fixes in informal housing in the Global South, *Antipodes*, 45(4): 789–808.

Vannini, P. (ed.), (2015) *Non-Representational Methodologies*. London: Routledge.

Vannini, P., Hodson, J. and Vannini, A. (2009) Toward a technography of everyday life. *Cultural Studies – Critical Methodologies*, 9(3): 462–476.

Vattimo, C. (1988) *The End of Modernity*. Cambridge: Polity.

Veloso, C. (2003) *Tropical Truth*. London: Bloomsbury.

Vidal, J. (2016). What's in the water? Pollution fears taint Rio's picturesque bay ahead of Olympics. *The Guardian*, 3 August. Available at: www.theguardian.com/sport/2016/aug/03/pollution-fears-taint-rio-bay-olympic-games [accessed: 5 September 2016].

Viola, E. (2013) Transformations in Brazilian deforestation and climate policy since 2005. *Theoretical Inquiries in Law*, 14(1): 109–123.

Virtanen, A. (2004) General economy: The entrance of multitude into production. *Ephemera*, 4(3): 209–232.

Wacquant, L. (1989) Towards a reflexive sociology: A workshop with Pierre Bourdieu. *Sociological Theory*, 7(1): 26–63.

Wager, J.B. (1999) *Dangerous Dames*. Athens: Ohio University Press.

Wallerstein, I. (1974) *The Modern World System*, vol. I. New York: Academic Press.

Wallerstein, I. (1980) *The Modern World System*, vol. II. New York: Academic Press.

Walter, T. (2009) Dark tourism: mediating between the dead and the living. In: R. Sharpley and P.R. Stone (eds), *The Darker Side of Travel*. Bristol: Channel View Publications, pp. 39–55.

Waters, C.N. (2016) The Anthropocene is functionally and stratigraphically distinct from the Holocene. *Science*, 351(6269): 2622.

Watson, I., Cotonio, V. and Kehl, J. (2016) Trash creates obstacles for Rio 2016 Olympic sailors. *CNN*, 2 June. Available at: http://edition.cnn.com/2016/06/02/sport/brazil-olympic-bay-pollution/ [accessed: 5 September 2016].

Watts, J. (2015). Museum of Tomorrow: A captivating invitation to imagine a sustainable world. *The Guardian*, 17 December. Available at: www.theguardian.com/world/2015/dec/17/museum-of-tomorrow-rio-de-janeiro-brazil-sustainability [accessed: 11 August 2016].

Weaver, D. (2011) Celestial ecotourism: New horizons in nature-based tourism. *Journal of Ecotourism*, 10(1): 38–45.

Weber, M. (1985) *The Protestant Ethic and the Spirit of Capitalism*. London: Unwin Hyman.

Weibel, P. (2011) Sloterdijk and the question of an aesthetic. In: W. Schinkel and L. Noordegraaf-Eelens (eds), *In Media Res*. Amsterdam: Amsterdam University Press, pp. 83–98.

Weiner, M. (ed.), (2008) *Japan's Minorities*. London: Routledge.

Wenning, M. (2009) The return of rage. *Parrhesia*, 8: 89–99.

Wetzstein, S. (2013) Globalising economic governance, political projects, and spatial imaginaries. *Geographical Research*, 51(1): 71–84.

Whatmore, S. (1997) Dissecting the autonomous Self: Hybrid cartographies for a relational ethics. *Environment and Planning D: Society and Space*, 15(1): 37–53.

Whitefield, M. (2014). Porto Maravilha: Reclaiming Rio de Janeiro's neglected port. *Miami Herald*, 3 June. Available at: www.miamiherald.com/news/nation-world/world/americas/article1965447.html [accessed: 9 September 2016].

Wikipedia (undated). Martinho da Vila. Available at: https://en.wikipedia.org/wiki/Martinho_da_Vila [accessed: 10 November 2016].

Will, S., Grinevald, J., Crutzen, P. and McNeill, J. (2011) The Anthropocene: Conceptual and historical perspectives. *Philosophical Transactions of the Royal Society A*, 369(1938): 842–867.

Williams, R. (1977) *Marxism and Literature*. Oxford: Oxford University Press.

Wilson, G. (1992) *Patriots and Redeemers in Japan*. Chicago, IL: University of Chicago Press.

Witzgall, S. and Vogl, G. (2016) *New Mobilities Regimes in Art and Social Sciences*. Abingdon: Routledge.

Wolff, J. (1984) *The Social Production of Art*. New York: New York University Press.

Wolff, K.H. (ed.) Simmel, G. (1959) *Georg Simmel, 1858–1918*. Columbus: Ohio State University Press.

Wojan, T.R., Lambert, D.M. and McGranaghan, D.A. (2007) The emergence of rural artistic havens: A first look. *Agricultural and Resource Economic Review*, 36: 53–70.

Wong, J.K. (2016) A dilemma of green democracy. *Political Studies*, 64(15): 136–155.

Wood, J. and Shearing, C. (2007) *Imagining Security*. Devon and Portland, OR: Willan.

Wynne, B. (2010) Strange weather, again: Climate science as political art. *Theory, Culture & Society*, 27(2–3): 289–305.

XIII Olympic Congress – Copenhagen 2009 (undated). The Olympic Movement in society. Available at: www.olympic.org/olympic-congress [accessed: 19 October 2016].

Yamamoto, A. (22 May 2012). Tokyo Sky Tree takes root as world's second-tallest structure', *NBC News*. Available at: http://worldnews.nbcnews.com/_news/2012/05/

22/11809861-tokyo-sky-tree-takes-root-as-worlds-second-tallest-structure   [accessed: 15 December 2016].

Yoshimoto, M. (1989) The postmodern and mass images of Japan. *Public Culture*, 1(2): 8–25.

Young, C. (2003) Kaiser Franz and the communist bowl: Cultural memory and Munich's Olympic Stadium. *American Behavioral Scientist*, 46(11): 1476–1490.

Young, C. (2006) Munich 1972: Representing the nation. In: A. Tomlinson and C. Young (eds), *National Identity and Global Sports Events*. New York: SUNY, pp. 117–132.

Young, I.M. (2005) House and home: Feminist variations on a theme. In: I.M. Young (ed.), *On Female Body Experience*. Cary, NC: Oxford University Press, pp. 123–154.

Young, I.M. (2006) Responsibility and global justice: A social connection model. *Social Philosophy and Policy*, 23(1): 102–130.

Young, R. (2008) The void of misgiving. In: K. Ikas and G. Wagner (eds), *Communicating in the Third Space*. London: Routledge, pp. 81–94.

Zeitlyn, D. (2015) Looking forward, looking back. *History and Anthropology*, 26(4): 381–407.

Zeuner, L. (1999) Culture and agency. The place of culture in social theory by Margaret S. Archer. *Acta Sociologica*, 42(1): 79–86.

Zhu, W., Zhang, L. and Li, N. (2014) Challenges, function changing of government and enterprises in Chinese smart tourism. In: Z. Xiang and L. Tussyadiah (eds), *Information and Communication Technologies in Tourism*. Dublin: Springer.

Zimmermann, A. and Favell, A. (2011) Governmentality, political field or public sphere? Theoretical alternatives in the political sociology of the EU. *European Journal of Social Theory*, 14(4): 489–515.

Zimmerman, R.E. (2013) Transforming utopian into metopian systems: Bloch's Principle of Hope revisited. In: P. Thompson and S. Žižek (eds), *The Privatization of Hope*. Durham, NC: Duke University Press, pp. 246–268.

Zipes, J. (1988) Introduction: Towards a realization of anticipatory illumination. In: E. Bloch, (1986) *The Principle of Hope*, vol. II. Cambridge, MA: MIT.

Žižek, S. (1999) *The Ticklish Subject*. New York: Verso.

Žižek, S. (2013) Preface: Bloch's ontology of not-yet-being. In: P. Thompson and S. Žižek (eds), *The Privatization of Hope*. Durham, NC: Duke University Press, pp. xv–xx.

Žižek, S. (2014) *Event*. London and New York: Penguin.

Zolberg, V.L. (2015) A cultural sociology of the arts. *Current Sociology*, 63(6): 896–915.

Zournazi, M. (2002) *Hope*. Annandale: Pluto Press.

Zukin, S. (1982) Art in the arms of power: Market relations and collective patronage in the capitalist state. *Theory and Society*, 11(4): 423–451.

Zukin, S. (1988) The postmodern debate over urban form. *Theory, Culture & Society*, 5(2–3): 431–446.

Zukin, S. (1995) *The Cultures of Cities*. Malden, MA: Blackwell.

Zukin, S. (2010) *Naked City*. Oxford: Oxford University Press.

Index

Abe, Shinzō 140, 158, 163, 164; Abe/
  Super Mario 155, 156, 158, 163, 164;
  Karōshi 156, 157, 158
Abreu, Zequinha de: *Tico-Tico no Fubá* 127
Academia Imperial de Belas Artes (*Escola
  Nacional de Belas Artes*, ENBA) 76
aesthetics 40; aesthetic of darkness 67,
  73, 118, 131, 159; aesthetic reflexivity
  26, 27, 40–1, 80, 115; artistic
  imagineer 35, 36, 38, 39; Brazil 15, 40;
  gender, racial and class inequalities 48;
  heritage aesthetics 102; 'hipster cool'
  aesthetics 151; political action 45
Albertsen, N. 62
Alexander, J.C. 11
Amazon rainforest 58, 103
Amin, A. 135
Andrade, Oswald de: *Manifesto
  Antropofago* 130
anime see *manga* and *anime*
Anitta 98
ANT (Actor-Network) 82
Antunes, Arnaldo: *Saudade* 131
Aomori team 158–9
Appelbaum, Ralph 76
Appiah, K.A. 11
Aravamudan, S. 15
Archer, Margaret 10, 35
architect 3, 13, 24, 29, 35; *see also* artistic
  imagineer
architecture 13, 12, 61; architectural
  morphogenesis 61; Brazil 16, 76;
  capitalism 13, 68
Arendt, Hannah 7, 38, 45, 122, 153, 171
art/artistic creativity 13, 34, 88–9; capit-
  alism 13; degrowth 52; interpretation
  and 50; *oeconomie artificialem* 20, 28;
  politics 46, 55; technology 28, 33;
  utopia 35

artificial economy see *oeconomie
  artificialem*
artistic *imagineer* 3, 27, 29, 31, 172, 173;
  aesthetics 35, 36, 38, 39; affluent tourist
  29, 173; aims 32; artistic/architectural
  labour 9–10, 29, 40; artistic worldmaking 89, 91, 100, 171; capitalism
  43; cultural capital and 99; cultural
  enclave/network 36, 38; experts 24, 25,
  38; friction among the artistic
  imagineers 36–7; gender and 37–8;
  homo mobilis 30–1, 33; mediating
  between policy and ideational
  planning 36; *oeconomie artificialem* 37;
  see also imagineering
artistic and social critique 39–43, 45, 46,
  117–18
Asada, Akira 162
Asano, T. 154
Athens 2004 Olympics 3, 5, 42, 130
athletes 1, 120, *120,* 127, 151, 153, 158,
  168
atmosphere 13, 14; *Carioca*-samba
  atmospherics 14–15, 125–6; Rio's
  atmosphere 15, 125, 132
Augé, M. 4, 16
Avatar 103–104
Azuma, H. 142, 153

Bach, Thomas 120–1, 133
Bacharach, Burt Freeman 162
Ban-Ki Moon 121
Barber, B. 27, 139
Barcelona 1992 Olympics 5, 53
Barreto, Hugo 80
Bataille, G. 42
Bauhaus 76
Bauman, Z. 7, 29, 74, 89, 90, 167–8, 171,
  172; *Otaku* 153

Beck, U. 38, 141
Beijing 2008 Summer Olympics 4, 42, 130, 140, 163; 2008 Olympic Handover Party 27, 143; budget 92; Olympic Stadium/Bird's Nest 80, 164
belonging 4, 5, 18, 32, 35, 90; Brazil 69; communal belonging 26, 68; Handover Ceremony to Tokyo 2020: 3; human belonging in ecological sphere 111; imaginaries of belonging 33, 39; Rio 2016 Olympics 91; social belonging 114
Benjamin, Walter 46, 80, 116
Berlant, L. 172
Berlin 1936 Olympics 5, 75
biopolitics 25, 32, 78, 91, 123; Foucault, M. 38, 137, 171; post-biopolitics 38, 122
Bird, Brad: *Tomorrowland* 63–4
Bloch, Ernest 68, 90, 165, 168, 172
Böhme, Gernot 14, 157
Boltanski, L. 39, 62, 174
Botafogo 17, 70
Bourdieu, P. 25–6, 37, 99
Brasília 1, 17, 40, 76, 103, 107
Brasilidade (Brazilian-ness) 17–18, 76, 115, 117; artistic *Brasilidade* 128; *Carioca Brasilidade* 97, 116
Brazil 15–16, 40; *abertura* 17, 40, 58, 109, 126, 129, 170; architecture 16, 76; *branqueamento* 16, 107, 110, 132; *buen vivir*/well-being 55, 59, 69, 75, 89, 113; capitalism 39, 111; cinema 107–109, 110; crisis 2, 33, 43, 51; culture 33; dictatorship 16, 96, 101, 105; economic recession 88, 92, 111; environmental issues 56–7, 59–60, 86; globalisation 107, 116; heritage 16, 19, 22, 34, 40, 41, 67, 93, 123, 125–6, 133; identity 37, 89, 103; ideology 17, 76; modernism/modernisation 15, 16, 18, 33, 69, 70, 76, 95, 104, 108, 109, 127, 129, 131, 169; nationalism 16, 63, 95, 116; neoliberalism 19, 40, 58, 110, 115; popular culture 22, 31, 32, 44, 95, 101, 111, 113, 115, 128; populism 63, 117, 123; security issues 21; tradition 16, 17, 98, 113, 116, 125–6, 127, 131; 'tropicopolitanism' 15, 69; *see also* Rio de Janeiro
Brenner, N. 4
BRICS (Brazil, Russia, India, China and South Africa) 55
Brun, C. 122

Buarque, Chico: *Construção* 105
Bulcão, Athos 102–103
Bündchen, Gisele 107, 108, 110
bureaucracy 59, 145, 146, 167, 173, 174; bureaucratic failure in mega-event host territories 168, 169
Büscher, M. 28
Butler, J. 6, 45

Caetano, Leonardo 92
Calatrava, Santiago 60, 62–4, 91, 103, 123; 'Byzantium', Athens 2004: 64; City of Arts and Sciences 63–4; Ground Zero 65, 66, 125; ideology 63; Montjuic Communications Tower, Barcelona 62; Museum of Tomorrow 13, 37, 38, 43, 53, 66, 71, 86, 87; Quadracci Pavilion, Milwaukee Art Museum 63; St Nicholas Greek Orthodox Church 64, 66–7, 75, 125; *see also* Museum of Tomorrow
'Camp' 10, 18, 35, 37, 129, 163; 'Camp' reflexivity 45; Miranda's 'Camp' 128
cangaceiros 131–2
O Canto de Ossanha 111–12
capital: capitalism and 45–6; cultural capital 99, 110, 125; ethical capital 37; ethno-racial capital 38; gendered capital 38; human capital 25, 29, 83, 129, 163; network capital 21, 22, 99; symbolic capital 13, 37
capitalism 8, 121, 168–9, 171, 174; architecture 13, 68; artistic *imagineer* 43; Brazil 39, 111; capital and 45–6; capitalist development 3, 19, 136; capitalist ideology 8, 39, 43; crony capitalism 20; environmental issues 56; global capitalism 65, 86, 111; Handover Ceremony to Tokyo 2020: 146, 150, 156, 157; *imagineering* 26; IOC 121; Japan 136–7, 139; mega-event 3–4, 5, 8; Museum of Tomorrow 54, 60, 67, 68–9, 75, 84, 87; Rio 2016 Olympics 41, 122; 'thana-capitalism' 43, 94, 156, 167, 174
capoeira 15, 23, 89, 99, 115; black ethnic practice 112–13
Carioca 3, 12, 13, 22–3, 109–10; accent 13; *Carioca Brasilidade* 97, 116; *Carioca feminine mystique* 22; *Carioca*-samba atmospherics 14–15, 125–6; *Carioca*-samba ethno-style 13, 14; *mulatta Carioca* 15, 112; Rio 2016

Olympics 3, 18; stereotype 18, 22; technology 36, 131
carnival 18, 22, 41, 110, 113, 125, 155
Carter, P. 71
catastrophism 5, 67, 172, 173–4
Chiapello, E. 39, 62, 174
Christ the Redeemer 60, 126
chronopolitics 55, 65
Cinema Novo 89, 94, 95
Citade Maravilhosa 22, 116
cittaslow, Italy 7–8, 160
City of Men 118
climate change 3, 11, 55–6; Brazil 57; Museum of Tomorrow 54, 56, 78, 79; perspectives on 56; Rio 2016 Opening Ceremony 118–20, 123, 124; *see also* environmental issues
Cohen, Erik 14–15, 90
Colker, Deborah 89, 93, 98–9
colonialism/colonisation 10, 11, 15, 25, 34, 92, 98, 104, 106, 149, 169; de-colonisation 34, 85; 'internal colonisation' 59; Japan 138, 146
Commonwealth Games 4
communism 16, 56, 76; Brazilian Communist Party 127
Connell, R.W. 45
consumption 7, 9, 17, 22, 24, 25; spaces of consumption 22, 25; spectacular consumption 27
Copacabana 17
Copacabana 127
Copacabana Palace 105
Cordeiro de Lima, Vanderlei 123
Correa, Andre 60
corruption 18, 20, 93, 129
cosmopolitanism 11, 15, 26, 39, 73, 107, 111, 129; cosmopolitan ethos 43; cosmopolitan togetherness 129, 131, 164; Japan (*kyosei*) 136–47, 149, 153; Olympic event 129, 172; rebuilding homes for humanity 172; 'tropicopolitanism' 15
Costa, Lúcio 76
Coubertin, Pierre de, Baron 5, 123
Couldry, Nick 89–90, 126
Cowan, J.K. 99
Cresswell, T. 23
crime 4, 28; *favela* 20, 21, 59, 93, 114, 116
crisis 13, 42, 43, 51, 122; artistic and social critique 117–18; Brazil 2, 33, 43, 51; existential crisis 5, 42, 43

cultural sociology 10, 11, 47, 89
culture 10, 11, 33; *anthropofagia*/'cultural cannibalism' 17–18, 115–16, 128, 143; Brazil 33; cultural hybridisation 18, 29, 33, 73, 98, 128–9, 142, 149; culture and society 34, 78, 139; Japan 33, 34, 139, 142, 143, 149; *see also* popular culture

Da Vila, Martinho 127
DaMatta, R. 128–9
dance 98–9; Handover Ceremony to Tokyo, acrobatics and dance 144, 158–9, 161, 162; Rio 2016 Closing Ceremony, dance and music 125, 126, 129, 131, 133; Rio 2016 Opening Ceremony 98, 102, 103, 105, 111, 112–13
darkness 15, 35, 43, 119; aesthetic of darkness 67, 73, 118, 131, 159; dark tourism 66, 73, 86, 131, 156; Museum of Tomorrow 67, 82, 83
Dascal, M. 135
De Beauvoir, Simone 122, 163
Debord, G. 27, 30
degrowth 43, 173–4; Handover Ceremony to Tokyo 2020: 164; Japan 73; Museum of Tomorrow 55, 82, 84; as *predicament* in art and architecture 52; Rio 2016 Ceremonies 89; Rio 2016 Opening Ceremony 96, 102, 119, 126
Degues, Carlos: *Orfeu* 97–8
Deleuze, G. 32, 98
Dench, Judi 119, 120
depénse 42, 67, 72, 120, 149, 173, 174; *oeconomie imaginationis* and economy of *dépense* 175
Derrida, J. 20, 38
Deslandes, A. 40
digitality 2, 24, 38, 44, 80, 169; digital ethnography 49; digital sources 49–50; digital surveillance 25; green face 79; Handover Ceremony to Tokyo 2020: 145, 146; Museum of Tomorrow 37, 80, 81, 82–3; Rio 2016 Olympics 79; tourism 83; *see also* technology
Diken, B. 62, 90, 94, 118
Dimitrova Savova, N. 102
director 3, 24, 29, 93, 170–1; Handover Ceremony to Tokyo 2020: 38, 50, 146; Rio 2016 Olympics 38, 50, 89, 91; technology 38; worldmaking 50; *see also* artistic *imagineer*
Doraemon 153, 154–5
dreaming 32, 35, 53, 61, 175

Drummond de Andrade, Carlos 119
Dussel, Enrique 21–2, 104, 113, 127
Dutch Development Bank 60
dystopia 35, 43, 54, 55, 56, 84, 86, 157

earthquake 141; Great East Japan
  Earthquake 134, 143, 146, 149, 159
economy of artifice *see oeconomie
  artificialem*
economy of imagination *see oeconomie
  imaginationis*
Edmonds, A. 110
EMBRATUR (Brazilian Tourist Board) 84
Enlightenment 71, 114, 136; progress 5,
  54, 61
environmental issues 28; Brazil 56–7,
  59–60, 86; capitalism and 56;
  democracy and 57; eco-technocracy
  57–61; environmental racism 27, 58,
  59, 72, 93, 111, 175; environmental
  rights 58–9; media 55, 57, 83; Museum
  of Tomorrow, environmental ethics 70,
  79–80; Rio 2016 Opening Ceremony
  105, 111, 118–20, 123; *see also* climate
  change; sustainability
epistemology 25, 44, 47, 48, 71, 85;
  epistemic community 47; hybrid
  epistemology 50
ethnicity: *Carioca*-samba ethno-style 13,
  14; ethnicity and globalisation 92;
  ethno-culture 7, 14, 16, 22, 24, 25, 35,
  99, 171; ethno-national/nationalism
  36, 44, 89, 116, 117, 135, 144, 150,
  153, 156, 163, 172; ethno-politics 33;
  ethno-racial capital 38; ethno-social
  morphogenesis 116; Japan 137, 144,
  150, 153, 156, 160, 163; Rio 2016
  Closing Ceremony 129–30, 131, 132–3;
  Rio 2016 Opening Ceremony 104,
  105, 112; *see also* race/racial issues
Ettema, J. 49
Europe 7, 109, 111; heritage 64, 73;
  modernity 33, 34, 76, 109, 111, 119,
  131; tradition 15, 33, 119
Evans, P.B. 102
Ezralow, Daniel 158

Fagge, N. 119
Fanon, F. 114
Fassin, D. 121
favela (shantytown, Rio de Janeiro) 12–13,
  17, 22, 76, 166, 170; *baile funk* 113–14,
  115, 117, 173; cable car over 78–9;
  Carioca Brasilidade 97; *City of God*

94–5, 118; crime/criminalisation of 20,
  21, 59, 93, 114, 116; displacement and
  eviction 167; *favela* gangsters 116–17;
  favelados 15, 31, 91, 114; festivalisation of the host city 24; futurising 21;
  imagineering 21; inequality 21, 117;
  mega-event regeneration 68, 79;
  mobility 169–70; police pacification
  21, 31, 59, 79, 118, 167; popular
  culture 31, 32, 95, 115; race/racial
  issues 21, 22, 23, 166; Rio 2016
  Opening Ceremony 94, 107, 111,
  113–18; samba 15, 22, 113, 116;
  security issues 20, 21, 114; slavery 20,
  115, 116; social protest 22, 23;
  surveillance 31, 32; tourism 167;
  tourismification 79; utopia 114;
  violence 20, 32, 114, 116–17, 118; *see
  also* UPP
femininity 110, 163, 172; artistic
  activities 114–15; body 107–10, 117;
  effeminacy 37, 128, 173; feminised
  post-modernity 97; feminised Rio 108,
  109, 111; feminised urban 'aesthetics
  of attraction' 109; *see also* gender
  issues; *Melindrosa*; *Moga*
Fernandes, Alexandre 69
FIFA World Cup 4, 5, 84, 88, 128, 146
Ford, H. 50
Foucault, M. 30, 31, 48, 50, 105, 168;
  biopolitics 38, 137, 171; Panopticism
  76; surveillance 25, 27, 30
Frankfurt School 26
Freeman, J. 59
Freyre, Gilberto 16, 107
Fullerton, L. 49
Fundação Roberto Marinho 79
funk/funkeiros 107, 110, 113; *baile funk*
  111, 113–16, 117, 131, 173

gambiarra 102, 107
gaze/gazing 10, 38, 81, 128, 133, 145,
  150; artistic *imagineer* 31; empathic
  gaze 38; gaze of pity 152; global gaze
  117; a green alternative 79; militourism
  27; objects of the 'gaze' 31; post-tourist
  gaze 143; public gaze 156, 157; tourist/
  visitor's gaze 15, 27, 30, 58, 91, 123,
  165
Geiger, R.S. 50
gender issues 129–30; artistic *imagineer*
  37–8; beauty and 22–3, 110; discursive
  cinematic trope 96; ethno-cultures and
  22; gendered capital 38; gendered 'risk

regimes' 122; hermaphrodite 10, 22; Japan 156–7; Rio 2016 Ceremonies 97–8; Rio 2016 Closing Ceremony 129–30, 132–3; Rio 2016 Opening Ceremony 107, 122; *see also* femininity; masculinity
Germann Molz, Jennie 8
Giddens, A. 20, 74
gift-giving 42, 43, 149
Gil, Gilberto 89, 96–7, 103, 110; *Aquele Abraço* 101
Gilroy, Paul 114, 115
Global South 4, 7, 19, 53
globalisation 2, 5, 10, 14, 86; *anthropofagia/* cultural hybridisation 18; Brazil 107, 116; cultural globalisation 140; global capitalism 65, 86, 111; globalisation pessimists 46; host city 2, 10; Japan 137, 140, 142, 144, 153; multi-scalar globalisation 53; neoliberal globalisation 88, 102; the urban and the global 17; 'world citizenship' 38–9
glocalisation/glocalism 4, 12, 33, 55, 89, 135; methodological glocalism 42
Gomes, Jorge 123
Gonzaga, Luiz: *Asa Branca* 133
Goodman, Nelson 46–7, 50, 88, 167
governance 5, 30, 59, 149, 163; eco-technocratic model of 58; global governance 18, 24, 66–7, 111, 122; neoliberalism 27, 170; urban governance 4, 27
Graburn, N.H.H. 136, 154
Ground Zero 65, 66, 73, 123, 125
Grupo Corpo 133
Guanabara Bay 70, 86; pollution 2, 60, 86
Guattari, F. 32, 98
guest/tourist 11, 50, 132, 165; mega-event's 'cinematic tourist' 154; tourist/visitor's gaze 15, 27, 30, 58, 91, 123, 165
Gyurta, Dániel 133

Habermas, J. 132
Haiku travel 154
Hamaguchi, Osachi 152
Handover Ceremony to Rio 2016: 95
Handover Ceremony to Tokyo 2020: 3, 14, 33, 40, 51, 136, 168; acrobatics and dance 144, 158–9, 161, 162; *anime-manga* 137, 144, 145, 151, 153–5, 157, 158, 163; an artistic statement 136, 147; athletes 151, 153, 158; atmospheric 'heritage attraction' 164; *bricolage* 150,

158; capitalism 146, 150, 156, 157; choreomobile arrangement 146–7; degrowth 164; digitality 145, 146; directors 38, 50, 146; from *oeconomie artificialem* to *oeconomie imaginationis* 159; *Hinomaru*-Japanese national flag 148; host city's landmarks 14, 151–3; ideology 147; *Kimigayo*/national anthem 148; *Moga* 151; *Mura*/village 160; music 162; neoliberalism 147; *origami* 148; popular culture 163; public revelation of the inner Self 41; romantic tourist 145–6, 158; 'solidarity by anxiety' 141; sustainability 143; synecdochical (dis)connectivities 135; *tatemae* 145; technology 37, 147, 148, 149, 158, 159, 164; technoromanticism 146; Tokyo Sky Tree 162–4; tourism 151, 164; tourismification 151–2; utopia 143, 147; *see also* Handover Ceremony to Tokyo 2020, segments; Japan; Tokyo; Tokyo 2020 Olympics
Handover Ceremony to Tokyo 2020, segments: 'Arigato from Japan' 148–9; 'The City of Festivals' 161; 'The City of Waterways' 159–60; 'Grand Finale' 162, 164; 'Tokyo is Warming Up' 150; *see also* Handover Ceremony to Tokyo 2020
Hannam, K. 112
Hara, Takashi 152
Hayek, Friedrich 56, 58
health-related issues 28, 60
Heidegger, Martin 43, 87
Heidemann, Britta 133
Henze, Stefan 131
heritage 13, 57, 58, 71, 89, 137, 152, 171; Brazil 16, 19, 22, 34, 40, 41, 67, 93, 123, 125–6, 133; Calatrava, Santiago 66; dark tourism 66, 86, 131; Europe 64, 73; heritage aesthetics 102; heritage attraction 164; heritage event 172; heritage interpretation redux: evotopianism and the war of worlds 165–70; heritage pilgrimage 162; heritage synaesthetics 102; *homo mobilis* 30; Japan 41, 138, 139, 141, 144, 145, 150, 153, 158, 161, 163; Olympic heritage 7, 46; tourism and 25, 59, 123; Western heritage 93; *see also* tradition
Herzfeld, M. 90
Holliday, R. 128
Hollinshead, K. 33, 48, 161, 168

Homo Faber 7, 122, 133, 172
Homo Mobilis 9, 29–33, 122, 133, 157,
172; empathy 31; explanation of the
term 30; *see also* artistic *imagineer*
Homo Mundis 172
honne 37, 138, 139, 154, 155; individualisation of 73, 143, 145; inner self 73,
136; *tatemae/honne* duality 136, 157,
161; *see also* Japan; *tatemae*
hope 3, 27, 34, 35, 42, 168, 172; Brazil/
Rio 2016 Olympics 97, 117, 120, 121,
122, 133; 'educated hope' 172; Japan
149, 159; mega-event 38, 52; societal
hope 169; *Ubuntu* 89; utopia 38;
worldmaking 100
hospitality 7, 12, 28, 38; Brazil and
militourism 39; Olympic hospitality 7,
9, 126
host 4, 5, 134, 165, 171; bureaucratic
failure 168, 169; hosting a mega-event
in a 'zero-friction society' 11;
Olympic/host values relation 45
host city 5, 8; festivalisation of the host
city 23–4; globalisation 2, 10; impact
of mega-event on 2, 5, 167; *ontogenesis*
of the (*mega*) city 71; shaping of 10, 78;
see also Olympic city; Rio de Janeiro;
Tokyo
Howe, Anthony 123–5
humanitarianism 38, 40, 121, 123, 149;
IOC 120–1, 122
Hutchinson, J. 137

ICT (Information Communication
Technologies) 83
identity 25, 130, 148, 173; Brazil 37, 89,
103; China 130, 140; Japan 37, 137,
138, 139, 140, 144, 145, 150–1, 154,
155, 156–7; *see also Brasilidade*
ideology 36, 51, 61, 62, 89, 173; Brazil
17, 76; Calatrava, Santiago 63;
capitalist ideology 8, 39, 43; Handover
Ceremony to Tokyo 2020: 147;
imagineering of utopia 34, 58; Japan
136, 139, 144; militourist ideology 59;
Museum of Tomorrow 62; neoliberalism
174; Rio 2016 Olympics 44, 126
IF (International Federation) 1
ILO (International Labour Organisation)
157
imagineering 3, 6–7, 13, 26, 32; creative
labour 13; 'fantasmatics' 33; *favela* 21,
32; imagineering utopias 33–9;
oeconomie imaginationis 32; Olympic

engineering 8–9, 24–5; reflexivity 26;
segmentation 25; spaces: physical and
virtual 36; technology 37; worldmaking/
imagineering relationship 51; *see also*
artistic *imagineer*
inequality 4, 18, 107, 170–1; *favela* 21,
117
Internet 49, 56, 79, 99, 131, 142, 166;
Google 118
IOC (International Olympic Committee)
1, 11, 20, 107, 134; capitalism 121;
humanitarian initiative 120–1, 122;
IOC Athletes' Commission 133
Ipanema 17, 68, 95, 105, 106, 107
IPCC (Intergovernmental Panel on
Climate Change) 55–6
Isinbayeva, Yelena 133
Ito, M. 141

Jameson, F. 87
Jansen, S. 51, 52
Japan 134; *bunraku* 138; capitalism 136–7,
139; cosmopolitanism/*kyosei* 136–47,
149, 153; culture 33, 34, 139, 142, 143,
149; degrowth 73; ethnicity 137, 144,
150, 153, 156, 160, 163; gender issues
156–7; globalisation 137, 140, 142,
144, 153; ideology 136, 139, 144;
identity 37, 137, 138, 139, 140, 144,
145, 148, 150–1, 154, 155, 156–7;
internationalisation 141; *Kimigayo/*
national anthem 140; military-related
issues 138, 143; militourism 139, 152;
mobility 73, 136–47; modernity 33,
136, 150, 152; nationalism 136, 137,
139, 140, 141, 144; *Nihonjinron/*cultural
nationalism 139, 160; *oeconomie
artificialem* 140–1; *oeconomie
imaginationis* 140, 141; pilgrimage
141–2; popular culture 137, 139, 163;
populism 137; racism 141; rise of the
individual Self 139; *satoyama* 74;
security issues 141; surveillance 141;
technology 138, 139, 141; third
Self 136–7; tourism 73; Western
acculturation 136; *see also* Handover
Ceremony to Tokyo; *honne*; Japan,
history and past; *tatemae*; Tokyo
Japan, history and past: Edo period 148,
152, 163; heritage 41, 138, 139, 141,
144, 145, 150, 153, 158, 161, 163;
post-Meiji Restoration 138; postmodernism 142, 143, 144; tradition 73,
142, 143, 145, 148–9, 153, 154; war/

post-war period 51, 140, 142, 156;
World War II 139
Japanese National Tourist Organisation
142
Jardim Botânico (Botanical Garden) 17,
69–70
Jobim, Antônio Carlos: *The Girl from
Ipanema* 106–107; *Samba do Avião*
105
Jobim, Daniel 106
JOC (Japanese Olympic Committee) 134,
135

Kabuki drama 146, 161, 162
Kant, Immanuel 38, 47–8
Karol Conká 113
Karōshi (death by overwork) 155–6, 157–8
Katagiri, M. 137
Keino, Kipchoge 122–3
Kermode, F. 63
kinaesthesia 102
King, D. 40
kitsch 22, 34–5, 128; 'kitsch man' 35;
kitschification 34, 45, 156
Kleist, N. 51, 52
Koike, Yuriko 133
Koizumi, Junichiro 140
Korstanje, M.E. 43, 73
Kristeva, J. 138
Kuma, Kengo 134
Kygo 129
Kyoto 141, 142, 149, 152, 161

Lampião: *Mulher Rendeira* 131–2
Lash, S. 20, 40, 80, 115
Lashley, Conrad 161
Latin America 58, 60, 94, 113, 127
Laustsen, C.B. 90, 94, 118
Lazzarato, M. 24, 25, 99
Le Corbusier 76
Leahy, T. 56
Lefebvre, H. 4, 30, 45–6, 92, 107
Lenine: *Jack Soul Brasileiro* 133
Lenskyj, H.J. 26
Levy, Sidney 88
London 2012 Olympics 2, 27, 42, 130;
2008 Olympic Handover Party 27,
143; ArchelorMittal Orbit 164; budget
92; urban regeneration 59
Los Angeles 1984 Olympics 145, 150
Lost in Translation 142, 151
Ludmilla 113
Lula da Silva, Luiz Inácio 2, 17, 40, 96,
170

Lund, Kátia 94, 95
Luxembourg, R. 30
Lynch, Paul 10, 164
Lyon, D. 168

Machado, Marcelo 97
Mackenzie, A. 75
Magalhães, Rosa 89, 96, 125–6, 131
malandragem/malandro 18, 22, 112,
151
Malthus, Thomas 56, 58, 78
manga and *anime* 34, 135, 137, 139, 142,
143, 144, 155, 158; Americanisation of
141; characters 153; 'creolisation' of
Japanese subjectivity 153; Handover
Ceremony to Tokyo 2020: 137, 144,
145, 151, 153–5, 157, 158, 163; *honne*
138; *Manga Eiga* 158; multipanel
animation 154; sentimentalism 154;
stiffness 158, 163; a worldmaking tool
155
Mannheim, K. 138
Maracanã/Maracanã Stadium 59, 78,
105, 107, 137, 155, 160, 163
Marcelo D2: 113
Marcuse, H. 30
Mardini, Yusra 121, 122–3
Marx, Karl 56, 58
Marxism 10, 19, 39, 43, 45, 103
masculinity 110, 115, 130, 172;
machismo 18, 107, 117; 'masculine
capital', diminution of 37; *see also*
gender issues
MC Sofia 113
media 49, 99, 102, 117, 148, 166–7, 174;
artistic *imagineer* 18; contemporary
event 51; environmental issues 55, 57,
83; imagineering 36; media ecology
172; mega-event 44, 165; Museum of
Tomorrow 82, 83, 85; new media 36,
83, 129, 165; Olympic Ceremony 90,
92, 129; social media 121
mega-event 1, 3, 49, 144, 168, 174; artistic
economy, dual impact of 3; capitalism
3–4, 5, 8; cultural economic approach
12; disruptive media event 165; ephemerality of 5; hope 38, 52; impact on
the host 2, 5, 51; literature on 5; media
44, 165; mega-event art, exilic worldmaking and post-modern pilgrimage
171; mobility 9, 169; *ontogenesis*
of 71; organisation of 5; security issues
26, 28; staging 28, 44; surveillance 30;
technology 2, 167; time, double

conception of 5, 7, 8; tourism 8, 25, 68;
transnational enterprise 9; utopia 171
Meirelles, Fernando 14, 37, 38, 43, 89,
91, 92; aesthetic of darkness 67; *City
of God* 94–5, 118, 122; *The Constant
Gardener* 118; *Domésticas* 93;
Museum of Tomorrow 53, 69, 74, 75,
81, 84, 86, 105, 119; Opening Ceremony
78, 94; realism 94; *Tropicália* 97
Melindrosa 108, 109, 110, 150
Melodia, Luiz 101
Merleau-Ponty, M. 38, 138
Mexico 1968 Summer Olympics 4, 5, 78,
129–30
Michaels, Julia 129
migrant 7, 22, 29, 30, 108, 133, 141;
arrival of Japanese labour migrants in
Brazil *104*; labour migrant/migration
7, 89, 104, 108, 116, 170
military-related issues 27, 28, 138, 143;
see also militourism; security issues
militourism (military tourism) 13, 27,
39, 51; Brazilian hospitality 39;
consumption 109; Japan 139, 152;
'looking-as-devouring' technology 27;
mega-event's 'militourist' rationale 27;
militourist ideology 59; surveillance
27; utopian thesis 27, 28, 43; war
frames 13, 27, 51; *see also*
military-related issues; security issues
Mills, C.W. 104
Miranda, Carmen 127–8
Miyake, Issey 158–9
Miyake, Jun 149; *Pina* 150
Miyazaki, Hayao 154
Mizuno, Mikiko 38, 146, 159, 161
mobility 9, 29–30; *choreomobility* 93, 94,
98, 146–7; cultural mobility 2, 3, 13,
18, 89, 99, 135; cultural politics and
11; *favela* 169–70; ideological
immobilities 173; Internet 99; Japan,
provincialised cosmopolitanisms and
cosmobilities 136–47; mega-event
industry as mobility apparatus 169;
modes of 152; power dynamics in the
Olympic city 28; slow mobility 5, 7;
smart mobility 36; social mobility 108,
169; systems of 5, 7; 'white' mobility
21; world mobilities 172–3
modernity/modernism 42, 113; Brazil 15,
16, 18, 33, 69, 70, 76, 95, 104, 108,
109, 127, 129, 131, 169; Europe 33, 34,
76, 109, 111, 119, 131; Japan 33, 136,
150, 152

Moga 150–1, 162
Montenegro, Fernanda 119
Montreal 1976 Olympics 5
Moraes, Vinícius de: *O Canto de
Ossanha* 111–12; *The Girl from
Ipanema* 106–107; *Orfeu da Conceição*
97
Mori, Yoshiro 134
Morris, William 68
Mostafanezhad, M. 55, 112
Mount Fuji 162
Munich 1972 Olympics 80, 86
Museum of Tomorrow (*Museu do
Amanhã*) 3, 14, 53, 59–60, *77*, 163,
164; Anthropocene 54, 74, 75, 80, 82,
105, 118; architectural design 76, 78,
80; architectural utopia in an
ornamental museum 67–71; *buen vivir/
well-being* 13–14, 55, 59, 69, 75;
capitalism 54, 60, 67, 68–9, 75, 84, 87;
choreographing mobility: between
Ubuntu and social thanatology 71–87;
cinematic/audio-visual techniques 63,
74, 75, 81, 82, 83, 85–6, 105; climate
change and environment 54, 55, 56,
78, 79, 86, 111; creative makers 60–1,
85; crisis, sense of 51; darkness 67, 82,
83; degrowth 55, 82, 84; digitality 37,
80, 81, 82–3; education 38, 55, 61, 69,
79, 85; environmental ethics 70, 79–80;
exhibition/display 75, 76, 80–5;
exhibition, epochal segments of 74, 80;
funding institutions 53; Gaia entrance
76, *77*, 78, 81; games/gamification 83,
84; 'gift economy' 37, 66; hybrid of
science/technology/nature and art 54,
69, 70–1, 78, 80, 85, 87; Meirelles'
collaboration 53, 69, 74, 75, 81, 84,
86, 105, 119; neo-futurism 3, 83;
partnerships 69; roof 79–80; the
suffering artist and his art-forms 61–7;
sustainability 69, 70, 74, 83; technology
37, 66, 68, 69, 70, 74, 75, 78, 79–80, 83,
85–6, 87; *tjurunga* 84, 85, 86; tourism
3, 55, 61, 67, 69, 80–2, 83–4;
transduction 75; worldmaking 61, 71;
see also Calatrava, Santiago

Nagib, L. 89, 118
nationalism: Brazil 16, 63, 95, 116;
ethno-national/nationalism 36, 44, 89,
116, 117, 135, 144, 150, 153, 156, 163,
172; Japan 136, 137, 139, 140, 141, 144,
160; methodological nationalism 171

Nederveen Pieterse, J. 18, 29
neoliberalism 17, 19, 22, 52, 147, 172,
    174, 175; Brazil 19, 40, 58, 110, 115;
    governance 27, 170; neoliberal
    globalisation 88, 102; privatisation 27,
    170; Tokyo 2020 Olympics 144;
    working-class/underclass 34
Nicolini, D. 43–4, 49
Niemeyer, Oscar 16, 76, 103, 107, 125
Nō theatre 138, 158
NOC (National Olympic Committee) 1
'non-places/spaces' 4, 5, 114, 125, 145,
    166; Museum of Tomorrow 69; non-
    spaces of capitalist production 5, 34–5;
    post-modernism 16, 65; Tokyo 144
Norum, R. 55

Obuchi, Keizō 140, 160
oeconomie artificialem (economy of artifice)
    27, 37, 135, 139, 152, 159, 167; art/
    artistic creativity 20, 28; artificial
    economy 1, 32; artistic *imagineer* 37;
    difference to economy of imagination
    171; hardening structural possibilities
    170; Japan 140–1; mega-event
    management 26; Rio de Janeiro 24;
    surveillance, security and control of
    leisure 1; Tokyo 2020 Olympics 135,
    152
oeconomie imaginationis (economy of
    imagination) 1, 26, 27, 140, 141, 147,
    159, 174; creating inclusive utopias
    170; difference to economy of artifice
    171; economy of *dépense* 175; ethics of
    care 28; *imagineering* 32; Japan 140,
    141; Tokyo 2020 Olympics 147, 153
O'Gorman, K. 7
Oliveira, Luiz Alberto 69
Olympic Ceremony 6, 14, 43, 50, 126,
    129; *choreomobility* 93; cosmopolitan-
    ism 172; 'exisience' 92; media 90, 92,
    129; narratives of gift-giving 42;
    'recreation' 90; *see also* Rio 2016 Cer-
    emonies; Rio 2016 Closing Ceremony;
    Rio 2016 Opening Ceremony
Olympic Channel 2, 129, 130
Olympic city 1, 5, 33, 167, 171, 172, 175;
    Rio de Janeiro 59, 102, 169; Tokyo
    159; *see also* host city
Olympic Congress (XIII, Copenhagen)
    1–2
Olympic flag 133
Olympic Movement 1–2, 7–8, 11, 12, 91,
    122

Olympic Torch 123, 166
Olympics 1, 169; European epistemological
    roots 6–7; hospitality 7, 9, 126;
    Olympic heritage 7, 46; Olympic
    holiday 166; Olympic mega-event as a
    travelling culture 168, 169; Olympic
    pilgrimage 166; principles 6
Olympism 9, 10, 45
Otaku 142, 151, 153–4, 155, 162; *Otaku
    Hikikomori* youth 154

PAC (Programme for Accelerated
    Growth) 59
Paes, Eduardo 60, 133
parkour 107, 113
pilgrimage 65, 171; heritage pilgrimage
    162; Japan 141–2; mega-event 90, 171;
    Olympic pilgrimage 166; post-modernity
    29, 132, 166
Pink, S. 49
Pixinguinha (Alfredo da Rocha Viana,
    Jr.) 126–7; *Carinhoso* 126, 127
Plastic Soup Foundation 60
Plato 145
political action 45, 141
political ecology 12, 20, 55, 97, 123
popular culture 102, 136, 174; Brazil 22,
    31, 32, 44, 95, 101, 111, 113, 115, 128;
    Japan 137, 139, 163; *see also* culture
population growth 56, 78
populism 44, 45, 174–5; Brazil 63, 117,
    123; Japan 137
Porto Maravilha 59, 67, 68, 79, 168
post-modernism 11, 54, 74, 80, 132–3;
    feminised post-modernity 97; Japan
    142, 143, 144; pilgrimage 29, 132, 166;
    post-modern non-places/non-spaces
    16, 65; Rio de Janeiro 101, 110, 111
Potts, T. 128
poverty 4, 21, 72, 123, 131
Powell, Baden 111–12
privatisation 27, 42, 46, 170
Putnam, Hilary 48

Qatar 2022 FIFA World Cup 5

race/racial issues 112, 170, 173; 'black'
    mobility 23; black population 17, 22,
    23, 97–8, 104, 107, 108, 110, 112–13,
    123, 128, 172; *branqueamento* 16, 107,
    110, 132; discrimination 166, 169;
    embodiment 23; environmental racism
    27, 58, 59, 72, 93, 111, 175; *favela* 21,
    22, 23, 166; Japan 141; *mestiçagem*

110, 112; *moreno* body 110; *mulatto/
mulatta* 15, 22, 108, 110, 112; racial
harmony 129; racialisation 21; Rio
2016 Ceremonies 97–8; 'risk regimes'
122; 'white' mobility 21; whitening 16,
23; whitewashing 19, 22; *see also*
ethnicity
Rainbow Bridge 152, 160, 162
Ranciére, J. 40, 46, 50, 112
rap 95, 97, 98, 113
realism 26
Rede Globo 13
reflexivity 22; aesthetic reflexivity 26, 27,
40–1, 80, 115; 'Camp' reflexivity 45;
cognitive reflexivity 20, 41; 'place'
reflexivity 143
refugee crisis 11, 51
Refugee Olympic Team 1, 37, 120–1,
133; body and technological
mediations of heroism 38
Reijnders, S. 153
resilience 102, 170
Richards, G. 171
Rickly, J. 112
Rio 2016 Ceremonies 90–8, 135, 154;
choreomobile 93, 94, 98, 146–7;
degrowth 89; economic recession and
budget 88, 92, 111; ethnicity and
globalisation 92; *favela/favelados* 91,
93, 95; gender and race 97–8; political
ecology 97; Rio's 'submerged centre'
90, 91, 106, 111, 117; utopia 91, 100,
117; *see also* Rio 2016 Closing
Ceremony; Rio 2016 Olympics; Rio
2016 Opening Ceremony
Rio 2016 Closing Ceremony 3, 89, 125–32,
168; 'The Art of the People' 130–1;
athletes 127; Brazilian National
Anthem 127; clay dolls dance 133;
cosmopolitan togetherness 129, 131;
dance and music 125, 126, 129, 131,
133; emotional and lifestyle plenitude
126; ethnicity 129–30, 131, 132–3;
gender issues 129–30, 132–3; great
Brazilian maestros 126–7; IOC
Athletes' Commission 133;
lace-making tradition 131–2; Olympic
Rings 126; *see also* Rio 2016
Ceremonies
Rio 2016 Olympic Cauldron 123–5, *124*;
Candelária's Cauldron 123, 125; *see
also* Rio 2016 Opening Ceremony
Rio 2016 Olympics (*Jogos Olímpicos de
Verão de 2016*, Rio de Janeiro) 1, 20,

27–8, 40; architecture 14; athletes 1;
budget 2, 88, 92; capitalism 41;
consequences/impact 2, 25, 167;
criticism and protest against 2, 23,
123; digitality 79; director 38, 50, 89,
91; frame 51–2; ideology 44, 126; joy
and play 37, 39, 44, 59, 101, 113, 117,
168; logo 78; mascots: Vinicius and
Tom 106, 107; security 23, 27;
technology 37; tourism 37, 84;
worldmaking 18–19; *see also* Rio 2016
Ceremonies; Rio de Janeiro
Rio 2016 Opening Ceremony 3, 18, 89,
101–25, 168; arrival of Japanese
labour migrants in Brazil *104*; athletes
120, *120*; *baile funk* 107, 111, 113–16;
'Birth of Life' 103–104; Brazilian
National Anthem 103; capitalism 122;
'Climate Change' 118–20, 123, 124;
crisis, sense of 51; dance and music 95,
98, 101–102, 103, 105, 111–13;
degrowth 96, 102, 119, 126;
environmental issues 105, 111, 118–20,
123; ethnicity 104, 105, 112; *favela/
favelados* 94, 107, 111, 113–18;
gambiarra 102; gender-related issues
107, 122; humanitarianism 120–1, 122,
123; 'Introduction' 101, 119;
'Metropolis' 105; *morro* cultures 116;
'moving cities' 118; Olympic Torch
123; 'Parade' 120, 122; samba 101,
102, 111, 113; sustainability 103; Tree
of Life *103*, 104, 119, 120; urban Rio
106; 'Voices from the *Favela*' 111;
worldmaking 117; *see also* Rio 2016
Olympic Cauldron; Rio 2016
Ceremonies
Rio de Janeiro 9, 11, 37, 51; atmosphere
15, 125, 132; bid winner 1, 2–3; as
Brazilian capital 16; 'de-criminalising'
enterprise 20; eco-technocracy 58;
feminised Rio 108, 109, 111;
festivalisation of the host city 23–4;
globalisation 107; as host city 19–20,
71, 88, 124; material urban development
for Olympics 14, 17, 67, 68, 167;
militarisation 28; modernity 108, 109;
oeconomie artificialem 24; population
17; post-modern, global city 101, 110,
111; tourism 17; *Zona Norte* 17, 108;
Zona Sul 17, 59, 70, 108; *see also*
Brazil; Rio 2016 Ceremonies; Rio
2016 Olympics
Rio World Heritage Institute 67

Rizomatiks 159
ROCOG (Rio Organising Committee for the Olympic Games) 36, 59, 92, 93
Rogge, Jacques 1
Romanticism 54, 111, 119; Japan 144, 145, 146, 156, 158, 161; romantic tourist 145–6, 158, 171; technoromanticism 145, 146, 171; violence 116
Rose, Nikolas 48
Rousseff, Dilma 2, 19–20, 40
Ruggiero, V. 40
Ruskin, John 68
Russia 2, 65, 133
Rutheiser, C. 26
Ryu Seung-min 133

Sá, Roberta 127
Salazar, N.B. 26, 144
Salles, Walters 95, 96
samba 89, 99, 112–13, 127; black ethnic practice 112–13; *Carioca*-samba 13, 14–15, 125–6; *favela* 15, 22, 113, 116; origins of 22; rap as evolution of Brazilian samba 98; Rio 2016 Opening Ceremony 101, 102, 111, 113; *samba-cançao* 22; *samba de morro* 22; samba school 101, 125, 152; sambadrome 112, 125; themes 22; *see also Carioca*
Santos-Dumont, Alberto 105–106, 126
São Paulo 1, 76, 93, 109
Sasaki, Hiroshi 38, 146
Sawai, A. 145
Seaton, A.V. 73
Sebro, T.H. 30, 93
security issues 51, 56; Brazil 21; *favela* 20, 21, 114; humanocentric vision of 26; Japan 141; mega-event 26, 28; *oeconomie artificialem* 1; Rio 2016 Olympics 23, 27; 'security field' 25–6; 'security iconographies' 26; technology 28; Tokyo 2020 Olympics 135; *see also* military-related issues; militourism
Seixas, Raul 133
Sennett, Richard 171–2
Serra da Capivara, National Park 130
sertão 89, 91, 131–2, 133, 160
Sewell, W.H. Jr. 102, 121
Sheena Ringo 38, 146, 162
Sheller, Mimi 15, 172–3, 174
Shibuya 150, 151
Shintaro, Ishihara 141
Silva, Rafaela 166

slavery 17, 23, 67, 97, 104, 108, 114, 115, 175; abolition of 22; *favela* 20, 115, 116
Sloterdijk, P. 47, 106, 136
Sneed, P. 114, 115, 116, 117
Soares, Elza: *O Canto de Ossanha* 111–12; *Mas que Nada* 111
Soares, L.E. 2, 18, 19
Sontag, S. 50, 66
spectacle 4, 30; mega-event 19, 27, 30
Stage One 124
staging 28, 44, 157
Steger, M.B. 56
Strange, S. 39
structuralism 43, 47
Sugano, Kaoru 38, 146
Sugarloaf Mountain 126
Super Mario 153, 154–5, 157, 159, 162; Abe/Super Mario 155, 156, 158, 163, 164
surveillance 14, 19, 28, 30, 100, 115; digital surveillance 25; *favela* 31, 32; Foucault, M. 25, 27, 30; Japan 141; mega-event 30; militourism 27; *oeconomie artificialem* 1
sustainability 8, 57, 173, 175; Brazil 60; Handover Ceremony to Tokyo 2020: 143; Museum of Tomorrow 69, 70, 74, 83; Rio 2016 Opening Ceremony 103; sustainable tourism 83–4; Tokyo 2020 Olympics 135, 144; *see also* environmental issues
Suzuki, M. 141
Sydney 2000 Olympics 5, 130
synecdoche 47, 135, 172; Brazil 71, 118, 122, 125, 132; Japan 135, 147, 148, 154, 159

Takeda, Tsunekazu 134
tatemae 145; *oeconomie artificialem* 139; public Self 74; *tatemae/honne* duality 136, 157, 161; *see also honne*; Japan
Tatil Design 78
Taylor, Charles 48
technicity 75, 148
technocracy 169; eco-technocracy 57–61
technology 37, 66; art/artistic creativity 28, 33; body as site of artistic technology 99; *Carioca* 36, 131; as creative comportment of irrealist worldmaking 171; enframing 87; Handover Ceremony to Tokyo 2020: 37, 147, 148, 149, 158, 159, 164; impact of 28; Japan 138, 139, 141; mega-event 2,

167; Museum of Tomorrow 37, 54, 66, 68, 69, 70–1, 74, 75, 78, 79–80, 83, 85–6, 87; security issues 28; 'technified natural man' 130; *technopoetic/ technological poesis* 70, 88–9; technoromanticism 145, 146, 171; Tokyo 2020 Olympics 135, 144, 159; as worldmaking process 41, 135; *see also* digitality
terrorism 3, 4, 28, 124
Teixeira, Humberto 133
thanatology: 'thana-capitalism' 43, 94, 156, 167, 174; *thanatopsis* 73, 74; thanatourism 122, 123, 153, 156, 162
Thomas, Daniella 14, 38, 43, 89, 95; *Midnight* 96; *Terra Estrangeira* 95
Thrift, N. 28, 135
time 4, 7; hyper-speed 5, 8; mega-event, double conception of time 5, 7, 8; slow mobility 5, 7; slow travel 8
Tokyo 141–2, 144; bid winner 134, 146; political engagement 9; techno-Orientalism 144–5; tourism 142; *see also* Handover Ceremony to Tokyo 2020; Tokyo 2020 Olympics
Tokyo 1964 Olympics 5, 134–5
Tokyo 2020 Olympics: 3; developmental programme 134; *honne* 145; the most eco-friendly Olympic Games 135; neoliberalism 144; 'non-places' 145; *oeconomie artificialem* 135, 152; *oeconomie imaginationis* 147, 153; security issues 135; sustainability 135, 144; technology 135, 144, 159; technoromanticism 145; *see also* Handover Ceremony to Tokyo 2020; Japan
tourism 28, 166; Afro-Brazilian heritage, transformation into tourist commodity 123; creative tourism 171–2; dark tourism 66, 73, 86, 131, 156; digitality 83; 'fantasmatics' 33; *favela* 167; Handover Ceremony to Tokyo 2020: 151, 164; heritage and 25, 59, 123; Japan 73; mega-event 8, 25, 68; Museum of Tomorrow 3, 55, 61, 67, 69, 80–2, 83–4; non-spaces of capitalist market 34–5; Rio 2016 Olympics 37, 84; Rio de Janeiro 17; romantic tourist 145–6, 158, 171; slow tourism 8; sustainable tourism 83–4; thanatourism 122, 123, 153, 156, 162; tourismification 79, 84, 96, 109, 151–2; 'tourist gaze' 30

tradition 175; Brazil 16, 17, 98, 113, 116, 125–6, 127, 131; European tradition 15, 33, 119; Japan 73, 142, 143, 145, 148–9, 153, 154; *see also* heritage
transmodernity 21–2, 104, 120, 132, 149, 174; transmodern ethics 22, 175
transnationalism 11, 36
Tropicália (documentary film) 97
Tropicália movement 96
Tropicalismo 96, 97, 127, 130
Truman, Harry S. 19
Tyfield, D. 55
Tze-Yue, H.G. 137–8, 158

Ubuntu 72–4, 78, 82, 88–9, 131
UN (United Nations) 11, 55, 60, 102, 121, 122
UN Commission of Human Rights and the Environment 58–9
UNEP (United Nations Environment Programme) 83–4
UNESCO (UN Educational, Scientific and Cultural Organization) 11, 161
UNWTO (World Tourism Organisation) 83–4
UPP (Police Pacification Program) 21, 31, 59, 79; *see also favela*
urban area 4, 78, 132; 'military urbanism' 27; the urban and the global 17; urban ecology 10, 12, 20, 58, 152; urban governance 4, 27; urban renewal 5, 11, 40
Urry, J. 14, 20, 30, 31, 36, 40, 43, 55, 80, 115, 125, 143, 152, 157
utopia/utopianism 19, 34, 68, 114, 168; artist 35; artistic utopia 40, 117; *baile funk* 114; *evotopian* doctrine 56, 102, 147; *favela* 114; Handover Ceremony to Tokyo 2020: 143, 147; hope 38; imagineering utopias 33–9; mega-event 171; militourism 27, 28, 43; *oeconomie imaginationis* 170; Rio 2016 Ceremonies 91, 100, 117; utopian thesis 12, 22, 27, 28, 43; utopic transgression 35

vagabondage 133
Vargas, Getúlio 15–17, 76, 96, 109, 112, 123, 127
Veloso, Caetano 89, 96–8, 128, 133; *Tropicalismo* 96, 97
Vila Olímpica program 123
violence 3, 4; *favela* 20, 32, 114, 116–17, 118; Rio de Janeiro 2, 18; romanticising violence 116

Waddington, Andrucha 14, 38, 43, 89, 97
WHO (World Health Organisation) 60, 122
Wikipedia 49–50
Wittgenstein, Ludwig 43, 47, 61
Wolff, J. 81
working-class 22, 24, 34, 106, 114, 128
World Bank 60
worldmaking 15, 17, 51, 68, 171; artistic worldmaking 89, 91, 100, 171; critique of 47–8; director 50; hope 100; Museum of Tomorrow 61, 71; Rio 2016 Olympics 18–19; Rio 2016 Opening Ceremony 117; technology 41, 135; 'world versions' 46; world-making/imagineering relationship 51; worldmaking and the methodology of post-growth imaginaries 43–52
Wurzel, Daniel 82

youth 34, 134, 150; Brazil 107, 123, 124; Japan 142, 143, 154
YouTube 98, 129, 166, 167, 170

Zeca Pagodinho 113
Zika virus 2, 60
Žižek, S. 87, 90
Zolberg, V.L. 46

Printed in Great Britain
by Amazon

33185414R00139